THE OLD BOYS

THE
OLD BOYS
THE DECLINE AND RISE OF
THE PUBLIC SCHOOL

DAVID TURNER

YALE UNIVERSITY PRESS
NEW HAVEN AND LONDON

For information about this and other Yale University Press publications, please contact:
U.S. Office: sales.press@yale.edu   www.yalebooks.com
Europe Office: sales@yaleup.co.uk   www.yalebooks.co.uk

Typeset in Minion Pro by IDSUK (DataConnection) Ltd
Printed in Great Britain by Gomer Press Ltd, Llandysul, Ceredigion, Wales

Library of Congress Control Number: 2015930854

ISBN 978-0-300-18992-6

A catalogue record for this book is available from the British Library.

10 9 8 7 6 5 4 3 2 1

Contents

Illustrations

Note on Pricing

Historical prices are converted into 2012 prices using indices produced by the Office for National Statistics, which go as far back as 1750. For prices before that point, the Phelps-Brown and Hopkins index of the price of consumables, which goes back to the thirteenth century, before Winchester's foundation, is used to calculate the 1750 price. This is then converted into today's prices using the same method as prices for 1750 onwards.* The indices used to arrive at today's prices are far from perfect, but they are the best available.

* See the Office for National Statistics Composite Price Index; Jim O'Donoghue and Louise Goulding, 'Consumer Price Inflation Since 1850', Office for National Statistics Economic Trends 604, March 2004; E. H. Phelps-Brown and Sheila V. Hopkins, 'Seven Centuries of the Prices of Consumables', *Economica*, November 1956, pp. 311–14.

Introduction

In 2011 David Cameron was derided by Ed Miliband as 'Flashman', that dastardly bounder from *Tom Brown's School Days*, the 1857 public school novel by Thomas Hughes, who bullied younger boys with a mixture of physical pummelling and verbal laceration. The nickname has stuck, because of a lingering suspicion that public schools still produce men like him. In the original book, and in the bestselling series of novels based on the character by George MacDonald Fraser, Harry Flashman is cursed with many faults: he is arrogant, lacks compassion, abuses his power as an older boy, has a flashy approach to spending his family's large fortune, and is, to put it mildly, sexist. After expulsion from Rugby School, he becomes an army officer through family help rather than merit, since his father buys him a commission. All these faults have been levelled by their critics at today's generation of public school old boys; most of them have been levelled at public school old girls. Cameron himself, an Old Etonian, has been attacked for a bullying style in parliamentary debate, a condescending attitude to female politicians, and a lack of concern for the poor. Andrew Mitchell, erstwhile member of Cameron's cabinet and Old Rugbeian, has been lambasted for a high-handed approach to police officers in an argument over a bicycle, with the claim that he called one of them a 'pleb' upheld in a libel case. At least neither man has, to the relief of their wives, been charged with two of Flashman's greatest faults: cowardice and philandering. Thank heaven for small mercies.

Even the eponymous hero of Hughes's novel, set in the 1830s, is hardly an exemplar of the appropriate elite for a modern society. Tom Brown is a morally upstanding boy: brave, kind and loyal to his friends. During the course of the tale, he plays a part in improving the school's moral tone. However, he attaches little importance to academic work. 'The question remains whether I should have got most good by understanding Greek particles or cricket thoroughly', he muses at the end of the novel as he recalls school days spent largely in playing the latter. 'I'm such a thick, I never should have had time for both.' Tom conforms to another popular image of today's public school old boy: a man more concerned with sport and play than knowledge.

The late eighteenth and early nineteenth centuries marked the nadir of the public schools, a time when boys such as Flashman were given free rein to terrorize the school, and even many well-meaning boys like Tom Brown learned little in the classroom that was useful. Given this, there are two central questions in this book. First, how did the public schools sink into the state described in *Tom Brown's School Days*, and in more purely factual accounts of the period? Second, have they improved, since the days of Flashman and Tom Brown, to the point where they are an asset to the nation?

If they have not, Britain is in trouble. More than half of the top medics, civil servants, lawyers, media figures and Conservative MPs went to public school. If these people are being educated in modern versions of Tom Brown's Rugby, where the bad boys learned habits of cruelty and authoritarianism, and even the good boys thought more of sport than of learning, British society is being led by people who are not up to the job.

Some of the scenes in *Tom Brown's School Days* are genuinely harrowing. Most disturbing of all, perhaps, is the passage where Flashman and his partners cruelly roast Tom Brown in front of the fire, giving him such bad injuries that he is confined to the sick-room for a couple of days. This scene is not exaggerated: junior boys were dangled over the fire at Rugby and other schools. If anything, Hughes is sparing his public from the worst atrocities – roasting was far from the worst thing that happened at the public schools of the period. In 1885 a boy was killed by bullies at King's College School. As late as 1930, a boy committed suicide because he could no longer face the treatment meted out to 'fags', the younger boys who did duties for the older ones, and were often treated by them with appalling callousness or downright sadism. *Tom Brown's School Days* does not, moreover, look at the most troubling phenomenon of all that was prevalent at the time when it is set: the inclination for senior boys to usurp the authority of the masters themselves through open, organized rebellion.

To see how public schools reached such a bad state, I have travelled back to the very beginning: the founding of Winchester College in 1382. The book then plies a chronological course that leads up to the present day, though certain issues, such as sport, homosexuality, and the schools' treatment of foreign pupils, are dealt with in a way that spans the centuries, in chapters covering the periods when these issues were most crucial. Chapter Nine looks at future risks to the public schools, with Chapter Ten considering the issue of whether they are, in the present day, a curse or a blessing for society: dangerously dominant or benignly pre-eminent.

From the beginning I need to establish my definition of a public school. 'Only three people ... have ever really understood the Schleswig-Holstein business', the British politician Lord Palmerston is reported to have said, 'the Prince Consort, who is dead – a German professor, who has gone mad – and I, who have forgotten all about it.' Over the past hundred years, it is highly unlikely that as many as three people have understood fully what a public school is, including insiders at the very heart of the system. 'He is a bold man to-day who ventures to define what is and what is not a public school', the Master of Wellington College wrote in 1932. In defiance of such a warning, however, here is my attempt.

This book defines a public school as a school independent of state control which has primarily educated members of the elite, with the purpose of providing, to some of the pupils at least, an academic education aimed at preparing them for university study. Nowadays these schools all charge high fees; in the past some did not, but admission to these schools was still, through patronage, tilted heavily towards the elite. I define 'elite' in a broad sense. These days perhaps a tenth of the population may have some hope of paying public school fees. This group includes the upper middle as well as the upper classes, and the well-off as well as the genuinely rich. This is my elite.

The grammar schools are excluded, until they reach the point where their client base resembles that of the public schools. By this definition, many of them, including Oundle and Dulwich College, became public schools in the nineteenth century, when they started basing entry mainly on high fees. Many of the rest became so in the 1970s. Although many grammars are ancient, as public schools they are quite new. King's School, Canterbury tentatively traces its ancestry back to 597; as a public school, however, it is a relative newcomer; it only became one in the nineteenth century.

The book's definition of a public school also excludes small establishments which did not last for much longer than the career of the individual who founded them. Occasionally one of them would build a sizeable stable of customers from establishment families, but too few of them for us to consider these schools as training-grounds for the upper echelons. Contemporaries usually described these establishments as 'private schools' or 'academies', to distinguish them from public and grammar schools, and I have made the same distinction. Girls from the broad elite who were educated at school were, until the late nineteenth century, generally educated at academies aimed at teaching the social graces, with little or no pretence at an academic education. The book charts the change, and the development of girls' schools from that point on.

In writing this book, I have tried hard, through analysing government and school data, to address a failing common to the bulk of writing about the public schools: the lack of hard, cold numerical facts to back anecdotal evidence. However, anecdotal evidence is also vitally important. I have sought this by trying to understand the experience of heads, teachers, pupils and governors. Some of their views are buried in history books, in particular the histories of individual schools. Sometimes their experiences are in school archives. I have interviewed many heads and old boys and girls, too – initially during my stint as the *Financial Times'* Education Correspondent in the 2000s and more recently when writing this book.

Where possible, I have also visited schools, in an effort to understand the history buried in their walls. During the past two years spent working on this book I have suffered indigestion from the strain of trying to understand Notions, the Winchester College argot, while lunching with the scholars. I have been jostled by unruly boys in a corridor as an entire school rushed to its next lesson after the bell. I have bent my neck far backwards while admiring the detail in the ceiling carvings at Westminster School; I have bent my neck far forwards over governors' minutes from the era of Tom Brown, while both the archivist and I tried to ignore loud rock music from the adjoining pupil common room and pretend to each other that we had not noticed the noise at all. I have clumsily tried to dissemble when ensconced in the armchair of a majestic study, after a headmaster sought my opinion on whether he or the head of a rival school had a more magnificent room. It has been quite an adventure.

I have also wondered, sometimes, what the characters in *Tom Brown's School Days* would make of the public schools I see now. Tom would, I am sure, be heartened by the continued importance of sport. Thomas Arnold, the real-life headmaster of Rugby who also appears in Hughes's book, would be saddened by the massive decline in the importance of religion at most public schools. Flashman would be appalled by the end of fagging and the decreased power of the older boys. On the other hand, he would probably be pleased by the convenient proximity of women, following the arrival of co-education at the majority of boys' schools.

What of my own experience of public schools? As a young man I had thought surprisingly little of how I personally had been shaped by my public school education. That changed when I became the *Financial Times'* Education Correspondent in 2007. A belated revelation came in 2014, when my family had lunch with the family of a man of roughly my age who had, like me, grown up in the professional classes, won a scholarship at a boys' public school and gone on from there to Oxbridge. His donnish habit of never answering a question with a simple yes or no, his reticence, and the slightly juvenile streak in his nature that made him get on well with little children made him seem familiar, but I could not think why. Then I realized that he reminded me of myself.

Each nation has different monikers to describe different elite social groups: the US talks of people with the 'Ivy League patina', after the top New England colleges; the French talk of the 'énarques' – members of the elite who, having been to the select École Nationale d'Administration, have the arrogance of men and women who feel born to rule; the British, by contrast, talk of men shaped much earlier in their education: 'public school boys'. I believe that the typical 'public school boy' has already changed in the couple of decades or so since I left public school, most of all, perhaps, because of the arrival of girls at my school and others. However, my experience one lunchtime reminded me of how the school shapes the boy and the boy is father to the man.

It is now time to read about the schools that still shape more than half of Britain's elite.

CHAPTER ONE

An Idealistic Cynic and the Birth of a System

1382–1603

WILLIAM of Wykeham was an idealist and a cynic; a man who strove to help the poor but worked hard to do favours for the rich and powerful; a servant of the Church and one of the richest men in England, taking rental income from green agricultural land and the grimy brothels of Southwark alike. He was a bishop but far from a saint. He transmitted the tensions and contradictions in his character and circumstance to the great British institution which he accidentally founded: the public school movement. The public schools would bear the mark of Wykeham for centuries.

Wykeham took his surname from the Hampshire village, ten miles from Winchester, where he entered the world in the mid-1320s into a family at the wealthier end of the peasantry. After a local education, probably at the grammar school at Winchester, in his twenties he somehow came to the attention of the powerful Bishop of Winchester, William Edington; through Edington and other powerful local figures he entered the world that revolved around King Edward III. By his mid-thirties he had become a close confidant of the king and the keeper of his signet seal, used to mark his royal approval to actions. By 1367 he was Chancellor of England, bishop of Edington's old see of Winchester and the most powerful commoner in the country.[1] His income from the Bishop's lands – £4,000 a year (£3.6

million in 2012 prices) – made him immensely wealthy. 'Everything was done by him, and nothing was done without him', wrote the contemporary chronicler Jean Froissart, wryly imitating the description of God in St John's Gospel.[2]

Wykeham was a likeable man, but in common with many powerful people he tended to be most likeable to those whose liking for him might pay dividends. He pressed, in a gently and compassionately worded letter, for the readmission to her convent of Isabella Gervays, a nun expelled for falling pregnant. Gervays came, perhaps not without coincidence, from a Hampshire gentry family with whom Wykeham had business dealings. He was harsher, however, towards another naughty nun, Marion de Rye, who lacked such connections, in this case simply agreeing to let the abbess do as she thought fit rather than intervening on Marion's behalf. Wykeham could also be ruthless: in 1388 he bought, for a fire-sale price, the London house of Robert Bealknap, which had been forfeited in the Merciless Parliament when many members of Richard II's court were convicted of treason.[3]

He seems, at first sight, to be the ultimate insider: a man constantly at the king's side, a man whose keeping of the signet seal meant that he could, literally, never be far from the monarch. In some ways, however, Wykeham remained an outsider. He did not come from an aristocratic family, like many of the court figures and some of the bishops. He had not even gone to university. By the mid-fourteenth century, the post of bishop was already rapidly becoming England's first graduate-only profession, some six-and-a-half centuries before government policy imposed the same fate on nursing, one of the last professions to remain open to non-graduates. When Wykeham had been promoted to the see of Winchester, he had faced accusations of a lack of learning because of the absence of a university background, even though he was a highly intelligent man with a particular gift for languages.[4]

Wykeham did receive an education of sorts. The details are sketchy, but he probably attended the local grammar school in Winchester. The cost of the education would have been modest – perhaps 4d

(£15) a quarter – but the additional necessary expense of boarding the child in the town would have been onerous. A further burden was the labour forgone in allowing him to attend school rather than work on the land.[5] This sacrifice shows that Wykeham's parents were more ambitious for their child than most peasants, largely because they were richer. Most children in the poor and middling classes were either not schooled at all, or given a rudimentary education through sporadic attendance in what were known as 'petty schools': informal schools, run by a single teacher, imparting the basics of reading and perhaps writing and counting.[6] The education of the bulk of the population would remain extremely deficient until well into the nineteenth century.

England was not a complete educational desert, however, during Wykeham's time. The country had a network of grammar schools, which aspired beyond simple literacy and numeracy to teach Latin to a high standard. Until the sixteenth century many jobs would have been impossible without a knowledge of Latin, the prevailing language not simply for church services, but also for legal documents, academic treatises, and communications between merchants of different countries requiring a lingua franca. It was the language of scholarship, the law and even international trade. These schools primarily taught children from relatively well-off families, who could afford the financial burden. The brighter or richer of these children sometimes went on to the two English universities, Oxford and Cambridge, for higher studies. The grammar schools also taught some boys from noble families, though many of these were educated, instead, in small groups in the palaces of bishops entrusted by parents with their care, in the houses of other nobles, or at home. The education of nobles outside the grammar schools often took on a more military bent, with the teaching of swordsmanship and other martial arts; they were, after all, still a warrior class.

By our standards, mediaeval education was cruel. In 1373 the bishop of Norwich forbade teaching in the churches of King's Lynn, on the grounds that the cries of beaten pupils distracted worshippers.[7] In mediaeval iconography the Virgin Mary was often depicted wearing a mantle of soothing blue, St Dorothy with a rustic basket of flowers, and the schoolmaster with a whip in his hand. In 1301 the teacher John Newshom was found drowned in the River Cherwell. The cause of his misadventure was firmly job-related: he was so focused on cutting willow from the riverbank with which to beat his pupils that he fell in. One can almost hear cheers from the legions of schoolboys victimized over the centuries.[8] However, education was not always something that was meted out; school textbooks of the time show attempts at rhyme, wit and humour designed to engage the interest of pupils.[9]

This system had certainly been good enough to produce enough men with enough learning to fill the ranks of the priesthood, but the Black Death, which hit in England in 1348 during Wykeham's early adulthood, broke this system down. The population halved, although the number of church posts to be filled remained the same. The half of the population that was left, moreover, was less inclined to enter the priesthood because of the growing opportunities elsewhere: shortages of labour pushed up earnings and increased opportunities in the secular world. In 1346, just before the outbreak of the Black Death, 115 men were ordained in a single ceremony at St Mary's Church Southwark, in the diocese of Winchester. When Wykeham was ordained in 1362, he was one of only nineteen men ordained that year in the entire diocese.[10] Wykeham realized he had to act.

His solution was to create two huge institutions to educate men to be priests. The first of these to be set up was New College, Oxford, established in 1379 for the study of 'Theology, Canon and Civil Law, and The Arts'. New College was to have seventy scholars, of whom fifty – the vast bulk – should study theology. The second institution was Winchester College, set up in 1382 to act as a feeder school for New College, with fellows at the Oxford college to come exclusively from Winchester once it had produced sufficient numbers to make this possible.[11] After many years of construction, Winchester College took in its first pupils in 1394.[12]

Winchester College was, in keeping with its purpose in educating boys to enter the clerical world, a very monastic institution, where boys led an austere and secluded life. They grew up in an all-male environment, enforced with a paranoid degree of strictness; the statutes decreed that 'every service to the said College' was to be done by males, before laying down the rules to be followed in the unfortunate and extreme event that a washerwoman must be used: 'She is to receive everything to be washed at the outer gate of the College from the hands of a servant appointed to the task by the College and bound by oath; and this washerwoman we wish to be of such age and condition as to be most unlikely to excite any sinister suspicion.' Furthermore, the boys were obliged to speak only Latin, the language of the Church, in school, and were commanded to 'wear a decent tonsure' – the haircut that distinguished the cleric from the lay person – 'under penalty of final expulsion'.[13] The religious nature of the institution was reinforced at every level: the schoolroom followed an east–west axis, in imitation of churches.[14] As late as the eighteenth century the old mediaeval fasts were still observed on Friday and Saturday at the school; Winchester and other boarding schools maintained some of the monastic characteristics established by Wykeham, such as the intensely male environment and ascetic conditions, into the twentieth century.[15]

The education demanded of a Winchester scholar, entering the school most commonly at the age of eleven or twelve, would have been unusually long and rigorous by the standards of the time. Wykeham's statutes envisaged a schoolboy staying on until the age of eighteen or nineteen.[16] By that point he would have been considerably better prepared for advanced study at Oxford than the many boys who went to the university at thirteen, fourteen or fifteen to use it as a substitute for an advanced education at school. Winchester's focus was, as the statutes make clear, on 'grammar', which at that time meant literacy in Latin, including speaking as well as writing. All the pupils were educated in a single large room, sitting on benches without desks.[17]

This education yielded results. Winchester was highly successful, even in its first decades, at producing not merely satisfactory scholars but eminent churchmen. The first alumnus to achieve notable worldly success not founded on his own family connections was probably Thomas Beckington. Admitted as a scholar in 1403, he became a useful lawyer to Henry V, making his name with legal treatises in favour of Henry V's claim to the throne of France, before becoming Bishop of Bath and Wells. As the first distinguished public school old boy, Beckington represents a milestone in the history of a movement that would have died out had it not been seen to produce successful men of the world on a regular basis. The next century was, for a school that often fell to below a hundred pupils, to educate a disproportionately large number of senior bishops, most notably of all William Warham, scourge of monastic corruption, Lord Chancellor, and Winchester scholar in 1469.[18]

It is in the admission of pupils that the conflict between Wykeham's ideals and his worldly life appear. He envisaged Winchester partly as an agent of social mobility, a place which could give to children of his humble background the rigorous education which he had never enjoyed. Winchester's charter laments the 'many poor scholars engaged in scholastic disciplines who, suffering from deficiency, penury, and indigence, lack and will lack in the future the proper means for continuing and advancing in the aforesaid art of grammar'. Wykeham's solution: in order that 'poor and needy scholars' may 'be able to devote more time and leisure' to study, 'we propose . . . to help and bestow our charity to support them'. The number of poor scholars to be educated and boarded for free at the college was fixed at seventy – the tally of disciples sent out by Jesus to spread the word of God according to the Gospel of Luke.[19] Wykeham's definition of poverty was not limited to below-the-breadline pauperism. His statutes specified that a scholar could not, unless a blood relation of Wykeham's, come from a family with an income of more than 5 marks (£3 6s 8d, equivalent to £3,500 in 2012 prices) a year. This was more than the earnings of many clergymen in the diocese of Winchester, or of a Fellow of Merton College,

Oxford, for example.[20] Nevertheless, this stipulation would have excluded genuinely wealthy families.

From the start the college attracted families far above the 'poor and needy', however liberally defined. The lands given to it by Wykeham made it one of the richest religious foundations in the country. Its size and wealth generated an endless stream of curious visitors, ranging from Oxford academics to the Duke of Brittany.[21] The twin institutions of Winchester and New College constituted an ambitious undertaking, which made the ruling classes take notice. They also wanted their children to attend.

Wykeham accommodated the rich and powerful by inserting an escape clause in the statutes: in addition to the scholars, 'we allow, however, sons of noble and influential persons, special friends of the said College, up to the number of ten to be instructed and informed in grammar within the same College, without burden upon the aforesaid College'.[22] They would, in other words, have to pay fees to the college for their upkeep. From the very beginning the school attracted these fee-payers from towards the top of society – known as commoners, to distinguish them from the scholars who were educated for free. By 1412 there were as many as a hundred of them, often sons of the local Hampshire gentry.[23] For most of Winchester's history these commoners would outnumber the scholars.

The most eye-catching names, however – the names of rich and powerful families – are often to be found not among the commoners but among the scholars. Although the lists of scholars do not show members of the high aristocracy at the beginning, they reveal a range of families from England's upper economic echelons. Mixed in with well-known local gentry families were upper-class families from much further afield, thus showing that from the start Winchester was more than a mere local school.[24] Early scholars included John, son of Sir Robert Cherlton, Chief Justice of the Common Pleas, Thomas, son of Philip Walwayn, Usher of the King's Chamber, and the sons of Robert Bealknap, the exiled former Chief Justice, and of John Cassy, Chief Baron of the Exchequer.[25] Scholars were not only excused any fees; they also had the chance of entering New College, which was barred to commoners.

Given Wykeham's requirement of relative poverty for scholars, the appearance of these names poses a riddle. The answer to this conundrum is that Wykeham appears to have broken his own rules. He did not die until 1404, leaving him many years to oversee the college's administration – and to receive visits from powerful figures lobbying for their sons' entry. The records show that Sir Robert Cherlton visited in 1392, and his son entered the following year. Cassy's son entered the college shortly after his father's 1393 visit, as did Walwayn's son.[26] Wykeham, who remained an active politician and major player in the affairs of state after the college's founding, seems to have used Winchester as a way of dispensing patronage – a standard method for politicians to increase and retain power. In doing so he ignored, at least to an extent, his own pious protestation that the school was for the 'poor and needy'.[27] There were, certainly, still some genuinely needy boys among the scholars, but there were many who were not.

The entry of large numbers of children of the elite clearly broke the college's rules; it was far from Wykeham's original stated intention. It is, however, a highly important historical moment. Wykeham's competing motives of idealism and cynicism had created, for the first time, a school where members of England's elite were educated together in large groups, with the aim of preparing a large proportion of them, at least, for a university education. Britain's public school movement had begun.

A connection with the monarch might today confer social cachet on a family or institution, or a certain competitive advantage for a manufacturer of oatmeal cakes. In the fifteenth century, long before parliament had clipped the wings of the Stuarts, monarchical favour was the route to all political power and a good deal of economic power to boot. It is not, therefore, hard to see why The College of Our Lady Mary at Eton, founded by King Henry VI in 1440 close to his favoured home of Windsor Castle, was an instant success.

Henry modelled Eton College very directly on Winchester; he visited the college in 1441 on a recce mission to see how the school was run. He poached its headmaster, William Waynfleet, to organize the newly born school, although there is some debate about whether or not Waynfleet formally became Eton's first headmaster.[28] The religiously significant figure of seventy 'poor and needy' scholars was also borrowed, as was the provision for commoners to board with the college at their expense – though in this case the maximum theoretical limit of commoners was raised to twenty, perhaps bearing the precedent of the high demand for Winchester commoner places in mind. By creating a sister college at Cambridge for Eton scholars – King's College – Henry also imitated Winchester's attempt to fashion a process by which young boys could be set on a comprehensive course of education that ended perhaps a decade later.[29]

The system of prefects – the appointment of older boys to supervise the behaviour of younger – was also borrowed from Winchester, where it had been set out in the statutes. However, the common belief that British public schools invented prefects is a myth. Wykeham had adopted the system from Merton College, Oxford, where older boys had taken care of the young teenagers who were common at Oxbridge colleges in those days.[30]

Given the royal connection, it is unsurprising that competition was fierce to become one of the scholars taught in the dark, plainly wrought classroom.[31] By 1447 the number had already reached the full complement, and by 1453 sixty-five boys were selected for possible admission to one of only fifteen places in the year to come.[32] The reason for the widespread desire to attend this institution is not hard to find: Eton enjoyed the mediaeval equivalent of glamour. From the beginning, several boys from the gentry – members of the upper classes whose families were neither members of the nobility nor titled aristocracy – were attending as commoners, such as the Catesbys of Northamptonshire. The nobility arrived later and in lesser numbers, but a fairly early representative a century and a half later was Robert Devereux, the future Earl of Essex and Roundhead general in the

English Civil War. By this time many other gentry families were sending their sons, including the Verneys, though Sir Francis Verney (1584–1615) went on to adopt an unconventional career path for the English upper classes by becoming a Barbary pirate.[33] Following in the tradition of Sir Francis, Captain Hook, another Old Etonian, became the pirate in Peter Pan; his last words before being swallowed by the crocodile are 'Floreat Etona', Eton's motto. Numinous relics that added to the glamour included the finger-joint and part of the spine of St John the Confessor, former Prior of Bridlington, and a segment of the True Cross that crucified Christ. No expense was spared by Henry VI, who closely monitored the school's continuing development.[34]

The royal connection and smattering of gentry names would have drawn families such as the Pastons, the most famous social climbers of the late mediaeval period, like bees to honey. The correspondence of this recently gentrified Norfolk family includes a 1479 letter lamenting the difficulties of Latin versification at Eton from William Paston, a rather superannuated public school boy of nineteen (he proves the difficulty by inserting an error in the missive).[35] It is easy to make fun of the Pastons until one realizes that their snobbish contemporaries mocked them too: one critic denigrated the founder of the family fortunes as a man who had married a serf and travelled to work 'on the bare horseback with his corn under him'.[36] An Eton education would help such arrivistes to acquire aristocratic connections at the same time as a smattering of Latin. Another family on the rise which patronized Eton from an early point was the Cavendishes, whose descendants would become Dukes of Devonshire and Newcastle. After the two sons of the late Sir William Cavendish, a senior courtier, were placed there in 1560, their stepfather Sir William St Loe reassured his wife with the bursar's promise that 'no jenttlemen's children in Ingland schalbe bettar welcum, nor bettar looked unto than owre boys'. Their voracious purchase of shoes – seven pairs each, according to their school bills – suggests that they were not short of possessions and comforts.[37] Eton College clearly educated the same mix of rich and humble as did Winchester.

However, the very royal favour which had given birth to Eton nearly proved its undoing. In 1461, twenty-one years after the school's foundation, while still lovingly engaged on making the magnificent Eton College Chapel even more magnificent, Henry VI found himself deposed by his Lancastrian rival, who had himself crowned Edward IV. The fan vaulting had not yet been completed – and, with that sense of eternity of which a really grand public school is capable, the college did not get round to finishing it for another five centuries.[38] Edward IV was a vindictive man, and Eton became the vehicle for his petty-minded sense of revenge. In 1463 he applied to Pope Pius II for a papal bull suppressing the college.[39]

Edward IV took many of the lands with which Henry VI had amply endowed the school. By 1468 the revenues had shrunk to a quarter of their former size and the number of scholars had been reduced to keep the college afloat. For a year Eton's most senior officials did not even draw a salary. It appears, however, that Eton's connections saved it. Regular records of small gifts from the college authorities to influential people, such as George Nevill, Archbishop of York and brother of Warwick the Kingmaker, the most influential noble in England, hint at the first clear instance of another motif of public school history: that assiduous and effective lobbying behind the scenes which recurs at crucial moments of public school history. Thanks, perhaps, to this lobbying, the bull was never implemented, and Winchester College's flashier younger brother was saved.[40]

A century and a half after the triumph of the Whiggish interpretation of British history as a steady progression from bad to good, it is common to view the Middle Ages as nasty, brutish, short and ignorant.

Eton and Winchester were no kinder to their charges than other schools in the Middle Ages. Each form at Eton had an official dunce, known as the 'custos', an unenviable title given to the weakest boy in the class, who was singled out for testing in front of his peers until he improved and the ignominy passed to another boy.[41] When it came to physical cruelty, the Winchester and Eton statutes at least called for punishment only in moderation, though public school history shows many cases of headmasters proving far crueller than the schools' governing authorities desired.[42]

The teaching was not based entirely on the fear of punishment. Both schools made an attempt to excite the interest of the boys, by at times using rather entertaining 'vulgaria': books composed of Latin sentences illustrating a grammatical point. This may sound deadly dull, but consider the famous 1519 *Vulgaria Puerorum* written by William Horman, headmaster of Eton from 1486 to 1495. It is, by the admittedly rigorously sober standards of modern Latin textbooks, rather bawdy and replete with attempts to create up-to-date material of topical interest – though the Latin itself was, according to the famous Tudor scholar Roger Ascham (1515–68), tutor to the future Elizabeth I, rather sloppy. The chapter 'On Piety' declares: 'It becomes not clerks to haunt a nunnery / Alone nor early nor late.'

A corresponding chapter 'On Impiety' warns: 'Some witches give man an enchantment in his meat or drink / That shall steer him to lecherous love.'

There are also several timely references to contemporary events, such as Henry VIII's capture of Tournai from the French only six years previously. In particular, the Turks, the bogeymen of Christendom until the end of the eighteenth century, are much mentioned. The chapter 'On War' notes rather forebodingly: 'There is a great rumour still / That the Turk is coming into Italy with a great host.'[43]

It would be stretching the facts to say that England's two embryonic mediaeval public schools contributed much to educational theory. The schools were, however, considered good enough to be held up as markers of educational excellence. In 1528 the master of Cuckfield Grammar School was instructed to teach 'after the practice of Eton'. In 1530 the headmaster of Saffron Walden School was expected to follow the example of Eton or Winchester, and obtained accounts from both schools of their educational system.[44] Moreover, from the beginning the two schools were sufficiently well regarded to attract significant numbers of boys from the upper echelons as boarders. This created a virtuous circle: the more prestigious the clientele, the more families wanted to enter their sons into the schools. The public schools had begun to chisel out a place in society.

St Paul's Cathedral had run a small school for centuries. John Colet, Dean of St Paul's, used the huge personal wealth inherited from his father, a Lord Mayor of London, to refound it on a larger scale in 1509 with an impressive total of 153 free scholars, supplemented, until the late nineteenth century, only periodically by paying commoners when the governors turned a blind eye to the rules. This number was probably a reference to the number of fish caught in the last chapter of St John's Gospel, which was supposed, by extension, to correspond to the number of species of fish to be found in the world – creating a numerology of internationalism appropriate to the statutes' pledge to educate 'all nations and countries indifferently'. There were, at this first British public school for day pupils, no rules governing who should be a free scholar. Pupils were expected to pay for the many extras, including, notably, the wax candles demanded by the school. Eight times the price of the usual tallow, they were the preserve of the wealthier Londoners from the merchant classes. The statutes made provision for 'one poor scholar' who would receive 4d from each schoolmate for sweeping the floor and other menial duties, but did not lay down any rules about the economic background of the other 152.[45] The wax candles show us, crucially, that Colet assumed the pupils would be comfortably off.[46]

Colet also created a constituency of families hungry for education by putting the school in the charge of the Mercers' Company, his father's old livery company, and the richest of them all. St Paul's quickly became a school largely for London mercers, and for those with connections to the company.[47] As at Winchester, the elite secured scholarship entry to the embryonic public school of St Paul's through contacts rather than cash. Purists might term St Paul's a grammar school at this early stage of its history, since it did not have fee-payers;

its economically and politically powerful client base makes it more logical, however, to treat it as a public school.

Colet was a well-connected man, a friend of no less a figure than Erasmus, high priest of the early Reformation, who recruited teachers and wrote textbooks for the new school. The first high master, as the headmasters are still known, was a good catch: William Lily was perhaps the first public school head at the very forefront of current teaching and scholarship. Under Lily, St Paul's became an early pioneer in the teaching at English schools of Ancient Greek. The language's spread during the Renaissance gave new life to philosophy by unlocking the key to the understanding of the great Greek philosophers and breathed new vigour into biblical scholarship.[48]

Despite becoming embroiled in controversies with other grammarians, Lily held on to his post until death released him from it ten years later, doing better than many other St Paul's high masters of the era. Four of the first ten were dismissed – reflecting the ruthless hiring and firing culture of the London merchant class that supervised the school.[49] Thus was established a tradition among public day schools, which has persisted to this day, of the cold-blooded culling of unsatisfactory heads.

Nevertheless, with the hindsight of history the most substantial public school head of the sixteenth century is probably not Lily but Richard Mulcaster, the first headmaster of Merchant Taylors' School, set up in the City of London in 1561 by the livery company of the same name. The statutes of this day school conceived the idea of 250 scholars: a hundred 'poor men's sons' to be taught 'freely', a hundred 'rich or mean [middling] men's children' paying 5s and a quarter (£100), and fifty further 'poor men's children' paying 2s 2d.[50] Mulcaster is noteworthy in public school history as an early pioneer of what would become one of the professed advantages of the public schools: the ideal of a rounded education, the virtues of which were not restricted solely to narrow academic achievement. After twenty-five years at Merchant Taylors', following a series of misadventures he went on to the headship at St Paul's, where he was able to apply the same principles.[51]

In common with the supposed invention of prefects, this presumed hallmark of the public school tradition was borrowed from elsewhere. Back in 1425, Vittorino da Feltre had established a school in Mantua which emphasized good manners, music and physical exercise.[52] Da Feltre and other humanists, such as Leon Battista Alberti, strove to resurrect the classical ideal of human excellence encapsulated in the Ancient Roman poet Juvenal's phrase, 'mens sana in corpore sano' – a healthy mind in a healthy body. They believed that the development of one's physique would help develop one's intellect. These humanists also emphasized the cultivation of an aesthetic sense, in line with their overarching aim that education should produce rounded individuals.[53]

Something approaching this philosophy of broad education gradually percolated through to English society, reaching the houses of some English nobles and even, improbably, London's Inns of Court, the training ground for lawyers. Writing about the Inns in the 1460s, the jurist Sir John Fortescue asserted that students 'learn to sing and to exercise themselves in every kind of harmony. They also practise dancing and all the games common to noblemen, just as those in the king's household are accustomed to practise them.'[54] A law student's life was clearly more fun than it is today. There are, moreover, traces of the broad education principle at Eton by the early sixteenth century: in 1528 Etonians were studying a didactic poem on hygiene and table manners written by Fra Giovanni Sulpizio da Veroli, the Italian fifteenth-century schoolmaster.[55]

Mulcaster took the principle of a broad education considerably further, however. His curriculum, expounded through two books on educational theory, *Positions Concerning the Training up of Children* and the *Elementarie* (which looked at the grounding principles or 'elements' of education), was unusually wide. It contained a cornucopia of exercises and activities, including drama and singing, dancing and wrestling, handball and football. Mulcaster justified such activities partly on the *mens sana in corpore sano* principle: he believed that physical training would boost mental powers.[56]

However, a more intriguing motivation also creeps in, which twenty-first-century public school heads have often found as hard to admit as their earlier counterparts: that it might be a good idea to undertake such activities simply because they are fun. In a chapter with a positively sybaritic title, 'That this Elementarie seasoneth the young mind with the verie best, and sweetest liquore', Mulcaster posed the rhetorical question: 'Doth not all our delite in times not busied ... protest in plain terms, that it is wonderfully indebted to either part of music, both by instrument and voice? That natural sweeter of our sour life in any man's judgement.'[57]

Mulcaster was, in particular, a devotee of drama. Parents across the country have for many years been forced to sit through school plays; Mulcaster imposed the same misfortune on nothing less exalted than the royal court, not once but four times, though the impressive list of future famous actors educated under him, including Thomas Kyd and Thomas Lodge, suggests that Merchant Taylors' school drama was a cut above the average. The London public schools, close to the theatrical amusements of the capital, were in the following centuries to build an impressive list of old boy actors and producers, their appetite often whetted by their experience of drama at school, including the annual Latin play, first shown by Westminster School in 1564 to an audience that included Queen Elizabeth I.[58] Two centuries later Merchant Taylors' educated the pioneering theatre manager and comic actor Charles Mathews; at the beginning of the twentieth century it would school Boris Karloff, the Hollywood horror film star.

Apart from providing a highly precarious career to a minority of pupils, this early incarnation of the notion of a rounded public school education secured a benefit for those who went on to conventional careers for the elite. Sir James Whitelocke began life as the son of a very ordinary London merchant, but won entry into court circles after a public school education under Mulcaster. Sir James, who became a barrister and distinguished judge, certainly credited Mulcaster with the formation of his social graces. Mulcaster, he said, 'presented some plays to the court, in which his scholars only were actors, and I among them; and by that means he taught them good behaviour and audacity'. A successful career at the bar certainly demands, even now, an element of dramatic skill, as well as the cultivation of self-confidence, or 'audacity', to which Whitelocke refers.[59]

Another of Mulcaster's contributions to English education was his love affair with the English language. 'I love Rome, but London better; I favour Italy, but England more; I honour Latin, but worship English', he wrote in the *Elementarie*, and his broad curriculum was certainly less exclusively focused on the Classics (Latin and Greek) than the conventional school curriculum of the time, though Mulcaster was also a good scholar in both languages.[60] It is to his credit that one of the greatest pioneers of early English literature in this period, Edmund Spenser, poet and author of the *Faerie Queen*, was his pupil. Mulcaster was imbued with a strong sense that although the English language was a worthy medium of literature, it was akin, as we might say, to a magnificent castle still under construction, which needed new words added to the existing edifice. Spenser, who gave the English language 'blatant' and numerous other neologisms by borrowing from Greek or Latin, was faithful to this theme throughout his career. The practice of enriching English by invention would be continued by men such as John Milton, scholar of St Paul's, whose new word 'pandemonium' was perhaps inspired by the noisy chaos of its large school room.

For centuries to come public schoolboys would continue the neologistical tradition through the development of highly sophisticated school argot. This reached its apogee in Winchester Notions: hundreds of slang words and expressions, often based on Wykehamists' love of irony, irreverence and abbreviation, which sharpened the boys' linguistic dexterity. The Senior Commoner Prefect is even now sometimes referred to as Sen: Co: Prae, a considerably less grandiose term.[61] Scholars trying to place Notions in the correct linguistic family can find a mixture of Latin, Greek – a maid in the main part of the school is a 'gallery nymph' – and Middle English – to laze around is to 'thoke', a word Chaucer might have used for his more supine colleagues in the embryonic English civil service. Notions even has some of its own grammar: adding 'ster' to a word denotes the person behind the action, thus making an idler a 'thokester'.[62]

In the London public schools at least, one can trace an unbroken line of support for organized drama over the centuries that began with Mulcaster. However, his other innovations did not take root; Mulcaster was a man too far ahead of his time. The public schools' continued concentration on Classics shows that at some schools headmasters worshipped Latin rather than English until well into the twentieth century. Moreover, organized sport – sport based on the patronage of the school rather than sport privately arranged and funded by groups of wealthy boys – did not take off at the public schools until well into the nineteenth century.

Mulcaster is probably the public schools' first great headmaster, despite a deeply flawed personal character. His deadliest vice was his greed for money at any cost. Perhaps the least of his crimes was to break the Merchant Taylors' rules by taking boys into the headmaster's house as pupils and boarders, until the company forced him to discharge them; this infraction was to become, in future centuries of public and indeed grammar school history, a common one. His decision to sell the office of under-usher while at St Paul's was far worse a sin, because teachers appointed through corruption rather than merit were less likely to be good ones. Moving on further down the moral hierarchy, he was accused of robbing a fellow student, John Caius, while studying at Cambridge University, a scandal which may be behind his decision to decamp to Oxford to finish his studies. Worst of all was his falsification of the records of a London church, while serving as warden, in pursuit of a scheme of embezzlement detected by the parish auditors. Explanation for this greed may lie in his attempt to keep up with the high company in which he moved in London. Mulcaster appears to have been inordinately proud of his membership of 'Prince Arthur's Knights', an exclusive gathering of archers akin to a sixteenth-century incarnation of the Marylebone Cricket Club.[63]

There is a final, curious possible first to Mulcaster's public school career: he may well have been the first man to fall foul of the authorities for not having the right public school accent. A year after Merchant Taylors' was founded, the Bishop of London and his underlings visited the school to examine the students and staff. The guests found fault with the 'Cumbrian accents' of the masters and students, complaining that the masters 'were northern men born, and therefore did not pronounce so well as those that be brought up on the school of the south parts of the realm'. Mulcaster was a member of the gentry, but he was Carlisle gentry: it seemed that he and his hand-picked men were giving the boys northern vowels.[64] The southerners would continue to win the battle over public school accents: a century and a quarter later, the Scottish mother of a pupil at Westminster School, by this stage a school at the heart of the establishment, wrote: 'I fear I lose a Scotsman, for he begins to get their words and accent.'[65] The public school accent would, over time, become firmly based on the pronunciations of the south-east, where so many of the public schools were based, to the point where at times it became synonymous with the term 'Home Counties accent'. The process of conformity, in this case conformity to the accent of the southern ruling class, began early in public school history.

It was another new school, Shrewsbury – founded in 1552, nine years before Merchant Taylors' – which supplied the first case of that important phenomenon in the history of the movement: the public school hero.

The high reputation of Thomas Ashton, one of the school's first headmasters, gave Shrewsbury a head start. Perhaps the school's greatest coup lay not in its headmaster, however, but in the grandeur of a small number of his boarding pupils from outside the town, most notably Sir Philip Sidney (1554–86), nephew of the Earl of Leicester, grandson of the Duke of Northumberland, poet and Renaissance man. It was Sidney's school friend, fellow poet and member of the upper class Fulke Greville (1554–1628), who proved that, at this stage in public school history at least, the connections of one's school friends were often more important than the quality of one's head-master. First forged at the school, the alliance between Greville and Sidney furnishes perhaps the first clear public school example of the old boy network. After leaving school, Greville built his political career through the aid of the Sidney family, who procured for him three Welsh sinecures providing an income that allowed him to pore over his poetry. It was in such matters artistic that Sidney gained, in return, from Greville: they experimented together in the composi-tion of poetry, in a friendly rivalry. At the end of an unusually intense friendship, which is hard to form outside the close daily proximity of boarding school or university during the character-forming age of adolescence, Greville's final and greatest repayment came with Sidney's death. The gesture that ensured Sidney's elevation to one of British history's heroes – the gift of his water-bottle to another wounded soldier as he lay dying after the Battle of Zutphen, with the gallant explanation that 'thy necessity is yet greater than mine' – came from Greville's biography of his friend. Greville himself was not there, and provided no source for this gentlemanly act; perhaps he simply felt that it was something which his idolized friend would very likely have done.[66]

The life after death of Sidney illustrates the importance of history, including the role of heroic old boys, in forging the identity of indi-vidual public schools. The memory of his valour was kept alive by the school, whose 1923 memorial to its fallen of the First World War was topped with a statue of the man, dressed in armour but with eyes downcast in the manner of a thoughtful scholar. Sidney served thus to commemorate the dead and inspire the soon-to-die Old Salopians (Shrewsbury old boys) of the next world war.

The final public school established in the sixteenth century, in the sense of a school educating the elite, was, like St Paul's and Merchant Taylors', in the very centre of the metropolis of London. It is believed the priests of Westminster Abbey had taught boys for centuries, but the grammar school was refounded by Elizabeth I under a new charter in 1560, with an allowance in the founding statutes for forty free scholars plus paying commoners. The scholars were to be chosen by giving 'the greatest weight' to 'gentleness of disposition, ability, learning, good character and poverty'. Under the rules, at least, no boy was to be elected scholar who could expect more than £10 (£4,000) a year as his inheritance, a rule which must have been so hard to check and enforce that it is likely it was treated with about the same respect as Winchester's scholarship rules had been regarded by the school's founder. Moreover, families had to pay the school's fees for at least a year before a boy won a scholarship, since a year at Westminster was a condition of taking the scholars' exam.[67]

Other public schools of the time had academic thresholds for entry, but these thresholds were often so low, until and even in cases beyond late Victorian times, that they have become the fuel for humorous stories fuelling ridicule against the schools. Westminster, however, is even now one of the most academic of all public schools. It got off to a fine start, with the public school movement's first truly competitive examination. Would-be scholars presented Latin work to the examiners in both verse and prose, though the school also tested less tangible qualities such as gentleness of disposition and good character.[68] This academic rigour was to pay off to spectacular effect in the following century.

Girls have been neglected in this chapter because they were sorely neglected by the public schools.

Until their dissolution in the 1530s and 1540s by Henry VIII, nunneries taught numerous girls from wealthy families, either as boarders or as day pupils. These nunneries were not, by most definitions, public schools or even proto-public schools, but their influence over the girls' public schools founded many centuries later would be profound. Their descendant schools would inherit many of their ancestors' educational DNA, including the shielding of girls from what were perceived to be the corrupting influences of the world; the emphasis on skill at music-making and needlework as badges of femininity and social accomplishment; and the accent on French rather than the classical languages. This was in part because this language was seen to be a less intellectually demanding subject suitable for a sex believed for many centuries to have lesser brain-power, and in part because of the close historical links between France and England. Some girls' public schools would retain much of this curriculum, and even the ghost of a sense that girls were inferior to boys, until well into the twentieth century. As always, Richard Mulcaster was far ahead of his time, arguing for more sophisticated women's education, including teaching the ability to 'understand and speak the learned languages' and to comprehend 'logic and rhetoric'. His, however, was a rare voice.[69] Most men, rather, would have been more sympathetic to the views of John Knox, the Scottish clergyman who in 1558 declared of women: 'Nature, I say doth paynt them . . . to be weake, fraile, impacient, feble and foolish'.[70] If women were foolish by nature, men saw little point in educating them beyond a certain unambitious threshold.

By the end of the sixteenth century there were six schools which might qualify as public schools, with at least some shared character-istics: Winchester, Eton, St Paul's, Shrewsbury, Merchant Taylors' and Westminster. Six is enough, certainly, to start tentatively to assess how good a job public schools, as a group, were doing for their pupils.

In the twenty-first century schools can be judged by their success in public exams. In the sixteenth century we cannot do this; a good substitute is to look at their record in producing distinguished old boys, though it is best to concentrate on boys not already placed by birth into an elite family on a trajectory towards leading positions in national life.

Winchester had a strong record in educating senior churchmen. In the arts the public schools had produced major figures, including Spenser, Sidney and Ben Jonson (1572–1637), the playwright and poet educated at Westminster; the public schools also retained their strong pedigree in producing great classical scholars. John Harmar

(1555–1613) was a Wykehamist who became both Regius Professor of Greek at Oxford and the headmaster of his old school. He worked on the New Testament for the King James Bible of 1611, the greatest collaborative work in British literary history. It was an undertaking that demanded close knowledge of the classical languages and an ability to render them into elegant English, which the early public schools at their best taught well. He was one of many outstanding classical scholars from the early public schools.[71] Six of the forty-seven translators of the King James Bible were educated by one public school master – Mulcaster – alone.[72]

The early public schools also produced men who combined impressive scholarship with strong courage in defending their religious principles. When Elizabeth I came to power after the death of her Papist sister Mary I in 1558, a band of Wykehamists fled abroad to become the chief intellectual supporters of the Church of Rome in England: Nicholas Sanders, Thomas Stapleton and Thomas Harding, former chaplain to the Duke of Suffolk, who had put his daughter Lady Jane Grey on the throne for nine days before Mary ejected her.[73] In 1581 Edmund Campion, an old boy of St Paul's, paid the ultimate price through one of English history's most famous Catholic martyrdoms.[74] The tradition of religious courage persisted: little over three centuries later, the school magazine of Bootham, the Quaker public school, reported at the end of the First World War that fifteen old boys had 'served in prison' as conscientious objectors.[75]

At this early stage of public school history, it is perhaps St Paul's which holds the most impressive record of any single school in producing a cluster of men who collectively played an important part in English life. Three leading statesmen, educated during a brief period under Lily, were Paulines (old boys of St Paul's). One was Edward North, who as Treasurer of the Court of Augmentations was a key official in dissolving the monasteries on behalf of Henry VIII (the court dealt with the former monasteries' estates).[76] Sir Anthony Denny became possibly the king's most trusted adviser of all: it was he who informed Henry of his impending death. William Paget was a key adviser to Henry VIII and a member of the Privy Council under Mary I.[77]

We cannot, of course, necessarily credit the later success of men to their schools, particularly not if they came from well-connected backgrounds. Denny was the son of a senior official and member of the Mercers' Company, though Paget, son of a shearman, was mocked by enemies for his humble birth.[78] A look through the old registers of the schools shows a marked tendency, both in the sixteenth century and in later ages, for the sons of grand men to pass on to grand careers, and for those plucked from obscurity to sink back into it. Who now remembers Nicholas Sturley, probable son of a London vintner and pupil at Eton from 1547 to 1551, or John Gravatt, probable son of an Oxford chandler who followed him six years later, their history so obscure that we do not even know for sure what their fathers did?[79] Their brief mention in this volume is the only time that history has taken notice of them. One cannot even necessarily credit later intellectual or literary success to the school's teaching. Sir Philip Sidney's Huguenot tutor, Johan Tassel, followed him to Shrewsbury.[80] In future centuries, many private teachers were to do this, compensating for deficits in the school's offering.

On the other hand, it is difficult to see how Richard Neile (1562–1640), the son of a tallow chandler – a maker of precisely the type of cheap, workaday candles which would not have passed muster at St Paul's School – could have risen to become Archbishop of York had he not been educated at Westminster School, followed by Cambridge University.[81] Richard Corbet, son of a gardener on the outskirts of London, became Bishop of Oxford and later of Norwich after attending Westminster in the 1590s.[82] Edward North, the Pauline, also came from a very ordinary family.[83]

There are, moreover, men who credited their success in part to their public school. One is Ben Jonson, who in later life acknowledged William Camden, the Second Master of Westminster who went on to head the school, as the source of 'All that I am in arts, all that I know'. Jonson also clearly benefited from Westminster's emphasis, like Merchant Taylors', on dramatic performance – he refers to Westminster's dramatic tradition in his work. Jonson honed his skills in poetry and play writing through the hard Westminster schooling of translating Greek and Latin verse into their equivalent English forms.[84] His Westminster friend, the collector of manuscripts Robert Cotton, was influenced by Camden's interest in history; former pupil and master collaborated in setting up the Society of Antiquaries. These are early cases of a public school master's enthusiasm for particular interests infecting his pupils.[85]

At first sight, Jonson illustrates the role of public schools, early in their history, as engines of social mobility, something whose alleged loss has frequently been lamented by modern observers of public schools. However, steep ascents from the lower to the upper reaches of society were relatively rare. A study of the scholars of St Paul's School that begins in the sixteenth century and goes as far as 1748, finds about fifty, out of about eight hundred scholars identified, from artisan backgrounds. These include eight tailors, five brewers, four printers and one baker, just 6 per cent of the total.[86] We cannot assume that they were all poor, however. Take the case of Jonson at Westminster. His stepfather was a bricklayer – which seems to us, today, to be a skilled working-class job. The man was probably Robert Prett, a wealthy contractor who rose to become master of the Tylers' and Bricklayers' Company. Although socially he was not a member of the upper classes, he would nevertheless have enjoyed almost the same status as the many mercers who seem, from looking through the St Paul's register, virtually to have monopolized the school in the sixteenth century. He would also almost certainly have been richer than most of them. Moreover, Jonson was not a free scholar; his stepfather had the money to pay his fees, and did so.[87]

Furthermore, any antediluvian idea that in the early years of the public schools the sons of nobles and artisans learned and lived in equal status is profoundly inaccurate. The Eton statutes specified that the progeny of noblemen should dine at the upper table with the senior college staff; the scholars sat elsewhere.[88] Sidney arrived at

Shrewsbury with a servant as well as a tutor.[89] Such circumstances created a multi-tier structure among the schools' pupils.

Even the case of Richard Neile shows a rather limited social mobility. His father had a very ordinary craftsman's job, but his grandfather had been a courtier under Henry VIII who had fallen from grace for religious nonconformity.[90] Westminster restored his family to the professional classes rather than taking a boy from a family that had never known anything else. This role of preventing downward social mobility, rather than encouraging upward social mobility, became, over the centuries, a regular feature of public school education. The Assisted Places scheme of the 1980s and 1990s, which educated middle-class children at reduced rates, is a modern example.

Nonetheless, the artisanal origin of men such as Jonson and Neile at least implies that at this time public schools were not snobbish about their children's professions. For much of public school history (though not for all of it) one man's (or woman's) money has been as good as another's when it has come to paying the school fees. As a result, public schools have been able to adapt to the ebbing and flowing of different sources of pupil revenue.

There were other ways to educate the wealthy, outside the public schools. Many of the grammar schools that educated local children of all classes provided a high-quality education during this era. It is difficult to criticize a class of school that educated William Shakespeare, who attended the local grammar school in Stratford-on-Avon. Private tuition of wealthy children at home remained common, and, at its best, was of high quality. Roger Ascham was educated at the home of Humphrey Wingfield, a lawyer and politician who modelled his household on the famous regime of private schooling at home created by Thomas More.[91] Ascham's masterpiece, *The Scholemaster*, was a teaching guide that ignored schools altogether in favour of giving advice on private tuition. Education at home followed by early entry to Oxbridge was a typical pattern, making Oxbridge another rival to the public schools until the late eighteenth century, when an older entry age of eighteen or so began to predominate. Francis Bacon, philosopher, scientist, politician and rascal, and one of the greatest Elizabethans of all, was educated at home, and then at Cambridge from the age of twelve.[92] However, the quality of home-based education was highly variable, judging by the caustic comment of Francis's father, Sir Nicholas Bacon, a courtier supremely well acquainted with the education of the elite on account of his role as the head of the Court of Wards and Liveries, which supervised the education and care of orphaned children of the upper classes: 'I may remember diverse gentlemen that gave gladly great wages to their horsekeepers and huntsmen than to such as taught their children, whereby they had very ready horses and perfect dogs, as that they had very untoward children.'[93]

The public schools certainly took greater care than this in selecting their masters – for the most part. However, there were already a handful of worrying tendencies among public schools which would, a couple of centuries later, become serious problems threatening their future.

The first problem was subtle: the schools were already drawing their headmasters and other officials from men educated within the small existing group of public schools, including their own institution. William Horman, the headmaster of Eton and composer of fruity Latin sentences, attended Winchester as a pupil; he later resigned the headship of Eton to return there as headmaster.[94] The first head of Merchant Taylors', Mulcaster, was educated at Eton; five of the early high masters at St Paul's were at both Eton and King's College, Cambridge. Eventually the system was to create great dynasties of public school heads. R. A. Butler, the 1944 Education Secretary who reformed Britain's school system (but not the public schools), was a scion of one such family, which in the nineteenth century produced George Butler (headmaster of Harrow), George Butler (Liverpool College), Henry Montagu Butler (Harrow again) and Albert Gray Butler (Haileybury).[95] Public school teaching was already showing signs of becoming rather a narrow sphere, where many in charge had seen little of the outside world. Eventually such narrowness breeds a conservative world-view, whether among Plymouth Brethren, inter-marrying royal families, or public school headmasters. The men who rise to the top of such systems cannot conceive of a different way of doing things, let alone seriously question established ways.

Another problem was more straightforward: the public schools were beating their children too much. By the sixteenth century, Renaissance thinkers such as Erasmus and Roger Ascham had started to question whether beating encouraged learning. Ascham's *Scholemaster* was prompted by the discovery that 'diverse scholars of Eton be run away from the school for fear of beating'. Ascham, in response, advised kind-ness in its stead: 'I assure you, there is no such whetstone, to sharpen a good witte and encourage a will to learning, as is praise', he promised. 'For, the scholar, is commonlie beat for the making, when the master were more worthie to be beat for the mending.'[96] Some might argue that the public schools were no more savage than any other schools – making any criticism of public school cruelty hopelessly naïve and unhistorical. However, at the beginning of the seventeenth century Alexander Gill the Elder, high master of St Paul's, was reprimanded by the governors for flogging too much. This suggests that the public schools actively resisted, rather than reluctantly followed, educated opinion on the issue.[97] Thomas Tusser certainly found punishment at Eton more severe than at St Paul's Cathedral, where he had been a chor-ister (with no connection to the school), writing:

> From Paul's I went to Eton set,
> To learn straightways the Latin phrase;
> Where fifty three stripes given to me
> At once I had,
> For fault but small, or none at all.[98]

As Tusser's lines show, in this and succeeding centuries boys would be beaten at public school, not only for misbehaviour but also simply for getting things wrong.

A third problem was, at this stage, still minor, but eventually it became perhaps the most serious defect of all. This was the issue of corruption. Mulcaster's wheezes for making extra money from Merchant Taylors' School cannot have been good for the pupils. Taking boys into his house as private pupils would have distracted him; selling staff positions is never the best way of getting the right man for the job.

These early cracks in the edifice were eventually to threaten the very foundations of the sector.

CHAPTER TWO

Earls and Shoemakers
1611–1767

THE next public school began with the mixture of high moral tone and hypocrisy which had accompanied the founding of Winchester. Despite this inglorious beginning, by the end of the seventeenth century it had already played a distinguished role in English public life.

In 1611 the will of the late Thomas Sutton, an Old Etonian merchant who had married judiciously and made a fortune from lending money to high-spending aristocrats, set up 'the Hospital of King James and Thomas Sutton in Charterhouse in the City of London'. Sutton, possibly the richest commoner in England, generously endowed the institution, like Winchester and Eton a mix of school and almshouse, with valuable land. Charterhouse was created, according to the founding statutes, 'for poor people, men and children', with forty scholars, their education paid by the hospital, to be nominated by individual governors. Revised statutes published sixteen years later allowed the schoolmaster and usher to take a further sixty scholars who were obliged to pay their own way, but the wealthy had in fact succeeded in infiltrating the school years before. The parental backgrounds of only six of the first thirty-five scholars are known, which suggests that some may have begun and ended their lives in social as well as historical obscurity. However, of the six that are traceable, all were from the professional classes, with one the son of a surgeon, one of a clergyman and one of a lawyer. A later order by the governors, that the surgeon's son was to be sent home if the report should prove true that his father was worth more than £400 (£85,000) a year, hints that the school's definition of poor was not of the most exacting rigour. Charterhouse had, it is clear, already become a public school: a school largely for the economic elite. It inherited the tensions of the Winchester College model when choosing its clientele.[1]

The rule that each scholar need be recommended by only one governor was a recipe for a system of admission based squarely on personal patronage, and the unusually exalted nature of the patrons made it a school largely, though not entirely, for well-connected members of the elite. The Charterhouse school play of 1761 was attended by one archbishop, five bishops, three dukes and the Lord Chancellor. By the eighteenth century the list of past governors included a high proportion of the most prominent politicians of the age, including five prime ministers: Robert Walpole, Henry Pelham, the Earl of Bute, Lord North and William Pitt the Elder.[2]

Patronage can, however, also benefit the well-connected poor, and at their best, governors acted as genuine talent spotters of boys from humble backgrounds. In 1714 the indebted and improvidently fecund clergyman Samuel Wesley, anxious to cut the costs of his children's education, used a governor to secure the entry of his academically talented son John, one of his nineteen offspring and the future co-founder of the Methodist movement, as a free scholar. In the same way, the Earl of Leicester had exerted his influence to win entry to Winchester for the brilliant John Harmar in the sixteenth century.[3] The Charterhouse records also show the regular admission in the school's early years of the sons of tradesmen who rubbed shoulders with scions of the professional classes.[4]

By and by Charterhouse fostered one of the most productive of all public school friendships and one of the great literary partnerships of British history: that of Joseph Addison and Richard Steele, the waspish early pioneers of magazine journalism, who co-founded the

Spectator and *Tatler*. To adapt the familiar modern zen riddle, would Addison have existed if Steele had not been there to hear him, and vice versa? Probably not: without their close relationship as working adults, building on a friendship forged at the school in the 1680s, they would probably have been considerably less successful. The two men produced a good advertisement for education among one's peers at school rather than in the seclusion of home.[5]

The new school of Charterhouse provided another option for ambitious London parents, but twenty-seven years after its foundation, a man walked into the long-established school of Westminster to begin a reign that would, for half a century or so, make Westminster the most alluring of all the public schools. Such achievements are hard to measure statistically, but Westminster managed to educate a sizeable minority of the most distinguished Englishmen of the seventeenth and early eighteenth centuries. At the centre of this accomplishment sat the cold, austere and intellectually brilliant figure of Richard Busby, headmaster of the school from 1638 until 1695, when in his ninetieth year he died in his quarters. His passing from this world to the next was marked, says a contemporary account, by sparks of fire.[6] Even fantastical myths hold a certain truth, in showing the regard with which men are held by their contemporaries.

Busby's ostensibly dull basic curriculum was not the cause of his unprecedented success. It was, outwardly, the educational equivalent of Monty Python's spam menu: a strict classical diet that consisted, to take the Second Form as an example, of the Greek story-teller Aesop on Monday, followed by the Roman authors Ovid on Tuesday, Terence on Wednesday and Martial on Thursday – and, for those rare boys who had not experienced enough of these authors by this time of the week, a repetition of some of their material on Friday.[7]

Be that as it may, contemporary accounts testify to Busby's charisma as an infectiously enthusiastic teacher of the Classics. The fact that he nearly gave up a teaching career before arriving at Westminster to go on to the stage reveals a large element of theatricality in his style, as has often been the case with the best public school teachers.[8] He also had a clever wrinkle that would have spurred on the more intellectually able Busby boys, though probably not inspiring the merely average: he encouraged his pupils to prove scholarly authority incomplete by finding obscure words or examples of uses for words not listed in the existing Classics dictionaries.[9]

The poetry and criticism of John Dryden, author of *Absalom and Architophel* and student of Busby, is steeped in a deep knowledge of Greek and Roman literature, including the poems of Ovid that had been taught by Busby. The 1685 Latin verses penned by Charles Montagu, the future Earl of Halifax and another Busby pupil, on the death of Charles II, were so outstanding that they gave him an entry into court society that he would use to build his successful political career. The 6th Earl of Dorset (another Old Westminster) invited Montagu to London after reading them, and introduced him to his friends.[10]

Busby's genius, however, lay in his cultivation of an unusually wide breadth of learning. His encouragement of mathematics, rare for a public school in this era, was all the more remarkable and creditable, given that he had no natural talent for the subject. Busby, who had been a Westminster scholar near the beginning of the seventeenth century, could not even add up: his papers include a valuation, wrong on both the weight and the value, which he made of the plate in his possession.[11] However, his distinguished pupils included Robert Hooke, the scientist and architect, who appears to have been allowed dispensation from the usual curriculum to concentrate on studying Euclid's *Mathematics* and other works. Hooke would probably have been taught by one of the maths instructors hired by Busby, an innovation for the public schools. Busby also introduced specialist assistants for modern and oriental languages, a rarity at the public schools of the time.[12]

Hooke erected the building that still houses Busby's famous library, blessed with an amazing range of works encompassing everything from astronomy to zoology, with architecture, maths, geography, the Classics and Hebrew included, though the most unusual of all the curios, the first version of the Bible written in Algonquin, was sold a few centuries later.[13] What is more amazing still is that Busby's school produced men remembered in all these fields and more. They included John Locke, the greatest English philosopher of his era, Dryden, the greatest literary figure, Henry Purcell, the greatest English composer until Victorian times, and Richard Lower, doctor, scientist and the first westerner ever to perform a blood transfusion.[14] Christopher Wren, the greatest architect of his generation, was a private pupil of Busby's, though not a member of the school.[15]

Busby's broad-minded approach towards education was founded on a particular religious sensibility, shared by some intellectuals over the centuries, which has done so much to enrich British history: the conviction not only that God existed, but that a rolling forward of the frontiers of knowledge into new spheres would show the workings of His wisdom to a steadily greater degree. Busby also appears to have exuded the air of a man who believed that the wise workings of the Lord were conducted largely through him. It is said that he refused to take his hat off to Charles II on the grounds that he did not want the boys to think there was a man greater than their headmaster.[16]

The positive side to his arrogance was a greater than usual degree of independence of spirit. Busby remained an open supporter of the king's side during the kingless rule of the Cromwells as Lord Protectors – even offering prayers for Charles I on the day of his execution in nearby Whitehall.[17] It was a bravish move in an era when headmasters were frequently ejected from their posts for holding the wrong political views; so too was his decision to retain the name of King's Scholar for the duration of the eleven-year republic that lasted until the restoration of the monarchy under Charles II in 1660.[18] Bravish if not quite brave: Busby judiciously attended Oliver Cromwell's funeral when Cromwell's son Richard assumed power, after staging this rather restrained semantic resistance.[19]

By this stage Busby was protected by his celebrity. By making Westminster the first public school with a stellar academic reputation,

Busby created a name for himself within the establishment. His name even took on symbolic value: much as great orators were referred to as 'the Demosthenes of his age' and such like, the speaker of the House of Commons was referred to in a 1659 diary as 'a Busby amongst so many school-boys'.[20]

Busby's staunch independence of mind was absorbed by his pupils. Philip Henry, non-conformist preacher and a favourite of Busby's during his time at the school, met Busby in St James's Park near Westminster, shortly after taking a huge gamble with his future by resigning his Church of England living to become a non-conformist. 'Prythee, child, what made thee a non-conformist?' asked Busby, who as a High Anglican was at the other end of the Protestant spectrum. To this Henry replied: 'Truly, Sir, you made me one, for you taught me those things which hindered me from conforming.'[21]

Busby produced an unusually high number of rebels who were active in political life as doers or thinkers, some of them with a roguish tint, though usually all the more lovable for that. Henry Stubbe was a famous Classics scholar who got into trouble with the authorities for, among other things, criticizing the universities, the clergy and the Duke of York's wife (though not all at the same time). Daniel Burgess was another famous non-conformist preacher, whose meeting house in Lincoln's Inn Fields was razed to the ground by an unappreciative mob. The 3rd Earl of Peterborough was a courageous and unswerving opponent of James II, and played a key part in the Glorious Revolution of 1688 which deposed James in favour of William III. John Locke was both independent-minded and a defender of toleration for others' independent views: he argued that a diversity of religious groups stabilized society, since it reduced the social unrest fomented by the denial of freedom of worship.[22]

Aside from Busby, other public school headmasters could also be shockingly independent. In 1726 the secretary to His Majesty King George I forwarded a request to the headmaster of Winchester to admit a certain John Brofield as a scholar, only to be given a resounding 'No' on the grounds that scholarships were in the gift of the governors alone, though, of course, 'this signification of your royal pleasure was received with a respect becoming the most dutiful of your Majesty's subjects'.[23] This reply is striking proof that England was not, in the eighteenth century, an absolute monarchy.

Locke is merely one of Busby's notable pupils. No single school in British history – not even Eton in its most glorious years – has contributed as large a share of the most distinguished members of society as Westminster did under this headmaster. At times, London society in the late seventeenth and early eighteenth centuries almost feels like a Restoration comedy of manners where the males are Old Westminsters – with accompanying music by Old Westminster Purcell. Two years after winning entry into London society, largely through the offices of Old Westminster the Earl of Dorset, Charles Montagu joined with fellow Old Westminster and school friend Matthew Prior to write a parody of *The Hind and the Panther* – written by Old Westminster Dryden, who also enjoyed the patronage of the Earl of Dorset.[24]

The attendance of the Earl of Dorset and other men from titled families at the school shows that Westminster even managed to breach one of the last great bastions of public school resistance: the high aristocracy, composed of the richest and most politically powerful titled families in Britain. As well as Montagu and the several generations of the Earls (later Dukes) of Dorset, pupils of Busby included the Earl of Nottingham, the future Lord Chancellor, who appears as Amri in Dryden's *Absalom and Architophel*.[25]

The key explanations for the flocking of the high aristocracy to Westminster are the academic brilliance of the school and its proximity to Britain's centres of power. The school was producing superbly educated men; that in itself provided a motivation to send sons there. In addition, many Old Westminsters were seen to progress to promising careers at court, both in politics and in the arts. It was useful even for the high aristocracy to send their sons to the place where many future members of the monarch's circle were congregating, a place which had become a kind of junior court. As increasing

numbers of the high aristocracy went to the school with every passing
generation, a virtuous circle took shape: the high aristocracy attracted
the high aristocracy, as well as ambitious families whose members
would, they hoped, one day depend on this class for patronage. This
was an age when the wealthy often enjoyed a potpourri of education,
consisting of a stint here and a stint there. A year or so at an academically distinguished public school would round off this experience.
The 6th Earl of Dorset spent a year at Westminster before leaving for
a Grand Tour of Europe with a tutor.[26]

The arrival of the high aristocracy was also the making of
Westminster as a school for the political class – and by the end of the
century this could be said for Eton too, and to a lesser extent St Paul's.
The make-up of the first cabinet of Robert Walpole, Britain's first
prime minister, illustrates the public schools' record in educating
politicians. Including Walpole himself, seven of the eleven members
had been to public school, with Westminster leading with a total
of three, though Walpole himself was an Old Etonian. Westminster
alone educated four of George I's and George II's First Lords of the
Treasury, predecessors to the prime minister, and a third of their
secretaries of state.

Busby's Achilles' heel was his 'devilish covetousness', to borrow the
description of the diarist Samuel Pepys.[27] He crammed as many
boarders into his house as possible to increase his profit from the
school. This was not against the rules, but another predatory practice
did breach them: the school's new governing committee, set up in
1645, complained about his habit of charging the free scholars £4
(£770) a year, which went directly to him. It would not have deterred
reasonably prosperous middle-class families from sending their sons
to the school, but it did rule this out for families in more straitened
circumstances. Deeming it 'a dishonour to the Parliament that those
poore boyes should be at that charge', the committee abolished this
practice and instead paid Busby £50 (£9,700) a year in compensation.[28]

For Busby, who, when he was most commercially successful,
earned perhaps £1,000 (£190,000) a year, the motivation for rapacity

seems to have been acquisition rather than extravagance.[29] He led an ascetic lifestyle, and was ready enough to assist some of those in need, such as the children of royalists who could not afford the cost of the school, although he surely cannot claim much credit for breaking the rules to filch money from scholars and then selectively giving some of it back.[30]

Busby maximized his income from the school so successfully that he left it in a dilapidated state. By the end of his reign his meanness was beginning to eat into Westminster's greatness from the inside. A document written, it appears, by an official connected to Westminster Abbey, found that 'meerly out of covetousness to avoid the expence' there were 'but two Masters constantly attending the Schoole'. As a result, 'the boyes can neither be soe well looked after, nor soe substantially grounded, or soe industriously forwarded in learning, as they are in other Schooles, and ought to be in soe eminent a Schoole as this, which was not only accounted, but was really heretofore the best in the Kingdome'. It was not merely their learning which suffered because of this neglect: the official also found that the commoners were prone to being beaten by the King's Scholars, 'not onely to bruises and bloodshed, but often even to wounds, and Scarrs, that remain al the daies of their life'. In conclusion, 'a great part of the most precious time of their whole life, and that which is the most flexible and fit for instruction, is squandered away and utterly lost'.[31]

The practical effect of Busby's neglect is revealed in a letter written in the 1680s by a worried mother. In words that could have come from a twenty-first-century parent fretting about her child's condition far from home, she writes: 'In the great cold school he sits the whole day over without a hat or cap, and all the windows broke, and yet thanks be to God he takes very well with it, though he never sees a fire but in my house.'[32]

The vices of covetousness and corruption, which would almost destroy the nascent public school sector in the following century, were apparent at other public schools as well. By the mid-seventeenth century Eton was in severe financial trouble, owing to the fellows' highly ingenious but also deeply dishonest wheeze of boosting income by charging all one-off costs as capital expenditure, and then dividing the surplus income among themselves.[33] In 1608 the commissioners who monitored Winchester College issued no fewer than two dozen injunctions against behaviour by the staff and fellows contrary to the statutes. One covered the taking of bribes to accept certain children as scholars: 'That no school-master, usher, chaplain, clerk, chorister, or servant be elected or accepted into the same [the school] for any money or reward, directly or indirectly.' Another dealt with the pocketing of revenue from the college's land. By 1620 the commissioners were ordering the provision of meat to the boys 'of due weight, that they may not be driven to get their food elsewhere' – corruption had reached such a point that the boys were being starved.[34] The public school asceticism first established by Wykeham, including plain food, cold baths and moderate fustigation, was acceptable to many parents, though it put others off. Outright privation was not, however, and would imperil the public schools' survival in the next century.

Harrow School was founded in 1572 in what was then a village outside London, but it took much longer to change from a grammar school primarily educating local boys for free to a public school that disproportionately educated boys from wealthy families. The key to the change was probably the 1669 occupation of the headmaster's study by William Horne, a man with good contacts in the aristocracy, including the Duke of Somerset. The 5th and 6th Dukes were educated under Horne; this was enough to entice other influential patrons. In 1690 his successor, William Bolton, described Harrow as a 'public school', in the sense of a school that educated the nation rather than just local people. A surer guide to Harrow's status than a headmaster's verbiage is probably the governors' brusque reminder in the same year to the master and his deputy that they had an obligation to teach the full complement of forty free scholars. The governors' minutes also hinted that – as in the twenty-first century – the bulk of the families who applied for free education at public schools were not working-class; the governors demanded that the full complement of forty should be met even if it meant enrolling children not exclusively from the poor, but from 'the richer sort' of Harrow and Pinner.[35]

Rugby School was set up in 1567, five years before Harrow, by the rich merchant Lawrence Sheriff as 'a free grammar school kept within the said school house to serve chiefly for the children of Rugby and Brownsover'. However, in the late seventeenth century it became primarily a public school, serving an elite client base rather than just local boys, at a similar time to Harrow's parallel transformation. In Rugby's case, as in Harrow's, the key to this was probably a distinguished headmaster, Henry Holyoake (who served from 1687 to 1730). During his time nearly 80 per cent of the boys were fee payers – though most were from nearby counties, suggesting that the clientele was not as grand as Harrow's.[36] Its time in the sun would come in the early nineteenth century under Thomas Arnold, still the most famous headmaster in British history.

In the late seventeenth century Harrow became a school for the sons of barristers, doctors, academics, vicars and landowners, a mixture of the upper classes and what were then called 'the learned professions' but are known today as the upper middle classes. These were not just London boys: they came from as far afield as Cornwall, Norfolk and Yorkshire. However, perhaps the most significant old boy of the period is, paradoxically, one of history's nonentities. John Girdler, who arrived in 1691, was the first of many Old Harrovian MPs.[37]

Harrow did not attract such exalted patrons by offering anything radically new. Nor could it have, since the men who made Harrow – its headmasters – hailed from the same narrow world as other public school heads. From 1608 to 1805 every one of them came to office having had previous experience of Eton, Westminster, Charterhouse or Harrow itself.[38] Instead of innovating, Harrow adopted the established pattern of à la carte public schooling and carried it to an extreme.

This was partly a question of living conditions, the result of a disparity in backgrounds that was, at Harrow, even greater than at other public schools. One might expect this from a school on the edges of a large capital city with great contrasts of wealth and poverty, which started as a very ordinary grammar but soon came to educate a large chunk of the political class. In 1769 Lord Althorp, an ancestor of Princess Diana, arrived at Harrow School 'with a suite and attendance of such state as even at that time to be considered an intrusion upon the uniformity of school life', in the words of a slightly shocked contemporary.[39] The following year William Peachey arrived as a free scholar. Althorp would, as the 2nd Earl Spencer, go on to be a leading politician. Peachey would become a local shoemaker and the (part-time) school porter.[40]

At Harrow money bought not merely a lavish lifestyle; it also bought a better education. By 1700 there was very little teaching in lessons, which were focused mainly on the oral repetition and imitation of classical texts and their translations.[41] This would have been helpful for pupils who already knew the text well and wanted to check their understanding. It would not, however, have imparted understanding, since boys were given little individual attention. As a result, Harrow in this era hardly fits with our modern definition of a school as a place where pupils are educated by the staff.

Apologists for this system might argue that the lack of teaching at Harrow was not necessarily a problem. This was the job of private tutors, who by this point were rapidly becoming not only standard but essential. Good tutors taught a veritable panorama of subjects, including maths and French, ancient history and metaphysics. Rich parents were able to afford intellectually impressive ones. At Harrow in the mid-eighteenth century, Adam Ferguson, historian, philosopher and one of the future leading lights of the Scottish Enlightenment, was tutor to Lord Bute's son – one of an increasing number of boys sent down south for their education in the decades after the 1707 Act of Union united England and Scotland.[42] The richer public school boys had long had private tutors, as the case of Sir Philip Sidney shows, but at Harrow the gulf in education between boys who had them and boys who did not seems to have been unusually wide.

The de luxe option from the Harrow education menu was expensive. Harrow pupils' bills in the eighteenth century suggest that careful parents could probably have whittled the cost of education down to about £30 (£4,600) a year, making it just about affordable, at a pinch, to relatively successful members of some professions, such as the law, the Church and engineering. However, total charges might be nearer £100 (£15,200) for a boy staying under the watchful eye of the head, in his own room, and hiring one of the more expensive tutors – well out of the reach of the average clergyman or even lawyer.[43]

These days there is much debate about how much of their business large corporations can outsource without losing their core identity. The practice of outsourcing one's teaching certainly left Harrow and other schools vulnerable. In the 1760s Harrow's hollow system almost caved in when the Revd Samuel Classe arrived in the town and began acting as tutor to sons of the nobility already attending the school. Classe took the concept of teaching by private tuition to its logical but dangerous conclusion – dangerous for the school, at least – by declaring that his tutees were exempt from the school roll-calls, made several times a day to exercise a modicum of control over pupils who frequently enjoyed but a tenuous connection to the life of the institution. Classe's attempts to live by eating Harrow's insides were foiled only when the school governors, rejecting the support given to him by some powerful parents, ruled that 'all the young gentlemen who shall be admitted into the Free Grammar School shall conform to the rules thereof'. This included the exacting task of turning up at the school.[44]

Harrow's case underlines the fact that other than at Westminster the standard of education at public schools was often less than satisfactory in the seventeenth and early eighteenth centuries.

Following the tradition of Eton College's William Horman, farsighted educators gave further thought to the challenge of how to make education interesting. Many responded by buying the 1659 English edition of *Orbis Sensualium Pictus*, history's first illustrated school textbook, which included an introductory Latin vocabulary based on pictures of common objects.[45] It did, not, however, become common reading at public schools. Despite signs that thought was being given to how Latin left the brain of the schoolmaster on its uncertain journey into the cerebellum of the schoolboy, John Milton, Britain's greatest seventeenth-century poet, was critical of his classical education at St Paul's School. He thought that too much time was spent on the mysteries of Latin grammar, with 'seven or eight years merely in scraping together so much miserable Latine and Greek, as might be learnt otherwise easily and delightfully in one year', though it should be pointed out that Milton was, all his life, an unusually waspish and critical character.[46]

At least Latin was taught, even if not always well. Critics were also volubly aware of the serious gaps in their educational offering throughout this period. One was the frequent emphasis on the memorizing of facts rather than on the intellectual exploration of ideas and concepts which might educate a boy for the real world. Remembering his three years at Westminster from 1749, Edward Gibbon, the historian, wrote: 'I left school with a stock of erudition which might have puzzled a doctor, and a degree of ignorance of which any schoolboy would have been ashamed.'[47] The neglect of mathematics at most public schools is reflected in the arithmetical ignorance both of Busby – though he rectified this at his old school – and of Pepys, who had been at St Paul's. Though a senior civil servant in the Admiralty, Pepys did not acquire the basic mathematical skill of multiplication until he was twenty-nine, when with some difficulty he learnt it from the mate of the *Royal Charles*.[48] By this time Pepys's admiration for his old high master at St Paul's, Samuel Cromleholme, had been somewhat dissipated by his encounter with Cromleholme in a drunken state in a London tavern – though Pepys was not the first or last ex-public schoolboy in history to see a former head with his mask of virtue stained by alcohol or other forms of vice.[49]

Several issues militated against adequate teaching. Boys of different ages were often taught together in one big form. This made pupil–teacher ratios at public schools very large when compared with modern times.[50] It was a textbook example of a flawed incentive structure: taking on new staff would reduce the profit made by the headmaster from the school's education.

Despite these problems, parents, even from the highest classes, continued to send their sons into the nascent public school system. This was probably partly because, in many cases, both the education and the quality of life at school were, for the wealthy aristocrats who began gracing the schools more frequently in the seventeenth century, a step above the average pupil's. In addition to having their own private tutors in many cases, such boys received special treatment from the school itself because of their high status, and frequently better provisions and living quarters because they proffered more for their upkeep. Robert Devereux, the future Earl of Essex, later one of the leading parliamentary generals in the First English Civil War (1642–6), was put in the charge of Sir Henry Wotton, Eton's provost – roughly speaking, the chair of the governors.[51] Sir Henry also found a man to teach the sons of the Earl of Cork to play the viol and sing while at Eton.[52] The provost took steps to cure one of the sons, the future scientist Robert Boyle, of his stutter. Boyle was grateful to Wotton for his kindness, recalling that he was 'not only a fine gentleman himself, but very well skilled in the art of making others so', though his father, reluctant to take any chances, also hired a private tutor.[53] It is hard to see these grander pupils, monitored by tutors or by the provost himself, being bullied.

Under Sir Henry's regime at Eton from 1624 to 1639, the college developed a practice which was to recur frequently when particular public schools were at their best in the coming centuries: the cultivation of certain talented boys, who were in this case chosen by Wotton to eat and live with him.[54] Wotton was not merely a brilliant but also a worldly man, no doubt with much to teach the boys; in a previous life he had been a diplomat, an envoy who had coined the much-quoted phrase, 'an ambassador is an honest gentleman sent abroad to lie for the good of his country'.[55] His background must have been attractive to parents.

One might ask how effective school was for the average boy of average ability from an average family, who did not enjoy such patronage. At many schools, he would have struggled to make a success of himself – and the fate of boys of average talent remained one of the weaknesses of the public schools until the second half of the twentieth century. One might also question whether public schools changed the future lives of aristocrats educated at them, notwithstanding the case of Boyle, whose confidence was clearly boosted by his kind treatment at Eton. Aristocrats might have had the most fun; at the very least they ate the best food. For the most part, however, they gained less from their time at school – because they had everything already – than the minority of boys from more humble backgrounds who were able to parlay their school days into successful careers.

Nevertheless, there are sometimes spectacular cases of boys who owed their future success to their public school experience, boys who fulfilled Wykeham's ambition of helping the 'poor and needy' into distinguished careers. Matthew Prior's father had prospered as a carpenter, to the point where he could afford to send Matthew to Westminster as a paying pupil. After his father's death, however, Matthew had to be withdrawn from the school, to earn his crust by working in his uncle's tavern. A year later the Earl of Dorset came to the tavern for sustenance, to find the twelve-year-old boy behind the bar reading the Roman poet Horace. Dorset set him an extemporaneous exam: the translation of a Horatian ode into English. Prior passed, and in 1676 was sent back to his old school, with the Earl paying for tuition and his uncle for clothing and other necessities. At school he befriended the future Earl of Halifax and George Stepney, son of a court official. Both men would gain greatly from Halifax's friendship – it was Halifax who secured Stepney's entry into the diplomatic service. Prior's association with Halifax helped him to break into the same profession, by providing him with a profile in court and literary circles.[56]

Half a century later William Whitehead, son of a baker, entered Winchester as a scholar. While there he took care to make friends with the rich and aristocratic, including Lord Charles Douglas, adumbrating a future career which would greatly depend on aristocratic and eventually royal patronage. The crowning glory came in 1757 when he became Poet Laureate, an acceptable candidate because of his upper-class connections.[57]

William Sherlock, son of a Southwark tradesman living in the unusually evocatively named Gravel Lane, entered Eton in 1653, probably as a King's Scholar. After going on to Cambridge, he enjoyed a brilliant career, becoming Master of the Temple and chaplain to James II and then William III, showing a certain deftness given the two kings' radically different religious sensibilities.[58] His royal link would have made it easier for him to procure the King's Scholarship for his son Thomas, who went to his father's old school in 1689 before achieving even more career success than his father by becoming a bishop and Vice-Chancellor of Cambridge University.[59]

These personal histories show how life-changing a public school education could be, but it remained difficult for boys of humble origin to enter most of the public schools. At times schools kept to the statutes by educating scholars for free, but at times they did not – Busby's was simply one among many cases over the centuries of a headmaster admonished by the governors for milking pupils. Even if genuinely free scholarship places could be won, for the labouring classes the barriers to entry remained. They included the extras for which a scholar usually had to pay, such as books and bed linen. The obstacles also included the connections needed to secure a scholarship place, the cost of the forgone wage of the boy sent away to study rather than work, and the knowledge of Latin, however basic, required to secure acceptance from the headmaster. Finally, there was the struggle to take full advantage of one's long school education by going on to university, which in the days before government grants was expensive.

Between the genuinely wealthy and the working classes lay a large portion of the population who could, by scrimping, saving and settling for a very basic level of provision, just about put their sons through public school. This was made possible by the absence of standard school fees until the mid-nineteenth century. Instead, commoners paid different rates for boarding depending on whose house they were staying at – with a place at the headmaster's usually the most expensive, and a place at a 'dame's house', a boarding house run by a woman close by who kept a loose, unofficial affiliation with the school, somewhat cheaper. Boys also had to pay the school separately for tuition, and for a bewildering host of extras, including books, Christmas tips to the headmaster, Christmas tips to the second master, candles and, luxury of luxuries, the privilege of not having to share a bed with another snotty boy.[60] However, some of these costs could have been avoided, or at least reduced, by the most determined of economizers.

The records in school ledgers and boys' account books of fees paid are, therefore, confusing – but also revealing. They confirm the à la carte nature of public school life in this era, not only in terms of education, as at Wotton's Eton, but in living conditions. The differences between the conditions enjoyed by individual boys within the same school could be almost as stark as in society as a whole. The notion of grand living at a public school had scaled new heights by 1730, when ten noblemen living with the headmaster at Winchester paid £200 (£37,000) each a year – many times above public schools' typical charges during this era, and a tad above the average earnings even of lawyers.[61] There was, doubtless, never a day when they failed to receive meat 'of due weight', and they must, unlike the Westminster boys, have seen a fire on every wintry day that called for one.

On the one hand, the three examples above of boys from humble origin doing well out of going to public school are not isolated; there are plenty more. On the other hand, if one leafs through the schools' registers of old boys relating to this era, it does not take long to ascertain that boys from elite families were far more likely to enjoy illustrious careers.[62] Public school was an engine of social mobility for the less socially elevated pupil; it was, however, a wheezing, sputtering engine rather than a smoothly running machine.

Parents who did not think much of public school education had plenty of alternative options.

In the early 1600s Thomas Farnaby, a former mercenary and survivor of Sir Francis Drake's last voyage, created a school in the City of London that soon attracted a stream of pupils. At times the school employed three teachers besides himself, putting it on a par with the public schools of the time. Key to all was the man's personality. Farnaby had a talent for enabling pupils to flourish through gentleness and encouragement. One among many pupils from the political class, the future MP Sir John Bramston, son of one of England's leading judges, was transferred there from a brutal schoolmaster in Essex. 'Oh heavens! Where have you been brought up?' cried Farnaby with theatrical joy on seeing his first sample of Bramston's work. 'I think he was unwilling to discourage me too much', recalled Bramston laconically. Farnaby also pioneered the practice, not adopted at most public schools until well into the nineteenth century, of putting each form in a separate classroom, an innovation which improved the boys' ability to concentrate on their study.[63]

Farnaby's venture is merely the most successful seventeenth-century example of what were then called 'private schools' – establishments set up by one person or a small group of individuals to make a profit, which usually folded after the retirement or death of the founder. Individual schools periodically became fashionable amongst the aristocracy, and were able to charge high fees: in 1657 the Earl of Westmorland paid £100 (£18,000) a year to keep his two sons at one such school in Twickenham.[64] However, these institutions' ability to threaten the public schools was limited by their inherent mortality. In essence this made them more like particularly successful ventures for the private tutors who established them, rather than schools which had a life of their own that continued after the departure of one key man. Few of these schools lasted sufficiently long enough to become 'public schools', in the sense of schools which taught the wealthy class for an extended period.

A more radical alternative remained. This was not to send children to school at all – not, at least, once they had reached a certain age. The army was the school for gentlemen, an army officer told the writer Jonathan Swift: 'Do you think Lord Marlborough beat the French with Greek and Latin?' In his 1729 *Essay on Modern Education* Swift declared that the gentry and nobility thought public school education useless, and 'that to dance, fence, speak French, and know how to behave yourself among great persons of both sexes' – not a set of skills taught in the private or grammar schools either – 'comprehends the whole duty of a gentleman'.[65] It is a view of education which owes far more to the tradition of the aristocratic houses of the Middle Ages, and far less to the monastic, ascetic and relentlessly male environment of the public boarding schools.

It was not just the upper classes who were sceptical about the virtues of school education. Until at least the end of the seventeenth century, the majority of the most famous thinkers who wrote about the subject, including Ascham, Erasmus and Locke, recommended private tuition over schools. John Locke may have been one of Busby's most successful pupils, but his writings show little sense of gratitude. 'It is impossible to keep a lad from the spreading contagion, if you will venture him abroad in the herd, and trust to chance, or his own inclination, for the choice of his company at school', he warned.[66]

Locke's reference to contagion is apt: the fear of social infection was the most powerful cause of opposition among the upper classes to schooling, whether at a public school or elsewhere. To say that someone has been educated at a famous public school has, in our time, become a way of insinuating that, having been brought up within a narrow, socially elite stratum of society, they know little of the rough and tumble of ordinary life. Such was the origin of the Cameron-Osborne pasty controversy (of which more in Chapter 10). It is, therefore, ironic that an earlier barrier to the acceptance of public schools was the widespread view that they introduced boys to a little too much of ordinary life. Far from being too posh, the boys at Eton and elsewhere were not posh enough. 'Are you sufficiently upon your guard against awkward attitudes, and illiberal, ill-bred, and disgusting habits; such as scratching yourself, putting your fingers in your mouth, nose and ears . . .?' warned Lord Chesterfield, the politician, in a famous letter to his son. They are, he says, 'tricks always acquired at schools, often too much neglected afterwards; but, however, extremely ill-bred and nauseous'. He was writing not of the local village or grammar school, but of his son's stay at Westminster.[67]

Richard Hurd, an eighteenth-century writer and churchman, ventured even further in undermining the idea that what would become known as the public-school manner could be taught at public schools. Writing of public school boys, he wailed: 'Bring but one of these grown boys into a circle of well-bred people, such as his rank and fortune entitle him, and in a manner oblige him, to live with: and see how forbidding his air, how embarrassed all his looks and motions! His awkward attempts at civility would provoke laughter, if, again, his rustic painful bashfulness did not excite one's pity.'[68] Little more than a century later, much the same would be said about boys on the grounds that they had *not* gone to public school.

Nonetheless, there were writers who favoured public school over private tuition, largely because of the view that being thrown into the society of other children was good rather than bad for character. Francis Coventry's *The History of Pompey the Little* portrays a brother and sister who, having been brought up at home by parents and tutors, were 'proud, selfish, obstinate and cross-humoured'. Parents should instead, says the author, have sent them 'to schools, where they would have been whipped out of many of their ill tempers, and perhaps by conversation with other children, might have learnt a more open generous disposition'.[69]

The modern reader might praise the perceptiveness of the sentiment that children are trained out of meanness through having to share with their peers, but they would question the curative powers of the birch. So, too, did many contemporaries. The public schools' academic fossilization was disturbing, despite some brilliant teachers even in the eighteenth century; it was their cruelty that was horrifying. In 1747 the father of one William Roberts brought a formal complaint, backed by a surgeon's affidavit, that George Charles, a high master of St Paul's, had visited on William a 'most severe correction of a great number of stripes on his back and face, inflicted with the utmost violence'. Charles was dismissed by the governors. Eton's reputation had become so bad by the late 1760s that the Earl of Huntingdon told the Earl of Moira not to send his sons there (or to Westminster) because of 'the risk of debauching their morals'. He instead recommended Harrow, which shows a certain lack of basic research given the violence to cats, carriages and persons which the school was to continue to see in the coming years (and the coming chapter).[70] Amidst the cruelty, sometimes the more humanitarian headmasters treated ordinary boys with kindness, and others treated their clients well simply out of rational self-interest. Accepting a new boarder from far away Lancashire, Samuel Cromleholme, high master of St Paul's from 1657 to 1672, told his wife: 'Sweetheart, you must take this child as mine and yours.' When a sensitive, or rather, perhaps, admirably independent-minded boy, who had run away to avoid a whipping from one of the masters, was about to be transferred to Merchant Taylors', Cromleholme made sure he was never touched again.[71] Many intelligent headmasters realized it would not do to lose boys to a rival school because of a reputation for harshness, though others carried on beating with no thought to what damage this might do for school numbers as well as boys' backsides.

The London borough of Hackney has a claim to fame incongruous with the relentlessly urban, tough inner-city image which it holds today. In the seventeenth century it was, as much as anywhere else, the birthplace of the primitive early ancestors of girls' public schools: small institutions of usually no more than thirty pupils, set up for profit in some verdant district a little way outside the city, where girls would be spared the unseemly horrors of life in the capital. Pepys, in a typical display of lechery, mentioned going to Hackney Church in April 1667 'chiefly to see . . . the young ladies of the schools, whereof there is a great store, very pretty'.[72] Hackney even earned the sobriquet of 'The Ladies' University of Female Arts', a name which elegantly encapsulates the purpose of most of the schools. One of the most successful – though like most of these schools, it did not outlive its founder – was the establishment run by Mrs Prestwich from 1643 to 1660. The emphasis was on music, dancing and needlework, with sixteen visiting masters teaching singing and an assortment of instruments. Other places deemed suitable for such ladies included Putney, mentioned by Pepys as a centre for girls' academies, and Chelsea, where the well-connected proprietor Josias Priest, originally a teacher of dancing, persuaded Purcell to write the opera *Dido and Aeneas* for the girls of a school called Gorges House. Sir Edmund Verney, the royalist courtier, and his daughter Mary, who arrived at the school at the age of eight, were, in both background and expectation, typical clients of such schools. When Mary asked if she might practise the feminine art of enamelling, her father approved, 'for I admire all accomplishments that will render you considerable and Lovely [*sic*] in the sight of God and man'.[73]

A rare exception to the educationally unambitious norm was a school set up in Putney by Bathsua Makin, former tutor to Charles I's daughter Elizabeth. Makin castigated the 'barbarous custom to keep women low'. She offered as a scholastic remedy Latin, Greek, French, history and arithmetic, while judiciously compromising by teaching the feminine arts as well. For the most part, however, academic education even for wealthy girls remained unimportant, and possibly even undesirable – in the view, at least, of the seventeenth-century paterfamilias.[74]

By the eighteenth century a small number of men and women were beginning to question the knowledge-lite orthodoxy of women's education. In 1729, the cleric and writer William Law formulated what was, in the next century, to become a common argument for girls' education: 'As they are mothers and mistresses of families that have for some time the care of the education of their children of both sorts, they are entrusted with that which is of the greatest consequence to human life.'[75] The idea that this made their own education important was, however, to make little headway for some years.

The seventeenth and early eighteenth centuries were, though not a glorious time for the public schools, at the very least glorious for some of the schools some of the time. Occasionally, under brilliant men such as Busby, they became breeding-grounds of intellectual independence. Given their erratic quality, it is not surprising that the total number of public school boys remained small. St Paul's was down to thirty-five in 1748, and in 1719 Shrewsbury reached a low point of only twenty-six.[76] Numbers at other public schools often surged, even while other schools were suffering a rapid decline in pupil rolls, and a school that had become very small indeed under an unpopular headmaster could quickly recover its fortunes again under a new one. However, these vagaries suggest that rather than being firm pillars of the establishment, the public schools were still more akin to the flame of a candle that sometimes burned brightly and at other times was in danger of being snuffed out. It is unlikely that the total number of public school pupils ever exceeded 2,000 in the early and mid-eighteenth century.

However, this small tally of pupils was becoming steadily more elite. Looking at the education of eighteenth-century peers with the right to a seat in the Lords, of those born before 1680, 16 per cent were Old Etonians, Wykehamists, Westminsters or Harrovians, but for those born after 1740 the proportion rises to a striking 73 per cent.[77] A public school education had become, with the aid of men such as Busby and Wotton, almost the standard education for the ruling class.

CHAPTER THREE

Of Frogs and Men

1768–1827

ADVOCATES of the public schools' ability to serve as agents of social advancement might talk of the rise of the Foster brothers.

The sons of a bricklayer who had risen far enough to afford the costs of Eton, John and William entered the school in the 1750s as commoners (or 'oppidans', to use Eton argot, from the Latin for 'townspeople'). William became chaplain-in-ordinary to two British kings. In 1765 John became the headmaster of his old school, entering society's upper echelons 167 years after Ben Jonson, stepson of another successful bricklayer and Old Westminster, had entered the establishment with the staging of his first hit play.[1]

From this point, however, the fairy tale starts to dissolve. In 1768 John Foster was the subject of the first of a series of rebellions at public schools across the country which would imperil their survival, though there had been isolated rebellions before. At the heart of this public school revolution was an arrogance based on social class. Foster, who as the son of a Windsor tradesman was held in open contempt by many of the aristocratic boys, was its first casualty – limping on as head until, weakened by a halving of pupil numbers at the school, he resigned in 1773.[2]

There had been at least a couple of infamous precedents for such revolts in school history, both inside and outside the public schools.

In 1710 the scholars had staged a mutiny at Winchester over beer rations.[3] In around 1690, the boys and masters of Manchester Grammar School had disagreed violently – in a literal sense – about the length of the Christmas holiday. Locking themselves into school and the masters out, the boys enlisted the aid of townspeople who supplied them with food and firearms, which were used to fire warning shots at anyone who tried to enter the premises. The rebellion lasted a fortnight.[4]

It was, however, the Eton rebellion, triggered by an argument over prefects' rights, which uncorked the bottle. Over the following seven decades there were six full-scale revolts at the school, with the last in 1832. Winchester also saw six – the first prompted, like the Manchester rebellion, by disagreement over a holiday, only two years after Eton had first rebelled. Rugby followed close after with five.[5]

Some of these rebellions, such as Eton's first uprising, were entirely peaceful, with mass walkouts and collective demands but no real violence against persons or property (unless we count the rebels themselves, who were often soundly thrashed afterwards). Other incidents, however, involved physical intimidation and serious damage to the school. In several cases, the boys conquered part of the school, wresting temporary control from the masters. Cases of serious injury to the staff were rare, though this was because staff, regarding discretion as the better part of valour, took the risk of injury seriously enough to escape. On several occasions external agencies, such as the local militia, had to be called in to restore the headmaster's sovereignty over the school.

In at least some cases the word 'rebellion' is no exaggeration: the worst of these were serious affairs. In 1797 the boys of Rugby School took staff prisoner at swordpoint; the Riot Act was read by the local authorities; and a force of soldiers, special constables and farmers armed with horsewhips was mustered.[6] Winchester's 1818 great rebellion ended only after the warden, the overall head of the school, was held hostage in his rooms overnight by boys armed with axes.[7] The year 1818 was an intensely worrying one for public schools in general, as it turned out to be the public school equivalent of the 1848 wave of discontent across Europe that earned it the moniker of The Year of Revolutions. Revolt in one educational institution appears to have sparked revolt in another – with uprisings at Winchester, Eton and Charterhouse and the Royal Military Academy at Sandhurst, where the young men put their training to practical use by drawing up in full battle array against the staff.[8] There was the ghost of a rebellion even at Shrewsbury, which was, uniquely for one of the public boarding schools, otherwise untouched by revolt during this period. Samuel Butler, headmaster of Shrewsbury, responded by seeking the advice of his counterparts at Eton and Winchester. 'I am very sorry to perceive that the contagion of rebellion has reached your school also', responded John Keate, the head of Eton from 1809 to 1834, before noting, in a wounded manner: 'I am sorry too to be thought to have sufficient experience to be referred to as an authority on these occasions.'[9]

The spirit of sedition was not limited to the old public schools: the 1851 Marlborough College mutiny, timed by the rebels for Guy Fawkes Night and announced to the world with fireworks and the explosion of a barrel of gunpowder behind the head's back, took place only eight years into the school's history. The rebellion did for him, as it did for Foster: he retired to a quiet country parsonage.[10] King's College School, a day school (though with a few boarders) that had been set up in the Strand in London in 1829, also suffered a rebellion in 1848, prompting it to set up a Committee of Inquiry into the matter.[11]

In short, the entire public school system was in danger of becoming ungovernable, the rebellions being merely the most spectacular manifestations of a permanent atmosphere of violence. Westminster saw uprisings in 1786 and 1791, and even after this second and final revolt, the atmosphere was not exactly sunny. Speaking of pupil life at Westminster in the 1810s, the future Bishop of Adelaide wrote: 'The boys fought one another, they fought the masters, the masters fought them, they fought outsiders; in fact we were ready to fight everybody.'[12]

At times the public school rebels borrowed the iconography and language of their international counterparts: on the queen's birthday in 1796 a Merchant Taylors' boy flew the French revolutionaries' Tricolour over the Tower of London; during the 1793 Winchester rebellion the Red Cap of Liberty, symbol of the French revolutionaries, fluttered over the school.[13] This suggests that some pupils may have seen their uprisings as justified, like the French and American Revolutions, because they were rational and virtuous revolts against excessively tyrannical regimes.

A couple of cases matched this description. Younger boys often chafed at the institution of fagging, under which they acted as servants to their 'fagmasters' among the older boys – particularly the prefects. The system, which lasted at many public schools until the 1980s but has now almost gone, could make the seniors very cosseted indeed at the expense of the juniors. George Keppel, the future 6th Earl of Albemarle, recalled a typical day's duties as a fag at Westminster School in the 1810s. He rose as the day broke, brushed his master's clothes and cleaned several pairs of his shoes, went to the pump in Great Dean's Yard to fetch hard water for his teeth, went to the cistern at Mother Gran's for soft water for his hands and face, prepared his breakfast, bought bread, butter, milk and eggs 'for the great man's tea', and then prepared his tea. This hard life was an inversion of what Keppel would have experienced at home.[14]

The Winchester insurgency of 1828 was instigated by six younger boys chafing against such servile duties, imposed on them by the seniors. The headmaster supported the head prefect against the boys, but liberals in the world outside denounced the cruelty and absolutist regime of the school.[15] The Rugby reign of Archibald Tait (1842–8) saw the Fags' rebellion: a group of fags assembled to attack the fagmasters; this was defeated by dint of a thrashing from three members of the sixth form.[16]

Most of the rebellions were certainly about power. They were not, however, about boosting the power of the downtrodden. In many cases they were, to the contrary, about upholding the power of prefects and other senior boys. In other words, they served as Tory rebellions aimed at buttressing the power of those already in authority rather than Whig rebellions aimed at establishing a greater degree of liberty for the ordinary boy. The Eton uprising of 1768 was triggered by the head's decision to flog a prefect for being out of bounds, the decision being, according to the prefects, a breach of their privileges.[17] The Harrow revolt of 1808 was an uprising by the prefects who were peeved that they were not allowed to flog their charges.[18]

These occasions were worrying enough. Still more disturbing, however, were the revolts that arose when boys tried to expand their role within the school – to become alternative centres of power that would rival the head and governors. Winchester's 1808 revolt broke out when the head cheekily tried to make a saint's day a holiday without asking the prefects. There was little the boys at the public schools did not consider beyond their rightful authority; two Harrow rebellions were triggered by the school's failure to appoint their favoured candidate as head.[19] If the boys had managed to accroach to themselves such levels of power, the schools would quickly have died.

Boys came to believe in such an unsustainably exalted role for themselves partly because of the extreme degree of power which the fagging and prefect systems gave them over other boys. Senior boys gained the powers not of constitutional monarchs, with powers limited by strict rules, but of despots circumscribed only by a mixture of convention and the fear that excessive cruelty would spark a rebellion. It was said that there were only three absolute rulers in the world: the Great Mogul, the captain of a man of war, and the Prefect of Hall at Winchester.[20] Total power over the boys within a senior boy's own house led, through ineluctable steps, to an exalted sense of his own power within the school in general, even (as an unseen presence) within the governors' meeting room itself.

The power of senior boys was buttressed by the awareness among masters of the possibility of preferment, in future life, from the families of the grandest pupils – mainly in Church posts, since heads were generally ordained. 'One very noticeable trait in the parson schoolmasters of those old days (and perhaps it still survives) was the subserviency of rank and wealth towards any pupils likely to give them livings', recalled the writer Martin Tupper of his time at Charterhouse in the 1820s. He told the story of a boy from a titled family who hunted and killed a stray dog. In retribution, other boys dumped him in a ditch. Tupper claimed that had the boy been 'a plebeian' the incident would have been ignored. However, as the playground monitor at the time, Tupper was held by his housemaster to be responsible for this heinous impudence against the upper classes, and was given an impossible task: to translate the longest book of the *Iliad* within a month, or face expulsion. The seventy boys of his house, showing a heart-warming sense of natural justice, each contributed to the translation – and within a week hundreds of pages, sewn together, were handed to the housemaster, who had no choice but to let the matter drop.[21]

The 1771 Harrow rebellion, which culminated in an attack on the carriage of a visiting governor and the closure of the school for nine days, provides a further clue as to why boys should have felt such an exaggerated sense of their own importance. In a petition to the governors that objected to the selection of Benjamin Heath as headmaster, the ringleaders declared that 'as we most of us are in some degree independent of the foundation' – commoners rather than free scholars – 'whatever may be your opinions we presume our inclinations ought to have some weight in determining your choice.'[22]

The Harrow rebellion set a strikingly dangerous precedent for the public schools, posing a far greater danger to their existence than any sense of burning injustice at oppression (justified though that was). No school can survive for long if a group of boys, many of them from aristocratic families that rule their local estates at the very least and the British Empire at the very most, feel they have a right to run the school predicated on their own social and economic circumstances. This sense of a divide between the grander and humbler boys was not merely limited to a few dramatic incidents; at many schools, at least, it permeated everyday school life.

Many boys lower down the social scale were singled out for ill treatment. The historian and churchman Charles Merivale (1808–93) was, as the son of a barrister, not from a poor family – but he was not from the upper classes either. He felt scarred for life by 'the sense of social inferiority which was impressed upon me at Harrow'.[23] Merivale's headmaster, George Butler, shouted insults at the writer Anthony Trollope, a free scholar, in the street because of his shabby appearance – in spite of knowing about Trollope's poverty.[24] 'As I look back, it seems to me that all hands were turned against me – those of masters as well as boys', Trollope recalled.[25] Remembering his time at Eton, the politician George Canning, captain of the oppidans in 1786, admitted to an 'insurmountable dislike' of the scholars, declaring that they were 'not looked upon in near so respectable a light'.[26]

Boys who were in any way different also suffered a tough time. At Eton in the 1800s, the poet Shelley, an individualist from an early age, endured the daily physical bullying of what his classmates called 'Shelley-baits'.[27] Such sensitive plants as Shelley are always more likely to have a hard time, no matter what school and era. It is their teachers' pastoral duty to minimize their persecution, but at many public schools of the period, the masters either neglected this duty or even approved of such ill-treatment. Quitting Westminster School in 1827, R. J. F. Thomas cited not only the tyranny of the school system but also the pointlessness of any appeal to adults to palliate it.[28] Joseph Drury, head of Harrow from 1785 to 1805, admitted that a particular boy may have been teased and bullied because of his eccentric and reclusive behaviour – and how many teenage boys are not eccentric and reclusive at some point? Nevertheless, Drury had a ready justifi-cation: that the victim should be 'indebted to them for their exertions in ironing the boy out'.[29] The boy's mother was more sympathetic, noting regretfully that her husband had always known that he was 'too delicate and weak and not fit for a publick school'.[30]

Apologists for public school cruelty have, over the centuries, argued that strong boys flourished in such adversity; that they were toughened up for future life. The physically hard regime certainly inculcated some boys with both physical toughness and wiliness. The 1832 diaries of the redoubtable George Pouchée, a pupil at Harrow School, are filled with his attempts to best his house master, Henry Drury, a respected opponent to whom Pouchée rather wittily refers, in a diabolical reference, as Old Harry. On one occasion he and his friends encounter Old Harry in the road while they are illicitly smoking a cigar. 'I clenched my hand with the cigar alight. Lucky for me I had a glove on', Pouchée relates. 'You three are after no good, I know', comments Old Harry before moving on, unable to catch Pouchée in the act. 'Harry then walked on. We struck light and finished our cigars', notes Pouchée. The incident is akin to the Spartan story of the boy who died after stealing a fox and letting it eat into his body rather than reveal the theft, showing a fortitude which made him a hero in a city-state whose upbringing of boys was often cited approvingly by Britain's public school headmasters. Old Harry would, very possibly, have approved of Pouchée's presence of mind and endurance of pain, though a Pouchée martyrdom would have been more than a little embarrassing.[31]

Nevertheless, Pouchée is far from a model character for modern readers. Even at the time, it was widely recognized that conditions in public schools did not suit the more sensitive boys – which, in reality, meant the majority: normal boys with normal human weaknesses. Speaking of his old school, Pitt the Elder declared that he had 'hardly known a boy whose spirit had not been broken at Eton; and that while a public school might be an excellent thing for a youth of hot and violent character, it was not the place for a tender or docile disposition'.[32] He responded to his own education by having Pitt the Younger educated at home.

A boy might have a hard time if he were poor, or even if he were not particularly grand; he might suffer if he were different; he might suffer if he were sensitive. He would also suffer simply for being new. The initiation rites at each school varied, but at Rugby novitiates were forced to stand on a table and sing; the penalty for failure to please was to swallow a pail of muddy water mixed with salt, which made victims ill for days.[33] A boy would have to work very hard indeed to have a tolerable time at a public school, and the route to survival would require an unhealthy process of brutalization. Writing of his departure from Westminster, R. J. F. Thomas expressed the fear that if he stayed he would in turn become a tyrannical senior boy, conditioned to 'despise the dictates of humanity'.[34] Other boys would develop serious emotional problems that would last well into adulthood. Commenting on his schoolmaster at Charterhouse in the 1820s, Martin Tupper wrote with a vivid bitterness six decades later, 'for this man and the school he so despotically drilled into passive servility and pedantic scholarship, I have less than no reverence, for he worked so upon an over-sensitive nature to force a boy beyond his powers, as to fix for many years the infirmity of stammering'.[35] William Cowper, the poet, developed depression while at Westminster in the 1740s, and later spent time in an asylum.[36]

Hannah More, the philanthropist and religious writer, who also ran a private school for girls for a while, summed up the experience well when lobbying (successfully) for the family of Thomas Babington Macaulay, the historian, to spare him from the public school experience: 'Throwing boys headlong into those great public schools always puts me in mind of the practice of the Scythian mothers, who threw their new-born infants into the river; – the greater part perished, but the few who possessed great natural strength . . . came out with additional vigour from the experiment.'[37]

Contemporary readers might wonder, living as they do in the present age of hot-housed public school boys fighting for good GCSEs, A levels and entry to a first-class university, how boys could have found the time to get up to such a wide range of highly inventive and imaginative cruelty. In the late eighteenth and early nineteenth centuries, the inherent indolence of many public school boys' lives was part of the problem: the devil finds work for idle hands. Pouchée's Harrow diary reveals a light lesson schedule, leaving him free to spend much of his time lounging around looking for trouble. This took the form of picking fights with locals outside the school, among other diversions. His diary records three brawls, described as 'baits', in as many days, culminating in 'a capital bait' – his term for an extra fun fight – 'with a Cockney'.[38] At least he did not stoop to the Harrow tradition, well entrenched by his time, of stoning the town's cats to death.[39] The weekends left even more time for the devil to tempt bored pupils into sin, since the public school mania for organized sports and other activities, largely an attempt to provide more salubrious alternatives to cat-stoning and other activities of that ilk, was to come later. *The Microcosm*, a witty magazine published anonymously by a group of Etonians including George Canning, includes a fictitious diary entry for November 1786 describing a lazy, irreligious Sunday spent by 'Narcissus', a boy at their school: 'Half past ten. Too cold for church. . . . Eleven to twelve. Took my Chocolate.-Read half a page of Henrietta Harville.-Mem. Never to read Sentimental Novels after the 1st. of May, or before 1st. of November.'[40]

The lightness of the timetable was linked to a deep structural problem, ingrained in the system by financial self-interest: the lack of masters. Just before the 1768 Eton rebellion there were twelve masters in 'control', to use the word in rather a broad sense, of about 520 pupils, or forty-three pupils per master.[41] All schooling is an exercise in crowd control, even at the best-behaved institutions. At the public schools the low number of masters made the taming of mob rule all the harder, and the required counter-measures all the more extreme. Richard Brinsley Sheridan, the writer, blamed the harsh tone of public schools' regimes on these adverse ratios, saying: 'When the number of boys is out of all proportion to the number of masters, nothing short of despotism can establish their government, no principle but fear can support it. Thus the torturer rod is introduced.'[42]

On occasion the daily violence meted out by masters to boys, or by boys to each other, ended in death – and scandal. In 1806 a Harrow boy drowned in mysterious circumstances that may have involved bullying.[43] In 1823 the son of the Earl of Suffolk died at Charterhouse during Pulling, a Good Friday custom endemic to the school which involved dragging senior boys across the green to goals on either side. It was quickly abolished.[44]

It is reported that the Captain of School of St Paul's once led a fight against the boys of Merchant Taylors' during this period, sword in hand. Nevertheless, at these two public day schools the atmosphere was, though far from ideal, certainly less riven with class conflict and governed less by physical force; it was also free from outright revolution. A later Captain of School at St Paul's in the early 1830s was Benjamin Jowett, son of a poor printer, and a boy of frail appearance and feminine manner. Jowett, the future master of Balliol College, Oxford, was already famed for his academic prowess. At any public boarding school of the time a boy of such uncommanding mien and humble origin might have been bullied mercilessly, but at St Paul's he became top dog.[45]

At the same time that the public schools were becoming nastier and more brutish places, parents from the upper and professional classes were becoming more protective towards their children and less tolerant of the harsh treatment visited on their offspring. This was partly because of deep-rooted intellectual changes. The eighteenth century saw the full flowering of the Enlightenment, whose exponents believed, in a break with Christian tradition, in the goodness of man. A boy imbued with innate goodness did not require harsh discipline in the judgement of the Enlightenment thinkers Jean-Jacques Rousseau and his fellow Swiss Johann Heinrich Pestalozzi, who exercised perhaps the greatest influences on educational thought at this time. In Britain, William Wordsworth's belief that children were capable of greater wisdom than adults became a popular truism among many educated families. The theme was later taken up by Charles Dickens.

A kinder approach to children in many aristocratic and upper middle-class families was encouraged by advances in human health: in the third quarter of the eighteenth century the infant death rate of children of this class dropped abruptly by 30 per cent. This was, perhaps, because of the growing custom for infants to spend more time with their mothers rather than in the care of servants, or, as had been common, with young women living somewhere else entirely.[46] This was the age when sentimental children's portraits arrived in British drawing-rooms, marking the mawkish spirit of the age. It is hard to imagine the parents of Master Charles William Lambton, commemorated for eternity lolling about in red velvet in Sir Thomas Lawrence's famous 1825 portrait, acquiescing in any privation.

Talk of a revolution in family relationships can, however, be over-emphasized; well into the twentieth century many upper middle-class parents saw some virtue in asceticism at school. Nonetheless, it did not require a particularly cosseting parent to write, as one did as late as 1841 to the head of Westminster after his son's first year as a scholar: 'You will grant, I am sure, that a parent has some little ground of complaint when he sees the face of his son disfigured, or his hand mutilated, or it may be his legs lamed, and that no notice of the circumstance has been taken by the Master or the Dame.'[47] At times the public schools were put under pressure by changing attitudes; at other times they were found wanting because of a physical regime that would not have been tolerated in the Dark Ages.

In an exemplary paradox to the turbulence elsewhere, there were no revolutions on Samuel Butler's watch.

Shrewsbury was a minor star in the public school firmament when Butler returned to his alma mater as head in 1798. The great political families did not send their sons there. There were, in fact, not many sons there at all when Butler arrived: between twelve and eighteen after a long period of decline under indifferent headmasters. However, by 1827 the roll-call stood at 285, though this figure was reached slowly and not until after Butler had despaired of his school and tried (but failed) to secure the headship at Rugby.[48]

The bedrock on which Butler's success was built was his talent in enforcing discipline, even while public school revolutions were raging at other institutions. In establishing the necessary order, Butler was no martinet. 'All extremes defeat their own ends, and especially that of rigour', he wrote to a master, later dismissed, who was prone to excessive flogging. 'Depend upon it, a fine perception of moral rectitude is better inculcated by example and exhortation than by blows.' Writing of the boy whose unsatisfactory work seems to have provoked the master's latest outburst of beating, he demonstrated to the teacher that encouragement worked better than dire threats. 'I had him in my library for an hour to do the derivations for his evening Greek lesson', Butler wrote. The work was done 'with some mistakes, but such as I considered venial, and in which it was much better to set the boy right by asking him a question or two, and making him think, than by intimidating him by threats and anger'.[49] Butler spoke from a position of good knowledge of the boy's disposition: he insisted on a weekly conference with masters, at which he demanded 'free and confidential communications respecting the conduct of the boys, not only at their lessons, but out of school'.[50]

The picture painted by Butler's correspondence reveals a humane, broad-minded man with a good understanding of human nature. He told an assistant that nineteen pages of Greek grammar was an unreasonably long punishment, knowing that if the boy did not detest the subject already, he certainly would by the nineteenth page.[51] To a clergyman who was trying to swim against the tide of the time by restricting the access of Unitarians and other Dissenters to the universities, he wrote: 'I dislike exclusive systems altogether, and I do not see why Unitarians should be excluded more than any other class.'[52]

Butler's ability to forestall a proper rebellion at Shrewsbury also owed something to the eighteenth-century equivalent of modern methods of zero-tolerance policing. He was strict in small matters. When two boys arrived late for school, the punishment was both severe and well-fitted to the crime. The boys were confined to the school gardens and ball courts for a month, and ordered to report to their house master three times an afternoon. A repeat offence was to be met with expulsion. Butler also pioneered the practice of increasing the responsibility of the prefects, which was to prove important in the resurrection of the public schools in general. He sent three of them to interview a man who complained that boys from the school had broken a window, rather than engaging with the man himself.[53] There was also, unusually for a public school dominated by boarders, no formal system of fagging under Butler. Its absence reduced two causes of potential rebellion: resentment towards the school among the younger boys, and an exalted sense of power among the older.[54]

And then there was the superlative nature of Butler's teaching, which clearly played a role in the school's orderliness since bad teaching produces resentful pupils. At the peak of Butler's glory, Shrewsbury probably outdid Britain's other schools in academic achievement to a degree higher than any other school either before or since. Every year reams of boys went to the universities. Butler calculated that by 1836, 629 of the 1,626 boys who had passed through his door, or 39 per cent, had gone on to Oxford, Cambridge or Trinity College, Dublin, with about 600 of those to Oxbridge.[55]

This does not in itself signify excellence at the school, since entry to Oxbridge was not particularly academically competitive until well into the twentieth century. Nevertheless, 39 per cent was an impressive figure for an age when attendance at Oxford and Cambridge, the dominant universities for the Anglican establishment, was in danger of going out of vogue among the gentry and professional classes. At least at Shrewsbury, Butler was keeping higher education fashionable and desirable among his pupils.

The real glory, however, lay in the Oxbridge prizes. At Cambridge, boys taught by Butler during his thirty-eight years at the school won sixteen of the annual Browne medals (for Greek and Latin poetry composition). In seven of these thirty-eight years, the first-ranked classicist in the university test was an Old Salopian (a former Shrewsbury pupil). In one year the top three places in Classics were taken by old boys. When it came to Oxford, in 1831 a boy won the highly competitive Ireland Classics prize while still at the school, showing the elevated academic level, equivalent to the top reaches of university achievement, which boys could achieve while still at Shrewsbury. The boy beat

William Gladstone, who had already developed a fearsome intellectual reputation though still only an Oxford undergraduate. Gladstone was not surprised, however: at this point Shrewsbury-educated boys had won the Ireland for five successive years. Writing to his father about his chance of clinching it, he lamented: 'There is, it appears, smaller chance than ever of it falling out of the hands of the Shrewsbury people.'[56]

This exemplary record at the universities was assisted by Butler's diligent courting of contacts.[57] 'Dr Butler comes here year after year', said Christopher Wordsworth, brother of the poet and master of Trinity College, Cambridge, 'just as a first-rate London milliner makes a yearly visit to Paris to get the fashions.'[58]

An air of nervy brilliance is conveyed in Thomas Kirkby's portrait of Butler in the school library. It is, in basic composition, a rather formulaic portrait of a scholar reading a book. However, the portrait also skilfully conveys the sense that Butler is veritably devouring the volume, with the air of a man turning its contents inside out in his brain for any infelicities of accuracy, style or argument. Paintings are paintings, rather than firm evidence, but we know from his university awards that Butler was a superlative classical scholar; several of his pupils also deemed him a superlative teacher. 'He was not one who was content with inculcating mere critical accuracy', remembered one. 'He also infused a lively spirit, a delicate taste, which I have been able to trace distinctly in all that made the proper advantage of his instructions.' Butler appears to have been a true chameleon of style. One former pupil conjured up an image of a lesson that would certainly have enthused the more academic boys: 'He would, as his manner was, work one eyebrow up and drop the other down, run his pen through an English-Latin sentence and make it Ciceronian, or an erased clumsy line would be rewritten by him, and a line put in you might mistake for Ovid.'[59]

Such was the reputation of his teaching that Henry Drury, a senior Harrow master, came to the school with an assistant to watch him in action. Both Drury and Edward Hawtrey, the reforming head of Eton, wrote to Butler to ask him about his system of internal exams.

Butler's 'emulative system', which was to spread across the whole country into the new as well as the old public schools, was one of Butler's greatest achievements. It consisted of regular exams governing the form order of boys, made eminently visible on a daily basis since it governed where they sat. Before Butler's time there was virtually no academic competition at public schools, thus setting a limit to one of the great alleged advantages of public school over private tuition: the spirit of competition. The emulative system must surely have jolted into activity a few bright but lazy boys who had previously maintained their classroom status by well-chosen quips and a studied air of indifference to the task at hand. It could be argued that it simply discouraged the less academic boys. Butler did not, however, ignore this group: he also introduced special tuition for boys behind as well as ahead in class.[60] Butler was, therefore, an early crusader for the cause of the average boy – more than a century before the public schools as a whole finally paid this unknown but totemic figure, the public school equivalent of the Great War's unknown warrior, his due attention.

Nonetheless, a man who flogged with his left hand instead of his right to minimize the severity, but still flogged all the same, could only be deemed a pioneer within the existing system that he found; he was not a revolutionary who tried to change the system itself.[61] This limitation was shown most dramatically in the case of his most famous pupil, one for whom Butler's regime was a failure. Charles Darwin could not be clearer on the subject – as if writing specifically to settle future historians' debates about whether Butler could claim any credit for his success. 'Nothing could have been worse for the development of my mind than Dr Butler's school, as it was strictly classical, nothing else being taught, except a little ancient geography and history', he wrote. 'The school as a means of education to me was simply a blank.'[62] His assessment was echoed by that of William Thomson, a future Archbishop of York educated at the school in Butler's last years, who recalled: 'It seemed as if it were thought necessary, in order to allow the great plant of Greek and Latin to flourish, that all other vegetation should be repressed, and that they alone should cover the whole ground.'[63]

Butler certainly opposed a significantly broader syllabus. Writing to Lord Henry Brougham, the politician and educational reformer, he averred that the school had been founded to teach the 'learned languages', and not 'English reading, writing and accounts'. Butler's justification for such a constricted curriculum was similar to that used by public school masters well into the twentieth century: an excessively crowded syllabus taught knowledge 'of that superficial kind which tends to foster vanity'.[64] However, English reading, writing and accounts would have benefited many of the pupils who did not go on to university, and in particular the hundred 'burgesses of Shrewsbury' from the 'lower grades' of society whom Butler estimated he had educated by 1836.[65]

One particular story, recorded with no sense of irony in a Victorian history of the school, encapsulates the other-worldly education given by Butler to a socially stratified clientele that had been receiving a similar education – sometimes deftly taught, more often clumsily so – for centuries. Dinah, a school housekeeper, lodged a complaint against the sixth form. She alleged that they had been using her name in conjunction with very bad language, though she did not understand the words – the language must be egregious indeed. On investigation, it transpired that the boys had been memorizing the text to be learned for repetition in their next Ancient Greek lesson – text from Sophocles' *Oedipus Rex* which included the famous line, 'Deina men oun, deina tarassei sophos oionotheta': 'The wise augurer disturbs us in fearful ways with his dreadful pronouncements.' Butler was greatly amused.[66]

Shrewsbury's record of innovation after Butler's departure was disappointing. His successor, Benjamin Hall Kennedy, was a distinguished classical scholar but a man with an unhealthy obsession with dry facts. History lessons, confined, of course, to the ancient period, consisted of boys filling in the missing words of sentences read out by the master from his textbooks. Kennedy once put to shame a visiting naval officer who regarded himself as expert on a particular naval

engagement, by naming to him all the ships engaged and their positions in the action; it was a feat of lengthy memorization that reveals
a sad waste of a marvellous mind.[67]

Aside from boredom, terror and the occasional revolution, were
Britain's public schools otherwise in a good state at this time? The
lack of basic personal security for the boys may have been their
greatest failing, but in general they were also doing a rather unsatisfactory job when it came to the main purpose of a school: education.

Classics teaching continued to dominate the curriculum, to the
exclusion of science, English, modern history and modern languages,
and many of the basics of maths, though geometry enjoyed some
favour since it was required for entry to the universities. In 1760
James Townley became head of his alma mater Merchant Taylors'. He
tried to introduce a modern curriculum, including maths, but met
with failure: the governing body objected. The author of *High Life
Below Stairs*, a farce not noticeably more subtle than other farces of
the period, he also attempted to revive the tradition of dramatic
performance that had begun with Mulcaster. By contrast this met
with success.[68] Such was the priority of public schools at the time,
though many grammar schools were not noticeably different.

As late as the 1830s at least three-quarters, and sometimes as
much as four-fifths, of the public school timetable was devoted to
the Classics.[69] 'At St Paul's School we teach nothing but the Classics,
nothing but Latin and Greek. If you want your boy to learn anything
else you must have him taught at home, and for that purpose we give
him three half-holidays a week', explained John Sleath, high master
from 1814 to 1837, with admirable clarity.[70] This restricted curriculum was justified by Thomas James, headmaster at Rugby from
1778 to 1794, on the grounds that 'young people are narrow-necked
vessels, into which you cannot pour much at a time without waste
and running over'.[71]

In defence of their methods, Classics masters could cite the
astounding capacity, by comparison with our own time, for learning

by heart. At the age of thirteen Thomas Arnold (1795–1842), future headmaster of Rugby, could recite 3,000 lines of Homer; Henry Butler, Victorian headmaster of Harrow, could recount the whole of Homer's *Iliad*. This is a talent which even the brightest children of today have lost.[72]

And yet some of the scholastic virtues of this era seem empty to the modern eye. Most educated people today would regard the committing to memory of thousands of lines of poetry as a waste of a good brain's time. Lord Halifax, who left Eton in 1818, had the weekly duty of reciting by heart to a master, every Monday morning, fifteen verses of the Greek Testament without interpretation or comment.[73] Moreover, although a minority of pupils learned the Classics well, such scholars all too often found themselves strangers in a foreign land. Some of these boys would go on to be public school masters, often speaking that strange hybrid language beloved of heads steeped in Latin and Greek who had no real need to be understood by the ordinary person. Henry Hayman, headmaster of Rugby School in the 1870s, famed for obscure expressions, would bellow 'adumbrate the scintillation' at boys who had not put out the light at bedtime.[74] Some would go on to become great classical scholars – but classical scholars had a greatly diminished literary value in an age when English had become the lingua franca for virtually the entire intellectual and literary life of the country. Having imbibed the Classics at Eton in the 1830s, William Johnson Cory, a famous Eton master, became one of the greatest writers of Latin verse of the nineteenth century, but few people would read his poems even during his lifetime, and none today. It is perhaps the emptiest public school achievement of all.

The narrow-necked vessel could, moreover, be very narrow indeed. A boy who stayed at Eton for long enough during the headship of John Keate would go through Virgil's *Aeneid* twice, a necessary evil for masters who felt that nothing had been written since the first century BC that was worth studying.[75] The *Edinburgh Review*, the leading mouthpiece for Whig intellectuals, was, in its 1830 tirade, as critical of the lack of a good classical education as of the dearth of other learning, noting that the Eton boy 'has not read a single book of Herodotus, or Thucydides, or Xenophon, or Livy, or Polybius, or Tacitus; he has not read a single Greek tragedy or comedy'.[76] It was in this academically fetid environment that Eton's final rebellion was hatched two years later. After months of boredom, the punctuation of sheer terror must have come as a welcome relief.

The public schools' argument that only Classics provided a true education left much of the public unimpressed. Many intellectuals, steeped in the new thinking of the Age of Enlightenment, which questioned and tested established tradition, whether in education, religion or politics, were positively vituperative. Thomas Campbell (1777–1844), the poet and educational reformer, lamented: 'It is a vestige of barbarism in our language that learning only means, in its common acceptation, a knowledge of the dead languages and mathematics.' The *Edinburgh Review* complained in 1830 that a boy at Eton 'is utterly ignorant of mathematical or physical science, and even of arithmetic; the very names of logical, moral, or political science, are unknown to him. Modern history and modern languages are, of course out of the question.' A rival Whig journal, the *Westminster Review*, complained in 1824 that 'boys are taught nothing of the age or country in which they live nor of science'. The following year it returned to the attack. In language that would soon be echoed by a century of official government reports, it asserted that when it came to the curriculum, 'there must be science, on which the wealth and power of Britain depend'. Adam Smith, the Scottish economist, said that at the end of a public school education, a boy might 'come into the world completely ignorant of everything which is the common subject of conversation among gentlemen and men of the world'.[77] Many parents, too, were unimpressed. In 1778 Mrs Barret removed her son from Harrow after three years' digestion of its almost exclusive diet of Latin and Greek and placed him with a private tutor, on the grounds that 'at publick Schools very little is to be learned'.[78]

Even the narrow curriculum that was taught was often taught badly. Remembering his experience at Harrow and Winchester,

Trollope wrote: 'During the whole of those twelve years no attempt had been made to teach me anything but Latin and Greek, and very little attempt to teach me those languages.'[79] The appalling pupil–teacher ratios made it hard to provide a sophisticated teaching system. At St Paul's each master was in charge of two classes, leaving one to its own devices while he taught the other.[80] An Eton pupil during the Keate regime recalled in later years that he was only called up by the master to have his work assessed twice a term.[81] This is not altogether surprising, since Keate taught up to 190 boys at a time – possibly the highest and worst ratio in public school history.[82]

The dearth of masters was not the only educational problem. Public schools still lacked a powerful intellectual motive force, which scholars would provide later in the nineteenth century. Patronage still ruled. The Revd John Russell tried, after becoming headmaster of Charterhouse in 1811, to create four new places for scholars based on a competitive exam. This, however, was blocked by the old guard, who were anxious to retain their patronage.[83]

When it came to providing a good academic education, the best that can be said about the average public school of the period is that at least it was not a grammar school. Had the grammar schools been in a better state, the public schools might have disappeared altogether.

In 1804 the son of the steward in charge of the Duke of Norfolk's Glossop estate entered Manchester Grammar School, to be taught Latin by rote for day after day 'without understanding one syllable of what we were repeating'. He complained that 'nothing was explained to us: even such words as nominative, genitive, dative, indicative, potential, subjunctive were left to our own ingenuity to discover, stimulated only by the powerful inculcation of the cane'.[84]

Many pupils felt little motivation, beyond the fear of physical punishment, to penetrate the mysteries of the Classics, and their parents were often sympathetic. Humphrey Repton (1752–1818), the landscape gardener, recalled that he abandoned Norwich Grammar School because his father 'thought proper to put the stopper in my vial of classic literature, determined to make me a rich, rather than a learned, man.'[85] Parents responded to the prevalence of poor teaching in irrelevant subjects by shunning the schools. Bristol Grammar, once the premier educational institution of one of Britain's biggest cities, had no more than a handful of boys on its rolls at any given time between 1811 and 1848 – and sometimes none at all. When Thomas Bullen arrived at Oundle, a once-thriving grammar school in Northamptonshire, he discovered that he was headmaster of an entirely empty classroom. In 1795 Lord Kenyon, the Lord Chief Justice, said that most of the grammars had been 'reduced' to 'a lamentable condition'. At grammars throughout the country, Kenyon found 'empty walls without scholars, and everything neglected but the receipt of emoluments'.[86]

The decline of the grammars from their heyday in the age of Shakespeare is partly a tale of legal unscrupulousness that was mostly perfectly legal and partly of political apathy verging on incompetence. The tragicomic history of Bristol Grammar provides a master class. For many years the headmaster continued to draw his salary even when there were no pupils at all, while pocketing fees for teaching on the school premises a healthy number of private pupils who paid him personally. When the incumbent head, the inappropriately named John Joseph Goodenough, was asked by the Charity Commission in 1821 why there were so few scholars enjoying a free education on Bristol Grammar's foundation, he had a well-crafted but narrow-minded reply: 'The only reason assigned for this small number of free boys is, that the inhabitants of Bristol may have less want of an exclusively classical education, than of a general education, to which this institution does not extend'. His protestation that he was only obeying the rules – 'he considers himself bound only to teach the learned languages, or what is considered as coming within the description of learned literature' – was greatly to his financial advantage. It was not until 1840 that the Grammar Schools Act made it lawful to apply the income of grammar schools to purposes other than the teaching of classical languages, and even then the schoolmaster's consent was still required.[87]

Christ College, Brecon, provides an egregious Welsh example of a grammar school destroyed by cupidity. In the early eighteenth century the college, an ecclesiastical foundation, had enjoyed an annual income of £8,000 (£1.5m). The Church, however, saw this monetary fund primarily as a means of providing income to local clergymen. As a result, after a number of local church personages had been paid various amounts, the total left to educate the boys was a mere £52 7s 8d – less than 1 per cent. The cash-starved school fell into such a state of disrepair that by the nineteenth century the church attached to the school was being patronized by grazing sheep rather than pupils. The school room itself was, according to a visitor, 'perfectly unfit for the purpose and would indeed be a disgrace to the smallest population in any parish'.[88]

If the old public and grammar schools were so bad at academic education, one might ask how Britain managed to serve as the birthplace of the Industrial Revolution, the crucial period of technological and economic advance that, roughly speaking, began in about 1780 and ended in around 1830. Those who were involved must have been educated somewhere.

In many cases they were not, or at least hardly at all. Many of the greatest inventors and engineers of this revolution were largely self-educated, including the scientist Michael Faraday, the railway pioneer George Stephenson, and the canal engineer James Brindley. The Industrial Revolution's technological advances were largely the work of practical men rather than theoretical scientists, who paid Britain's internationally renowned legions of skilled craftsmen to put them into action. The civil engineer Isambard Kingdom Brunel once said he would never employ a man who could read; he would have had even less use for a man who could also recite a hundred lines of Virgil.[89]

Many other technological innovators, and theoretical scientists to boot, were educated at 'academies', which were generally short-lived private schools set up mainly to educate religious Dissenters whose parents did not want them to imbibe the Anglicanism of the public schools. Virtually all the academies offered a broader curriculum than the public schools, often including science. The academy teachers of the period include a few of the great scientific and engineering names of the age. Joseph Priestley, who discovered oxygen, taught at two of the most distinguished: the Warrington Academy in the 1760s and the Hackney Academy in the 1790s.[90] John Dalton, the pioneer of atomic theory, instructed pupils at an academy in Manchester while Priestley was in Hackney.[91] Distinguished academy pupils who made their mark in British science in the late eighteenth and early nineteenth centuries include Henry Cavendish, the aristocratic discoverer of hydrogen, the chemist William Henry, and the astronomer John Goodricke.[92]

Many of the technocrats of the Industrial Revolution came from outside England. Scotland had an education system more geared to science than England; a number of talented boys went to local universities, which tended to provide more science teaching than Oxford and Cambridge, at around the age that they would have started public school in England. The physicist David Brewster attended Edinburgh University from the age of twelve. Other men of talent and achievement from north of the border were James Watt, the mechanical engineer, and the chemist Joseph Black. Still other key figures, such as the French-born engineer Sir Marc Isambard Brunel, father of Isambard Kingdom Brunel, hailed from outside the British Isles.[93]

The old public schools did not have a good record in producing the revolution's technocrats; they were not, moreover, the primary breeding grounds of the great entrepreneurs of the age – the far-sighted businessmen who commercialized the technological breakthroughs and exploited the opportunities generated by the growth of international trade. The majority of industrialists came from the existing business middle class; few were from the landowning upper class and professional upper middle class, both of which were very likely to attend the old public schools.[94]

It is necessary to start to have to use the term 'old public schools' because, by the final quarter of the eighteenth century, new public schools were springing up, mainly to serve pupils outside the Anglican Church: both Dissenting non-conformists and Catholics. Such schools were encouraged by the repeal of several laws discriminating against each group. These included the 1791 Roman Catholic Relief Act, giving Catholics the right to open schools on condition that an oath of allegiance to Britain's Protestant monarchy was sworn, and the 1779 Dissenters' Relief Act, which permitted tutors and school-masters to teach without needing to be licensed by their local Anglican bishop. This removed the sword of Damocles hanging over Dissenting academies, allowing them to be established on more secure foundations.

The first of these new Dissenting institutions to be set up on a permanent basis was Ackworth, the Yorkshire school established to educate Quaker boys and girls in 1779. Other non-conformist schools dating from this period include Mill Hill (founded 1807), Caterham (1811), Silcoates (1820) and Bootham (1823).

The word 'public school' must be used guardedly about these new, more permanently established, Dissenting institutions. They are all public schools now, primarily educating upper middle-class children for high fees, but Ackworth was founded as a boarding school 'suit-able for the education of children whose parents are not in affluence', with annual fees of £8 8s (£1,200), about a fifth of Harrow's.[95] Bootham's founding committee stipulated that the school should provide for 'that class of society to whom the expense of other schools is too great a burden', though it should also be able to educate 'the children of the opulent'.[96] An exception is Mill Hill School, conceived from the beginning as a national institution. Nearly half of the first 150 pupils were sons of businessmen, another third were the sons of professionals such as army officers and solicitors, and many of the rest had fathers who owned their own shops.[97]

When compared with the innovation of the best academies under the best teachers such as Priestley, the new Dissenting public schools were rather disappointingly devoid of revolutionary principle. Joseph John Gurney, a successful Norwich banker, philanthropist and supporter of Ackworth, criticized teaching at the school which appeared calculated to 'exercise the powers of memory while it left those of reflection untouched' – a barb which could just as easily have applied to the old public schools.[98] Mill Hill initially promised to teach an impressively wide syllabus, including English, French, maths, geography and history, as well as the usual classical education, but the day-to-day classroom life of the 1840s consisted primarily of classical and mathematical components.[99]

Despite Mill Hill's conservatism, many of the new Dissenting public schools tended to provide a more practical, less exclusively classical education than the old public schools – for the highly practical reason that Dissenters were, more or less, excluded from the same fields as Catholics until 1828. The founding committee at Bootham, which educated great industrialists such as Sir Joseph Pease and Joseph Rowntree in its early years, decided 'that the course of English Instruction' should include 'a knowledge of reading, writing, arithmetic, English grammar, geography, history, mathematics, and the elements of natural philosophy [that is, natural science]'.[100] At Ackworth, James Wilson, founder of *The Economist* newspaper and Standard Chartered Bank, developed his passion for figures which has left its mark in the statistics-based journalism of his newspaper even today. After finding himself excluded from becoming a barrister because of his family's Quaker background, Wilson instead built a successful business career.[101] As well as Wilson, Ackworth old scholars from its first half-century include famous industrialists such as the cotton master Henry Ashworth, as well as intellectual advocates of the free trade system which played an important role in creating a modern, wealthy economy, including the politician John Bright.[102] The Industrial Revolution owes more to Ackworth than to Eton – at least in terms of the direct contribution of old boys to commerce and technological innovation, without taking any account of the role in political and social stability played by old Etonians.

When it came to the new Catholic schools, two in particular, Stonyhurst (1794) and Ampleforth (1802), began to draw numbers of the Catholic aristocracy who had previously been educated at seminaries abroad.

Ampleforth College, situated in a cold stone abbey in northern Yorkshire, would never have suited boys of a sensitive physique. It was originally founded in Germany, but although the king of Prussia decided to suppress the school in 1802, he humanely allowed the boys to stay until the Easter of 1803, after hearing that the North Sea littoral to which they were destined was not a pleasant place in the winter. The Benedictine monks who kept the new school at Ampleforth in winter and summer had fewer reservations. Despite this inauspicious start the school had rather an impressively modern curriculum by the standards of the old public schools, including French, Italian, Spanish, history, geography, botany and ornithology, as well as the usual Latin and Greek – the modern European languages serving as useful Catholic tongues for future priests. In an 1815 letter to parents, the school declared itself 'confident that without any detriment to the classical part of education, a comprehensive knowledge of the most useful sciences can be communicated in the time that is usually given to languages alone'.[103] Stonyhurst set up what it claims to be the first chemistry lab in any English school as early as 1808; certainly it is one of the earliest, and predates its counterparts at all the old Anglican public schools.[104]

The early, highly creditable enthusiasm at Catholic public schools for a practical education makes sense, given the circumstances of the time. Until 1829 Catholics were barred from most of the professions, including politics, the senior civil service and the judiciary – and they were to remain barred from Oxford and Cambridge Universities for longer still.[105] Stonyhurst's new Prefect of Studies (a master rather than a boy) responded to this in 1814 by adopting a common-sense view: 'On looking over the list of scholars, it appears that far the greater part of them are to be employed when they leave the college, in some sort of mercantile business. To all of these Arithmetic is the science, which will be most useful and most interesting.' Stonyhurst remained a school strong in maths well after 1829, educating not only Sir Arthur Ignatius Conan-Doyle but also Sherlock Holmes's arch-enemy Moriarty, described as 'endowed by nature with phenomenal mathematical ability'. Moriarty was the name of two of Conan-Doyle's contemporaries, who both won maths prizes.[106]

The old public schools generally failed to produce future entrepreneurs and technological innovators during this era. However, they provided good vocational training in the most important job of all: ruling Britain.

Although public school numbers fell to crisis low levels at individual schools in many years, much of the political class continued to be sent to them. Robert Walpole, Britain's first prime minister, was the first of nineteen prime ministers to learn about politics at Eton. In 1866, almost a century and a half after Walpole was ejected from office, the Earl of Derby came to power and formed a Conservative cabinet which would play a role in shaping the Second Reform Act – a great Victorian achievement which pushed democracy forwards by extending the right to vote to millions of new people. Eleven of this cabinet's sixteen initial members had been educated at public schools in the early years of the century. Eton had educated a scarcely believable nine of these eleven, with one apiece schooled at Rugby and Shrewsbury, and one of the nine at Rugby as well as Eton.

The public schools did not just educate boys who would subsequently become politicians. It also educated boys in the art of politics, and provided them with useful friends who might help them in that field. 'A boy who forms parties, and makes himself popular in a school or college would act the same part with equal ease in a senate or a Privy Council', concluded Eustace Budgell, the writer and politician, in 1712.[107] Budgell took the view that their very imperfections would prepare public schoolboys for politics better than the more rarefied environment of tuition at home. Private tuition 'would furnish out a good subject for Plato's *Republic*', he wrote, referring to the fifth-century BC work which focused on how to be a good ruler. A public school would, however, furnish 'a member for a community overrun with artifice and corruption', preparation which Budgell deemed useful, given the state of British politics at the time. One boy who went on to hold a senior position in ecclesiastical politics as an archdeacon was more idealistic about his training. Recalling his time as a prefect at Winchester at the beginning of the nineteenth century, he and his friends devised, in their minds, a special parliament to deal with fellow prefects who became tyrannical. 'What delightful talks we had about it! How we returned to the subject again and again!' he remembered fondly.[108]

It is certainly difficult to see George Canning, son of a failed wine merchant and an actress, becoming one of the greatest Tory politicians of his age – foreign secretary and briefly prime minister – had he not gone to Eton in 1782 courtesy of his uncle's generosity. At the school he gathered round himself a circle of useful and lasting friends, including John Hookham Frere and Charles Ellis, who would become, respectively, diplomat and MP.[109] Canning not only excelled at the Classics but also distinguished himself in public speaking at the school. 'Canning knew nothing of frogs, and yet he could rule men', wrote his ever-loyal friend Frere, with the disdain for scientific inquiry typical of Etonians of his generation.[110]

A generation later Eton was divided into Canningites, who supported free trade and Catholic emancipation, and orthodox Tories, who did not. The future Liberal prime minister William Gladstone was on the side of the Canningites, supported by a coterie of friends including James Milnes-Gaskell, a future Tory Lord of the Treasury, who defended Canningite policy on Ireland with apposite quotations from Caesar. One schoolboy ally at Eton, the poet Arthur Henry Hallam, was to prove important in his political life: Hallam, the son of Whig historian Henry Hallam, introduced him to Whig ideas and people. Gladstone honed his debating skills in 'Pop', the still extant Eton society which then functioned as its debating forum, though it has since assumed more of a prefectorial role within the school.[111] It is telling that Kurt Hahn, the educationalist who in 1934 founded Gordonstoun School, based his principles for training for leadership partly on Pop, having met some of its former members at his old college, Christ Church, Oxford.[112] Gladstone seems to have dived headlong into Eton's growing club scene, which provided the training for the versatility of political life, where men must learn to work alongside each other. Improbably, given his future reputation for humourlessness, he wrote perhaps the wittiest account of the peculiarities of school clubs in a parody of a school magazine, *The Eton Miscellany*. In the fake minutes of the Eton Dull Club, Rule Number 6 decreed: 'That loud talking be considered disorderly, and that any member (the chairman excepted) who shall wake another, shall be subjected to a fine of two-and-sixpence, unless he can lull him to sleep again in five minutes.'[113] It sounds similar to many a parliamentary meeting, as anyone who has sat through a two-hour House of Commons Select Committee session can testify. After these varied experiences Gladstone left the school 'proficient in Greek and Latin, competent in French, barely adequate in mathematics, and largely ignorant of the sciences', as the *Oxford Dictionary of National Biography* notes.[114]

The journey that took William Gladstone to Eton was a long one. Thomas Gladstones had been no more than a moderately successful Scottish corn merchant, but his son, Sir John, became immensely rich through trading in corn, cotton and sugar. In politics, however, John was never more than a backbench Tory MP. The transformation (and truncation) of the Gladstone name (minus the 's' from 1835) took two generations, but its second act was consciously planned by Sir John. Determined that at least one of his sons should succeed in politics, he saw an education at Eton and Christ Church, Oxford, as the best preparation for that. The spectacular rise of William Gladstone suggests that his tactics paid off, though William's identically educated elder brother Sir Thomas only became a politician of roughly the same status as his father.

Cynics might argue that a tyrannical school system may teach lessons in politics, but does not teach lessons that one would want to see imitated by one's future political masters. Recalling his time at

Winchester in the 1780s, Sydney Smith, the writer and cleric, wrote that public school boys were 'alternately tyrant and slave'.[115] As head boy, Smith himself reached the exalted position of arch-tyrant. At their worst, the senior boys were not even tyrants with honour. The unhappily abbreviated actor W. C. Macready recalled, as a Rugby schoolboy in the first decade of the nineteenth century, how a boy sent by his prefect to steal an ash plant to be used for his own beating was seen by chance by the head, and expelled for refusing to reveal who had sent him. The prefect did not confess that it was him.[116]

There were certainly large numbers of public school men who presided over intolerance and espoused reactionary policies over the centuries. Three of the seven bishops who formally opposed James II's 1687 Declaration of Indulgence, which called for religious freedom for all Christians, were Wykehamists.[117] A century and a half later, Wellington, an Old Etonian, opposed the Reform Bill of 1832 which extended suffrage – allegedly noting, after its passage resulted in the election of more MPs outside the upper classes, that 'I never saw so many shocking bad hats in my life'.[118]

Later intellectuals complained that the public schools' classical curriculum generated excessive conservatism. 'A culture based wholly on the past will seldom be able to pierce through everyday surroundings to the essential splendour of contemporary things, or to the hope of still greater splendour in the future', fretted the philosopher Bertrand Russell in 1910, in an attack on the notion of a predominantly classical education.[119] Dean Frederic Farrar, Classics master at Harrow, made a similar point in 1866 with more than a mite of melodrama, noting that in 'an age of observation and experiment . . . we keep bowing and scraping to mere authority'. He posed the rhetorical question: 'Are we alone to follow the example of the Chinese in a changeless imitation of our ancestors, and to confine our eager boys for ever between the blank walls of an ancient cemetery, which contains only the sepulchres of two dead tongues?'[120]

Advocates of the Classics can counter that all human life is in the subject, if well taught. Moreover, although many classicists regarded

Ancient Rome and Greece as representing a golden age, this belief was no call for social stasis – as the very word 'revolution' implies, as many revolutions have been caused by a desire to return to a mythical arcadian period, as by a desire to progress to an uncharted Utopian future. The seventeenth-century philosopher Thomas Hobbes warned that Classics might teach political radicalism. He would be proved right by Robert Sumner, a chain-smoking, hard-drinking rebel with an immoderate love for the works of fellow Old Etonian Henry Fielding, the sharp-eyed satirist of British politics and society. In the eleven years between becoming headmaster of Harrow in 1760 and his death at the early age of forty-two, he became Britain's most brilliant headmaster.[121]

In a subtle way, Sumner deliberately prepared his pupils for future lives in politics, partly through monthly declamations, introduced earlier in the century at Eton, which taught boys the art of rhetoric, and partly through the study of Greek and Roman history. This included the Greeks' stand against the despotic and aggressive Persians, and the story of Aristogeiton and Harmodius, the sixth-century BC Athenians who became known as the Tyrannicides after killing Hipparchus, an abusive dictator. Surviving essays by his pupils show that many absorbed well the principles of these early proto-Whigs. Philip Yorke, the future 3rd Earl of Hardwicke, wrote: 'That man is truly wise who, emerged from the power of custom, is swayed only by the arguments which offer themselves to his unprejudiced judgment.' He would later fight for Catholic Emancipation as Lord Lieutenant of Ireland. One pupil wrote that he and his peers had been taught the virtues of democracy – introduced to humanity by Athens in the sixth century BC – by voracious reading under Sumner's charge.[122] Another man taught by Sumner was William Jones, founder of the field of comparative linguistics and political radical who supported the American Revolution.

A forward-thinking politician from another public school was Bertrand Russell's grandfather, the 1st Earl Russell, an Old Westminster and one of the champions of the 1832 Reform Act which extended the suffrage. He claimed that 'the democratic character of the nobility of England . . . is very much to be attributed to the gregarious education they receive'.[123] A contemporary, Sir Robert Peel (who went to Harrow), contributed to the emergence of a more economically efficient free market system by supporting the repeal of the Corn Laws, and helped preserve social stability by laying the foundations of a modern police force.

Public school politicians provided the peace and continuity that allowed the entrepreneurs of the Industrial Revolution to succeed, and which encouraged them to come, like the Brunels fleeing the French Revolution, from unstable countries which lacked peace and stability. There were also enough far-sighted public school men in the eighteenth and nineteenth centuries to keep the British locomotive of industrial and democratic progress going in the right direction. For that, the public schools deserve some credit.

'I am glad you intend to send my eldest neice [sic] to a boarding-school', wrote Mrs Montagu, an English aristocrat, in 1773. 'What girls learn at these schools is trifling, but they unlearn what would be of great disservice – a provincial dialect, which is extremely ungenteel.' Clearly setting out her order of priorities in education, she noted approvingly that at boarding schools, 'the carriage of the person, which is of great importance, is well attended to, and dancing is well taught'. However, 'as for the French language, I do not think it is necessary, unless for persons in very high life'.[124] For most girls from wealthy families, the purpose of an education remained to boost both their femininity and their ability to blend in with men and women of the upper classes. One could argue that, given the social circumstances of the time, in strict economic terms this was the best that schools could do for their girls: deprived of the opportunity to make their own money, their best chance of a life of material comfort lay in attractiveness rather than achievement. The object of education remained 'to increase a young lady's chance of a prize in the matrimonial lottery', observed Maria Edgeworth, the Irish novelist and feminist (1768–1849).[125]

The living conditions at girls' schools were, at times, as frightful as anything in the boys' public schools. At the Clergy Daughters' School at Cowan Bridge in Yorkshire, the Brontë sisters suffered from the terrible cold and cruel treatment of staff. However, the worst outrage was perhaps the most incompetent cooking in history, including rice puddings boiled in dirty and foul-smelling water taken from a rain butt, and burnt porridge full of unidentified fragments. In this insanitary environment two of the Brontë sisters fell ill and died.[126] The school was commemorated with bitterness in Charlotte Brontë's *Jane Eyre*.

And yet we can detect a smidgeon of progress in the education of women at this time. The average school for girls from wealthy families remained focused primarily on the outward manners and superficial accomplishments of young ladies, but a few schools appeared whose headmistresses showed a genuine interest in education. One of them, the Great School in Queen Square, Bloomsbury, was to become known as the Young Ladies Eton some while after its foundation in the mid-eighteenth century, underlining its strong claim to be called England's first girls' public school rather than a mere fly-by-night finishing school. It lasted for a century, and at its acme educated as many as 220 pupils at about 100 guineas (£13,500) a year. At the peak of its prestige in the 1790s, Mrs Devis, the headmistress, wrote an English grammar and a geography textbook for her pupils, as well as teaching them lessons in deportment, music and French. Without these subjects the school could not, in that era, have stayed in business.[127]

The capacity for the boys' public schools to educate politicians was a virtue but not a saving grace. Repeat custom from the families of Britain's tiny political class, and those desirous of breaking into it, was not enough to prevent a marked slide in the already small number of boys entering the old public schools. The annual number of boys starting at eight of the schools – Winchester, Eton, St Paul's, Westminster, Shrewsbury, Charterhouse, Harrow and Rugby – fell from 575 in 1830 to 412 in 1835, a 28 per cent drop.[128] Even sharper slides in individual schools' numbers to nadirs in the 1830s, 1840s and even 1850s raised questions about their future existence. Charterhouse had more than 200 pupils in 1825, but fewer than 100 ten years later.[129] Rugby's roll slid from 245 in 1793 to 141 ten years after that. By 1827 it was a tad lower still at 120.[130] Westminster and Winchester took a little longer to reach even more dire low points: the former to 67 in 1841 from a peak of 332 in 1818, the latter to 68 in 1855 after a series of fluctuations.[131]

A number of these schools came close to outright extinction. At Harrow, where the fall in the intake of pupils was the most spectacular – from 351 in 1802 to only 69 by 1844 – the governors stared into the abyss, responding to this slide by acknowledging 'the probable dissolution of the school'.[132] There were no longer enough pupils for the masters to make a decent living; a heating system devised by the maths master in an unusually disastrous attempt at DIY had burnt down a chunk of the property; what was left of the school was shockingly primitive, with five waterless privies recognized as health hazards, and no bathrooms or even bathtubs in any of the boys' houses.[133] Harrow was a damaged, sordid, almost empty school, and many of the other old public schools had already slumped into a similar state.

The old public schools might have been able to limp on despite such low numbers by firing staff and lowering the salaries of those who were left. They would, however, at best have become backwaters, staffed by underpaid and underqualified masters teaching small numbers of boys. At worst they would have suffered the fate that befell many of the endowed grammars in the nineteenth century: the closure of the school and transfer of the assets to more successful charities.

Surveying the litany of failings at the established public schools in the early nineteenth century, one is entitled to ask why the public schools' response to their defects was so feeble. The reasons were threefold. The first was greed; the second was narrow-mindedness; the third was that universal cause of inertia throughout history: the undeserved veneration conferred on any system simply because it has survived for so long, even if no longer fit for purpose.

Greed had become a positively venerable vice, of centuries' standing. At Harrow, Joseph Drury perfected the process of squeezing as much out of the school as possible. His method was to take as many pupils as he could into the school (because heads continued to receive a capitation fee per boy), stuff the maximum possible number into his own house as boarders, and spend as little as he could on what had become slum accommodation. By the end of his time Drury had hit on the brainwave of moving out of the headmaster's house entirely to make room for more boys while he rented a nearby cottage to live in. During his twenty-year tenure he earned over £80,000 (£8.5 million), perhaps more, in real terms, than any other headmaster in British history who did not actually own a school.[134]

The narrow-mindedness derived from the exceedingly small world in which the old public schoolmasters continued to move. 'I am perfectly indifferent as to who comes here', Drury wrote to Samuel Butler at Shrewsbury about his successor to the Harrow headship, before setting out a list of conditions that indicated the opposite: he must, of course, be 'a gentleman, scholar, and a public school man who can do [Greek and Latin] verses'. He must also come from Eton, Harrow, Winchester, Shrewsbury, Rugby or 'perhaps Westminster, and from no other places whatever'.[135] The governors of Westminster took a still narrower view: between 1593 and 1846 every single head had been educated at the school.[136] In 1830 the *Edinburgh Review* summarized the situation accurately: 'Bred in the routine of Eton education, young men are sent to a college [King's College, Cambridge], inhabited solely by Etonians, where all, or nearly all, study is voluntary; and after a few years return to their old school to teach the things they were themselves taught, in the place, and in the manner, they had learnt them.'[137] Such a man would meet few others who might question the time-honoured Eton way of teaching.

He would also have found little to challenge his assumption of the primacy of narrow classical learning at any other college at Cambridge or Oxford, and this fossilization at the two universities encouraged fossilization at the public schools. Classical learning even gained in importance at Cambridge with the 1822 introduction of the Classical Tripos, the forerunner of modern degrees in Classics. The centuries-old dominance of the Classics at the ancient universities and ancient public schools produced an equilibrium where they were currently deemed to provide a good education precisely because they had previously been deemed to provide a good education. In the mid-eighteenth century Lord Chesterfield had told his Westminster-educated son that classical knowledge was absolutely necessary because everyone agreed to think so.[138]

Change was in the air, however. In 1836 Oxford and Cambridge lost their duopoly over English university education with the founding of the University of London, which from the first aimed to offer a broad range of learning not dominated by the Classics. The 1820s saw the beginning of a wave of new day schools to rival the old boarding schools as well as St Paul's and Merchant Taylors'. From the 1840s a new group of boarding schools was added to the mix. For old and new to serve both their pupils and the interests of British public and commercial life, the relevance and quality of education required improvement. More fundamentally, order needed to be imposed on chaos. In the public schools, the reform movement began to gather pace at the end of the 1820s; it was to prove sufficiently successful to instil the widespread assumption that the Victorian era was as golden an age for the public schools as it was for the empire. Closer scrutiny, however, indicates superficial gilding of the thinnest sort, or even mere ormolu. This intellectual inspection – of the public school in Victorian times and the eventful decade beforehand – takes place in the next two chapters.

CHAPTER FOUR

'First-Character. Second-Physique. Third-Intelligence.'

1828–1869

WILLIAM Conybeare, who welcomed boys through the gates of the newly opened Liverpool College in 1843, lived with a very personal and effective reminder of why Britain's public schools needed reform. He monitored the establishment of the day school, which provided a relatively humane education marked by a minimum of corporal punishment, through only one eye. The other had been lost in a schoolboy dispute at Westminster, a place where, he remembered with some bitterness, Sundays had been marked by a total absence of productive activity. As a result, 'we had nothing to do, and employed the idle time in reading novels or in quarrelling'.[1]

Conybeare was one of many headmasters scarred by their experiences of growing up within the old public school system, though not, usually, in such a literal sense. Some of these men founded new schools; others transformed the old ones. For some, idealism was the guiding force; for others, the motive power was the notion that, in an age when many would-be public schools disappeared within a few years, they had to compete or die. Christopher Wordsworth, who tried and failed to restore Harrow's fortunes in the face of its antiquated curriculum and even more antiquated facilities before being forced out in 1844, blamed the school's decline partly on new schools such as Cheltenham College and London's University

College School, founded as a school for University College London, Britain's first secular place of higher education. (Most of the new public schools, however, had religious affiliations.[2]) By the 1860s Cheltenham's principal, Alfred Barry, was telling the governors he needed better boarding houses if the school were to compete with new public schools such as Marlborough, Clifton and Malvern. What had been considered acceptable accommodation a mere twenty years ago was no longer so, he counselled.[3] Matters continued in this vein for many subsequent years. In 1883 one of Brighton College's governors drew attention to 'the great competition between schools' in 'appliances, such as boarding houses built for the purpose, with every convenience and perfect drainage', and in the provision of 'ample space for games'. 'Parents think much of these things', he concluded. 'They see them at one place and expect them everywhere.'[4]

Ultimately these reformers saved the public school movement, which not only survived but thrived. The 1820s, 1830s and beginning of the 1840s saw the foundation of many of what are now the leading public day schools, including the Edinburgh Academy, University College School, King's College School and the City of London School (though the last-named did not really become a public school, in terms of clientele, until well into the twentieth century). As for the boarding schools, there were two peaks when the mania for foundation was particularly strong during the period covered by this chapter: the 1840s and the 1860s, with thirteen such schools founded in each decade.[5] The rapid growth in schools was assisted by the tailwind of economic change. Britain was not only becoming wealthier; the end of the Napoleonic Wars in 1815, combined with a boost to productivity fostered by the Industrial Revolution, nurtured a period of high economic growth. The wealth was also becoming more concentrated, to the benefit of the public schools' core client base. By 1867 the top 5 per cent of the population of England and Wales received almost half the national income, compared with only one-third at the beginning of the century.[6]

The favourable economic climate undoubtedly increased the public schools' potential pool of patrons. It could never, however, have saved the public schools on its own unless they had raised their game, since there were plenty of alternative models of elite education. One was the smaller private schools. Another alternative was private tuition with a local scholar or at home; as late as 1893 this was still the background of almost one-fifth of Cambridge undergraduates.[7] However, the view survived that public schools, where large numbers of boys were thrown together, could provide the necessary educational ingredients which other forms of education could not. In the 1841 inaugural ceremony of Cheltenham College, the Revd Francis Close, vice-president of the founding committee, declared that the new institution would be big enough to give the boys as much competition with each other as the traditional public schools provided, furnishing them, he concluded, with the best possible chance of getting into university.[8] Boys do not just compete with each other, of course: they also bully and abuse. Nonetheless, enough parents saw the virtues of a public school education, amid the rough-and-tumble of the public school environment, to give a new lease of life to the movement.

The most famous of the public school reformers was Thomas Arnold. He inherited a school of only 120 pupils in 1828, and set the foundations for a rise in the Rugby roll to almost 500 in the years after he died, still at the helm, in 1842, a time when schools such as Harrow and Westminster were still scrambling to keep alive.[9] Arnold's awakening to the faults of the public school system came early; he was attacked on his first night as he knelt to pray at his bed at Winchester College by boys who took a dim view of such religious display.[10] At the Anglican public schools of the time religious devotion did not loom large, even though the headmasters were as a rule ordained, and some, including Samuel Butler, went on to become bishops. Butler and other heads exhibited that characteristic English horror of the display of strong religious emotion, a proclivity which was customarily condemned with the then pejorative word 'enthusiasm'. 'Religion was non-existent then at Eton', Gladstone remembered of his 1820s school days.[11] Arnold would, however, help to change this. His Rugby reforms would be seeped in an intensely and very publicly devout approach to life, retained despite, or perhaps because of, attempts by Wykehamists to beat it out of him. In *Tom Brown's School Days*, Hughes wrote stirringly of his sermons: of 'the tall gallant form, the kindling eye, the voice, now soft as the low notes of a flute, now clear and stirring as the call of the light infantry bugle, of him who stood there Sunday after Sunday, witnessing and pleading for his Lord'.[12] It sounds quite a performance.

In practical terms, public school Christianity largely meant deracinating sins that had taken root at Rugby and elsewhere, sins which Arnold astutely identified. His classification of the 'evils' which might exist in a school included 'systematic cruelty', the type of 'general idleness' which the one-eyed Conybeare had seen at Westminster, and a bond of evil 'by which a boy would regard himself as more bound to his companions in ties of wickedness, than to God or his neighbour in any ties of good'.[13]

Arnold's solution to this sinfulness was not revolution but reformation, and his tool was the system of boy government. Boy government, where boys took part in the running of the school, had existed from the very beginning of public school history, but the system had gradually grasped more authority for itself, responding to the power vacuum within schools that arose from the scarcity of teachers. One facet of this was the fagging system, which Arnold described as a necessity in providing for 'regular government' and avoiding 'the evils of anarchy'. Another facet was the closely allied prefect system, and the most eloquent description of the system in its ideal form comes from one of the prefects themselves. Writing three years after Arnold's death, the prefect described the sixth form, from which the prefects were chosen, as 'an aristocracy of talent and worth, created by neither birth, interest, nor personal strength ... [It turned] those who should otherwise have been the ringleaders in every disturbance into an organized and responsible nobility, with power, privileges, and a character of their own to preserve.'[14]

Rather than diminishing the authority of the older boys, Arnold tried to make this authority benign. This was done partly through religious exhortation, and partly by treating the boys almost as equals. Four prefects were invited to dine with the Arnold family every week – providing them with almost as much access to the throne, and hence prestige within the school, as the teachers themselves. A regime of constant proselytizing, punctuated by the occasional lunch sitting face-to-face with the head, may sound hellish to many a modern reader. However, Arnold was popular with his boys. In 1839 sixty-one signed a petition that persuaded him not to give up running the house for the senior boys. 'We venture to say that the personal regard we feel for you would make us extremely lament [sic] your leaving us', they pleaded.[15]

Arnold's ideas were implemented at other schools by a generation of men who were either educated by him or came under his influence as adults, including Charles Vaughan, the arch-reformer at Harrow, Conybeare in Liverpool, and Thomas Priestley at Mill Hill. The second, much larger, generation consisted of men who came into contact with this first generation, or were educated at Rugby after Arnold's 1842 death when the school still bore his stamp – men such as George Cotton, head of Marlborough (known at the school as the 'master'). The list of heads influenced by the hagiography that sprang up after Arnold's demise is even larger. Thomas Jex-Blake, principal of Cheltenham College before going back to his old school Rugby as its head in 1874, was down to go to Eton. However, his father transferred the boy to Rugby after reading Arthur Stanley's heavily sold *Life and Correspondence of Thomas Arnold* and declaring that hitherto 'he had no idea that any school attempted to act on the Christian ideal'.[16] Summarizing his alleged influence shortly after his death, George Moberly, headmaster of Winchester and an apostle of Arnold's, claimed to have seen an 'improvement' across public schools, including 'a general improvement in respect of piety and reverence', 'mainly attributable' to 'Dr Arnold's personal earnest simplicity of purpose, strength of character, power of influence, and piety'.[17]

However, Arnold's reforms did not entirely succeed in creating a school of upstanding Christian morality and benign boy government. Although he bequeathed a powerful ideal of headship, his influence over his own school was transient. Poaching and vandalism against local farms became less common, and the school was spared major disturbances during his period in office.[18] Nevertheless, the Fags' rebellion took place a few years after Arnold's passing, during the term of his successor Archibald Tait.[19] Furthermore, Lewis Carroll, who arrived at Rugby as a clever and sensitive boy with a stammer four years into Tait's rule, suffered severe bullying at night during the peak hours of boy government when the masters were elsewhere. He recalled: 'I cannot say that I look back upon my life at a Public School with any sensations of pleasure or that any earthly considerations would induce me to go through my three years again.'[20]

Given the limited effect of Arnold's reforms even within his own school, it is hardly surprising that they were only patchily effective in the schools of his disciples. Fettes' school historian alludes to 'a good deal of bullying, both moral and physical', during the headship of Arnold's disciple Alexander Potts.[21] At Cheltenham College, the principal Alfred Barry movingly described the virtues of boy government at the 1868 speech day, declaiming: 'You know how I have always desired to give you liberty and responsibility of action, because it seemed to me that any English school should be an epitome of England herself, in which the rulers shrink not from their burden, and yet they who are ruled leave them not to bear it alone.' By the 1880s, at least, this liberty and responsibility had become abused: a special committee, established in response to a sharp drop in pupil numbers, found lax discipline and severe bullying by the boys; the head promptly resigned after it published its report.[22] On the other hand, both Marlborough and Harrow flourished after introducing reforms to the prefect system in line with Arnold's principles – though at the same time as other changes, to be considered later, which may have been more crucial. Arnold's prefect system assisted competent headmasters; where headmasters were less effectual it does not seem to have made a difference.

Despite Arnold's preoccupation with eradicating 'sin' at public schools, he was guilty of an excessively optimistic view of the perfectibility of human nature. Boys, girls, men and women who are put in positions of trust and power may use it well, if they respect the person who has dispensed that power; they are just as likely, however, to abuse it. The man government model of the new Catholic boarding school of Stonyhurst was more realistic. Certain teachers were appointed as prefects of discipline, patrolling the playground in the daytime and the dormitories at night. Even this system is clearly not foolproof, however, given the risks of child abuse by a tiny but dangerous minority of masters.[23]

Arnold's mixture of boy government and religious exhortation worked only up to a point. His most complete success lay in setting out a powerful myth of public school paradise. This attracted parents such as the Revd Jex-Blake, father of Thomas, and boosted the numbers at Rugby and other schools which adopted practices that worked well in sermons and in letters to parents, but less reliably on the ground. Myths can, nevertheless, be powerful, because if they are sufficiently inspiring they start to affect reality. Such was the case for Arnold, who provided an ideal which headmasters strove to reach – making the public schools less consistently cruel, at least, than a generation earlier.

Marlborough College, opened in the Wiltshire countryside in 1843, the year after Arnold's death, was conceived as a cheap imitation of the old public schools, down to the faux-ancient buildings added to the original eighteenth-century country house by Edward Blore. The latter was a specialist in country houses of counterfeit antiquity, and the man who had won the sobriquet of 'the cheap architect' for his cut-price completion of Buckingham Palace after the dismissal of the more distinguished John Nash on the grounds of his excessively expensive building plans.[24]

What went on inside the buildings was, initially, all too accurate an imitation of the public schools at their worst. Marlborough's *raison d'être* was to provide a public school-style education at bargain prices to the sons of clergymen who could not otherwise afford it, with fees of 30 guineas (£3,400) for the offspring of clerics and 50 guineas for sons of the laity.[25] In response to high demand, the cash-strapped school authorities made the serious, though understandable, error of cramming the buildings with as many boys as possible. They announced a rise in targeted numbers from 200 to 500; by 1848 the tally had risen to 521. Faced with such a large pupil roll but only limited resources, the school had little choice but to adopt the traditional public school model of keeping in poor conditions boys who were taught by an insufficient number of teachers. There were only fourteen of these, and each of them stuck to the conventional, though hardly satisfactory, public school model of teaching one huge class while the other, nominally under his control, worked on an assignment, with the boys chatting idly, or worse. Life outside the classroom was also bad: a boy who had arrived in 1843 remembered 'suffering from almost chronic hunger'. Moreover, for mutual protection against the tyranny of the crowd, boys organized themselves in groups, known ominously as tribes, which took their names from their leaders. The traditional public school defects led to the traditional public school outcome: a full-scale rebellion in 1851. In response the head resorted to a mixture of flogging and negotiation – to no avail: the boys rebelled again days later. By the following term the pupil roll had fallen to only 400, and the school's long-term future was in doubt.[26]

The disgraced master was replaced by George Cotton, who had taught at Rugby under Arnold. His solution was to reform the school on several fronts, including the prefect system. These boys led, he complained, 'a life of privilege without duty or responsibility', and so their responsibilities were increased. In return for the newly benign government of the prefects, Cotton told the boys, pupils must 'either submit to the prefects, or be reduced to the level of a private school, and have their freedom ignominiously curtailed'. In summary, 'The prefects are and shall be, so long as I am head, the governors of this school.'[27] The boys must also be found something to do, to keep them out of mischief, in much the same way that prisons where the inmates are kept idle become breeding-grounds of discontent. Most school circulars to parents are as dull as ditchwater. However, Cotton's 1853 'Circular to Parents' was, improbably, an important historical moment. It proposed changes to the syllabus that would lead to the formation of a 'Modern' side: a concentration by some boys on maths, modern languages and (to a certain extent) natural science. This was still a novelty at the time. However, even more importantly, its call for organized games gives it a strong claim as the document which started the mania for sport at public schools. Such activities had the virtue, asserted Cotton, of keeping boys 'as much as possible together in one body in the college itself and in the playground'.[28] It was, in other words, a perfect way to exert crowd control.

Boys can always find ways of making their own sport, but hitherto this had often taken an unwholesome form, including poaching at Rugby, cat stoning at Harrow, and bullying across the length and breadth of Britain. By making sport a core part of the curriculum, organized by the school itself, Cotton and other heads gave it a much more central role in the lives of public school boys. Over the succeeding decades three sports were to become particularly deeply rooted in public school culture. Rugby, devised at the school of the same name in the early 1800s, offered a sublimated violence which made it an especially powerful substitute for the knightly training of earlier centuries, though Arnold, who arrived at the school after its invention, took little interest in sport. Cricket offered an attractive blend of team-playing and individualism. Dearest of all in the hearts of many Classics masters, however, was rowing, the foundation of Athenian military power. Lord Rosebery, prime minister from 1894 to 1895, arranged to have the 'Eton Boating Song', written by his mentor, the Eton master William Johnson Cory, played at his funeral.[29]

Although organized public school sport began as a way of controlling the mob, public school headmasters' enthusiasm for it was sharpened by the blessings bestowed on sport by classical writers, who in practice often wielded far more influence on the outlook of headmasters than did biblical texts. In their discussion of how to educate a governing elite, Plato's *Republic* and *Laws* insisted on the importance of athletics as a counterpoint to the study of literature. Physical activity would, thought Plato, strengthen character. The display of physical prowess would, moreover, form one of the criteria for selection as members of the Athenian ruling class.[30]

Over the succeeding decades, organized sport came to exercise an ever more important role in the public schools, though more uniformly in the boarding than in the day schools. By the end of the 1880s, boys played compulsory football every day at Uppingham School. By the turn of the century Eton had fifty courts for the sport of fives, compulsory football for every house four or five times a week, and a cornucopia of other sports including beagling, rowing and athletics.[31]

Sport was largely organized by the school house – a semi-accidental public school invention of the early nineteenth century. Centuries previously, these units had started off as houses in the literal sense – places run by 'dames' with no educational role, by housemasters who derived the vast bulk of their income from them, or by the headmasters themselves. The school house now found a new lease of life as a vehicle for sporting competition within the school, and as a means, at least at the more enlightened schools, of preventing boys from becoming lost within the broad mass of pupils. The school house would also become a means of policing the school to guard against deviant behaviour.

Over the next century and more, sport did a great deal of good for the public schools and for their pupils. Paul Jones, an ex-Dulwich College boy, was no brainless athlete: he won a scholarship to Oxford, though he did not take it up because he joined the army during the First World War. 'Your sportsman joins the Colours because in his games he has felt the real spirit of unselfishness, and has become accustomed to give all for a body to whose service he is sworn', he wrote. 'Besides this, he has acquired the physical fitness necessary for a campaign', argued Jones. However, physical fitness did not, of course, save him from being killed by a bullet.[32] Sport could also teach men to be leaders. C. B. Fry (1872–1956), quondam cricket captain of England and old boy of Repton, was once sounded out about the possibility of becoming king of Albania, according to some sources.[33] A famed and handsome scholar-athlete is not quite such a preposterous idea for kingship if one is drawing from a blank sheet of paper. There is no hard evidence that the Duke of Wellington ever said one of the most famous of all quotes about public schools: that the Battle of Waterloo was won on the playing fields of Eton.[34] However, recalling his time at St Paul's, Field Marshal Bernard Montgomery, the Wellington of the twentieth century, praised the role of sport at the school, saying: 'By the time I left school a very important principle had just begun to penetrate my brain. That was that life is a stern struggle, and a boy has to be able to stand up to the buffeting and set-backs.'[35] It is a sentiment not so very different from that expressed in former Clifton College head boy Henry Newbolt's famous but rather clumsy 'Vitaï Lampada' (1892). The British lines have been broken, 'The Gatling's jammed and the Colonel dead' . . . 'But the voice of a schoolboy rallies the ranks: / Play up! play up! and play the game!'

Sport is not the only activity that imbues pupils with unselfishness and resilience. However, for some boys who failed to engage with other aspects of school life, it proved the best vehicle for teaching these virtues and others. Sport can retain that power in the present day. A 2007 study of 11,000 pupils aged between eleven and sixteen, published by academics at Loughborough University, found that three years of extra physical education and after-school activities improved behaviour, increased self-esteem and boosted school attendance.[36] Sport became, and remains, one of the virtues of a public school education.

Sport can even smooth a career path. 'Sport probably led straight to my career in a strange way', says a man who was at Hampton School (now Hampton Grammar School) in London in the 1980s. He was coached in rowing by former Olympic gold medallists, a situation he describes, with public school understatement, as 'quite handy'. He rowed for England while at the school, and credits this to be the reason for his election as president of his college's Junior Common Room at university. He thinks that his rowing credentials helped him with his successful application for the Foreign and Commonwealth Office Fast Stream; he was also able to impress while chairing a discussion during a group interview for the FCO, because he had done this so many times before for his JCR. His public school rowing led, step by step or stroke by stroke, to an elite job.[37]

Despite the beneficial effects of sport, however, the schools' concern with it went too far – to the point where it began to interfere with the other virtues of the system. 'Mens sana in corpore sano' implies a duality: that the mind and body are equally important. However, sport came to crowd out intellectual and cultural matters. Recalling the Marlborough of the 1900s, the poet Siegfried Sassoon remembered suffering a rant from his housemaster after revealing that he was taking organ lessons – 'You play the organ to get out of playing games, you wretched brute'.[38] In the same era, a Harrow boy was let off lightly for poor work in a letter from housemaster to father: 'I don't think too much attention need be given to the very bad report he has received from Mr Roebuck his Classics master. He has played exceptionally hard, and for the second year running we won the cock-house match', an important Harrow football fixture.[39] A Jesuit father at Stonyhurst complained in 1907 that 'studies do not hold the place of honour which is their due'. He lamented that various other activities 'always take precedence over studies', including gymnastics, boxing and cadet corps. There was not much space left for scholarship.[40] A decade previously, Clement Attlee, the future Labour prime minister, entered

Haileybury College. 'Nobody was considered anything unless he was good at games', he recalled.[41] The role of sport at public schools had gone far beyond what Mulcaster, its early pioneer, had envisaged.

H. H. Almond, headmaster from 1862 of Loretto, a public school near Edinburgh, was unusually frank about the low status of scholastic activities compared with sport. He listed the order of priorities at Loretto as 'First-Character. Second-Physique. Third-Intelligence. Fourth-Manners. Fifth-Information.' Almond added: 'Games in which success depends on the united efforts of many, and which also foster courage and endurance, are the very life blood of the public school system.'[42] Many parents agreed with him, until the advent of mass higher education changed their priorities. Malcolm Lees, who entered Ellesmere College in 1945, was told by his father that he wished him to become a 'good citizen in post-war Britain and a sportsman in the true sense of the word'.[43]

One can see why character should be considered important, particularly given the opportunities during the recently ended public school revolution for those of low and vicious character to wreak havoc. It was, however, not healthy for the headmaster of a school to list information – another word, more or less, for 'knowledge' – as a mere fifth. The word 'cult' is used too often; however, by the late Victorian era there truly was a 'cult of the athlete', a phrase often used at the time. Like all cults, its adherents claimed for it special powers which had no basis in reason. At the Brighton College old boys' dinner of 1888, Henry Smith Wright, a Conservative MP, declared: 'Our national sports seem to be the one feature which distinguishes us from all other nations on earth. Germany and France cannot colonize much because they have no cricket or football.'[44] At times sport even took on the religious elements of a cult. In the period between the world wars at Fettes, prefects chose special hymns for house prayers before and after key fixtures with rival public schools. Before-the-match choices included 'Christian, seek not yet repose', with an after-match favourite, if Fettes was victorious, 'For all the saints who from their labours rest'.[45]

Cotton became ambivalent about the monster he had created, even though it helped Marlborough's numbers to recover. He warned, astutely: 'The applause here bestowed upon success in games is apt to blind a person to his own ignorance, to make him indifferent to the faults of his character, to prevent him from realizing the fact that he will be judged very differently when he passes from boyhood to manhood.'[46]

Just as importantly, the rules will not be the same; an excessive devotion to the strict rules of sport can create complacency. James Welldon, headmaster of Harrow from 1885 to 1898, criticized workers' strikes, saying: 'It might well be wished that all persons who take part in public life would learn the lesson of "playing the game". It is a lesson which has been regularly taught upon the playing fields of our public schools.'[47] This may have been a noble aspiration, but strike leaders felt no compulsion to fulfil it. In politics, business and war, the rules invariably change with every generation, and those playing the old game lose. The kind of boy whom Welldon had in mind was described by John Hay Beith, ex-master at Durham School and Fettes. Manby, his archetypal image of the head of house, a senior prefect, 'fears nothing – except a slow ball which comes with the bowler's arm'. A Manby of his acquaintance once came upon a group of boys committing the sacrilege of playing tip-and-run at cricket. He chastised them one by one; the next half-holiday, he made them perform it 'under broiling sun and his supervision two till six'. Beith concluded: 'A House with a Manby at the head of it is safe. It can even survive a weak Housemaster. Greater Britain is run almost entirely by Manbys.'[48] Perhaps so, but in 1914, the year he wrote this, advances in firearms changed the old rules of war to provide overwhelming power to the defender. Britain's generals – many of them public school boys, though by no means all – did not sense this change in time. The Manbys were mown down.

Perhaps the greatest failing of the obsession with organized sports is that it stifled creativity and individuality by imposing a strict frame-work on boys' lives that allowed little room for other pursuits. 'I think that boys are now less ready to take the initiative than formerly. Organized games coached by masters are probably responsible for this change of attitude', wrote M.D. Hill in 1928, after spending the bulk of his life at Eton as scholar and then master. 'Boys again are eager to consult and obey masters in matters in which they used to resent interference.' Hill also recounted a story which hinted at resentment by the boys against games mania. Watching a cricket match between 'indifferent performers', he saw two batsmen in succession deliberately knocking down their wickets to end the match. 'A boy in my house, a member of that particular club, told me that this performance was by no means unusual. "We are fed up with cricket".'[49]

It is difficult to know what these boys would have done if they had not spent the time playing cricket. That mystery is itself a virtue: some would have idled, but many would have done whatever suited their interests and talents. They might have indulged in the idiosyncratic pleasures of an earlier generation: collecting fossils like T. G. Bonney, the geologist, at Uppingham School, or exploring the Thames like Shelley at Eton, before sport really took off at the school. Defenders of organized games could riposte that if Shelley's schoolmates had spent more time on the sports field, they would have spent less time on 'Shelley-baits'. The lightness of the timetable could have a good side. Boys had the freedom to be inordinately horrid to each other; they also had the freedom to indulge in their own private passions, and the tolerance of their masters was sometimes impressive. At Harrow in the 1770s the young Lord Althorp enjoyed the opportunity to collect grubs and silkworms and to rear squirrels and greenfinches.[50] In the 1810s Harrow's indulgent headmaster, George Butler, set aside part of his greenhouse to allow Henry Fox-Talbot, the polymath and photography pioneer, to grow his own botanical specimens – and even to conduct chemical experiments in the head's house until an explosion exhausted the master's liberality.[51] These were time-consuming passions, requiring considerable leisure each and every day, which would not fit in easily with the more academically punishing pace of modern boarding school life.

Christopher Barnett, head of Whitgift School at the time of writing, puts a persuasive modern case for the role of sport, when sport is encouraged within prescribed limits. He cites the case of Victor Moses, the Whitgift-educated Chelsea Football Club player, whom the Football Association selected for the European Under-17 Championship. Barnett, who as Moses's headmaster had the power to refuse to release him, told the FA to take him by all means, as long as it paid for an accompanying Whitgift master to prepare him for his forthcoming GCSEs. With this condition agreed, Moses went on to win the championship's Golden Boot. Whitgift has also educated Lawrence Okoye, a modern-day C. B. Fry who became a professional American football player after earning two A*s and two As at A level. Barnett cites research by the school showing a link between 'over-achievement' – exam results higher than expected on the basis of IQ scores – and strong performance in sport, drama and other extra-curricular activities at the school. He credits this to the confidence and positive approach to life generated by achievement outside academic work, agreeing '100 per cent' with the old 'mens sana in corpore sano' dictum. Answering the oft-posed critical question as to why academic institutions should get involved in sport at all, he argues that they are, to the contrary, the very best places to nurture sporting excellence. Drawing a contrast with British tennis professionals withdrawn from ordinary schools to concentrate on the sport, only to fail to pass muster on the professional circuit, he says that boys who perform brilliantly at sport in their early years but do not make the ranks of the professionals still have their academic credentials to fall back on to earn a living.[52]

To the charge that sport stifles creativity runs the counter-argument that the public schools were impressively creative when it came to inventing sports, including the Eton Wall Game, Eton and Rugby Fives, Rugby, Winchester, Uppingham and Rossall versions of football, and Rossall Hockey. At their worst these sports were vehicles for the megalomania of a particular head: at Victorian Uppingham Edward Thring, the headmaster, insisted that his boys stick to a particularly violent form of football of his own invention, devised to discourage teamwork in favour of dogged and rather masochistic self-reliance.[53] At their best, as in Rugby Football, they were so entertaining that they became mass-participation sports. Men educated at schools which practised their own unique activities might think nothing of inventing or improving sports, to the benefit of millions of future aficionados. W. C. Wingfield, one of the inventors of lawn tennis, was at Rossall before Rossall Football and Hockey were created, but an environment of creative sporting invention was probably already there.

In 1854, a year after Marlborough's birth, Charles John Vaughan took over as headmaster of Harrow School when it was practically in its death-throes. He was to effect the most spectacular transformation of all in a public school's fortunes: by the time he left in 1859 there were 438 pupils – six times as many as when he had arrived.[54] Vaughan would prove, in many respects, a brilliant headmaster, until, with his reforms unfinished, he resigned in shadowy circumstances that may or may not have involved a homosexual affair with a pupil – the evidence is strong but not quite compelling.[55]

Vaughan's greatest achievement was the upgrading of the almost mediaeval physical structure of the school. Objective observers might have considered it easier to shut the school down rather than to rip out its insides and install something more acceptable in a modern country, but Vaughan managed to persuade the pupils' parents and other friends of the school to sponsor an extensive reconstruction programme.[56] He did so under pressure from the government, which had begun a clean-up of Britain (in the expression's original literal sense) because of a growing realization that squalid conditions were killing people. The General Board of Health ordered 'certain alterations in the school privies' in 1853 – spurring the governors into action.[57] The absence of the miasma of human excrement was, in the struggle conducted by public schools to gain and retain pupils, a distinct competitive advantage in the health-conscious Victorian era; the promotional pamphlet of Eastbourne College, founded in 1867, dwelt on a curious mixture of snob value and earthier benefits. It boasted that the school enjoyed the patronage of the Duke of Devonshire, and that the district's sewage outflow had recently been removed to a point three miles outside the town's furthest limits.[58]

Parts of Eton were possibly in even greater need of improvement than the ancient 'facilities' (to use the term broadly) of Harrow School. 'Please God, I will do something for those poor boys', the new provost, Francis Hodgson, is said to have exclaimed on first catching sight of the buildings where he had lived as a scholar in the closing years of the century.[59] The cold and insanitary Long Chamber where the scholars lived, with no adult supervision between evening and morning, was notoriously bad. 'Cruel, at times, the suffering and wrong', remembered Edward Thring, who as headmaster of Uppingham (1853–87) revamped the school to create better conditions for the boys than he had suffered as an Eton scholar.[60] 'Cries of joy or pain were equally unheard; and excepting a code of law of their own, there was no help or redress for anyone.' Edward Hawtrey, Eton's headmaster during Hodgson's time as provost, prudently deflected a request from the visiting King of Prussia to see where the scholars slept, and acted against the bullying and privation by building separate rooms for the boys, installing heating and improving the food.[61] In response to Hawtrey's reforms the number of applications for scholarships increased, allowing the school to return to its full complement of seventy scholars; similar improvements to the school as a whole reversed a decline in its overall numbers, boosting them from a low of 444 in 1835 to a record high 777 in the 1840s.[62] The creation of palatable conditions in public schools was a response to competition within the system, as well as a reaction by headmasters who had suffered at such schools in previous generations. The 1865 prospectus for Bloxham School, opened in Oxfordshire five years previously, declared proudly that 'every boy has a single bed', as did many other prospectuses.[63] This was progress indeed.

Vaughan went beyond improving the buildings. As befitted a disciple of Arnold, he expanded Harrow's prefect system to give the 'monitors', as they were called, almost complete power, on the understanding that it ultimately derived from him and could be taken away by him if abused. The monitors were employed by Vaughan to stamp out savagery by meeting it with officially sanctioned brutality. On one memorable occasion, the head of school was permitted to deliver a sound thrashing, in front of the whole school, to two boys caught in the traditional Harrow sport of torturing a cat.[64] Vaughan also advanced further than Arnold – who had a rather limited interest in curriculum reform – by introducing an army class which received extra teaching in maths and military science. By 1857 this innovation, which deftly played to Harrow's historical strength as a cradle for future army officers, had attracted a respectable forty-five pupils.[65]

The growth of specialist classes learning specialist syllabuses, with a greater concentration on maths, science and modern languages than the standard classical syllabus, is one of the great educational changes of the Victorian era. An early exponent was Cheltenham College, which espoused specialist classes from the day the school's doors opened, to both boarders and day pupils, in the Gloucestershire boom town in 1841. In the classical department boys adhered more or less to the usual public school curriculum, which, as well as Latin and Greek, included maths, a little modern history and a little Hebrew. In the 'modern' department the list of available subjects from which pupils could choose included – as well as the usual Latin and maths – French, German, history, geography, drawing, experimental science and Hindustani, useful for future civil servants in India.[66] The public schools had educated many generals in the past, but until the formation of army classes well into the nineteenth century, they had not directly educated them in military affairs, unless one includes the practical training provided by the many public school rebellions. One of the ringleaders of the Rugby revolt of 1797 was the future Lieutenant-General Sir Willoughby Cotton, GCB, who later put down a slave uprising in Jamaica.[67] The public schools' dominance of the higher military ranks has continued until the present day: eight of the ten men promoted to full general status since 2003 went to public school.[68]

The growth of specialist classes came largely on account of the modernization of entry into the civil and military services, which began in 1853 with the opening of appointments in the Indian Civil Service to competitive examination. Two decades later there were similar exams for entry to the Home Civil Service, the Indian Civil Service, the officers' training college at Sandhurst, and the military academy at Woolwich where the engineers and artillery – the technical whizzes of the army – were trained. In 1870 the purchase of army commissions, long the conventional way for the upper classes to kick-start their army careers, ended completely. The social elite could no longer use either their money or their connections, made at public school and elsewhere, to secure automatic entry to a wide swath of public service posts.[69] From now on, men such as Flashman would have to prove their worth.

Despite the cases of Harrow and Marlborough, the public day schools, or hybrid day-boarding public schools founded in the first half of the nineteenth century, were the most likely during this period either to establish modern sides or to introduce a broader, less Classics-based curriculum via other methods. In 1851 King's College School in London split its teaching in two: a division of Classics, mathematics and general literature, and a division of practical instruction. The syllabus of the latter included English, French and German, history and drawing, and even 'mathematics with applications', a branch of the subject far from the abstract maths taught at most public schools. Perhaps most innovative of all was the introduction of Chinese as an optional subject, though for quite a high price – £5 5s (£620) a term, which came fairly close to doubling the school fees.[70] Clifton College, which took in boarders and day boys in a suburb of Bristol from 1862, began, like Cheltenham, with a modern and classical side.[71] George Butler (son of the eponymous headmaster of Harrow) split Liverpool College in a similar fashion after becoming principal in 1865.[72]

The thinking behind modern sides is set out in the King's College School prospectus for 1856–7, which explains the mooted potential advantages with admirable comprehensiveness: 'The object in view in this Division is to prepare pupils for general and mercantile pursuits, for the departments of engineering, architecture, civil services, and military science in the college [King's College, London, its sister university college], for the military academies at Woolwich, Sandhurst, and Addiscombe, and for the royal navy and the commercial marine.' Moreover, to fulfil the school's aim of producing pupils with a genuine facility in modern languages, French and German conversation classes were set up, with the aim of 'superseding, as far as possible, the necessity of a residence on the continent'.[73]

These innovations were, given the previous centuries of public school conservatism regarding change, positively revolutionary. New day schools, new boarding schools, and even the old public schools were shifting the very foundations of their education. Among the old schools Harrow was perhaps the most radical, but others were changing too. There was even some movement at Winchester, among the most conservative of all schools, where science was introduced in 1857.[74]

Parent power was crucial to this seismic change. Garnering support for the new modern side, Cotton at Marlborough wrote to parents: 'I receive an increasing number of requests from parents that I will permit their sons to give up some part of the regular Classical work.'[75] At the Edinburgh Academy, a day school though with some boarding founded in 1824, James Hodson established a modern side soon after taking up his duties as rector (headmaster) in 1854, on the grounds that boys were being removed from the school because parents wanted them to spend less time on Classics and more on subjects that would be useful to them in their future working life.[76] This explains why the modernization was particularly marked at day schools. 'You understand that we are not like the old public schools, isolated and autocratic', Butler of Liverpool College told his wife, the famous social reformer Josephine. 'This is an immense day-school, and the wishes – even the prejudices – of parents cannot be wholly ignored.'[77]

Any reader who senses a soupçon of reluctance in Butler's comment to his wife is not being excessively sensitive; headmasters were, for the most part, reluctant reformers, responding to, rather than leading, parental opinion. At times the governors took the head's side; at times they fought the head tooth and nail to implement what they considered to be the modernizing impulses of their client base. Butler's zeal for imparting the classical languages, acquired as a schoolboy at Harrow, extended even to his dog, who rejoiced in a passable understanding of the Latin and Greek suitable for an educated canine. The Liverpool head refused to give way to the demand of governors to substitute modern languages and science in place of the Classics. 'The want of sympathy with higher studies which commonly exists in commercial life acts upon the rising generation', complained Butler. 'They wish to get on in life as quickly as possible, and they would gladly be excused all work which they think unnecessary, and not likely to pay immediately. This is utilitarianism.'[78] The public schools were in terrible danger of providing a useful education.

The struggle for survival of many schools which initially tried to plough a narrow classical furrow suggests widespread dissatisfaction with the old public school educational model. At King's, the syllabus changes were a reaction to a fall in pupil numbers from 500 to 423 in only three years.[79] At Liverpool College, the number of boys in the upper school – the 'public school' part of the institution, based on clientele and fees – fell from 185 in the year Butler arrived to only 122 boys in the year he left. It had, by then, slipped into the vicious circle common to all declining schools, of cuts in staff numbers and salaries, the loss of the more able masters, and a reliance on the moribund and incompetent who were unable to abandon the sinking ship.[80]

The Edinburgh Academy shows how a school could be brought to its knees by excessive conservatism – as one might expect for a school whose façade would not leave it looking out of place in the Parthenon.

'To attempt to introduce any other branch of education would interfere with the success of the direct object of the Institutions, which is
to be a school for Classical Instruction', its governors stipulated from
the beginning, despite the qualms of a minority of them, including
the local celebrity and author Walter Scott. 'We still carry the pedantry
of former times a little too much into education, and boys are apt to
think that learning Latin is the exclusive business of life and that all
other acquisitions are of little consequence in comparison', complained
Scott, who called for a separate master to teach the four subjects of
English, spelling, geography and history. The school's chequered early
years suggests that many potential parents agreed. Pupil numbers
dropped from 440 in 1825 to just over 300 in 1836 – far from the 500
which the founders had deemed necessary for the school's long-term
sustainability. The janitors' wages were cut, the cleaners fired, teaching
assistants dismissed, and a mortgage taken out on the school. 'The
tide is setting strongly against classical education', wrote Henry
Cockburn, one of the school's founders, in 1834. 'Meanwhile, other
establishments, both private and public, are springing up now, which
as yet have in general succeeded chiefly, as it appears to me, because
they disdain these two languages [Latin and Greek], and profess to
teach what they call useful knowledge.' By 1848 due to falling rolls the
school's finances were so bad that Lord Cockburn wrote: 'The state of
the Academy fills me with sleepless alarm'.[81]

The expansion of the public schools' syllabus was a crucial moment
in their history; without this change few if any would have survived.
We should consider, therefore, who these exacting parents were, with
their own firm views of the curriculum, who so annoyed Butler and
other conservatively minded heads. It was not a change in the parental
base that led to change; rather, it was the traditional client base which
wanted change.

The patrons at the bulk of the old boarding schools varied from
school to school, but had for centuries consisted, more or less, of a
mixture of the professions first and foremost (including the law, the
clergy and the army), the landowning class (which furnished the

political class), and the more successful end of the business class. The business class had sent the Pastons in the Middle Ages, Ben Jonson in Tudor times, and William Gladstone and Robert Peel (the son of an immensely wealthy textile merchant and self-made man) in the early years of the nineteenth century. The client base remained similar in the mid-nineteenth century. The son of George Hudson, the self-made Railway King, started at Harrow the year that Vaughan did, two generations after Peel was sent to the same school – and Hudson's son was there at the same time as the future 4th Earl of Mount Edgcumbe, the courtier and politician.[82] The clients at the new boarding schools – many of them from the professions – were not radically different. Marlborough was set up with the clergy in mind, while Wellington College, founded in memory of the Duke of Wellington, concentrated on the sons of army officers when it opened in 1859.[83]

Turning to the old day schools, St Paul's and Merchant Taylors' continued to educate few landowners' sons, filling their rolls instead from the capital's highly varied middle class, including the sons of business men. Westminster still catered to an eclectic mix that included the high aristocracy as well as the London urban elite. The patrons of the several new London public day schools were similar to the traditional client base of St Paul's and Merchant Taylors'. Analysis of the period at King's covered by the first headmaster, John Major (1831–66), reveals that the bulk of fathers were lawyers, clergy and substantial businessmen; there were also, in the school's early years, various scions of the growing government bureaucracy centred on the capital. King's parents did not have the glamour of Eton's or Harrow's. One of the school's most distinguished early parents was Sir Joseph Bazalgette, the architect of London's (literally and meta-phorically) ground-breaking sewage system, which is still with us today: it was that kind of school.[84]

The early and mid-nineteenth century also saw, for the first time, a fairly large number of public day schools in Britain's growing urban centres, including Bristol, Liverpool and Edinburgh. Many of the first boys on the register of Liverpool College were sons of merchants.[85] Of Edinburgh Academy's first 372 boys, the fathers of a strikingly high 67 were lawyers, with 20 doctors, 27 in the army or navy, and 64 in business or international trade.[86] As in the case of King's, these were members of the broad rather than the high elite.

Finally, the non-conformist schools founded a generation or two previously continued to cater to the largely business-focused non-conformist elite, with the Catholic schools set up in Britain at a similar time educating a fairly small number of the Catholic upper and upper middle classes.

The public schools' clientele was, therefore, not radically different in social composition from previous times. There were, on balance, probably proportionately more fathers in business, but the professions remained strongly represented.

The professional classes were pressing as much as any other group for changes in public school education. By the mid-nineteenth century, members of the professional classes who hoped for a similar career path for their sons could see that their sons' interests would be best served if they gained a broader education than the public schools had previously provided. At Marlborough, Cotton told parents that the syllabus was to be broadened because families wanted children to 'devote themselves to special subjects connected with their future professions'.[87] At the Edinburgh Academy Hodson cited parental demands for subjects useful in the civil service and army as well as commerce.[88] Lieutenant Colonel J. P. Kennedy, a governor of Cheltenham College in its early years, sent his sons to the school because he believed that Germany and France were ahead of England in science, and that Cheltenham was the best school in Britain to help redress this balance by providing a scientific education.[89] Many members of the intelligentsia believed that scientific awareness was increasing both in British society and in countries that rivalled Britain; the nation's upper and upper middle classes could not, they believed, afford to be left behind. Baden Powell, Professor of Geography at Oxford and Anglican priest, declared in 1832: 'Scientific knowledge is rapidly spreading among all classes except the Higher, and the consequence must be, that that class will not long remain the Higher.'[90]

In reality, some of these fears were overdone, even though a more balanced curriculum was in England's interests. Although in some respects Germany was indeed ahead in science, many of its brightest scholars were classically trained, with Germany itself experiencing a revival of interest in Greece and Rome. One of the early prospectuses for University College School (founded 1830) boasted that German was offered – but no mention of its modern commercial advantages was made. Instead, the language was taught 'for the specific purpose of enabling the pupil to avail himself of the valuable assistance afforded by the labours of German philologers towards the right study of classical literature'.[91]

When it comes to the patron base of the public schools there is, however, one clear difference between the public school movement of the early to mid-nineteenth century and that of earlier generations: the emergence of a Celtic clientele. Scottish schools founded by the mid-1840s included the Glasgow as well as the Edinburgh Academy, Loretto, Merchiston Castle and Glenalmond. Ireland had the Royal Academical, Belfast. Cheltenham attracted considerable numbers from Ireland, though Wales remains to this day comparatively bereft of public schools. We can, for the first time, talk about British rather than merely English public schools.

Or can we? In the 1820s the Edinburgh Academy generated a brouhaha and spawned proto-Scottish Nationalist fervour within the city when it changed the pronunciation of Latin in school lessons from the mainland European style, also favoured in Scotland, to what was known as the 'Eton style', the pronunciation dominant in England and England alone. One might argue that it would have been more logical for Eton to change its sound to match the European manner; but the alteration in the Academy's Latin style, combined with a rigorous discouragement of the Scottish dialect and accent in the speaking of English, prompted criticism. 'There are Scottish schools (the Edinburgh Academy, for example) from which Scottish is almost entirely banished, even in the pronunciation of Greek and Latin', wrote Cockburn, the co-founder. 'I could name dozens of families, born, living and educated in Edinburgh, which could not produce a single son or daughter capable of understanding even The Mouse or The Daisy' – poems in Scots dialect by Robert Burns. However, the rector justified the policy of conforming to English pronunciation, whether in Latin or in English itself, by declaring: 'All classes seem desirous that their children should, at least, read with a pure English accent.' By the 1840s, after many years of debate, the Anglicizers had won the battle. When a boy pronounced the name Menelaus, husband of Helen of Troy, in the Scottish way, the master asked: 'Who is Menelaws? I only know an excellent tea-merchant of that name.' Three centuries after the inspectors had baulked at Mulcaster's Cumbrian accent at Merchant Taylors', the public school accent was again being imposed.[92]

Another way of insisting on the 'right' accent was to bar any pupil likely to have the wrong one; at some of the new schools in England, this was ruthlessly enforced. At a public meeting setting up Cheltenham College, it was resolved that no one could become a shareholder of the school (giving them a right to nominate pupils as well as a share in the profits) 'who should not be moving in the circle of gentlemen. No retail trader being under any circumstances to be considered.'[93] This bar was stricter than the one at Eton, alma mater of the Foster brothers, sons of a Windsor tradesman (though John Foster's Eton career was not entirely happy). Despite the modernity of Cheltenham's curriculum, it, like some other newer schools, had a strangely mediaeval, caste-ridden view of each boy's place in society.

In practice, however, attempts to impose strict rules on who could and could not enter public schools tended to founder on the rock of economic reality. Brighton College began a policy of social segregation even before it was founded: at the 1845 inaugural meeting to discuss its establishment, the founders of Rossall and Malvern, both public schools, were unseated because, as a hotelier and factory manager, they were not gentlemen, according to Brighton College's official historian. Having taken advice from Cheltenham on whom to exclude, the College initially barred the sons of wealthy tradesmen, but still admitted the offspring of a wine merchant, a hotel manager and a silversmith. Its 1893 bankruptcy forced it, however, to abandon the restriction on tradesmen altogether.[94]

In practice, the boys' schools were eventually always forced to follow money, rather than class, when deciding whom to admit. The public schools thus played a useful role in raising thousands of families from wealthy plebeians to wealthy patricians. In *The Newcomes*, William Makepeace Thackeray's wittily knowing 1855 novel charting the rise of a family in society, Clive Newcome, a boy at Gray Friars School (modelled on Thackeray's old school Charterhouse), contrasts the fine appearance of his father, Colonel Newcome, with the father of his schoolmate. The Colonel 'looks like a gentleman, every inch of him – not like Martin's father, who came to see his son lately in highlows, and a shocking bad hat, and actually flung coppers among the boys for a scramble. He burst out a laugh at the exquisitely ludicrous idea of a gentleman of his fashion scrambling for coppers.' Perhaps so, to Clive's eye, but Gray Friars would doubtless, over time, give Martin the mien of a gentleman.[95]

Powell's sense of foreboding about the perils of upper-class scientific ignorance was not shared by the masters of Eton College. In 1861, when asked by the Public Schools Commission to assess the relative value of Classics, maths and modern languages, the school's headmaster, Charles Goodford, responded wittily with a mathematical formula: 15:3:1.[96] He also noted, scarcely less tersely, that 'physical science is not taught', before moving on to discuss other subjects of more burning interest to the college.[97]

The Public Schools Commission, also known as the Clarendon Commission after its chairman, the 4th Earl of Clarendon, was a Royal Commission set up in response to public criticism over alleged corruption in the financial management of the old public schools.

Instead of finding any smoking guns when it gathered testimony from the schools in 1861, it described convoluted and long-standing practices of dastardly ingenuity, through which the fellows of Eton had pocketed revenue that could have been put to better use if spent on educating the pupils.[98] This proved in the end, however, to be a minor part of the report. The bulk of the text was instead devoted to looking at the quality of education in the nine old public schools it chose: Eton, Winchester, Westminster, Harrow, Charterhouse, Rugby, Shrewsbury, St Paul's and Merchant Taylors'.

In its 1864 report, the commission threw a couple of consoling morsels into pages of criticism so severe that it bordered at times on the comical. One was its view that although the education these schools provided was generally bad, it had previously been even worse. Another was that although the bulk of pupils were ill-served, the system was narrowly effective for a small minority of clever pupils. The most telling criticism came in its description of the quality of undergraduates sent to Oxford and Cambridge by the Clarendon Nine, as the schools are even now sometimes termed with that sense of an elite brotherhood conferred accidentally by the commission. 'A fair proportion of classical honours at least is gained by the public schools', and 'those who enter the Universities from the highest forms of these schools are on the whole well-taught classical scholars', found the report, before adding: 'These however, notoriously form a small proportion of the boys who receive a public-school education.' A specific investigation into standards at Christ Church, Oxford, which according to the commission had taken more than one-third of its undergraduates from Eton and about 10 per cent each from Harrow and Westminster, prompted withering comments from the dons about the quality of the students they received. 'The answers we get to simple grammar questions are very inaccurate', said one about new undergraduates' classical training. 'The answers to the questions in arithmetic do not encourage us to examine them in Euclid or algebra', said another with a certain tact. When looking at Oxbridge undergraduates from the Nine as a whole, the commission concluded: 'These facts and figures do not indicate an average of classical attainment which can by any stretch of indulgence be deemed satisfactory'. Furthermore, 'the knowledge of history and geography, though better than it was, is still very meagre'. There were, in addition, 'great deficiencies observable in English composition, reading, and spelling'.[99]

The greatest gap of all was in natural science; the modern scientific subjects including physics, chemistry and biology, but not maths. This field was 'practically excluded from the education of the higher classes in England', it found, echoing Powell's words a generation before. 'This exclusion is, in our view, a plain defect and a great practical evil. It narrows unduly and injuriously the mental training of the young, and the knowledge, interests, and pursuits of men in mature life'. Furthermore, education in science among the elite was 'narrower than it was three centuries ago, while science has prodigiously extended her empire'.[100]

Casting around for reasons why the schools had sunk into this state, the Clarendon Commission ventured astutely that 'it must be disadvantageous' for 'any school to be officered exclusively by men brought up within its walls all imbued with its peculiar prejudices and opinions, and without experience of a system or any methods but its own'.[101] The schools were too incestuous.

The commission found, therefore, that the old public schools provided a confining curriculum which had failed to keep up with advances in knowledge over the centuries, left the higher classes hardly able to express themselves even in their own language, and did not even do a good job in their restricted core aim of teaching the Classics. The report did not make for encouraging reading. There were, clearly, still too many boys like Eugene Wrayburn, the indolent though honourable barrister, educated at public school, in Charles Dickens's *Our Mutual Friend*, which began serialisation in the year the Clarendon Commission's report was published. 'When we were at school together', Wrayburn tells another character, 'I got up my lessons at the last moment, day by day and bit by bit; now we are out in life together, I get up my lessons in the same way.' Wrayburn does not seem to have been traumatized emotionally by his public school experience. He was, however, cursed in another way: he picked up the habit of laziness.[102]

Another report, published in 1868 by the Schools Inquiry Commission, also known as the Taunton Commission, put pressure on the rest of the public schools – though this Royal Commission's broad brief also included grammars and small private proprietary schools, with roughly equal amounts of criticism devoted to each. It made the general point, for schools as a whole, that a more varied syllabus, including natural science, Classics, maths and modern languages, 'may be of the greatest advantage to young men proceeding to the Universities, or to professional training, or directly to the business of life', echoing the justification made by Cotton and other public school heads for broadening the syllabus.[103]

The Taunton Commission's report led directly to the Endowed Schools Commission, which, by reforming the remits of endowed grammar schools, set the winds of change blowing through this sector. Forced, during the mid-Victorian period, to look at whom and what they were for, many schools, including Oundle and Dulwich College, responded by turning themselves from local grammar schools serving a wide range of social classes into public boarding schools charging high fees and catering to the elite – the elite in a broad sense, including the professional and more successful commercial classes. This transformation accentuated the growth in the number of public school boys.[104]

The Clarendon and Taunton Commissions did not say much about the public schools that had not been said before by the schools' critics. The reports must be considered, however, in the context of the time. Between 1850 and about 1870, Britain's rulers transformed entry to the top posts in the civil service and army from a system founded on patronage and purchase to one based on academic achievement and competition. This put pressure on the public schools to raise their standards, as did changes in parental expectations. The extra pressure created by high-profile reports, such as the Clarendon and Taunton Commissions', was all the more important because it did not come from isolated sources. A clamour for change could be heard outside the walls of the schools.

The Taunton Commission's report also castigated the teaching given to the sisters of public school boys. 'It cannot be denied that the picture brought before us of the state of Middle-Class Female Education is, on the whole, unfavourable', said the report, before going on to list its cardinal sins: 'Want of thoroughness and foundation; want of system; slovenliness and showy superficiality; inattention to rudiments; undue time given to accomplishments, and those not taught intelligently or in any scientific manner; want of organization – these may sufficiently indicate the character of the complaints we have received.'[105]

The dead and heavy weight of tradition had for many years prevented the boys' public schools from reforming themselves to meet the needs of each new age. So it was, too, with the girls' schools – which, because of their generally small size, transient nature and frequent lack of academic ambition, were 'private schools' rather than 'public schools'. Most of those which taught girls from well-off homes were not very old, since these schools tended, still, to last the working lifetime of the founding headmistress before folding. Despite the rapid turnover in schools, the almost unchanging nature of parental expectations for middle- and upper-class girls encouraged each new school to stick to principles which can be traced back to the nunnery education of mediaeval times. In fact, convents remained rivals to the girls' private schools, since they continued to educate middle- and upper-class children.

Parents prized social accomplishments which they deemed feminine over academic education. They also approved of the severe social segregation, with girls kept in small schools among other girls of their same class, though usually as lay pupils rather than religious novices. 'We have had much evidence, showing the general indifference of parents to girls' education, both in itself and as compared to that of boys', reported the Taunton Commission. There was, as a result, 'a long-established and inveterate prejudice, though it may not often be distinctly expressed, that girls are less capable of mental cultivation, and less in need of it, than boys; that accomplishments, and what is showy and superficially attractive, are what is really essential for them; and in particular, that as regards their relations to the other sex and the probabilities of marriage, more solid attainments are actually disadvantageous rather than the reverse.'[106]

The piano-list, which dictated which pupil used one of the school pianos and when, was 'always the guiding, and sometimes the only, time-table', wrote H. A. Giffard, the commission's inspector for girls' schools in Surrey and Sussex, with classes 'constantly broken' by the arrival of pupils' turns on the instrument. 'Young ladies', he wrote, 'are made to devote themselves to what are at most the graces of life, and merely nibble at the bone and sinew of sound instruction in the moments which can be spared from the piano and the easel.' In an introduction to a separately published book consisting of edited evidence from the girls' schools, Dorothea Beale, principal of Cheltenham Ladies' College and one of the grandes dames of female education, estimated that at private girls' schools as a whole, though not her own, 'one hour in every four of schoolwork is devoted to exercising the fingers' in playing musical instruments.[107]

There might have been some compensations in this narrow focus, had the girls been taught sufficiently rigorously. The boys' public schools had, after all, turned out some great classical scholars, even though a more enlightened approach to teaching the Classics might have produced a greater number. The hours devoted to art and music, however, did not generally produce ladies of culture. One headmistress of a school for high-class ladies told the commission that all her pupils were taught instrumental music, but only because of 'the prejudices of parents', described as 'my greatest hindrance'. The result was underwhelming: 'During the whole of my experience I have only had four or five girls who became really good musicians.' This partly reflected the fact that only a minority of children, even in well-run schools, would ever be genuinely good at music. 'I have often remonstrated with parents', one headmistress lamented, 'on the folly of teaching music to the hopelessly unmusical; their time might be so much better spent; but the parents are inexorable.' It also, however, reflected a culture of mediocrity. 'It is not thought worth while [*sic*] to tune practising pianos, or those which are used by the junior girls, who usually get the broken down hacks which have ceased to be fit for work', found Giffard, who concluded: 'It would be an act of mercy to a child with a musical ear to take out the wires; it certainly cannot improve an imperfect ear to leave them in untuned.' The teaching of art was equally flawed, with girls often drawing in oils or watercolours before they had, through drawing, mastered the basic elements of perspective. Giffard blamed this on parents' insistence that the measure of educational success was the ability to draw 'pretty pictures' and not much else.[108]

There was, to be fair, a good deal of French taught, as well as some Italian and German, since these were regarded as social accomplishments. Giffard found, furthermore, that in the girls' schools he inspected in Surrey and Sussex Latin was, in his carefully measured phrase, 'professed to be taught' in forty-five of 'the more expensive private schools for girls', with four other headmistresses anxious to introduce it but unable to overcome the opposition of parents. Moreover, 72 per cent of pupils in the more expensive schools learned 'some branch of natural science'. This was most commonly botany, long regarded as the most feminine science since it involved pretty flowers, though he also found lessons in natural history, chemistry and even physics.[109]

Superficially this range of subjects sounds impressive, but across the country as a whole many schools continued to offer a highly attenuated curriculum. From the age of twelve, the report noted, 'a girl becomes subject to many influences which tend to check her improvement. She is told that Latin is not a feminine acquirement; that arithmetic and mathematics are only fit for boys; that science is not useful to a woman; and that she must begin to devote her chief attention to "ladylike accomplishments."' It added: 'Any fondness she may have conceived for the pursuit of other studies is frowned on or repressed.' Moreover, even where the education was more ambitious, the quality of teaching was often poor. Giffard found that science teaching was chiefly oral rather than experimental, a method that would have inspired few girls. The problem lay largely in the calibre of the teachers themselves. 'The two capital defects of the teachers of girls', declared the report, 'are these: they have not themselves been well taught, and they do not know how to teach.'[110] A bad system was perpetuating itself.

To many people this was not a matter worth worrying about at all, since middle- and upper-class women had no economic role. Moreover, a wife who showed herself in company to be more knowledgeable than her husband was an embarrassment. 'I do not think girls less capable than boys', one headmistress told the commission. However, 'men are afraid of clever women. I have met many of my old pupils after they have left school. As a rule, the clever ones remained unmarried; those who get married are the vapid and the frivolous.' Given this backdrop even the most loving father might have preferred his daughter to concentrate more on social accomplishments, which would maximize the chances of her procuring a doctor or lawyer to keep her in a middle-class mode of life.[111] It is thought-provoking that many of the headmistresses of the girls' public schools founded in the middle and late nineteenth century remained single – virgin queens of their institutions.

This view of the purpose of women's schooling came to be challenged vigorously in the 1870s, but early attempts to provide a more academic form of education for middle- and upper-class girls can be unearthed as early as the 1840s and 1850s. In 1848 Frederick Denison Maurice, professor of English literature and history at King's College, London, founded Queen's College in the capital's Harley Street – a highly ambitious venture to secure a stable career for future governesses through lectures to its pupils in a cornucopia of subjects, from mechanics to Italian. North London Collegiate School, founded in 1850 by the education pioneer Frances Buss and largely serving upper-class and professional families, had a different aim: to educate future mothers, in line with William Law's eighteenth-century philosophy that an educated mother was a better mother. The curriculum was equally academic, with classes in Latin and a broad range of science, but very little music. Buss, knowing how much damage it had wrought to girls' education, detested music teaching.[112]

The key female figure of this era within the public school movement is Buss's friend Dorothea Beale, who in effect refounded Cheltenham Ladies' College after taking over a struggling school in 1858, five years after its establishment by local dignitaries including the principal of Cheltenham College. By the time of her death in harness in 1906, it had become a leading school for families from the elite who wanted a thoroughly academic education for their daughters. Many of the girls went on to the small number of female Oxford and Cambridge colleges by then in existence – one of which, St Hilda's in Oxford, was set up by Beale.[113] Under her headship, the college produced a host of distinguished old girls, including Jane Harrison, sometimes described as Britain's first professional female career academic, Maude Royden, a pioneer of the campaign for the ordination of women, and Dame Helen Gwynne-Vaughan, naturalist and Controller of the Women's Army Auxiliary Corps in France during the First World War.

Beale was in many ways an admirable character. She found a school with an identity crisis: the first head of the day school (though it was later to become primarily a boarding school), Annie Procter, had insisted on a highly academic education, including a thorough grounding in the intricacies of Latin. However, the year before her arrival the governors' minutes recorded criticisms by parents of their daughters' poor facility for sewing, showing the uphill struggle she faced in selling the virtues of female learning to her patrons. In Procter's final year, owing to a dearth of pupils she was told that there could be no replacement for a departing member of staff; the school looked set to be trapped in a vicious circle of a decline in the school roll and a corresponding fall in the quality of education. Some parents, moreover, were griping about their daughters' poor grasp of conversational French, that venerable accomplishment of private girls' schools. Shortly after Beale arrived she was warned that she should not introduce advanced maths (a stricture she ignored) because some parents objected even to basic arithmetic. One father said this was fine if his daughters were to be bankers, but this was not what he had in mind for them – and he removed them from the college, unswayed by Beale decrying 'the old rubbish about masculine and feminine studies'.[114] Beale had overcome, through her own personal study and through attendance at Queen's College, the appallingly deficient (though no worse than normal) education of much of her girlhood, including time at a fashionable Paris school where she had learned history and grammar by rote. She now insisted on doing a better job for her girls. In 1859 the governors praised her teaching skills and her ability to win the affection of pupils; by the 1870s the number of Cheltenham Ladies' College girls had risen above three hundred, from a low of only sixty-nine when she had first entered the gates.[115]

Beale was not, however, a rigorously academic schoolmistress, a consequence, perhaps, of her own patchy education. 'In teaching, Miss Beale's definite aim was to inspire. She sought but little to inform, but much to kindle a thirst for knowledge, a love of good and beautiful things, and to awaken thinking power', wrote her biographer Elizabeth Raikes, a former pupil. 'When there was a question of preparation for examination, or of the definite knowledge such as was required in mathematical subjects, it was necessary to supplement the lessons of the Principal.'[116]

Moreover, Beale's career shows how it is possible to be too moral. Morality made her incapable of cruelty: 'I never remember her raising her voice, scolding us, being satirical or impatient with dullness or inattention', recalled one pupil. Morality also made her notoriously incapable of humour, whether satire or otherwise, and morality corrupted her teaching with excessive high-mindedness. Beale was immoderately fond of imposing her view of virtue on others. It was a proclivity that may have derived from that common mid-Victorian affliction, religious doubt, doubt strong enough to provoke a long and deep depression in middle age, though she was to recover both her faith and her equanimity. Beale once summoned a mistress teaching the Tudor period to impart her strongly held views on the cowardly nature of Thomas Cranmer, the archbishop and arch-realist who tried to escape martyrdom by recanting his Protestant faith several times.[117] Her favoured heroine was, rather, Britomart, the mythical warrior-princess of Spenser's *Faerie Queene*. She is commemorated, earnest and unsmiling like the headmistress who championed her, in a series of Beale-era stained glass windows at the college.[118]

The one moral lapse for which Beale can arguably be attacked is her decision to keep the college highly socially exclusive. Beale told the Taunton Commission that girls from 'a lower class of society', as the commission put it in its question, 'would not be admissible'.[119] This is, however, on balance an excessively fussy criticism. Outright social segregation, a legacy of the nunnery origins of the schooling of girls from the elite, was at the time standard in girls' private schools, because headmistresses assumed that without it schools would lose their credibility and go out of business. 'All the sharp lines of demar-cation which divided society into classes, and all the jealousies and suspicions which help to keep these classes apart, are seen in their fullest operation in girls' schools', found the commission. After each school had 'fixed' its 'particular social grade', it was 'next to impossible for the mistress to get a new pupil from a family which considers itself to belong to a higher stratum, while the mistress not infrequently promises the parents that she will not receive pupils from a lower.'[120] The girls' schools were, therefore, in another sense, 'private' rather than 'public', because they were not open to all comers who could afford to pay. In fact, events in the late Victorian era were to prove that girls' schools which were socially fairly mixed could survive. However, Beale was not to know this. After arriving at the college she had refused to compromise on academic standards, despite parental objections; to enable the school to survive, however, she had to compromise on something. It was unrealistic for her to fight two battles against parents at the same time.

Public commissions, exams and the force of public and parental opinion were forcing change in the boys' public schools, but attempts to reform them were, by the mid-point of the Victorian era, not always effective.

The comments of staff and former pupils underline the fact that curriculum reforms were often rather half-hearted. At some schools the head or an individual master was genuinely enthusiastic, but unable to defeat the conservatism of the school as a whole, with Classics masters unwilling to lose pupils who showed an aptitude in the subject to the modern side. At other schools even the reforming head did not take the mooted changes very seriously.

John Percival, the first headmaster of Clifton College, belonged to the tribe of zealots, trying assiduously to build up the school's modern side after it opened in 1862. However, his successor, Canon James Maurice Wilson, wrote that by the time Percival left in 1879, 'it had become a refuge for the less cultivated and the less capable . . . for the unambitious, the unliterary, the stagnant'.[121] George Ridding, headmaster of Winchester, was less enthusiastic about change in the first place. When J. S. Furely, a classical scholar, joined the staff in 1878 he was told by Ridding – under pressure to introduce changes in the wake of the Clarendon Commission – that he would have to teach French. '"But I know no French, Dr Ridding", I said. "That does not signify", he answered, "it is only a matter of common sense".'[122] Although Marlborough introduced science in 1871, it proved difficult to get the governors to pay for the apparatus. A year later, a letter to them from the science master, trying to cope with the primitive conditions, pleaded: 'Please let me have a fire in my classroom on damp or wet Wednesdays or Thursdays, otherwise I fear my electrical experiments will all fail.'[123] Marlborough's approach to modern languages was also amateurish. Considering the question of whether language teachers should be native speakers, George Granville

Bradley, master from 1858 to 1870, ruled: 'The answer is decisive and final. A foreigner, in the vast majority of cases, cannot control, understand, or stimulate a large class of English boys.'[124] 'Marlborough French', the term in the Middle Ages for badly spoken French, seemed equally appropriate in the Victorian era.

To be fair to the public schools, the amateurish approach to science was a British rather than a purely public school problem. 'In our Public and Endowed Schools, Science is as yet very far from receiving the attention, to which in our opinion, it is entitled', wrote the 1874 Royal Commission on scientific instruction and the advancement of science. 'Considering the increasing importance of Science to the Material Interests of the country, we cannot but regard its almost total exclusion from the training of the upper and middle classes as little less than a national misfortune.'[125]

There were still, however, enough examples from both inside and outside the public school movement to show public school headmasters how much they could have achieved had they taken science and other non-classical subjects more seriously. Within the public schools, Cheltenham College gradually built up a strong pedigree in getting boys into Woolwich, the military academy for cadet engineers and artillery officers, who had to show good mathematical knowledge to win a place. Thirty-six boys entered Woolwich from Cheltenham in 1900 alone. Throughout the late nineteenth century at least half the boys were on the military side, and sometimes nearly two-thirds.[126] The college was to educate many distinguished army engineers, including Lieutenant-General Sir Philip Neame, who made up for the deficiencies of First World War hand grenades by manufacturing his own, and Glubb Pasha, who was to become head of the Jordanian army in 1939. At Manchester Grammar School, Frederick Walker, the brilliant head from 1859 to 1877, introduced physics and chemistry as well as revamping Classics teaching. The school gradually built up a superlative reputation for the mathematical and natural sciences. One-third of the eighteen natural science scholarships offered by Oxford from 1869 to 1871 were won by Manchester Grammar boys.[127]

The City of London School, founded in 1834, provided a template for genuine innovation that was disappointingly rarely taken up by the public schools. It is now a fully fledged public school educating boys primarily from wealthy families. However, in the mid-nineteenth century initial annual fees of £8 (£880) were markedly lower than those at King's or University College Schools, making it a school for a broad range of social classes rather than a public school for the upper middle classes and upwards.[128] During this period it did strikingly well. Much of the Clarendon Report reads like a 'how not to' guide to education, but the City of London School (along with King's) 'presents an example of a great metropolitan school educating a large number of day-scholars with distinguished success'.[129] The Taunton Commission gushed that all 600 boys were taught natural science, and 'some of them have acquired distinction in several of its branches at the University of London'.[130]

The syllabus described by the Taunton Commission sounds like that of a twenty-first-century public school. Latin was begun at the age of twelve and Greek at fifteen, only after the boys had been 'well-grounded in arithmetic, French and perhaps also German, and received some elementary instruction in mathematics and chemistry'. The result was described by the commission: 'Their minds have now been opened, they have begun to think and compare, Latin and Greek can now be taught them on philological principles; they make rapid strides, and by eighteen or nineteen they have just as good a chance of being elected to open [Classics] scholarships at the universities as if they had begun the dead languages at the age of eight or nine years.'[131] It was a far cry from University College School, founded as a public school four years before City of London School with the aspiration that 'the school shall not be designed for the instruction of pupils in science . . . but in those branches of knowledge which are at present commonly understood to be implied in the term liberal education'.[132]

The school's success can also be measured by the large number of very Victorian heroes it produced: men who invented or improved various unglamorous but essential products of the modern world which are now taken for granted. William Perkin, a City of London boy who at the age of only eighteen discovered the first aniline dye, mauveine, owed his success entirely to the school. Perkin's builder father disapproved of his specialism in science at the institution, but the boy was allowed by his father to follow his heart after several talks between father and science master. Two of the most distinguished boys, Sir Alexander Kennedy, a pioneer of electric lighting in England, and William Unwin, who harnessed the hydro power of Niagara, were the sons of churchmen. Had they joined the thousands of other sons of the clergy who attended Victorian public schools, would they have achieved so much in science?[133]

The public schools' record in the professional examinations was decidedly mixed at this stage in their history.

With the exception of Woolwich, generally speaking the posts opened to competition required proof of strong, but not necessarily broad, knowledge from successful candidates – and they did not necessarily require good mathematical or scientific knowledge. The design of the exam for Sandhurst allowed candidates to focus entirely on the public school specialities of Latin and Greek, although they could alternatively choose to concentrate on experimental sciences and geography, or languages, or to be examined in a broad range of subjects. The examiners for most of the civil and military posts were interested primarily in general ability rather than specific technical knowledge. They built on the dictum of Lord Macaulay, who pioneered the reform of the civil service in the 1830s, that the character of the education was immaterial: suitability for high office could be shown by ability in 'the most correct and melodious Greek or, for that matter, Cherokee verses'.[134]

The public schools' most talented pupils did very well indeed. Of the eleven top clerkships awarded in 1877 to entrants to the Home Civil Service exam, seven went to public school men, including three from Winchester alone.[135] However, looking at the new exams as a whole, the public schools' overall performance was mixed, though not disastrous. For Indian Civil Service candidates, a public school education in itself was usually not sufficient. An investigation of its candidates for 1874 shows that 84 per cent had not come directly from school; rather, after their school education – sometimes in a public school, sometimes in a grammar, and sometimes elsewhere – they had gone to a specialist crammer, spending an average of fifteen or sixteen months there.[136] Although this pointed to a wider failing that went beyond the public schools, nevertheless this statistic does not show the public schools in a good light. The exams had been designed largely with the public school curriculum in mind; the landowning class which supplied many of the public school pupils had also for centuries provided many of the empire's rulers.[137] The public schools educated the country's future leaders, but they could not do so adequately on their own without the aid of crammers.

When it came to these public exams, it was not primarily the lack of knowledge of maths and science which let down the public school boys (as well as grammar school boys); it was the lack of a strong knowledge of anything. They were not taught Greek well; it is unlikely that they would have been taught Cherokee verses any better had these been on the syllabus.

Despite these criticisms, the public schools had made progress by the mid-point of the Victorian era. Virtually all of them, both new and old, had introduced an education system much more familiar to twenty-first-century public school pupils than the earlier orthodoxy, a system which both provided a more general education and allowed for specialization in a wider range than previously. Moreover, facilities were modernized, sport organized, the prefect structure systematized. The result was, on balance, a less brutal form of schooling. The early Victorian period was crucial for the public schools. They had fought off the prospect of extinction. They were, moreover, after centuries of decline, at least on the road to improvement.

The next four chapters of this book tell the story of this continuing progress.

CHAPTER FIVE

'The Monastic System is Getting on My Nerves.'
1870–1902

THE year 1870 was a time of exciting feats of technology and science, from the completion of the huge Fréjus railway tunnel through the Alps to the linking of Britain and Australia by telegraph. However, Alexander Potts would, on balance, probably have preferred the year to have been about 350 BC, or perhaps even a touch earlier. The first head of Fettes, founded in Edinburgh in 1870, kept a commonplace book, filled with inspiring sayings, which included the famous observation from Plato's *Philebus*, published in the middle of the fourth century BC: 'The ancients were better than us. They lived nearer the gods.' Potts tried to keep pupils as near to the ancients as possible by inserting a strong classical bias into the school.[1]

Potts's commonplace book also contained a solemn series of twelve 'Arnoldiana' (sayings of the great man). Inspired by this, he introduced Arnold's system of prefects and fagging, as well as the ancient Spartan regime and the more recent sporting emphasis of its Sassenach counterparts. During the first, harsh winter, each boarder rose at seven for a cold bath in his cubicle, breaking the ice with a brush if necessary. The cold was, in any case, good for the boys, in the view of Clem Cotterill, a master at the new school: 'The keen wind serves but to brace and harden them; to clear their brains and sweeten their tempers; to purify not only the blood, but surely to help in so far as we can be helped by such agencies, to purify also their hearts.' Cotterill had no time for weak-bodied scholars – since the mere scholar who did not keep his body strong was 'half-man half-ghost'. To be fair, though, he had no time for the mere athlete either, whom he cursed with the description of 'half-man half-beast'. Should their spirits threaten to weaken under the impact of such a harsh regimen, assistance was available in the shape of H. H. Almond, who jogged seven miles each way from the headmaster's quarters at Loretto to preach at Fettes. Life was a little easier for the prefects – they were allowed hot water, on the grounds, one presumes, that warmth alone would not weaken the morals of the most upstanding boys in the school.[2]

Fettes started primarily as a day school, but soon became an establishment mainly for boarders.[3] In this respect, the city of Edinburgh illustrated a growing national trend. One might have expected Fettes and the Edinburgh Academy, its biggest rival, to establish comfortable existences through demarcating and dominating completely separate markets within the city, with the former taking the commanding heights of boarding and the latter concentrating on day pupils. Instead, Edinburgh Academy tried as far as possible to go the same way. In the 1890s its reforming rector (headmaster) Robert Mackenzie helped to reverse declining rolls by turning it largely into a boarding school. He also tried to ape, as far as possible, the customs of the boarding schools. Mackenzie introduced prefects, entitled with the exotic name 'ephors', after the ruling officials of Sparta.[4] It was in many ways an apt epithet, given the resemblance between the boarding schools' way of life and the *agoge* ('raising') of Spartan boys – taken from doting parents at a young age and toughened up, until the age of eighteen, by means of an upbringing with packs of other boys, where harsh physical training and a lifestyle of extreme austerity were imposed.

The Edinburgh Academy's response was not exactly fleet-footed, since the school had to wait for a new head before it fought back. Other day schools were slower still. They were hobbled by the common handicap of public schools throughout the ages: most were free-standing schools with little capital, rather than forming part of great chains, the stronger members of which could collectively provide enough capital to allow a single school to transform itself (exceptions were the schools set up by Woodard from 1848, by the Church Schools Company from 1870, and by the Girls' Public Day School Company in 1872). At Liverpool College, every head from Butler onwards pressed the governors to expand the boarding side in reaction to the national trend. 'With a new building on a fair site and two or three boarding-houses it may yet be raised to a level with Cheltenham or Clifton Schools', wrote Edward Selwyn, Butler's successor. Mixing emulation with excoriation, he added: 'It may yet be a school of which Liverpool will be proud, and to which she will send her sons instead of blindly obeying the fashion as she does of boarding them away from home and home influences at enormous expense on unhealthy swamps and desolate hill-sides in remote parts of England.' He was, at least, to get one of his wishes in 1884 when the college was moved to the decidedly undesolate Liverpool suburb of Sefton – a development which boosted numbers.[5] The governors did not open a boarding house, however, until 1918.[6]

Cotterill of Fettes would not have thought much of the half-man half-ghost products of King's College School in London – and neither did some of the school's parents. In 1887 a pair of them sought to remove a son from King's on the ground that he required 'more recreation', a growing strength of the boarding schools, whose often plentiful rural acres could be used to create ample sporting facilities to stop boys cooped up together for entire terms from killing each other. In response the head, Thomas Stokoe, acknowledged: 'We lose plenty of boys just now for want of this.' Discussing the near-extinction of the school, his successor, Charles Bourne, complained to the governors in 1901 that all the London day schools faced the same problem: parents preferred to send their boys away. Early in the new century the possibility of turning the institution into a boarding school was mooted, but made no headway. The next best thing short of this was to move it out of the urbs to greener pastures in the suburbs, where it might be able to offer amenities approaching those of boarding schools. Bourne forced a move to the leafy London suburb of Wimbledon in 1897, after scaring the governors into submission. 'The present rage for athletics makes it practically impossible for us to hold our own against schools which have playground facilities', he warned. As a result, 'only two courses seem open – either to abolish the school, or to remove it to Wimbledon', which had room for facilities that its cramped Strand location did not.[7] If anything, Westminster School faced even worse problems. 'The space is so inadequate for purposes of instruction, that even with our present numbers the work of the school is seriously impeded and no examination can be conducted satisfactorily', a 'Memorial from the Masters' to the governors lamented in 1881. 'At Easter the only manner in which the Examination for Exhibitions can be carried on at all, is by borrowing a room which the Civil Service Commissioners are kind enough to lend for the purpose.'[8] At this point the day schools were far from the lavish facilities of the twenty-first century.

The conservatism of the day school governors is understandable: they were in a bind. Those at Liverpool College were for many years reluctant to take the risk of moving the school's location or expanding the range of possible patrons through boarding, given the substantial cost which either of these changes required. There was, after all, no guarantee that such a change would attract sufficient numbers of new pupils to pay for itself. Many day schools did, despite such risks, move to the suburbs or even the countryside in the late nineteenth century. Some saw an upturn in numbers, including Charterhouse, a day school with some boarders, whose roll surged in 1872 after its transfer from the City of London to Godalming in Surrey.[9] However, the temporary rise in rolls at the new King's site was not sustained, forcing the school to limp along until rescued by the government on the eve of the First World War.[10]

In some cases trains on the expanding railway network chuffed to the aid of day schools by increasing the radius of their hinterland. John Howson, the entrepreneurial principal of Liverpool College from 1849 to 1865, persuaded directors of the local railways and river ferries to offer concessionary prices to all schoolboys. The second step was to shower south-west Lancashire with maps showing railway lines and principal residential centres, marked with concentric circles that placed the college at the centre of the universe. It was brilliantly successful, helping to double the numbers in the upper school.[11] Despite such individual acts of organizational heroism, however, on balance the railways probably did more harm than good to the day schools, by making boarding schools more accessible. This was the period when the system of two school terms a year was replaced by three, precisely because this new accessibility made it feasible – even though Eton stubbornly retains the name of the old terms, giving it three 'halves' a year. The improvement in train timetables enabled Uppingham School in Rutland to transform itself from a regional to a national boarding school under Thring. 'We don't know whether Mr Thring trains the boys' minds; but he makes them mind their trains', quipped *Punch* magazine, reporting on the sorry case of two brothers who had done nothing wrong at the school, but were punished simply for arriving late for term. A generation earlier Thring could not have insisted on such punctuality.[12]

It was not, however, primarily the rail network which drove the surge in numbers of pupils in the boarding schools. Nor were the schools boosted by any clear academic advantage: of the top six with the most Oxbridge scholarships in 1885–92, only two – Eton (benefiting from its huge size) and Marlborough – were primarily boarding schools. A further two, St Paul's and Merchant Taylors', were primarily public day schools, with Clifton offering a large measure of both, and Manchester Grammar School completing the picture. Looking further down the list at the sixteen other schools with twenty or more Oxbridge scholarships in the period, the boarding schools did not do noticeably worse or better than their rivals.[13]

What, then, aside from sport, was the boarding schools' special ingredient, which drew families to send their sons to them? Perhaps the most eloquent explanation was made in 1932, ironically at a time when such schools were struggling under the yoke of an economic crisis. Frederick Malim, master (equivalent to headmaster) of Wellington College, saw this special ingredient as the housemaster – an institution which the day schools tried to copy, though in these schools the housemaster, lacking the same twenty-four-hour responsibility for his pupils, never quite had the same intense relationship with them. Education 'is the last activity to which methods of mass production should be applied', wrote Malim with a poignantly elegiac tone in the knowledge that this situation might not last for much longer, 'for education depends for its success not on the discovery of some treatment which can be brought to bear on large numbers of patients, but on the contact of one mind with another and of one spirit with another'. He added: 'The head master looking for recruits cannot forget that he is looking for the house masters of the future; in his eyes no technical skill in the presentation of a subject will atone for the absence of the sympathy, the insight, and the personality without which no man can win the loyalty and confidence of his house.'[14] The relationship became, at times, almost parental: in the modern day, Anthony Seldon, the current master of Wellington, estimates that the relationship between house master or house mistress and their pupil has 'maybe a third' in common with that of parents – 'but if a parent is somehow deficient the teacher becomes even more important'.[15] Even wives were frequently regarded as an encumbrance to this intense relationship. 'In most public schools the assistant masters lead a life which is essentially monastic', wrote H. Lionel Rogers, an assistant master at Radley in the Edwardian era, clearly in reference to boarding schools such as his own rather than day schools. 'Marriage is possible for but few'. For the master who did marry, thus diverting himself from an exclusive focus on his school duties, 'how great' must be 'the loss to his pupils in direct teaching and example'.[16]

The monastic style of life – together with its costs and drawbacks – is borne out by diaries and memoirs. 'There is something monastic about the life here: only one other master except the Chief [headmaster] is married: women are obviously not encouraged', writes

S. P. B. Mais, a master at Rossall and future professional author and broadcaster, in a diary entry from 1909. Two months later, his tone is considerably less detached. 'The monastic system is getting on my nerves. I find myself longing to hear a baby crying, a girl laugh, or any noises of the street. We are too much aloof from the outside world.' His solution is a regular Saturday night out in the local town, including dinner, a show and a gawp at the shopgirls and their boyfriends at the dance.[17] Sometime after returning to his old school, Marlborough, after the First World War, a young housemaster called Ronald Gurner decided to marry, 'but we found soon enough that marriage and my duties were almost incompatible', in particular with his evenings spent supervising prep or simply in perambulating to 'exude good fellow-ship about the house'. Gurner confessed in his memoirs: 'I would slope round to see my wife after "lights out", and return to apologize to my fellow house-master and explain that I had only been away a few minutes.' His rapid solution was to resign his post for the headship of a state school.[18]

Day schools tried to make up for this lack of influence in the life of their pupils. University College School in London introduced 'Consulting' masters with pastoral care for boys in the 1880s after a teacher complained: 'The fact that we draw our pupils from various parts of London and that we have no control over them out of school hours, tends to minimize our personal influence over them.'[19] This was a perceptive assessment: by exerting control over boys' lives for twenty-four hours a day, the boarding schools inevitably had more personal influence over the average boy. This was, however, frequently not used to the good.

The cosy house run by Oscar Browning at Eton between 1862 and 1875 provided just the right atmosphere that a highly cultured and fairly protective family wanted for their son. Browning had nearly starved while a scholar at Eton in the 1850s; as a result the boys in his care ate nourishing and plentiful food, behind curtains designed by William Morris, in an environment feminized by the presence at meal times of his mother and two twenty-something sisters. Browning spent so much on the catering that he provoked the ire of other housemasters who felt pressured to keep up. It was, as one boy put it to his father, 'awfully jolly'.[20]

It was more than that. Browning banned the Victorian equivalent of today's Manchester United posters – prints of Tom Cribb the bare-knuckle boxer and Mad Jack Mytton the reckless hunter – and filled the empty spaces with engravings of European masterpieces. The works of Brahms and other controversial modern composers not yet sanctified by age were performed by local musicians. Poetry readings and the acting of plays were encouraged. Outside the house and inside the classroom, Browning became a star, introducing a conversational style which demanded, and received, strong intellectual contributions from his pupils. In 1868 Eton made it compulsory for older boys to study a modern subject every week; Browning's offering, modern history, became the most popular topic. How could it have been otherwise, when a witty and urbane master had chosen to delve into such scandalously hot topics as the French Revolution, a choice of which the head, James Hornby, heartily disapproved? Browning also espoused smaller class sizes, because of his belief that good teaching required personal contact – in keeping with Malim's principle that mass production was the enemy of teaching.[21]

Browning was adored by a large and influential group of people, both within and without the Etonian empire. Inside the school, when Hornby tried to take him off modern history, a colleague complained, writing that 'whatever protest has been made against this muscle worship' of the cult of athleticism, 'whatever effort has been made to promote culture and industry and thereby improve morals, Browning has taken a leading part in it ever since I have known Eton as a master'. Hornby relented. Browning also formed the habit of picking boys he liked from outside his house, to become an intellectual mentor to them. The most famous of these relationships – to last as long as they were both alive – was with George Curzon, the brilliant future viceroy of India and foreign secretary, who carried off a plethora of prizes at the school. Browning in effect poached him from his official house-master, a rather intellectually dull man who would have done little to develop Curzon's mind. 'Whatever I am,' said Curzon to his wife, 'I owe it all to Mr Browning.'[22]

Many of Browning's acolytes, including Curzon, were to write about him with the deepest affection, which was reciprocated by the master. Of Gerald Balfour, the politician, who was to be a friend for life, Browning wrote to Balfour's mother: 'He has the most entire purity of mind and character and at the same time is not at all unfitted for contact with the world. . . . I quite dread his leaving this half.'[23] Browning had learnt to form such strong attachments from his own mentor at Eton, William Johnson Cory – himself regarded as a bril-liant teacher and tutor who read the characters of his charges with great facility. The weak-voiced, short-sighted Johnson excelled not at teaching Eton's still large and unruly classes, but in encouraging the boys to think for themselves in his wide-ranging tutorials. This was particularly the case for his favourites, on whom he lavished great attention.[24]

The strong emotional attachments continued into the next Eton generation. M. D. Hill, who joined Eton to teach science in the 1890s, later recalled a stubbornly recurrent dream from his days as a house-master. Taking his usual tour of the house after prayers, he finds an unknown face. 'I ask him who he is and what he is doing here. He replies that he is a boy in my house. " 'Why", I remark, "I have never seen you before." To which he replies: "You have never been in my room till to-night." I am so amazed and concerned at this dereliction of duty that I awake.' Eton had come a long way from the callous neglect of the Long Chamber.[25]

From mid-Victorian times onwards, boarding school masters increasingly tried to form sympathetic bonds with their pupils. Much of this was probably in reaction against the horrors of the Long Chamber and its ilk. Thring's career was largely an attempt to provide a more humane system for his pupils at Uppingham than he himself had experienced at Eton. It was a measure of Thring's high-minded humanitarianism that the head's entire concept of the school's size and design was founded on the happiness of the boys. Each school house should have no more than thirty pupils under the care of each house-master, so that each housemaster should know his boys well.[26] The conventional high pupil–teacher ratios were anathema to Thring because, in his words, 'sixty or seventy pupils to one master become as nominal as ten thousand parishioners to one clergyman'.[27] Uppingham should have no more than 300 to 330 boys, so that he could know enough of each boy to form a personal opinion of him.[28] Moreover, Thring took the unusual step of providing each boy with his own personal space – a cubicle where he could sit, read and think in privacy, free from the tormenting of others.[29] 'You don't live in a prison here', he declared, having had the school rebuilt literally as well as metaphori-cally. 'We make your life free and pleasant, we trust you, we make your temptations few, we make it easy to live a true life.'[30] His housemasters often had different ideas, however, favouring the 'mass production' attacked by Malim, since their income was largely based, as at many boarding schools at this time, on how many boys they took in. But although Thring's diaries reveal a constant battle with the masters over admission numbers, he never gave in to what they wanted.[31] 'A fall in the pupil-teacher ratio at Uppingham and other public schools provided an essential underpinning to the improving relationship between master and pupil. At Thring's old school there were nine masters to 570 boys at about the time he arrived as a boy: 63 to every master. By the time of the Clarendon Commission, a large increase in the number of masters had pushed the ratio down to twenty-four, with twenty-four for Rugby, too, and twenty-one for Harrow.[32] Changing ratios made institutional violence less necessary. Thring was not averse to beating, but he beat less than had many public school heads of previous generations. He noted realistically: 'The ablest man over-matched in numbers, with all things round him dislocated and imper-fect, must punish.'[33]

If some of the above descriptions of relations between masters and boys sound slightly sexual, however, the reader has judged well. The first two masters, Browning and Johnson, were both homosexual, though Thring was not. Johnson was forced out of Eton in middle age for this reason; disapproval of his sexuality contributed, at least, to Browning's departure, though his inability to stick to any kind of school rule whatsoever was the prime cause.[34] Homosexuality within the boarding schools is a tough topic to investigate, given the understandable attempts by headmasters and school historians to suppress all but the vaguest references to it. The reluctance of schools to refer to this sexual preference over the centuries is, nevertheless, all the more reason for us to do so.

Latent, unconsummated homosexuality appears, from the rumours, hints and confessions skulking in this murky area, to have been common throughout much of public school history, though even the research on this is sourced and written in a rather cloak-and-dagger style. Perhaps the earliest reference to it is the 1541 confession by Nicholas Udall, headmaster of Eton, of a charge of buggery – though Udall's biographer has cast doubt on this by having advanced the ingenious theory that this may be the sixteenth-century equivalent of a typo by an overworked scrivener. Udall made the admission while being questioned about the theft of college property, which suggests that he may have been guilty merely of 'burglary'. From such errors are historical reputations formed.[35]

Writing in the 1920s, the sexologist Havelock Ellis quoted an unnamed expert who wrote of the many cases where 'a physical sexual attraction is recognized as the basis of the relation, but as a matter of feeling, and partly also of theory, the ascetic ideal is adopted'. The expert added that 'no one can have passed through a public school and college life without constantly observing indications of the phenomenon in question'.[36] Recalling his time at the boarding school Stowe in the 1930s, the journalist Peregrine Worsthorne recalled: 'Romantic friendships abounded, but only occasionally were they physically consummated'.[37] This notion of same-sex attraction but without physical expression was even given a limited respectability by the development among late Victorian intellectuals of the concept of 'Greek love' – non-sexual love between men – extracted from the study of Plato and other venerated classical authors. It found a ready audience among some masters serving in the all-male environment of the boarding schools, including Browning. However, the discovery that some of its champions, including Oscar Wilde and Browning's close friend Simeon Solomon, had followed this to its logical conclusion by actually having sex with men finally discredited this movement in conventional society.[38]

When it comes to active homosexuality, some old public school boys say they never saw it at any time in their school careers; others say it was endemic. At Eton, shortly before Johnson's departure, seven boys were expelled for homosexuality.[39] Another source quoted by Ellis, writing in 1882, declared that he had since met many of the 'vicious' (the standard code for homosexual) boys he had known at Eton, and that 'these very boys had become cabinet ministers, statesmen, officers, clergymen, country-gentlemen, etc, and that they are nearly all of them fathers of thriving families, respected and prosperous.'[40] This implies that the source had encountered a good many of them during his education. Recalling his time as a pupil at the school in the early 1870s, Edward Lyttelton, who would return as its headmaster in 1905, lamented 'a hideous amount of vice.'[41] Frequent references to homosexuality in public school novels and memoirs show that it was common enough. *Tom Brown's School Days* refers to 'little pretty white-handed curly-headed boys, petted and pampered by some of the big fellows'.[42] Frederic Harrison, the jurist, was one of the 'little pretty' boys at King's College School in the 1840s – and he did not like it at all, though he was never sexually molested. 'On many a scrimmage where the petting grew intolerable, I would strike, kick, and even bit like a dog', he remembered.[43]

In *David Blaize*, written in 1916 by E. F. Benson, the novelist and Old Marlburian, the eponymous protagonist experiences a different fate from Harrison's. He hero worships his older school friend Frank, and has some sort of sexual encounter with him (or so it is implied), though only once, after meeting him by chance in the bathrooms.

'David had always avoided the thought of that; it remained a moment quite sundered from the rest of his intercourse with Frank, embarrassing and to be forgotten, like the momentary opening of a cupboard where nightmare dwelt', he wrote. 'Anyhow, it had been locked again instantly, and the key thrown away. Never a sound had again issued therefrom.' This poignant painting of how homosexual urges – in this case, probably not abusive – are repressed probably describes many public school relationships.[44]

It is perfectly possible that those who saw no homosexuality and those who saw a good deal are both telling the truth: many young men have an impressionable sexuality and may follow the lead of a few of the alpha males in the group. Ellis concluded: 'The prevalence of homosexual and erotic phenomena in schools varies greatly at different schools and at different times in the same school.'[45] Perhaps the most spectacular case was in 1892, when Brighton College closed an entire boarding house in an effort to root out homosexuality, as well as expelling eleven boys, including two prefects.[46]

Homosexuality was illegal in England and Wales until the 1960s, when it became permissible on the recommendation of a government-appointed report led, appropriately, by a former public school headmaster, Lord Wolfenden, who had been in charge at Shrewsbury. Nowadays most Britons would not regard it as wrong. Sexual abuse, however, whether homosexual or heterosexual, is clearly immoral. Sexual behaviour is abusive, of course, when it involves children rather than young men, or when it involves an approach from someone in power towards someone lower down the hierarchy. It is equally abusive – no more and no less – whether it involves same-sex relationships, or sexual relations between men and girls. However, opportunities for abusive heterosexual relationships were rather limited at boarding schools for most of their history. The key question is, therefore, how much homosexual abuse there was in the Victorian age and the early twentieth century, before changes to the schools, and to society in general, opened up this closed and intense system.

1 Where the public schools began: Chamber Court, one of Winchester College's original buildings from the fourteenth century.

2 The first image of a public school boy: John Kent, who died while still a scholar at Winchester in 1434. Note the priestly appearance in this memorial brass in a local church.

3 The first public school hero: Sir Philip Sidney, an old boy of Shrewsbury, in pensive mood in this statue on the school's grounds.

4 Seat of learning: an allegorical portrait of Richard Busby, Westminster's famous seventeenth-century headmaster.

5 Making their own devilish entertainment: the arcane and cruel custom of bumping, typical of the barbarous practices of the unreformed public schools of the early nineteenth century.

6 Westminster boys participating in the Pancake Grieze in front of a bemused audience, 1919.

7 The most successful head in public school history? Samuel Butler, who led Shrewsbury from 1798 to 1836.

8 An intense relationship between master and boy, tinged with sexuality: the brilliant Eton housemaster Oscar Browning with George Curzon, future Viceroy of India.

9 'First-Character. Second-Physique. Third-Intelligence': H. H. Almond, Loretto's redoutable Victorian head.

10 Tradition with a hint of menace: Winchester College Football teams arrive on the field of battle.

11 Sporting excellence: Bob Tisdall (far left), gold medal winner in the hurdles at the Los Angeles 1932 Olympics, at Shrewsbury School.

12 Ross Hockey, a form of the sport peculiar to Rossall School in Lancashire.

13 Making men of them: a boy on Sedbergh School's famously tough Wilson Run, 1917.

14 The magnificent Rugby School Chapel, dating from 1872. Religion played an important role in the moral reformation of many public schools in the nineteenth century.

15 King's College School prefects in 1898, rather dour and unsmiling.

16 King's College School prefects of 1996–7, exuding bonhomie. Note the ethnic mix that was absent in the earlier King's photo.

17 Admirable but humourless: Dorothea Beale, principal of Cheltenham Ladies' College 1858–1906 and pioneer of academic education for girls.

18 Britomart, the mythical warrior-princess who was Dorothea Beale's favoured heroine, commemorated in the stained glass windows at Cheltenham Ladies' College.

19 Cheltenham Ladies' College girls lining up for prayers in about 1930. The scene testifies to the tightly controlled environments of the girls' public schools of the time.

20 Roedean senior prefects, 1913. Far less intimidating than the prefect photos of boys' public schools of the era.

21 Teaching the feminine graces: 'Sketching Class at the Rose Temple', from a 1920s prospectus for St James' School, Worcestershire.

22 A Roedean lacrosse team on a windswept day in 1920. 'Special pains will be taken to guard against overwork, and from two to three hours daily will be allotted to out-door exercise and games', its first prospectus noted.

23 Alone with Teddy: a touching photo of a Roedean girl in quite a comfortable-looking, though rather plain, boarding cubicle, 1931.

24 Teddy in luxury: a plush and cheery shared room at modern-day Sedbergh School.

25 The first of many: Brighton College's first girls with the chaplain and his wife, 1974. By the mid-1980s two-thirds of boys' public schools had female pupils.

26 The reinvented public school boy: Brendan Bracken (centre), a trusted adviser of Winston Churchill and chairman of the board of governors of Sedbergh. He attended the school as a nineteen-year old, posing as a fifteen-year-old orphan. In this 1954 photo, Bracken is flanked by General Sir John Stuart Mackenzie Shea GCB KGMG DSO (left) and Headmaster Logie Brucc-Lockhart (right).

27 An early chemistry laboratory at Christ College, Brecon, populated with apparently rather enthusiastic boys, 1909. Christ College took science seriously from the late Victorian era, earlier than was the case for many public schools.

CHARLES DARWIN

28 'Nothing could have been worse for the development of my mind than Dr Butler's school, as it was strictly classical, nothing else being taught, except a little ancient geography and history.' Such was Charles Darwin's assessment of Shrewsbury, which he attended in the early nineteenth century. He is, nevertheless, used heavily in its marketing. This bust of him adorns the school.

29 Training the next military genius: military manoeuvres at Cheltenham College, alma mater of tank pioneer Sir Ernest Swinton and fourteen Victoria Cross holders.

30 An antidote to the Combined Cadet Force: Peace Day at Bootham, the Quaker public school.

31 How times have changed: pupils of both sexes, and all races and colours, cheerily waving to the camera at Downside School.

32 Bird of war: the addition of Black Redstarts, one of which is pecking at the corn, was the only change made to the ceiling carvings of Westminster School's Busby Library when it was recreated after the Second World War – an acknowledgement of its taste for bombed buildings. A good metaphor for the public schools' adaptation and evolution over the centuries?

The nature of boarding schools certainly created tensions which might have bred inappropriate behaviour. The rigid sense of hierarchy created blind obedience; the survival of the fag system fostered opportunities for a good deal of cruelty and humiliation in boarding schools; for a young boy, previously innocent about sex, often suddenly transplanted to a world of savagery, sexual cruelty might have seemed merely one among many forms of persecution that had to be endured with forbearance. There are parallels with the young adolescents beginning their *agoge* in Sparta, who routinely accepted the convention of sexual initiation by older boys. Another potent ingredient was the intense relationship between master and pupil, which Malim and other advocates of boarding schools valued so much. Intense relationships carry the risk of triggering sexual feelings, if the potential for sexual attraction already exists.

Such seems to have been the case for Browning and Johnson. Browning was repressed to the point of attacking homosexuality, seeking out good-looking or charming boys to make them confess their sexual anxieties, warning them against sentimental attachments to other boys, and reminding them of the sacred beauty of male virginity.[47] The repressed homosexual interest which prompted this behaviour must have been obvious to all but the most naïve boys, making his behaviour inappropriate, though not perhaps abusive. The pattern of repression repeated itself: as an older man, having taken refuge in a scholar's life at his alma mater King's College, Cambridge, Browning insisted that a muscular young man sleep in his bed in case he was seized by a sudden illness and needed to be whisked off in strong arms.[48] Johnson sought intimacy through embraces and close physical contact which were not only inappropriate but crossed the line into abusiveness, because they were sexual. 'Elliot and I lay together on the long morocco sofa. He put his strong arms around me and his face against mine', he wrote of one boy – though, according to his diary entry, at least, this encounter did not progress from there.[49] In engaging in inappropriate or abusive behaviour, Browning and Johnson were in a minority. They were outnumbered by men such as

Arthur Benson, the Eton master (1885–1903) who satisfied himself merely by choosing the company of the better-looking Etonians, and by masters who went no further than stabs at rather literary innuendo, like Tempest, the gay master in Alan Bennett's 1968 play *Forty Years On*, who exclaims, while organizing the end-of-term entertainment, 'I wish I could put my hands on the choir's parts'.[50]

However, the 'contact of one mind with another and of one spirit with another' attempted in the intense environment of the boarding schools had its downside, particularly in an era when homosexual men were denied an outlet through relationships with men of similar age. This downside was an occasional sexual obsession with their pupils.

It is common to assume that anyone alive in the Victorian era had an irrational, confused and misguided attitude towards sex. However, it is to the credit of public school headmasters such as Arnold that they saw abusive sexual behaviour as a problem which needed addressing. Aside from taking a lead from Arnold in reforming boy government, other headmasters tried a variety of stratagems to police the system and to prevent pretty curly-headed boys from being more than petted and pampered.

One solution was sport. 'My prophylactic against certain unclean microbes was to send the boys to bed dead tired', declared a late Victorian headmaster of the United Services College.[51] At Eton, James Hornby, headmaster from 1868 to 1884, also stepped up sport partly in response to signs of increasing homosexual activity.[52] It was probably an ineffective solution. Any activity which displays the physical attributes and athletic skills of healthy young men would, if the sense of attraction was already felt, sharpen rather than blunt sexual feelings towards them. While he was a master at Rugby, John Percival, the future head of Clifton College, sensed the danger: he made boys lengthen their football shorts and fasten them with elastic bands over their knees, so that no flesh in the lower, more lascivious part of the body was showing at all.[53] There was, admittedly, probably only a small number of knee fetishists benefiting from an education in the Bristol suburb. Nevertheless, Percival's appreciation of the dangers of sport was realistic, even if his solution was eccentric.

A widespread policy of segregation was probably more effective than sport at preventing sexual abuse. As the first headmaster of Wellington College, Edward Benson, father of Arthur, ordered wire entanglements to be placed on top of the dormitory cubicles – which could not be fastened on the inside – and issued a fiat that when the younger boys were undressing, 'steward and matron to walk up and down in the middle of the dormitory and report any boy who goes out of his own dormitory to another.'[54] Moreover, close friendships between boys in different houses were at the very least kept under surveillance, and often discouraged, since relationships that did not develop under the watchful eye of the housemasters posed greater danger. There was clearly monitoring, too, though unsystematic, of the relationships between boys and masters: one of the immediate triggers for Browning's dismissal from Eton was his friendship with Curzon, a boy whom Browning had sought out and cultivated as a friend even though Curzon was not in Browning's house.[55]

Segregation exacted its costs. Writing in 1934 about his education at Malvern, founded in 1865 in Worcestershire, an old boy described poor relations between master and pupil as 'one of the main defects of public school life'. 'There can only be a completely satisfactory result from teaching when affection is permitted to exist between master and pupil', he wrote. 'The boy who is indifferent to his master's general personality can react to his teaching only in a restricted way.'[56] Recalling, in the same year, his life at Wellington in the first years of the twentieth century, the diplomat Harold Nicolson wrote that despite numerous changes, 'one thing, however, did remain – a thing which I still regard as the main and the most stupid defect of the whole Wellingtonian system ... In my day it was not thought proper that boys should become acquainted with other boys not in their own house or dorm.' As a result, he estimated, one knew the thirty or so boys in one's house; of these about ten qualified, through age, as possible friends. 'This reduction was most damaging, as I found to my bitter cost when I went up to Oxford. We learnt a great deal about Demosthenes and the acts of the apostles; we learnt but little about life.'[57] The claim is overwrought, but echoed, in substance, by the memory of a 1950s Brighton College head of house who recalled that because of 'the grip of the House system', when a Brighton boy from a different house came up to his Oxford college the year after him, the two spoke for the first time in their lives.[58] In an earlier age, writers had declared public schools educative precisely because they were public: exposing sons to the influence of many other boys, from whom they might learn. By mid-Victorian times, however, how public were they? On the other hand, competent headmasters did not have much of a choice. Homosexuality was often common; the risk of homosexual abuse was always loitering in the background; the injection of a little paranoia into the conduct of school government was therefore inevitable.

Homosexuality was not, in any case, the only reason for masters to adopt a much more watchful approach to their pupils. The death of a public school boy from bullying in 1885 suggests not too much but too little control over the lives of pupils. It was all the more shocking because the fatal incident took place at a day institution: King's College School. If a boy could die in the supposedly less rough-and-tumble world of the day school, what on earth was happening to boarders?

One could, at first sight, make a case for writing off the fatality of Charles Bourda as an isolated, freak incident, based on a personal grudge between one boy and another. However, an inquest found that this was far from the case. A dozen boys in the upper form had decided, it transpired, to administer a blow to the back of each small boy as he passed them – a systematic form of violence directed at their juniors in general. Returning a verdict of 'death by misadventure', the inquest added 'that the attention of the authorities at King's College should be called to the evident want of supervision over boys during the intervals of school hours, which, in the opinion of the jury, led to the death of Charles Fisher Bourda'.[59] Unsurprisingly, the accident provoked a political storm. Sir William Harcourt, the Home Secretary, declared in the Commons: 'I do not think there is any greater blot on our social system than the abominable practice of bullying which takes place in the great schools.' At King's itself, the incident prompted the withdrawal of a large number of young boys from the school and the firing of surplus staff, though the fact that the school did not collapse altogether engenders a sneaking suspicion that some fathers who had themselves been to public school felt that such an incident might, perhaps, have happened during their schooldays, too.[60] There had, after all, been the odd death by misadventure in earlier ages, as has already been shown, but none had been as clear cut and as well documented as this. It showed that the public schools were far from tamed.

The view that girls were not suitable vessels for academic education received a body blow in 1872, with the launch of the Girls' Public Day School Company, the brainchild of four feminists with a practical bent, at a meeting attended by the great and the good in the Albert Hall. The initial syllabus set out by the company, which was to grow to a mighty empire of 33 schools educating 7,000 pupils by the end of the century, shows that it was able to avoid two competing and not very happy traditions: the heavy concentration on social accomplishments which it might have inherited from earlier girls' schools, and the emphasis on the Classics, albeit less unremitting than before, at boys' public schools. The planned curriculum included English grammar and literature, French, German and elementary physical science, with Classics and elementary economics for the older pupils – though there was also some drawing and class singing, in line with the precedent set by earlier schools.[61]

Schools' initial prospectuses have often, historically, given the impression of a scheme of education considerably broader than reality. However, the practice of the company schools over the following decades matched the curricular rhetoric. By 1900 Notting Hill High School, set up in the second year of the company's existence, had won sixty-five open scholarships to the universities of Oxford, Cambridge and London, with consistently strong performances by other schools such as Oxford and Putney High (originally East Putney High).[62]

The question of whether schools wanting to do their best for their girls needed a feminized syllabus, rather than one identical to that of a modern boys' school, was to remain a dilemma for decades. Opportunities for a middle-class woman to have a career similar to a man's were just beginning to appear in the late nineteenth century; there were, for example, 264 female doctors by 1895.[63] Nonetheless, 264 was not a very large number for a large and sophisticated country. The bulk of even the best-educated women still became full-time wives and mothers rather than salaried workers. Agnata Ramsay, an Old Girl of St Leonard's School, St Andrew's, caused a tempest in the teapot of Cambridge University in 1887 when she came top in the Classics Tripos, though technically, since women were not then awarded full degrees, she was merely 'above the Senior Classic', who was a man. She, more than anyone, proved the limited career horizons of women, however. Her public life ended when Montagu Butler, the aged master of Trinity College, Cambridge and a proponent of women's education, married her the following year. It does at least sound as if she had the consolation of a wild honeymoon – they 'read a good deal of Greek together', according to a biography of her husband.[64]

The solution at North London Collegiate, founded in 1850, was to offer a broad academic syllabus, while adding to this some subjects which might be useful to a woman who as an adult concentrated on domestic work. In 1872 it provided courses in the philosophies of business, dress and food. Frances Buss, its first headmistress, also made book-keeping a regular subject, and introduced dress-making 'on scientific principles'.[65] This might sound old-fashioned, but it represented definite progress. These were not superficial social accomplishments likely to attract a husband; they were useful skills for women engaged in the job of mistress of the household. Maria Grey, another of the Girls' Public Day School Company founders, wrote of the traditional girls' private school education, 'they are not educated to be wives but to get husbands'. At North London Collegiate they were taught the skills of the former rather than the arts of the latter.[66]

Some old girls of these schools would have preferred a more uncompromisingly sexless syllabus than this. On the other hand, others, such as Molly Hughes, a future educationalist taught by Buss in the 1880s at North London Collegiate, thought it was not feminized enough.[67] It was a difficult balancing act.

Roedean School was set up in London in 1885 as a day and boarding school, but soon moved to a windswept location on the outskirts of Brighton. It is one of several schools which stuck to a considerably more conservative and feminized pattern than North London Collegiate and the Girls' Public Day School Company. Roedean endorsed the still popular myth that girls' health would be damaged by excessive mental effort. Consequently, 'special pains will be taken to guard against over-work, and from two to three hours daily will be allotted to out-door exercise and games', boasted its first prospectus – though it did also pledge that girls could be prepared for Newnham and Girton.[68] The fear of mental overstrain exerted a powerful influence, too, at Wycombe Abbey, founded in 1896 by Frances Dove, previously headmistress of St Leonard's. 'The hours of study will be strictly limited', promised an early prospectus from 1897.[69]

Even so, the new girls' public schools had without doubt moved on from the traditional private school model. One of the greatest differences was the wholesale embracing of sport at many schools, though to a more limited degree by the Girls' Public Day School Company. Sport was regarded, at Roedean and other schools, as a bulwark against overwork. Dove extolled Wycombe Abbey's virtues in language similar to that used by its champions at boys' public schools. She believed games would develop 'powers of organisation, of good temper under trying circumstances, courage and determination to play up and do your best even in a losing game, rapidity in thought and action, judgement and self-reliance, and above all things, unselfishness.'[70] A particular favourite at the girls' public schools was lacrosse, a game invented by Native Americans as a kind of symbolic warfare and played by many a British schoolgirl in the same martial spirit. Sceptics such as Olive Willis, a Roedean pupil of the 1890s and future founder of her own school, complained that, as at the boys' schools, the emphasis on sport went too far.[71] However, the idea that women from well-off backgrounds should be healthy, active and vigorous had for the previous few hundred years been anathema to many males, who had regarded such virtues as unfeminine. The clashing of jolly hockey sticks was a Victorian feminist triumph.

At this stage of their history, in some ways girls' public schools were better than boys' schools. The physical cruelty which peppers the memoirs of old boys, both officially sanctioned beatings by masters and prefects and illicit bullying, is mainly (though not entirely) absent from the memoirs of old girls. The lack of an almost sacred respect for the Classics frequently also made the curriculum better balanced, even if at times there was immoderate concern not to tax the girls excessively. Comparing the education she and her sister received at Wycombe Abbey in the 1890s with that of her brothers educated at boys' public schools including Eton and Rugby, the writer Winifred Peck found her brothers' wanting: boys' schools 'still breathed out the last disenchantments of the Middle Ages'.[72] In some ways, however, girls' schools simply absorbed the practices of boys' schools, including their virtues and vices, with a good headmistress able to maximize the former and minimize the latter. Ada Benson, headmistress of Oxford High when it opened in 1875, introduced the prefect system under the influence of her brother Edward, the former Wellington headmaster, and many other schools would follow suit (Arthur and E. F. Benson were her brothers).[73]

In other respects, however, girls' schools tended to be worse than boys' schools. They were often veritable factories of rule-making, a legacy of the convent origins of female education. Molly Hughes claimed that during her time at North London Collegiate, new rules were displayed in the corridor 'almost every day'. These included bans on getting wet on the way to school, walking more than three in a row, dropping a pencil case, hanging a boot-bag by only one loop, and so on almost ad infinitum. 'Can't remember using the front gate, or not changing my shoes, or talking on the stairs, or–' says Gwen Gascoyne, the heroine of the 1913 Angela Brazil story *The Youngest Girl in the Fifth*, as she races to meet a command to appear before the headmistress – though, in fact, the bright young girl, a mere Remove pupil, has been called up to meet the glorious destiny revealed in the book's title.[74] At Gateshead High School, part of the Girls' Public Day School Company, the ban on talking in the halls and stairs was enforced so rigidly that new girls lost in the building remained so for ever, wandering around like female terra firma versions of the captain of the Flying Dutchman.[75]

The strictest rules were often reserved for conduct outside the school: specifying who could and could not be spoken to and when, a consequence of the fear of social infection which parents harboured towards their daughters. Given the social segregation which had been the priority of many girls' private schools, the Girls' Public Day School Company's most revolutionary step of all lay not in curriculum policy but in its relaxed approach to social class: it sailed precisely the opposite course to most older girls' schools by not vetting its pupils by family background. In this sense the company's schools were, unlike Cheltenham Ladies' College in its early years, truly 'public'. The Duchess of Northumberland had refused a request to support the venture shortly before the company's launch, declaring that 'to help to make girls' education like that of the boys, public', would 'never have assistance from me, for I believe such a system would be an unmixed evil'. Writing later about the company's beginnings, Maria Grey recalled, 'I was asked again and again whether I was mad enough to suppose that any gentleman would send his daughter to a public school'.[76] But many did, and to the company's schools.

In practice, there was a fair social mix at its schools, though it was skewed towards the higher echelons of society. Fees were deliberately set low enough to maximize the number of families who could afford them, but they were still far from schools for the masses. At the Chelsea School, the very first, they were £4 4s a term for the youngest girls, rising to £8 8s (£770) for pupils entering at above the age of fifteen. This was out of range for all but the most successful of the skilled working classes, and even for particularly well-paid members of the middle class such as teachers. The fees were, however, well within the range of affordability for a fairly wide range of professionals.[77] Early pupils at the schools certainly remembered a broader mix than they would have found at Cheltenham Ladies', for example. 'Some were not of the upper class but were splendid people', Dame Meriel Talbot, daughter of an MP, recalled of her time at the first of the company's schools. 'I liked them all and my time at school left me with a facility for enjoyment of people of very different types.'[78] It provided, thus, a truly vocational education for Dame Meriel, whose career, as a member of a host of official committees, would be built on helping people of 'very different types' from herself, including deprived girls.

From the point of view of the schools' financial viability, however, they were not exclusive enough. Developing science into a properly taught subject would have been immensely costly. 'We had no laboratories at all and girls like myself who wanted to do science had nothing', wrote Dame Harriette Chick (1875–1977), who became a distinguished nutritionist, of her days at Notting Hill. But although science was therefore learned 'theoretically', 'it was exceptionally well done'. It clearly worked for her, but was hardly ideal.[79] The company was in a bind: science labs and adequate sporting facilities were expensive to build, and the schools lacked the endowments enjoyed by the old public schools, which might have made it easier to realize these ambitions. However, because it wanted to educate a fairly wide variety of children the company was reluctant to raise fees, and the large volume of parental complaints about even the existing fees suggests that it might not have been able to do so anyway without suffering falling rolls.[80] However, some other non-company schools, such as St Leonard's, a mixed day and boarding school founded in

St Andrews, Fife in 1877, had the money to take science seriously right from the start – an attitude which produced a steady stream of medics, including the epidemiologist Alice Stewart (1906–2002) and Louisa Garrett Anderson (1873–1943), the medical pioneer.[81] The company was, in comparison, in danger of falling behind. From the 1890s its response was to accept increasing amounts of state funding, which in the early twentieth century would leave the state with too powerful a role in the schools for them to be called public schools by our definition.[82] It was a fate that would befall many boys' day schools as well, during some difficult periods for the public school movement.

In 1900, two Old Etonian generals, Lord Methuen and Sir Redvers Buller, made a striking contribution to the annals of British military blunders by suffering one sound trouncing apiece on the South African veldt in the opening stages of the Second Boer War.

Britain had grown accustomed to winning, vanquishing frequently ill-armed and ill-trained foes in a series of small wars over the previous century. A good many of these wars had been won by old boys of the public schools. The country's initial defeat on the southern tip of the Dark Continent, though later redeemed by the victorious, if morally dubious, scorched earth strategy of Lord Kitchener – not a public school boy – was therefore all the more shocking. It gave birth to a wave of national self-questioning. This was given a greater sense of urgency by the fashionable Social Darwinist theory, which held that world affairs was a competition between powerful nations, with those which failed to adapt to the times facing oblivion. In this fearful atmosphere, the public schools were examined by social commentators and found wanting. The attitude of public schools 'towards the teaching of modern languages and the preparation of our future officers has been almost incredibly stupid and perverse', wrote G. G. Coulton, a former public school master teaching the army class. He repeated the now-familiar argument that too much Classics was taught, to the exclusion of modern subjects. Unless the curriculum and teaching improved, he asserted, there was every likelihood that Colenso and Magersfontein, which destroyed the reputations of Buller and Methuen, respectively, would not be the only battles lost on the playing fields of Eton.[83]

However, the 1902 Akers-Douglas parliamentary report on officer training, an official response to this national self-doubt, presented an assessment of the public schools which, far from being apocalyptic, was veritably positive. On being asked why the percentage of successful candidates entering from crammers had dropped from sixty-eight to fifty-two from 1895 to 1900, Sandhurst concluded: 'The decrease in those entering Sandhurst from "crammers" is believed to be due to the Army classes at public schools receiving better supervision and instruction than formerly.' It added: 'There is no question that the boys entering the R.M.C. [Royal Military College of Sandhurst] straight from public schools are certainly, as regards general educational fitness, physical fitness, general character and bearing, and aptitude for command, more desirable than those coming from "crammers".'[84]

Another charge would quickly be made against the public schools in the years following the Boer War, one that was, in a sense, even more serious, because it questioned the entire social structure that underpinned them. This was the claim that public school boys were out of touch because of the nature of their education. 'Instincts of caste that forbid sympathy and understanding between the well-to-do and the poorer classes' were fomented in the schools, asserted John Galsworthy, the writer and Old Harrovian.[85] Galsworthy blamed this for the severe industrial unrest in the years before the outbreak of the First World War in 1914. It is fair to ask how it could be that the political and military establishment, largely educated at such schools, was in such a state of ignorance about the conditions of the masses that it was shocked to find a huge proportion of working-class men rejected by the army as Boer War fighting material on grounds of ill-health. This was the case for three out of five of all men at the Manchester recruiting station.[86]

The headmasters of many boys' public schools could point, in their defence, to the many Christian missions set up by schools in working-class areas in the decades before the Boer War, including Clifton (1875), Cheltenham (1890) and Eton (1880), whose boys were inoculated before they made the trip from Windsor to the working-class districts of Hackney Wick.[87] The amount of money raised by boys and friends of the school to fund the activities of the missions could be impressively high. For the Cheltenham mission in London it came to an average of £500 or so a year (about £55,000) – enough to fund a full-time missioner and assistant missioner. A cynic could argue that these missions suffered from the common affliction of many good causes supported by the professional classes, then as now: money was given generously; time much less so. A regular complaint in the Cheltenham Missioners' Annual Report was that so few Cheltonians or Old Cheltonians visited the mission to assist in its work.[88] However, accusations that the missions did nothing to bridge the large social divide between Britain's classes comes up against the inconvenient truth that Britain's first prime minister of a fully fledged socialist government became a socialist after growing to understand the conditions of the poor while working at his public school's mission. Clement Attlee's eyes were opened at Haileybury House in the poor London borough of Stepney.[89] Moreover, some schools actually invited poor boys from the districts where the missions were located into their confines. In 1910 Bradford boys came to Sedbergh School for summer camp, where they developed an enthusiasm for bathing with the pupils in the river and walking with them in the Yorkshire fells.[90]

There were, however, still few working-class boys actually attending public schools. Schools which had awarded scholarships through patronage abandoned this from the early Victorian era onwards in favour of competitive exams. One might have expected this to broaden the schools' social base, by allowing bright boys of modest means to win entry through their brains rather than family connections. Scholars had, after all, tended to come from the establishment circles frequented by governors and senior masters who exercised this patronage – in the same way that Wykeham had let in the sons of

powerful men as scholars. At Charterhouse, the last scholar nominated before exams were introduced in the 1870s was the son of the
successful publisher Frederick Warne.[91] In reality, however, this new
development left schools no more and no less socially exclusive than
before, largely because it played into the hands of the growing network
of prep schools catering to the wealthy classes, schools whose *raison
d'être* was the preparation of pupils for public schools. Examining the
registers for Winchester College for 1836–7 to 1905–6, shows that in
1836–7, during the patronage era, fifteen of the seventeen boys were
the sons of men in holy orders. In 1905–6, six of the twelve were from
this background, with another the son of a justice of the peace, another
of a captain, and another of a father living at Number One Bryanston
Square in London – far from the tough districts where the public
schools placed their missions.[92] At Winchester, at least, the end of
patronage slightly broadened the astoundingly narrow base from
which the scholars were drawn, but only for the most part to include
other members of the professional classes.

The provenance of public school scholars was privileged in the
early part of the century, and remained so in the latter part. The
major difference was that the new boys were on average considerably
brighter than their forebears, to the point where they exercised a
beneficial academic effect on the whole school. At Eton, which introduced competitive exams in the 1840s, the headmaster told the
Clarendon Commission that of seventeen King's Scholars in his class,
'I find twelve clergymen's sons, two young sons, whose elder brothers
are provided for; two sons of naval officers, and one who is a solicitor's son.' The head added, with a sense of definition of the term 'poor
scholar' which would stretch the imagination of the most imaginative lexicographer: 'I take these to be, as near as may be, the class of
person whom our Founder meant to benefit; and the leaven of stead-
iness and diligence, which they impart to the rest of the School, is
most valuable to us.'[93]

Taking scholars and commoners together, public schools largely
catered only to a restricted range within Britain's broad and varied

elite classes. A study of boys at Winchester at the end of the century shows 61 per cent from professional backgrounds, with 31 per cent sons of businessmen. For St Paul's during the same period, 58 per cent were from the professions. At both schools, even boys who did not come from the professional class joined it after leaving: almost four-fifths of St Paul's boys in the period became professionals. Another study of 754 leading businessmen in Manchester, Birmingham and Bristol active between 1870 and 1914 shows that under one-fifth attended public school.[94] Many parts of the wealthier end of the middle classes had not, by and large, yet picked up the public school habit. One estimate puts the number of pupils at boys' public schools at 20,000 in 1902 – only about 1 per cent of the relevant age group at the time, roughly speaking.[95] This definition is based on classifying sixty-four schools as public schools, a fairly narrow definition, though it includes the majority of what this author would call 'public schools'.[96] With some exceptions, the world of boys' public schools was indeed a narrow one. It was not a caste system, since a wide variety of boys could attend if their fathers could pay. It was, instead, an island connected to the vast mainland of British society only by narrow and badly paved bridges.

There were alternatives to the public schools, at this stage of British history, but the strength of rival systems should not be exaggerated. The small private schools, often run by a single schoolmaster or mistress as for-profit ventures, remained in large numbers, with some catering to boys, some to girls, and some to both. However, the bulk of them provided only an elementary education, teaching children the three Rs – reading, writing and arithmetic – if they were lucky. 'None is too old, too poor, too ignorant, too feeble, too silly, too unqualified to be regarded by others as unfit for school keeping', a member of the Newcastle Commission on the state of popular education had written in 1858, though the conclusion would have applied equally well at any point in the century. School keepers included, according to the report, 'domestic servants out of places, discharged barmaids, vendors of toys or lollipops, keepers of small eating houses, milliners, consumptive patients in an advanced state, men and women of seventy and even eighty years of age'.[97]

In the late nineteenth century the place of these schools was taken increasingly by state-sponsored schools. The Education Act of 1870 gradually spread state-funded elementary education throughout England and Wales, with a similar Act for Scotland in 1872. Elementary education then was not the same as primary school education now. Although the education was basic, concentrating largely on the three Rs, classes included some older as well as younger children. In other words, the name referred to the nature of the education, rather than the age of the children being taught. The 1870 Act also led to the creation of 'higher schools', but limited numbers of children attended these. The higher schools can be seen as an early incarnation of the state secondary school system. But although the teaching was more advanced than for the elementaries, children did not usually go on to university from these schools – making it diffi-cult to see them as academic rivals to the public schools.[98] Meanwhile, the grammar school movement had been given new impetus by the Endowed Schools Commission, strengthening the potential compe-tition to the public schools.

The public schools were, on the death of Queen Victoria in 1901, in a considerably better state than at her accession to the throne. They had begun to train pupils for traditional upper-class careers in the army; the training was, belatedly, beginning to reach a high standard. The curriculum outside the military classes was also considerably broader, and more likely to be taught well. In reward for these reforms, the public school movement as a whole was thriving – with tens of thousands of pupils attending, instead of the few thousand of only a century before. Many of these pupils were girls, at institutions which shared at least some characteristics with their brothers' schools.

There were, however, still weaknesses. When compared with the grammar schools, the public schools were often weak in science. At boarding schools the boys were sometimes half-starved; the constant recurrence of public school novels of illicit feasts, including the 1947 tale of how Billy Bunter, the most famous Old Boy of Greyfriars School, was found in his schoolmaster's study eating jam with his ivory paper-knife, reflected a fantasizing about food generated by the lack of basic provisions.[99] At both boarding and day schools boys were often bullied. The reform of the public schools was half-finished. However, in very many ways, the new century would be faster than the old one. This greater sense of speed would apply, too, to public school reform.

CHAPTER SIX

Beware Greeks Bearing Gifts
1902–1945

DEFECTIVE systems are capable of surviving for long periods of time if the competition is equally addled; in many cases the flaws prove fatal only when a challenger becomes strong enough to deal a mortal blow. The public schools had been able to rise from their trough from the mid-nineteenth century, and to embark on reform at a rather stately, though steady, pace for the rest of the Victorian era, only because of the weakness of potential rivals; at this stage the rival grammar schools were prey to many of the same faults, and state funding of secondary education was in its infancy. From 1902, however, the environment was less forgiving. The Education Act of that year, passed by a Conservative government, marked the beginning of a massive expansion of secondary state education in England and Wales over the next thirty years. From this point onwards the public schools were to have a complex relationship with the state. Their existence would be threatened by competition from the parallel state system, but there were also to be times when a huge chunk of the public school system owed its survival to state assistance. By the end of the century, moreover, the Nietzchean principle that what does not kill you only makes you stronger had proved true: responding to the minatory presence of the state, the public schools were forced to raise their game.

The 1902 Act encouraged local government to increase the provision of secondary education, though without forcing it to do so. The councils of counties and county boroughs were required to 'take such steps as seem to them desirable ... to supply or aid the supply of education other than elementary'. Moreover, local authorities were to be held responsible for maintaining the existing voluntary schools, including the payment of teachers – a change which rescued the grammar schools from financial precariousness. Local government responded with unbridled enthusiasm: the number of secondary schools supported by state funding doubled from under 500 in 1904–5 to over 1,000 in 1913–14. Meanwhile pupil numbers almost tripled from under 64,000 to 188,000.[1] By 1937 there were 409,033 pupils between the ages of eleven and seventeen in state-funded secondaries – 10 per cent of the age group – though the vast bulk of children of this age who were still at school were in the less academically ambitious elementaries.[2] Total state spending on secondary education was boosted by the 1902 Act, and again increased towards the middle of the century – up 37 per cent between 1921 and 1944.[3] The grammar schools began to produce a steady stream of leading public figures, such as the future prime ministers Harold Wilson, Edward Heath and Margaret Thatcher, who were all educated during this period.

Much of this largesse was lavished on grammar schools, which were dominated by the middle classes. By 1944, 41 per cent of the money went to grammars – a higher proportion than two decades previously. The 'free-place' system, instituted by a Liberal government in 1907, made recognition for a government grant dependent on the school concerned taking a certain proportion of children for free from state-funded elementary schools. However, this left the leading grammar schools, accustomed for most of their history to charging fees for some of their wealthier pupils, free to continue doing so.[4] The school rolls were skewed even further towards the bourgeoisie by the fact that poorer families often rejected even free places as unaffordable, given the cost of books and uniform, as well as of an adolescent's wage forgone for the sake of continuing education; it was reported in 1926 that in Bradford about 60 per cent of free place winners turned down their scholarships.[5]

Some of the older state-aided grammar schools were reassuringly similar to the public schools, for parents seeking a cheaper alternative. John Lewis Paton, high master of Manchester Grammar School from 1903, was an Old Salopian and former headmaster of University College School. His public school background shone through in the style of education he imposed at Manchester Grammar School. 'A strong body is your servant, a weak body is your master', he declared to the boys on his first speech day. A biography of Paton written by his son concludes that 'he saw that in the great public schools the moral tone was fostered by the corporate life, the organized team-games, the personal influence of masters, the continued attachment of scholars after they had left'. At King Edward's School, Birmingham, another leading grammar school, boys' initials were placed before their surname in school lists only if they were a member of the football First XI or rugby First XV.[6]

Officials in local and national government also agreed to give grants to an increasing number of public schools in return for free places. Without doubt, for some public day schools already holed in the water long before the 1902 Act, this was a life-saver. In 1912 King's College School, London, was placed on the grant list by Surrey County Council, in return for taking up to 10 per cent of its new pupils from elementaries. King's had wanted the higher grant that was eligible for schools which offered to take at least 25 per cent, but it is a measure of how far the institution had sunk that Surrey was not prepared to take the risk of spending so much money on an institution which might not, in the council's opinion, survive.[7] It is also hard to see how North London Collegiate, already running a deficit before the Act and afflicted by the steady deterioration of its Camden neighbourhood, could have struggled on indefinitely without state subvention. After initially turning down a grant, the governors were forced by the parlous state of the school's finances to change their mind in

1907. By the end of 1914 nearly one-third of the pupils were free scholars sent there by London County Council.[8]

A considerably larger number of public day schools were stable before the Act, only to be cast into crisis by the arrival of new state schools with striking new science and art facilities which they could not match. Their solution was to feed from the mouth that bit them. The governing council of the Girls' Public Day School Trust (the new name for the Girls' Public Day School Company from 1905) protested to the Board of Education against the establishment of new state-funded secondaries near its Dulwich, Streatham Hill and Shrewsbury High Schools, prompting the Board of Education to reply disingenuously 'that the interests of the Trust [would] not be prejudicially affected to any degree'. The trust came to rely progressively more on state aid, however, as its finances worsened. 'Every feature of the business is dark', the Finance Committee moaned in 1914, at a point when the trust had accumulated a debt of £106,000 (£10 million) by mortgaging its property. The inability of the trust's schools to keep up with their state-funded rivals was revealed in inspections made by the Board of Education, a body which took on a steadily more powerful supervisory role in return for financial support. At East Putney High School (now simply Putney High School), it decreed that a basement room fitted up for science teaching 'cannot be regarded as really adequate for the purpose, as there is insufficient room for more than a few girls to do practical work, and the benches at which they sit are far too narrow'.[9]

The financial position of many public day schools worsened still further after the School Teachers Superannuation Act of 1918, which introduced pensions for teachers at state-aided schools, and the first report of the Burnham Committee on teachers' pay in 1918, which ramped up their salaries by establishing minimum rates. Public schools were forced to emulate both these gestures of largesse to keep staff.[10] In 1921 the headmaster of Arnold School in Blackpool told parents that he had been forced to raise fees to match the Burnham recommendations for state-funded schools, as 'only in this way is it possible for me to retain the services of fully qualified and experienced assistants'.[11]

Faced with such steadily rising pressure from government policy, a huge range of schools were obliged to accept grant status, becoming state-funded secondaries at least in part, in the period before the Second World War broke out in 1939. The list included, in addition to the schools mentioned above, University College School (1919), Robert Gordon's in Edinburgh (1920), and Arnold School (1937). Grant status created a fairly broad social mix. A quarter of the new boys at University College School in 1921 were from working or lower middle-class backgrounds, including the sons of railway workers, market porters, joiners, postmen and clerks.[12] 'I am grateful to University College School for teaching me to understand the lives of those who were poorer than myself', wrote the poet Sir Stephen Spender, who attended the school in the 1920s. 'When I was a child I was never allowed to play with poor children because my mother regarded them as not only rough, but also as perpetual carriers of infectious diseases.' However, 'some of the boys I most liked were of working-class parents and lived in very poor districts'.[13]

The effect of more and better state schooling on the finances of the public day schools was bad enough, but the arrival of state funding sounded the death knell for many of the private schools – small and transient establishments owned and run by a single individual. Some of the private schools had enjoyed high reputations in earlier centuries, but by the early twentieth century the bulk of them were mediocre at best. In an era of sparse state education they had at least served some purpose, but this purpose disappeared in the early twentieth century. 'In the majority of the schools ... the provision for playgrounds, classrooms, assembly halls, the teaching of physical exercises and practical subjects, sanitary accommodation, furniture, heating and lighting, ventilation, cloakrooms, etc, falls much below the standards of the grant-aided school', found the National Association of Inspectors of Schools and Educational Organisers in the early 1930s when examining the private schools. 'This is hardly to be wondered at for economic conditions, and the competition with grant aided schools [that is, state-funded schools] on the one hand and with one another on the other, operate to reduce fees to such a level that the schools are unable to provide the accommodation and equipment which are indispensable if the work is to proceed satisfactorily.'[14]

The boarding schools were not in direct competition with the state-funded schools, which were primarily for day pupils. However, the rise in state school salaries recommended by the Burnham Committee, and even more than that the new pensions system ushered in by the School Teachers Superannuation Act, also caused them financial headaches. The poor pay and lack of provision for old age for many masters had long been a weakness of the boarding schools. At successful schools – those with large numbers of pupils – headmasters and housemasters, at least, had done well financially. Many of the smaller schools, however, had long survived by paying staff meagre wages. Higher pay at the state schools now presented them with an alternative, and much better, way of earning a living. The prospect of higher financial reward was particularly enticing for the increasing number of boarding school masters who, like Ronald Gurner, the Marlborough teacher, were keen to end the monastic life and start a family.

Responding to their fears over the effect of shouldering these onerous demands for pay and pensions, the boarding and public day schools alike made a potentially epoch-making decision: they showed themselves ready to strike a deal with the government. In his memoirs Frank Fletcher, the influential and well-connected head of Charterhouse, recalled the public schools' response. In the aftermath of the School Teachers Superannuation Act, the leading public schools for boys agreed to make a proposal to the Board of Education: they would all offer places to free scholars from state elementary schools in return for state funding of the new pensions and other items. Crucially, the deal included schools which could afford to pay the pensions without assistance – a bid to ensure continuing parity of status among the different public schools by tarring them all with the same state brush. The board turned down the offer, at a meeting at which Fletcher was accompanied by the heads of Eton and Marlborough: 'We were told there was no demand for places in our schools for ex-elementary schoolboys.'[15]

The question of what would have happened to Britain's public schools had the board instead accepted the offer – and had both sides managed to agree the precise details of state supervision – is one of the great 'what ifs' of public school history. Public schools that have accepted large amounts of state aid – given in widely varying forms over the twentieth and into the twenty-first centuries – have generally ceased to be true public schools at all, because they have, in practice, lost their independence. The official historians of King's College School have written that from the time it accepted state-funded places to the time it exited the system in 1944, 'the school ceased to control its own financial destiny', an apt description for all schools that took government money. At King's College, 'the Board's authority had always to be sought, local councils' goodwill and support gained, before any activity could be undertaken'.[16] In commenting on the new offers of state assistance, the writer and ex-public schoolmaster John Hay Beith demonstrated the worth of the Classics in elucidating the present by quoting from Virgil. The larger and better endowed schools 'merely winked their rheumy eyes and shook their heavy heads. "Timeo Danos," they growled, "et dona ferentes [beware Greeks bearing gifts]." '[17]

If Fletcher's proposals had borne fruit, the leading boys' public schools would have ceased to be so, and the public school system would have been headless. It is going too far to say that the public schools would have become extinct: some of the public schools which became shadow public schools by accepting state aid in the early part of the century reinvented themselves as true public schools again in the 1940s, including King's. Others did so in the 1970s. This suggests that the public school movement could have roused itself from its self-imposed dormancy, rather than eventually dying in its sleep. However, it is also possible that, once virtually the whole movement had accepted a degree of state control, this would have come to be seen as a normal, sensible and permanent state of affairs. Looking outside the field of education and at British society in general, until the Thatcher era there was almost a consensus, even shared by many Conservatives, that the age of powerful and wholly private institutions, independent of the state, was inevitably coming to an end. A final possibility is that Fletcher and other headmasters agreed on the joint proposal to the board in ignorance of the large degree of control which the board would have demanded in return, and that once they had been disabused of this ignorance they would have abandoned all co-operation.

'Dulce et decorum est pro patria mori', wrote Horace in an ode studied by many a public school boy who went, from 1914, to die on Flanders fields: 'It is sweet and fitting to die for one's country'. We in the twenty-first century know only of Wilfred Owen's ironic kidnapping of the phrase to describe death by gassing, neither sweet nor fitting, on behalf of a mother country whose armies were run by incompetent idiots. Many public school boys of the age would, however, have agreed more with the Roman poet's original heartfelt sentiment.

The huge casualties suffered by the public schools made the First World War too sad a conflict to be called a good war, even by the most gung-ho of commentators. Death rates were 27 per cent among old boys from Harrow and Loretto, 20 per cent for several of the more famous boarding schools, and around 16 or 17 per cent for many of the public day schools, all above the national average of a little over one in ten. This can partly be credited to the schools' disproportionate share of the officer class – disproportionately likely to die – and partly to their well-organized Officer Training Corps at the war's outbreak. The OTC boys tended to join up quickly – cursing them with more years in which to be killed.[18]

Admiration for the readiness of old boys to die bravely muted criticism of the public schools in the First World War. Remembering Richard Levett, an Old Etonian lieutenant killed in the war, a rifleman

172   THE OLD BOYS

wrote: 'No one will ever be able to say that the upper classes haven't given their all in this just cause. The best and bravest have given their lives freely.' He was one of hundreds of Etonians killed in the conflict. In Flanders' Ypres salient alone – scene of some of the bitterest fighting of the war – 324 Old Etonians died. In response, old boys of the school funded the Ypres Memorial School, which educated the children of those who tended the local war graves until the area was overrun by the Germans in 1940.[19] Another Old Etonian killed during the war was American-born Henry Simpson. Returning to England to take part in the war, he became a British citizen with his mother's consent, 'freely given as soon as she realised his conviction that duty to England, which for him meant Eton, left him no choice'. Simpson became a member of the Royal Flying Corps, and died while testing new planes in 1916.[20]

If bravery is measured by medals, Eton led the public school field with thirteen Victoria Crosses, part of its total tally in British history of thirty-seven, which was more than any other school.[21] Eton is also, tellingly, the school whose old boys have contributed the most to the canon of patriotic songs, including 'Rule Britannia', composed by Thomas Arne, 'Jerusalem', set to music by Sir Hubert Parry, and 'Land of Hope and Glory', whose lyrics were penned by Arthur Benson. Another ex-public school boy, Rupert Brooke of Rugby School, composed a poem that would, by some, be regarded as a spoken anthem describing what Britain was fighting for. 'The Soldier' begins:

> If I should die, think only this of me:
> That there's some corner of a foreign field
> That is forever England.[22]

A cynic might argue that it stands to reason that boys from the grandest schools should fight so bravely and sing so well; they had the most to fight and sing for. Just as Vietnam has often been described as a white man's war – fought for the white man's interests – the First World War could be seen as a public school boys' war, fought to preserve an imperial system which had been good for public school boys but not for the working classes.[23] Brooke's poem was about England; however, in Benson's final version of 'Land of Hope and Glory', written in 1914, the lyrics are largely a celebration of the British Empire, including the lines: 'By Freedom gained, by Truth maintained, / Thine Empire shall be strong.'[24]

Cynics might also argue that courage does not, by itself, win wars. The Etonian Redvers Buller, whipping-boy of the press for his poor handling of troops in the Boer War, had won a Victoria Cross in the Zulu War. One of the most famous public school heroes of the First World War, John Vereker (VC, Harrow), had a dire record in the Second: he was in command of the British force that barely made it back to Britain after the 1940 defeat of the Allied forces in France.[25]

Industrial materials do, however, indubitably play a key role – often the deciding role – in winning wars. Britain's inability to produce enough of certain crucial resources, including optical glass and smelted tungsten, used to make steel, prompted disquiet about the role of the public schools and other parts of the education system in producing both enough specialist scientists and enough rulers with a scientific mindset. Thirty-six eminent scientists wrote to *The Times* in 1916 asserting that Britain's failures in the war were due to 'a lack of knowledge on the part of our legislators and administrative officials of what is called "science" or "physical science"'.[26] The growing discontent about the fitness of Britain's education system to enable victory in both war and peace gave birth to twin committees, on science and modern languages. Appointed by Herbert Asquith, the prime minister, they presented their conclusions in 1918.

The report on science, chaired by Joseph John Thomson, a Nobel Laureate in Physics, acknowledged the progress made by the boys' public schools in the past half-century. Its survey of fifteen schools found an average of 192 boys on the modern side, where 'the time given to Science is reasonable', for every hundred on the classical. However, it criticized both the quality of education on the modern side, including the lack of 'strenuous work', and the neglect of science among many of the brightest boys. The report pointed out that scholarships to the public schools were largely Classics-based. As a result, 'the curricula of many Preparatory Schools are unnaturally distorted' – pushing the sharpest minds from an early age on to a Classics track through prep school, public school and university. 'It is impossible to avoid the conclusion', the report found, 'that the effect of existing entrance scholarship examinations at the public schools' – which were focused largely on classical knowledge – 'is to divert to specialised literary and linguistic studies a particular kind of boy who might have been successful in other fields'. The inevitable end result, it pointed out, was a heavy bias towards Classics rather than science scholarships at university. In a survey of Cambridge colleges covering the previous ten years, it discovered that among the seven schools offering boarding which were covered by the Clarendon report – Eton, Winchester, Westminster, Shrewsbury, Charterhouse, Harrow and Rugby – 117 boys had won classical scholarships, with only 19 in science. It found, moreover, that at some schools 'the teaching of Science on the classical side is confined to the lower forms'. As a result, 'a clever boy who is placed on entry high up on the classical side may altogether miss instruction in Science', thus making total ignorance of science a badge of status among academically brilliant public school-educated men.[27]

This contrasted with state-funded schools, including grammars, where 'the provision of science teaching, which must include practical work, is not a matter of choice but of regulation', with each school submitting its curriculum to the Board of Education. It found that among sixth-formers, advanced teaching in science and maths was more common than in Classics. The result was a brilliant flowering of scientific achievement. Taking the same group of Cambridge colleges, of 113 scholarships won by boys in state-aided schools, 88 were in science. No longer could the public schools be defended for their scientific backwardness, as in the nineteenth century, on the grounds that the other schools were little better. The public school boys were the classically trained thinkers, while the grammar and state school boys were the boffins.[28]

The report on modern languages, chaired by Stanley Leathes, a senior civil servant and Old Etonian King's Scholar, covered similar ground. It found little to praise in the teaching, lamenting that the old tradition of Classics dominance 'has directly and injuriously affected modern studies. For a long time after French and German were introduced into the Public Schools they were taught like the dead languages and the results were very poor.' Even in 1918, 'though better methods of teaching are generally followed, the examinations in modern languages are modelled too closely on Classical tradition', which placed no importance on conversational ability.[29]

The low priority given to non-classical subjects in the early years of the twentieth century is apparent from many a tale. Fettes's casual approach to scientific scholarship reached comical heights when William Heard, the headmaster, appointed a mathematician in 1902 with the request, 'it would be an advantage if you could teach some chemistry'. After spending the summer working on it, the master was informed by the head, as term began, that he had meant to say 'physics'. Heard was a scholar of Latin and Greek, and chemistry and physics were all science to him. Heard's attitude to science was, in fact, more than merely indifferent: he referred to the boys in the sixth form's modern side as 'the barbarians'. As barbarians they were not, of course, allowed to sit at the sixth form table of classicists at lunch.[30] One would not have expected a Roman centurion to break bread with a Hun. At many schools one would not, either, expect a classicist to know much about history other than Roman centurions and their legions. On arriving at Wellington as a schoolmaster in 1929, T. C. Worsley was asked to teach history, English and divinity as well as Latin. 'This arrangement, however admirable it was in theory, had for me an alarming disadvantage', he recalled with horror. 'Marlborough', his old school, 'had taught me neither history nor English.'[31]

Neither report dealt with girls' public schools specifically, but other evidence from individual schools shows that their science teaching was often limited. As late as 1930 the Girls' School Year

Book entry for St Margaret's School, Bushey boasted that 'girls are trained in habits of nature study', but did not mention physics.[32]

More generally in the early twentieth century, girls' schools remained afflicted by the lack of a clear answer to the key question of the time: what was girls' education for?

In their annual Girls' School Year Book entries, Cheltenham Ladies' College, St Leonard's and Wycombe Abbey boasted of places won and exam honours attained at Oxbridge's women's colleges. Headmistresses at the Girls' Public Day School Trust attacked government attempts to make the feminine art of cookery a core part of the curriculum at state-aided schools, including their own; a 1907 memo by five of them argued that it 'cannot be justified on educational grounds. By it we can awaken or train no power not already reached by other means.' Since the trust schools were 'first and foremost, Literary Schools', 'to replace the subjects of a wide and comprehensive literary curriculum to an undue extent by the introduction of "Practical Housewifery" would be a retrograde step, and one which we should deplore'.[33] Trust schools also specialized in the decidedly unfeminine (in the standard view of the time) subject of mathematics; seven of its twenty-four headmistresses in 1914 were maths graduates from Cambridge.[34]

By contrast, Derby High School's list of 'successes' in the 1930 year book began first with the very feminine achievements of awards by the Royal Drawing Society and Operatic Association. The City of London School for Girls placed itself, like many schools, somewhere in the middle, mentioning in its 1930 entry an exhibition to St Hugh's College, Oxford, as well as its classes in hygiene and needlework.[35] St Paul's Girls' School, founded by the Mercers in 1904 as a sister school to St Paul's, would, over the following century, produce perhaps the longest list of eminent women of any school in the country. However, Frances Gray, its first high mistress (until 1927), declared: 'Every woman that is born into the world is given by God the duty of being a home maker . . . Those of you who are doing the adventurous things, as far as in you lies be home makers because in doing that you are doing the very best and highest and greatest thing that can be given to woman.'[36]

It would be wrong, however, to presume that headmistresses uniformly imposed conservative views of a woman's role on more modern pupils of a younger generation during this era. In 1914 Cheltenham Ladies' College issued a pamphlet on careers for women; in the same year a motion, put forward in a school debate, that paid work was more valuable to the community than unpaid work, was thrown out by a thumping majority.[37] The pupils could be more conservative than the teachers.

The thundering condemnation made by the Thomson and Leathes reports certainly gave further impetus to changes in the curriculum at the boys' public schools away from the primacy of the Classics. The process had begun in the previous century, and continued slowly but surely after the arrival of the new one. Several school entries in the 1902 *Public Schools Year Book* show an unabashed Classics bias: at Shrewsbury 'the work of the School is chiefly Classical', at Charterhouse 'the main teaching of the School is Classical', and at Winchester 'the course of study is principally Classical'. By 1938, however, the last year of peace before the Second World War threw curricula into chaos, emphatic statements that Classics dominated had been expunged from the three schools' entries.[38]

However, several schools conveyed subtle intimations that Classics still held the edge. Charterhouse specified that of its minimum of ten scholarships a year, a mere 'one or more' will be awarded 'without taking into account the marks for Greek', in line with the Thomson report's complaint about bright boys being put on a Classics track. In the 1920s the parents of Alan Turing, the Second World War code-breaker and computer scientist, were told by the headmaster of Sherborne that 'if he is to stay at a Public School, he must aim at becoming educated. If he is to be solely a Scientific Specialist, he is wasting his time at a Public School.'[39] There is no such bald statement of classical dominance at Sherborne in any *Public Schools Year Book* of the era; however, the 1938 entry included a detailed, year-by-year description of the classical syllabus which was not accorded to other subjects. Moreover, even in 1938 the public schools' entries still lacked the enthusiastic embrace of modern curricula to be found in some of the grammar school entries: Bedford Modern School's stated baldly that 'the curriculum has a strong bias in favour of modern studies'.[40]

Modern languages masters, meanwhile, were generally treated by the other teachers as second-class members of staff, and were often on lower pay. Their lower status percolated through the walls of the common room into the classroom. 'Pillingshot's views on behaviour and deportment during French lessons did not coincide with those of M. Gerard', writes P. G. Wodehouse observantly in *Tales of St Austin's*, a 1903 collection of public school stories. 'Pillingshot's idea of a French lesson was something between a pantomime rally and a scrum at football.'[41] Leathes was to make a similar point fifteen years later, albeit in a more scholarly way.

Classics did not quite rule at the public schools any more, but the subject was, as Turing's headmaster might approvingly have said, still sometimes *primus inter pares* (first among equals). It did not matter that it was not directly useful for a life in science or commerce. That was beside the point. 'I know ... that you boys are so fond of saying – that Latin Prose is "no use" ', booms Jolty, the Classics master, in *From a Pedagogue's Sketch-Book*, a series of fictional sketches from public school life written by Francis R. G. Duckworth a few years before Turing's time at Sherborne. 'That is shopkeepers' talk. We ought, indeed, to be glad if it could be shown that Latin prose is "no use" in the ordinary sense.'[42]

The boarding schools thrived in the years after the end of the First World War, despite the caustic comments of government reports – doing so well that the post-war period saw a mini-boom in foundations, including Canford and Stowe in 1923, and Bryanston in 1928. The numbers at existing schools also rose: by 1930 Durham School's roll was, at 265, two-and-a-half times its level of two decades previously. At the other end of the country, at Lancing in Sussex, numbers doubled from 195 to 385 over the same period.[43] 'The boarding-schools of the country, both of the first and the second rank, are at the present time enjoying a period of unexampled prosperity', wrote Cyril Norwood, headmaster of Harrow, in 1929. 'Applicants crowd to their doors, and parents sue humbly for the admission of their sons. They house themselves in buildings of increasing convenience and splendour, and lay out playing-fields with an elaboration which would astonish even our immediate forerunners.'[44]

Norwood's explanation for the 1920s prosperity of the boarding schools was that 'they "deliver the goods". They impart a character which is consistent, and can be trusted.'[45] This claim made for public schools' special character-building qualities may sound like mere empty cant to a sceptic, but the ideal counted for something among many parents, even parents patronizing the less grand schools whose children would have to make their own way in the world without any family connections. 'In these and future times, which are full of interesting and unknown possibilities it is my opinion that provided you can play the game and be fair, academic qualifications are not of prime importance', a businessman and old boy of Ellesmere College in Shropshire told the head when entering his son for the school in the 1940s. 'If Ellesmere can . . . guide him to stand on his own feet . . . and teach him to be true and to look after others first and himself last, I shall be satisfied.'[46] This was echoed by Duckworth, the public school master: 'A boy when he leaves a Public School at the age of eighteen will very likely imagine that Michelangelo was a musician, or that Handel wrote comic verse. He will be unable to tell you the difference between rates and taxes.' Yet Duckworth said he would still send his son to such a school: 'He can get in a Public School what he could not get anywhere else in any country . . . He will learn self-reliance, and will acquire certain other moral qualities, a sense of duty and fellowship, a knowledge of how to command and to obey.'[47]

The public school emphasis on character-building through the house system, governed by prefects, was increasingly picked up by

Catholic boarding schools, which had initially resisted it. Ampleforth switched to the house system in the 1920s. Father Paul, the headmaster who introduced it, argued in justification: 'Catholics are no longer regarded as pariahs by their fellow countrymen . . . they now find their way as a matter of course to the universities, into the army and the civil services, and are daily called upon to take up important positions and fill important posts.'[48]

Norwood also identified another, more modern and sinister reason for boarding schools' popularity: since the introduction of the free place system, 'there has been from the day-schools a steady transfer of a good type of boy, whose parents forty years ago would have been quite content to send him to the local school'. Norwood explained: 'When the day-schools were quite rightly opened to the "free-placer" and "ex-elementary" scholar, parents were quite determined that their own children should not "pick up an accent".' For a public school boy to pick up the 'wrong' accent would be disastrous: it would destroy the set of outer trappings which marked a boy as coming from the higher classes. Norwood noted, darkly: 'Less praiseworthy reasons for the success of these schools are that they confer a social badge, and they give easy rights to entry to circles which people do as a matter of fact very much desire to enter.'[49] Public schools sometimes vaunted their snob value, seeing it as a virtue. 'Even the flies at Stowe are snobs', J. F. Roxburgh, Stowe's first headmaster, used to explain to visitors, when justifying why he carried an elegant silver-handled fly swatter around the grounds of what must surely be the most beautiful public school in the country.[50]

The free place boys themselves sometimes had a hard time in the public schools, since pupils and even masters were often less than welcoming. They were, generally speaking, 'good pupils', the master of Dulwich College, George Smith, admitted in 1926. 'But when they come they have, again generally speaking, much to learn in the way of corporate spirit and they are unfamiliar with the idea of subordinating their individual interests (often selfish) to the interest of the school and the tradition of school discipline.' On balance, the number of free place boys 'is rather too large', he concluded.[51] Some school-masters retained a fine sense of the social distinctions even among the fee-paying boys. In *The Hill*, H. A. Vachell's best-selling 1905 novel about Harrow School, the boy-hero, John Verney, notices that the housemaster, toadying to a visiting duchess with a son in his house, introduces the boys in order of prestige: son of a guardsman first, son of a judge second, and son of an obscure parson third: 'These . . . are Egerton, Lovell, and-er-Duff.'[52]

Norwood's 'social badge' theory explains the bizarre and otherwise incomprehensible tale of Brendan Bracken. As a teenager Bracken was sent to a Jesuit boarding school in Ireland, though he soon ran away. Having made enough money as a teacher, he paid, as a vener-able nineteen-year-old, for a term's education at Sedbergh School in 1920, posing as a fifteen-year-old Australian orphan. This act marked the beginning of Bracken's reinvention. Using his new-found public school persona to win transient teaching posts at prep schools, and telling tall stories about friends in high places, he gradually climbed the social ladder, finishing up as Winston Churchill's minister for information and, in 1951, chairman of the board of governors of Sedbergh, the beneficiary of huge donations from Bracken.[53] 'There's a blessed equity in the English social system . . . that ensures the public school man against starvation', a roguish master at a godforsaken Welsh public school explains in Evelyn Waugh's *Decline and Fall* (1928) when describing his uncanny ability to find another job despite every disgrace. 'One goes through four or five years of perfect hell at an age when life is bound to be hell anyway, and after that the social system never lets one down.'[54] Public school may have been hellish for Bracken too – the cruel fagging regime led to the suicide of a boy at Sedbergh in 1930 – but people inside and outside the system believed that it conferred advantages.[55]

The lifetime achievements of boarding school old boys cannot be explained merely by scholastic achievement. An analysis of the number of 1961 entries in *Who's Who* put Eton at the top of the list among all schools.[56] After allowing for size, the next-highest placed were, in order, Winchester, Wellington, Rugby and Harrow – all public boarding schools rather than grammars. Compare this with Cambridge scholarships from 1929 to 1933, the rough point at which people at the peak of their careers in 1961 might have been expected to begin university. The list is very different, with Manchester Grammar second, King Edward's, Birmingham, seventh, and Bradford Grammar ninth.[57] The list measuring career success is dominated by the public schools; the list measuring academic success is more balanced.

When looking at the *Who's Who* figures, one must allow for the fact that hereditary lords were habitually included in the book, regardless of whether or not they had achieved anything. This boosts the number of Old Etonians, though not the old boy numbers for other schools to a great degree.

Even for ex-public school boys who did achieve something of note, this success can, of course, be explained partly by families rather than schools. Winston Churchill, scion of a powerful political dynasty, would probably have gone into politics had he never attended Harrow. Lord Grey of Fallodon, foreign secretary on the outbreak of the First World War, came from a similarly distinguished political family, whose ancestors had included a prime minister. Though intellectually brilliant at Winchester, he was extremely idle at Oxford, where he achieved a mere Third.[58] Nevertheless, he soon entered public service, as a junior civil servant, through the assistance of the squire of an estate neighbouring the Grey family's, Lord Northbrook, who happened to be the First Lord of the Admiralty. By the age of twenty-three Grey had made the most of his name and connections to become the youngest MP in the House. There are similar examples of political careers founded on family background for men of at least the generation that followed, and to a lesser degree the generation after that.

Churchill and Grey were, however, born into a remarkably narrow political class – narrower, even, than the client base of Harrow, Winchester and the other leading boarding schools. The question of what the schools did for the broad mass of less exalted classmates is more crucial.

Wykehamists born between 1880 and 1909 leave a reassuringly meritocratic message. Those with a First at university were the most likely to reach the elite levels of their profession afterwards – more so than those with lower degrees or with no degree at all. However, a striking figure also points to the power of the non-academic side of a Winchester education in generating success in later life. The senior commoner prefect, the leading boy among the non-scholars, was twice as likely as other commoners to reach elite positions, such as Queen's Counsel within the legal profession, or bishop or dean within the established Church – with a 65 per cent chance compared with 32 per cent for the rest. To an extent, this reflects the fact that boys who had already shown leadership potential were more likely to be chosen for an elite role. However, the boost in self-confidence from becoming a master over others at the impressionable age of eighteen, and the training for leadership which the role of the prefect brings, were valuable assets for these boy-men.[59]

When it came to the power of the vaunted Old School Tie, Attlee, too, was at the very least highly aware of men of promise from his old school. 'My Haileyburians are an able lot', he wrote to his brother Tom, who had been at the same school, before listing three who had been selected for various posts below cabinet level, including his new parliamentary private secretary Geoffrey de Freitas. Some MPs, at least, believed that a Haileybury education did confer an advantage. When Hugh Dalton, one of Attlee's cabinet colleagues, asked one of them about the general opinion on Attlee's 1947 ministerial reshuffle, he was told 'that it seemed that, to get on in this Government, you must have been at Eton, or Haileybury, or in the Guards, or in the Railway Clerks Association' – an interestingly eclectic mix of old boy networks.[60]

Old boy networks sometimes even existed on a semi-formal basis. In a section on 'Employment of Boys Leaving School', the Dulwich College Governors' Minutes for 1932 refer to the 'disappointingly small' number of notifications of vacancies, when compared with previous years, 'from O.A. [short for 'Old Alleynian', the term for a

Dulwich old boy] friends and others.'[61] Disappointing this may have
been, but the complaint shows the high degree of expectation placed
on former pupils to help with careers. The ties among contemporaries who had shared schooldays would have been stronger still,
often creating bonds between families, involving mutual career
favours, which would last more than one generation. Seven per cent
of married Wykehamists born between 1910 and 1919 lived in
wedded bliss – or, at least, as much bliss as the famously reticent tribe
of Wykehamists were pleased to show – with the sisters or daughters
of other Wykehamists. The proportion was, moreover, the highest in
at least ninety years, showing an even more rather than less close-
knit world.[62] Wykehamists even tended to name other Wykehamists
as co-respondents in their divorces: Wykehamist wives chose
Wykehamist bedfellows.[63]

A final career benefit of a public school education was the inculcation of a public school patina. The benefits of this rested partly on the
snobbery about accents which Norwood had criticized. The son of a
Lancashire businessman who had done well out of the Second World
War was sent to Ellesmere College soon after the conflict, but proved
unable to refine his working-class speech. After a term's merciless
ribbing by his classmates he left, but many more in the same situation
doubtless learnt the 'right' (in heavily inverted commas) way to
speak.[64] M'Turk, one of the heroes of Rudyard Kipling's 1899 public
school novel *Stalky and Co.*, was a linguistic chameleon: capable of
speaking in his native Irish accent outside the school, but then
switching to an English accent when back in the school grounds,
where his original way of speaking had been 'carefully kicked' out of
him by his friends.[65]

Leaving aside outright snobbery, ex-public schoolboys benefited
simply from the fact that other ex-public schoolboys in positions of
power understood them and felt at ease in their presence. Lord Grey
once wished aloud that all foreign statesmen could have gone to
public school, where they would have learned a common set of
ground rules. How much simpler it would have been to negotiate the

fate of nations with other Wykehamists, Harrovians and Etonians – the sort of chaps with whom Lord Grey mixed in London.[66]

The early twentieth century may well have been the time when the public schools reached their most dominant point, in terms of the proportion of people at the top of their fields educated at public schools. On the one hand, the virtual monopoly of the public schools in the prime minister's cabinet was diminishing, partly because of the arrival of powerful working-class politicians. On the other hand, it was becoming much more standard for the sons of industrialists and financiers, who were often the top industrialists and financiers of the future, to go to public school (though many, such as Robert Peel, had attended in previous ages). Largely for this reason, by 1939 61 per cent of the directors of clearing banks had been to one of twenty-six well-known public schools. This was also a time when public school-boys still predominated in the civil service and the Church – 46 per cent of under secretaries and above, and 57 per cent of assistant bishops and above in the Church of England, had been to one of these schools. William of Wykeham, who had straddled both these worlds, would have been pleased. One might think that even God was a public school old boy. In later decades, however, the public school dominance of these two fields would weaken, while public school dominance of business and finance would remain strong.[67] Public schoolboys became more prone to worship Mammon than God.

Norwood's 1929 comments about the 'unexampled prosperity' of the boarding schools proved wrong almost as soon as he uttered them. In 1929 the Great Depression crossed the Atlantic to reach Britain. The economy descended to its nadir in 1932, the year when the jobless rate peaked, but the depression did not really disappear until the outbreak of war in 1939 returned the country to full employment.

The effect of the depression on the economy was uneven, with the industrial north suffering particularly badly. It was a pattern of pain inflicted, in due course, on public schools. Numbers at St Bees, a boarding school in Northumberland, slumped from 310 in 1919 to a mere 120 in 1938, though after the possibility of closure was raised the school was saved largely by loyal old boys.[68] A slump in the local shipbuilding industry sent numbers at Sunderland High, a day school run by the Church Schools Company, plunging by 40 per cent in the final four years of peace, though it too survived.[69] Even St Peter's School, York, founded in 627 AD before Winchester College, parliament or England existed, came close to extinction: it is believed that the headmaster was fired for recommending its closure, though this particular incident is shrouded in mystery.[70]

Many schools in the wealthy public school heartlands of the south were hit too, though the suffering was less uniform than in the north. Norwood's Harrow was forced to close a boarding house, and a Harrow master wrote during the final months of peace in 1939 that 'the existence of Harrow is not assured'.[71] Dulwich High, a girls' school run by the Church Schools Company, put up its shutters in 1938. Tunbridge Wells High School, run by the Girls' Public Day School Trust, limped along until 1945, though talk of closing it had already begun in the 1930s.[72]

Depression was not the only cause of the public schools' travails. The sector was also suffering from a reversal of the 'winner takes all' concentration of income which had worked to its advantage in the nineteenth century. The share of national income held by the top 10 per cent – the main potential client base for public schools – had already dropped to half or just below by 1913; by 1949 it had fallen further, to one-third.[73] Another burden for Eton, Shrewsbury and other older schools endowed with rural land was the Tithe Act of 1936, which abolished the ecclesiastical tax they had collected.[74] Public schools were also damaged by demography: the number of live births had dropped sharply during the First World War, reaching its lowest point for children born in 1918 – the group which, had they gone to public school, would usually have started in 1931 or thereabouts. Aside from a brief surge in the aftermath of the war, the number of babies born – always above a million a year in the late Victorian and Edwardian eras – would drop below a million in 1922 and stay there permanently, forever shrinking the theoretical potential client base. Moreover, the time bomb set ticking by the depression-era dip in births was primed to hit the schools during the dark days of the Second World War, putting them under further pressure.[75]

Another source of financial pain was the existing debt which schools had incurred in improving facilities before the depression hit. This ranged from Harrow's purchase of local land and housing to University College School's move from its cramped central London quarters to a more spacious estate in Hampstead, chosen partly because of the lack of competitor schools in the area.[76] It is all too easy to criticize the schools for rashly spending too much before the depression hit; in fact they had little choice. The growth of state-funded education forced the public day schools to improve their own facilities, either to compete or simply to meet the standards required for them to receive state aid themselves, though in many cases a lack of funds kept some facilities astoundingly primitive. The two chemistry labs which had existed since University College School's pre-Victorian foundation remained essentially unchanged as late as the 1960s.[77] Meanwhile the boarding schools were under pressure from parents, whose concept of minimum acceptable standards for their offspring had risen considerably. While headmaster of Eton in the 1930s, Claude Elliott was confronted with a memo from twenty-five parents complaining about the condition of boarding houses. Responding to this and other gripes, including the discovery that in parts of the school there were more than ten boys to each bathroom or shower, Elliott spent money on improvements. Eton's finances remained secure in this period, making such amelioration more or less affordable; other schools, however, were less fortunate.[78]

For day schools, already straining under the weight of competition now that the state had decisively entered secondary education, the outbreak of the Second World War in September 1939 made a pretty parlous situation still worse – though the boarding schools, often in secluded rural areas less disrupted by the war, tended to fare better. The First World War had thrown into disorder the operations of some schools by prompting evacuations from coastal areas, but the overall effect had been fairly mild; such was not the case the second time around. The nation quickly descended into a state of officially sanctioned panic: seduced by the mistaken interwar orthodoxy that mass bombing campaigns waged on urban centres by the enemy would inevitably cause huge casualties, government planners had assumed 300,000 civilian deaths in the first fortnight of war.[79] Evacuations of inner-city public schools began. Many an urban school shared facilities with a rural one. The City of London School moved to Marlborough College – which was saved from peril by fierce lobbying from Old Marlburians, including R. A. Butler, president of the Board of Education. Because of the efforts of these friends in high places, the Ministry of Aircraft Production cancelled plans to commandeer the buildings.[80] It was a chaotic time, with public school children as well as grown-ups shifted from one location to another, in the name of safety and of victory. This generated all manner of anomalies and curiosities. A Roedean Old Boys Association still exists, peopled by naval officers planted there by the navy, which took over the school during the war. The officers were greatly amused by the sign by a bell push that said 'If you require a mistress, please ring' – a promise not, to the men's chagrin, backed up by reality.[81]

Whereas some schools not in officially sanctioned evacuation areas gained – the same number of children still had to be educated, after all – the mass migration of pupils immersed a large proportion of the schools in deep trouble. In 1941 the governors of Mill Hill debated the school's 'chance of survival after the war' under the heading 'Mending or Ending'; the governors of Liverpool College, faced with dwindling numbers and bomb damage, discussed whether the school should be closed down; the head of Westminster, evacuated to Hertfordshire, was found in his study, head in hands, saying to himself in despair, 'if we go below a hundred, we're finished'.[82] By the end of 1940 the Girls' Public Day School Trust was close to collapse; the council gave every member of staff provisional notice of termination, on the grounds that the overdraft had already reached the permitted limit.[83]

To the prospect of financial insolvency was added the accusation of moral bankruptcy. 'If the public schools are national assets because of their leadership training qualities, what are we to think of those qualities when we survey the mess into which their leadership has brought us?' fretted T. C. Worsley, the former Wellington master, in the year that John Vereker, the Harrovian war hero who had by this time succeeded to the peerage as Viscount Gort, narrowly escaped losing the British Expeditionary Force in France.[84] Worse was to come; in February 1942 an Old Rugbeian presided over the biggest capitulation in British history, when Lieutenant-General Percival surrendered Singapore. 'Probably the battle of Waterloo was won on the playing fields of Eton', Orwell had written the previous year, 'but the opening battles of all subsequent wars have been lost there'.[85] The barbs of Worsley, Orwell and others constituted a serious, potentially fatal, charge against the boys' public schools: the role of the schools in creating leaders capable of defending and governing empires had, in the speeches and memoirs of hundreds of headmasters up and down the land, been one of the chief justifications for their existence.

Public school boys presided over many of the war's greatest failures. Percival was not very ably assisted by Air Chief Marshal Robert Brooke-Popham, the Haileybury-educated Commander-in-Chief of British forces in the Far East. A few months after the fall of Singapore General Archibald Wavell, an Old Wykehamist, was relieved of command in North Africa after failing to defeat Field-Marshal Rommel.

However, many of the greatest heroes of the war were also public school men, including Field-Marshal Montgomery (St Paul's) and Air Chief Marshal Hugh Dowding (Winchester), who won the Battle of Britain. As well as providing some of the best senior military leaders, the public schools also educated some of the best theoreticians, such as Sir Basil Liddell-Hart (another Pauline) and John Fuller (Malvern), who held pioneering views on the use of the tank, a machine conceived and developed in the First World War largely by Sir Ernest Swinton (University College School, Rugby and Cheltenham). Moreover, the hard numbers show there was no clearing out of inadequate public school generals during the war. In 1939, 54 per cent of major-generals and above had attended one of twenty-six well-known public schools; by 1950, a few years after the war's end, this had fallen only to 49 per cent.[86] In wartime, in a reasonably well-run system, poor military leaders are gradually dispensed with in favour of better men. The numbers show that this process of discarding the incompetent did not really disfavour the public schools, however. It was largely public school men who lost the first half of the land war; it was largely public school men who won the second half.

Nevertheless, while Britain's top generals have, at least for the past two centuries, often taken the limelight, the service which played the most crucial role in defending the homeland and empire remained the less glamorous navy. The top ranks of the navy have, throughout history, been filled by a remarkably small number of public school boys compared with almost every other section of the British elite. Back in the seventeenth century, John King, a pupil at Charterhouse, had been press ganged after illegally going to the Lady Fair in Southwark, and put aboard a ship for Tangier. The school's master persuaded the monarch to act, and Samuel Pepys was dispatched to obtain his release. Since King's time, most public school boys have been scarcely less reluctant to agree to a life on the ocean wave.[87] In 1939 only 7 per cent of rear-admirals and above had attended one of the twenty-six public schools used in the research. The figure dropped even further, to 5 per cent, eleven years later.[88]

The public schools have played a role in the acquisition of empire, by men such as Clive of India (Merchant Taylors'). As civilians, they have often taken charge, with varying degrees of competence, of the governance of empire; nine of the twenty-two nineteenth-century viceroys of India were educated at Eton alone, with another three from Harrow.[89] However, the men who kept the convoys free in the Atlantic during the Second World War, starved Germany in the First, and kept the empire's maritime trading routes open for more than two centuries, were rarely public schoolboys. The low public-school contribution to the navy's higher ranks suggests that, despite the belated preoccupation among some headmasters of the newer public schools founded in the late nineteenth and early twentieth centuries with providing imperial servants, the sector's contribution to the preservation of empire has been exaggerated.[90]

The public schools' darkest hour had, in fact, already passed before the 1942 fall of Singapore, as the initial chaos caused by the outbreak of war dissipated. Schools which had been transferred for safety's sake to new areas started picking up more local pupils; some schools returned to their peacetime sites, as fears eased that Armageddon was set to rain from the skies. By 1941 numbers at the evacuated schools owned by the Church Schools Company were on the increase; by the end of the war all of its schools were full, and most had a waiting list, as pupils returned to their former homes.[91] Numbers at Girls' Public Day School Trust establishments began to rise from their trough in 1942–3.[92]

Just as their fortunes were recovering, another proposal was made to turn the rest of the public schools into the semi-state, semi-public schools which many of the day schools had become by taking the king's shilling and accepting government grants. In contrast to the proposal championed by Fletcher after the First World War, this time the move was made not by the public schools but by the state. The trigger was the attempt by R. A. Butler to create a post-war education system which matched growing wartime expectations among the populace, an attempt which was to culminate in the Education Act of 1944, considered in the following chapter. In 1942 Butler appointed Lord Fleming, a Scottish judge, to head a committee 'to consider means whereby the association between the Public Schools . . . and the general educational system of the country could be developed and extended'. In July 1944 the Fleming Report recommended that local education authorities form agreements with willing public schools to pay for places.

Had such agreements been made, the government would have gained considerable control over the schools involved: the report stipulated that the state would nominate one-third of the governing body. To give a flavour of the high and detailed degree of government control envisaged, one of the two proposed schemes recommended 'that reasonable variations shall be allowed in staffing ratios' by local education authorities, 'with due consideration for the character of the curriculum, the amount and variety of sixth form work, the necessity of a larger staff because of boarders, and other relevant factors'. The state would peruse virtually everything about the schools to ensure its money was spent as it saw fit.[93]

A few years earlier many of the public schools might have accepted this partial abdication of their independence. However, by this point most were not as desperate for a lifeline as previously. For its part, the wartime coalition government showed little interest in the proposals. Blame lies largely with Lord Fleming for his leisurely approach to the report, which was not published until two months after the Education Bill had received its third and final reading – making it difficult to slot the proposals for public schools into the new national framework set out by the eventual Act. As Butler was to put it in his memoirs, with a note of irritation, 'the first class carriage had been shunted into an immense siding'.[94] The Labour government which came to power in July 1945 showed no more interest in exercising control over the public schools than the coalition government had. The Labour Party as a whole would not adopt an actively aggressive anti-public school agenda until the 1960s.[95]

The public schools had survived a prolonged period of adversity in both peace and war. To ensure their survival, in the previous four decades they had made marked progress in broadening their curriculum and improving pupils' conditions. The majority had withstood the most severe economic depression in modern British history. Their old boys had won, or helped to win, the Battle of Britain and the Battle of Normandy, though not the Battle of the Atlantic. Most important of all, they had survived the onset of much greater competition from the state; indeed, they had emerged stronger from it. The following decades would prove the notion that what does not kill you only makes you stronger, and amplify it to an extreme degree.

CHAPTER SEVEN

Embracing the Examination Incubus
1945–1979

WINCHESTER College has an Elysian quality, doubtless appreciated by the classical masters who supplied its educational staple for most of its six-century history. It lies in the centre of a quiet market town whose relative importance in national events has declined a little more in almost every century since it lost its status as the nation's capital slightly over a millennium ago. As one strolls across its verdant lawns from one ancient building to another, one is imbued with a sense of confidence that this peaceful school is likely to survive for another few centuries yet, unharmed by whatever turbulent events are plunging the nation into turmoil outside its walls.

This was not, however, the view held by Canon Spencer Leeson, the college's headmaster, at the war's close in 1945. Most of the public schools had, it is true, recovered their pre-war numbers by the time the conflict had finished in September, if not a year or two previously. The public schools were also being assisted by the strong recovery of the domestic economy. Nevertheless, in his penultimate annual report to the warden and fellows, Canon Leeson was in melancholy mood. 'I imagine that we are at present living in a state of artificial prosperity, and that as the controls relax and the altered position of this country in the scheme of world economies becomes more apparent, our present comparative affluence will diminish', he feared.

'If and when that time comes, how long will it be possible for Winchester to keep herself accessible to that professional class from which she has drawn many of her strongest recruits in the past?' How many 'parents of the Winchester type' would be 'able or willing' to face the high cost of prep school, Winchester and university, 'when they can get State-aided education of a rapidly improving quality . . . for nothing or next to nothing?'[1]

Canon Leeson's thoughts were perceptive, but in the end proved to be unnecessarily apocalyptic. Over the following generation public schools would change more rapidly than ever before in response to state competition. New exams were embraced; facilities were transformed; the Classics were finally knocked off their pedestal, losing their status as the most important part of the public school curriculum. These changes produced a host of indirect, but almost equally important, changes. These included the decline of sport in the face of pressure for academic improvement, and the growth of co-education as the boys' schools responded to the loss of pupils to state education by expanding their market. Moreover, on top of the revolutionary effect on the public schools of increasing state competition, changes in society at large, including a declining respect for pillars of society such as the Church and the military, created a powerful impetus for change. It was a busy time for public school head teachers.

Canon Leeson's fears derived from the 1944 Education Act. This made it compulsory for local councils to offer secondary education free to everyone, a measure which boosted the state secondary school population from 1.1 million in 1944 to 2.0 million only eleven years later. Spending on state secondary education rose accordingly – by 80 per cent in real terms over the period.[2] This expansion increased the number of pupils at grammar schools, which, in the cosmology set out by the Act, were given the role of educating the more able children, while secondary modern and secondary technical schools took the less academically talented. In scholastic terms, at the very top of the state system were the 'direct grant' grammars. These were 180 or so schools which received a grant directly from central government rather than the local authority, in return for providing up to a quarter of places free of charge to children from state elementary schools, plus at least another quarter free to local authorities as long as the local authorities paid the fees. In the late 1960s and early 1970s education spending surged again, pushing up the share of the economy devoted to state and state-sponsored education from 4.6 per cent of gross domestic product in 1966 to a peak of 6.3 per cent in 1975–6.[3]

The impact on Winchester came not just from the prospect that parents could opt for one of the increasing number of places at a nearby grammar school. The growth in the number of grammar school children also created more competition for university places. Moreover, in the more generous post-war system of government funding for students, these places came within reach of a much greater number of bright grammar school boys and girls from humble backgrounds. Greater competition for university generated, in turn, a new qualification designed to mark individual students as fit for a university education: the A level, born in 1951.

Many public schools took a relaxed attitude towards the A level during its first decade or so – relaxed to the point of complacency. Instead, public schools continued to focus on the entrance scholarship exams of the various Oxbridge colleges, which catered to the minority of boys considered intellectually equal to the challenge. Etonians did not sit A levels until 1958.[4] Some schools were actively hostile towards them. ' "A level" is the enemy of scholarship', wrote the warden of Radley College in the first years of the new qualification. It was a veritable 'examination incubus'.[5]

By the 1960s, however, the public schools' attitude towards both A and O levels had begun to change under the twin pressures of parents and universities. O levels, also introduced in 1951, were typically taken at the age of sixteen. Parents were increasingly worried about their sons' futures in the more competitive post-war world, where the jostling for higher education places and good jobs was becoming tougher, even for well-connected Etonians. In 1960 a group of Eton parents, including such establishment figures as an air commodore, a member of the high aristocracy and a knight, put their names to a letter to the provost noting that because of 'a radical change of outlook' it was now 'difficult, and in some cases impossible', to get into a university, 'enter certain professions' or obtain a job with 'leading industrial and commercial firms' unless boys left school with two or three A levels. The letter then listed a series of complaints, including the high rate of failed A levels and 'the quality of some of the masters', which 'might be improved'.[6] A 1963 paper by Westminster School's Timetable Committee summed up the challenge. 'In the past we have been fortunate at Oxbridge; but we must expect greater difficulty in placing boys there in the future, and we must consider more carefully the requirements of other Universities', it warned. 'We must accept that good "A" Level results (possibly in three subjects) . . . are essential.'[7]

For some of those public schools, even those with a strong record in training their brightest to pass Oxbridge scholarship exams, A level results were initially remarkably poor. The Westminster paper just cited calculated a failure rate for different A level subjects of between 19 and 28 per cent. Average marks in English, biology, geography and even Greek, a staple Westminster subject for many centuries, were below the national average. History and Latin results fluctuated around the average, it found. 'Are we entitled to be pleased with "O" and "A" level results, particularly if we remember that our entrance examination is considered to demand a high standard?' the committee asked rhetorically. Lest the school forget its duty in this essential task of boosting results in these national exams, the committee noted that parents 'take a much keener interest in educational problems than their predecessors. They want us to be educational experts, they want results.'[8]

At Bloxham School Stanley Thompson, head from 1952, saw that his school only had a long-term future if it could guide substantial numbers of boys through A levels and on to university. Scions of farmers filled up much of the school, but many finished their education at sixteen, leaving only a small number of boys even attempting to get into university. Thompson also considered the teaching to be poor, particularly in science. It was not helped by the facilities: one master recalled having to wear gum boots in the science labs, because the floor was awash after rain. On becoming head, Thompson's first action had been to have a sign removed from the local village which read 'school slowly round the bend' – an unfortunate choice of words not becoming to the dignity of the institution. It must have seemed, at times, apposite to have kept it; after becoming head, Thompson was rejected from membership of the Headmasters' Conference of leading public school heads on the grounds of Bloxham School's small number of sixth formers, poor exam results and low number of university students. (The Headmasters' Conference, nowadays the Headmasters' and Headmistresses' Conference, or more commonly just HMC, represented the heads of the biggest and, for the most part, more academically successful boys' schools, including the leading grammars as well the public schools.) 'What has happened?' an irate Old Bloxhamist wrote to ask. 'If Bloxham is not a Public School, what exactly has it become?' Attempts to improve the academic tone of the school by discouraging the scholastically unambitious farmers' sons alienated the local community for many years, but Thompson felt he had no choice, telling an Old Bloxhamite parent, 'what I cannot accept is that a boy should be sent here for a short period, just to get snob value from the fact of having been to a Public School.'[9]

This sentiment was echoed by John Vallins, a housemaster at Cranleigh School in Surrey, a boys' school until it introduced co-education in the 1970s: 'Through the sixties, acceptance became less fashionable, and the future of the Public Schools became a matter for speculation. No longer was there a settled class of conservative people, automatically and unquestioningly packing off their sons for three months at a stretch and confidently choosing schools on the basis of family tradition or a big name.' Instead, 'it became necessary for public schools to strive to be more competitive, academically and otherwise, to look at their teaching methods.'[10]

The pressure on public schools to improve academic standards was heightened by a much more challenging approach to public schools from the media, which in a more irreverent age no longer assumed that public schools were by their very nature a good investment for parents. In a forerunner to the league tables introduced in the 1990s, in 1964 *The Times* published a survey by a sociologist of seventy-five public schools – mainly boys' boarding schools – which included a 'top ten' and 'bottom ten'. Turning next to the principle of 'value for money', the survey found that Eton, Harrow and Charterhouse, three of the oldest and hitherto highest-status public schools in the country, fell into the unenviable 'high fees low A levels' category.[11]

The public schools' anguish about O and A levels was largely a manifestation of its growing concern about the prospects of the totemic 'average child'. In the pre-war era he or she would have been highly unlikely to go to university. After the war he or she was progressively more likely to do so, though she was still much less likely to do so than him. However, the growing importance of a degree in the labour market, which both fuelled and was fuelled by a quadrupling in university student numbers between 1945 and 1985, forced schools to provide a high standard of academic education to a much larger group than previously.[12] The Westminster paper is peppered with references to children in the academic middle, newly elevated to a vital role. Good A level grades were 'essential' in its bid 'to help the average boy', who was surprisingly ill-served in a school whose record of success for the top boys hoping for Oxbridge scholarships was excellent.

Donald Crichton-Miller, head of Fettes from 1945, was earlier than most in realizing the need to cater to the average child, although he did not put it so politely. In his Founder's Day speech a year after taking office, Crichton-Miller pledged to give 'special attention to the mediocre people'.[13] It was not an inspiring vow, when compared with the Statue of Liberty's promise of assistance to 'your huddled masses yearning to breathe free'. Nevertheless, the view that one must do more to help the average child was to prove vitally important as Britain entered the era of mass university education. Crichton-Miller abandoned the practice – common at Fettes and other public schools – where

the headmaster taught only the elite classical sixth, in favour of minis-
tering to the lower forms for one period a week of history or letter
writing. That, and his habit of randomly choosing a batch of exercise
books from a different class each week for examination, was a good way
of keeping an eye on the academic standards of the broad mass of Fettes
pupils.[14]

Despite the realization among many masters that the average boy
had to do better academically, conservatives in the common room and
on governing bodies put up staunch resistance. At Eton, one of the
fellows (governors), the politician Lord John Hope, displayed ostrich-
like tendencies by noting in response to the previously mentioned
1960 letter, 'I should have thought industry badly wanted the sort of
man that Eton produces, if he is all right, whether he gets two A Level
subjects (let alone three) or not.' Hope added: 'I believe that the Navy
is already regretting its earlier insistence on academic standards to the
exclusion of character. It will be a tragedy if industry is going to make
the same mistake.'[15] Recalling his arrival to take up the headship of
Westminster in 1970, John Rae wrote: 'When I came here, the future
of the majority of boys was sacrificed to the pursuit of Oxbridge scholarships for the chosen few.' As for the rest, 'boys who could easily have
got good A-Levels ended up having to go to a crammer to take the
exam again. I am amazed parents did not complain.'[16]

The arrival of A levels and O levels had another important effect
in addition to ending the invisibility of the average boy at public
schools; it also dealt one of the final blows to the primacy of
Classics – eventually.

Even as late as the 1950s, the cleverest boys entering University
College School were leant on heavily by the head to concentrate on
the Classics – and those who did so did not study history or geography at all. In 1954 school inspectors visiting the school found that
some sixth-formers would not have been taught either of these
subjects ever since entering its junior branch before the age of ten.
The inspectors consequently deemed it 'hardly surprising' that they
'sometimes show themselves strangely deficient in what might well

be regarded as basic general knowledge of an historical or geograph-
ical nature'.[17]

However, getting a good brace of A levels and O levels, an important desideratum in the post-war world of much greater competition
from state-educated pupils, demanded a much wider range of knowledge than a heavily Classics-based curriculum. These qualifications
also offered pupils a choice between papers in different subjects, all of
them of roughly equal esteem among universities and employers. As a
result, the brightest boys could no longer be directed by the school to
concentrate on the Classics; the end had come for the elite institution
of the Classical Sixth. The consequent fall from grace was sudden and
spectacular. At Shrewsbury, where Classics had dominated more
perhaps than at any other school, by the end of the 1970s only seven
boys were sitting Latin A level – one-eighth the number taking mathematics, and half the number taking the new-fangled subject of business studies.[18] Samuel Butler must have turned in his grave. By 1975
the proportion of A level students taking only science or maths A level
at the 'efficient independent schools' – those deemed by government
inspectors to meet certain standards of 'efficiency', such as adequate
facilities for science and other activities – was, at 27.2 per cent, very
nearly the national average, and several public schools were among
the leaders in scientific education.[19] By the late 1950s one of them,
Oundle School, had scored a coup by becoming one of the first schools
to design a computer, prompting visits from more than a hundred
inquisitive institutions and two curious education secretaries, Mark
Carlisle and Keith Joseph.[20]

The primacy of Classics in the public schools had, in fact, been
under pressure for a long time, because of its dwindling status in the
world outside. Earlier in the century, Classics had already lost its
status as part of the shared cultural experience of Britain's more vari-
egated political elite. When Sir John Anderson, a member of
Churchill's wartime cabinet, stood on the floor of the Commons and
began a ponderous reference with 'as Horace has it, "if you drive out
nature . . .", the rest of the tag was drowned out by the ribald shouts

of Labour MPs, 'good old 'orace!'[21] By the end of the 1970s the Classics had lost its special place in the hearts and brains even of most public school parents and public school heads. 'The head of Classics [at Westminster] wants my help to ensure that enough scholars choose to do Latin and Greek at A-Level', John Rae confided to his diary in 1977. 'Will I have a word with this and that young scholar or with the parents? No, I will not.'[22]

The new emphasis on academic success for all boys, not just the brightest, was largely responsible for the breaking of the stranglehold of sport on the schools. With this stranglehold slackened, the inordinate power held by the Bloods – the boys who excelled at sport and were in the top teams such as the rugby First XV – also disappeared.

In many boarding schools the Bloods had filled many of the senior prefect posts, including the role of head of house. *The Hothouse Society*, Royston Lambert and Spencer Millham's 1974 book on boarding schools based on interviews over the preceding decade, contains a piece of advice from a head of house to his successor. The missive betrays – unless the boy was positively delusional – a high degree of power over the housemaster, a man who 'has many new and pretty odd ideas which, no doubt, he will try and spring on you. If you don't like them, don't have them. Just be politely firm and he will gently fade away.' The prefect goes on to warn, with a large dose of condescension, 'he does like to be kept in touch with the house and unless you do something about it, he will do this by wandering around it at all hours. It is worth half an hour now and then just to keep him informed and thus curtail his wanderings.'[23] At many schools of the 1950s, 1960s and even 1970s, it was not the done thing for masters to amble about the house.

A head of house was often appointed to this role because he was a member of the rugby First XV or other important team. Recalling his time at a public school in the 1930s, Oliver van Oss, headmaster of Charterhouse, spoke in 1969 of 'the reign of the "Bloods", with their special clothes and their privileges and their effortless superiority, before whom not only boys but masters cringed sycophantically.'[24]

At the other end of the power spectrum lay the younger boys, who acted as fags to the older, a form of servitude which tended to corrupt those who imposed it. Understanding the niceties of this hierarchy was essential for any new boy. In 1937 Guy Kendall, recently retired headmaster of University College School and a former Charterhouse master, imagined a boy already at school writing an advice-filled missive to a younger boy about to start: 'The great thing to remember is to leave the top button of your jacket unbuttoned whether the rest is done up or not', he counselled. 'To button that up is the privilege of a "beefer". And above all don't have the corners square. They must be round until you have got a colour or get into the Sixth.'[25] Alec Waugh describes both the power, and the comic potential that arises so often from the pompous nature of the powerful, in *The Loom of Youth*, a novel based on his time at Sherborne School in the 1910s. In the tuck shop, 'the real blood is easily recognised. He strolls in as if he had taken a mortgage on the place, swaggers into the inner room, puts down his books on the top table in the right-hand corner – only the bloods sit here – and demands a cup of tea and a macaroon.' On his departure, 'when he gets up he knocks over at least one chair.'[26]

The power of the Bloods – and at the same time the fragility of that power – is revealed in an anecdote by the writer Robert Graves, remembering his time as a Charterhouse pupil when Guy Kendall taught there (Kendall was one of the few masters he liked). Their authority had become institutionalized to the point where the rest of the school accepted their right to enter chapel on Sunday just before the masters but after all the other pupils. One Sunday three boys from the scholars' house dared to break this unwritten rule of the Carthusian constitution by entering after the Bloods, 'magnificent in light-grey flannel trousers, slit jackets, butterfly collars', and even that final ornate accessory to a Blood's garb, a pink carnation in their lapels. Graves claimed that the Bloods' prestige was permanently ruined.[27]

However, even by the time *The Hothouse Society* was published, government by the Bloods was on its way out. 'Team games and other organized activities have lost much of their mystique, the hierarchical system of government is no longer taken for granted', wrote the former head of Abingdon School in 1972. 'It may seem more important to a boy to get good "A" Levels than to be Head of House or row at Henley – and who is to say that it is wrong?'[28] The reign of the Bloods was ended 'not by any revolt of the human spirit, but by the advent of A-levels', claimed van Oss, since it was revealed that many a sporting idol among the younger boys had 'a head of clay'.[29] 'The athlete today neither expects nor receives the adoration of the small boy', claimed J. M. Peterson, ex-headmaster of Shrewsbury, in 1965. 'The main reason for this change is undoubtedly the higher academic standard required by the G.C.E. [A levels and O levels] and the consequent academic rat race for a place at the University.'[30]

The diminishing importance of team sports was part of a broader decline in what might be termed The Compulsory Life. Stowe School 'had as many rules and regulations as the army – many of them ... completely anachronistic and pointless', recalls Richard Branson, the entrepreneur, of his 1960s education. These included the Combined Cadet Force, or CCF (formerly the Officer Training Corps), 'in which boys dressed up as soldiers and paraded around with antiquated rifles', and compulsory attendance at school chapel on Sunday. Branson and his best friend 'were particularly incensed by the rule that anyone who wasn't playing games had to go and watch the school team when they were playing anther school'.[31] In 1954 a conscientious objector was expelled from the City of London School for refusing to stay in the CCF – or was he? Displaying exceptionally dextrous casuistry, the headmaster argued that he had not actually been expelled, telling *The Times*, 'the youth had the option of remaining in the cadet corps or leaving the school. He chose to leave.'[32] Four years earlier Peterson had censored a letter to the Shrewsbury school magazine which dared to suggest that the Force be made voluntary.[33]

In the next few decades, however, The Compulsory Life broke down, under pressure from the increasing diversity of the public schools' clientele and of society in general. At the City of London School, compulsory CCF ended in 1970, sixteen years after the conscientious objector was forced out of the school.[34] At Shrewsbury, seventeen years after Peterson had censored the letter about the CCF, his successor, A. R. D. Wright, implemented its recommendation.[35] Reverence for the military also declined. By 1996 Bloxham, a school which lost a large number of pupils on Flanders fields, was putting on a large-scale production of *Oh, What a Lovely War!*, a satire on the conflict.[36]

There were changes, too, in the religious aspect of The Compulsory Life. The founding committees of the public schools of the nineteenth century had been populated largely by clergymen, and the heads had often been ordained. However, by the late twentieth century Christian belief had declined among masters as well as pupils. The inevitable, though delayed, consequence of a declining adherence to Christianity was a partial, though not total, dismantling of the system of compulsion. At Shrewsbury compulsory daily attendance at chapel ended in the 1960s.[37] Even at Stonyhurst, a school with an extremely strong Catholic tradition, compulsory daily mass before breakfast had gone by the early 1970s.[38] By the end of the 1970s most boys enjoyed much greater freedom of choice: their school lives were dictated considerably more by their individual personal tastes and moral values.

The decline of the seemingly endless number of rugby and cricket fixtures within the school dealt a blow to the house system which had been so crucial to public school life. Fervent loyalty to the house also seemed anachronistic in an age when teenagers were questioning established creeds and loyalties in their lives in general. The school magazines of the City of London School record the growing sense of apathy. 'Unfortunately the House drops off in the Senior forms; at the moment it is considered "unfashionable",' lamented one pupil in the 1972 House Notes that detailed the achievements of the year. 'I have no doubt that in a few years the House system will collapse because of this feeling.'[39] The house system never quite collapsed, but it was hard for even moderately politically aware boys in the centre of the nation's capital to care too much about who had won the house rugby in a year when the government had declared a state of emergency and unemployment had risen above a million.

Fagging also appeared anachronistic in an age when the whole concept of a strict hierarchy was falling out of favour in the affairs of nations as much as in the affairs of schools. 'To learn to obey as a fag is part of the routine that is the essence of the English public school system', declared a Harrow master in 1928. 'Those who hope to rule must first learn to obey'. He concluded: 'Who shall say it is not that which has so largely helped to make England the most successful colonising nation, and the just ruler of the backward races of the world?'[40] By the end of the 1970s the empire had gone, and no one talked – openly, at least – about backward races. The 1960s ideal that the world should be governed by peace and love might have seemed hopelessly naïve at the time, but it has, in truth, left its mark on most people's views of how life should be organized. It made its mark on the public schools too.

Despite the new-found confidence of pupils in questioning various public school institutions such as fagging, the house system and chapel, public schools generally remained free from serious rebellions during the 1960s and 1970s, in contrast to the social unrest at several universities. At the end of Lindsay Anderson's 1968 film *If. . . .*, set in a boys' boarding school, Malcolm McDowell, machine-gun in hand, leads an armed insurrection.* The real public schoolboys of the era were considerably more muted in their criticisms. The nearest thing to a school-wide rebellion which the boys of Radley College could manage, in the year after *If. . . .* was released, was to try to turn the end-of-term celebration into a pop festival. Most of the posters were

---

* By chance, Malcolm McDowell enjoys a curiously important role in the cinematic expostulation of public school history. As well as the public school rebel in *If. . .*, he plays the Eton-prefect-turned-Great-War-fighter-pilot-hero in *Aces High* (1976), and the public school bully Flashman in *Royal Flash* (1975). One wonders whether McDowell is aware of this key role.

found and taken down, and the few revellers who did turn up were given a long tour of the school. Surely the worst gig in history, man . . .'[41]

The schools' heads deserve credit for the lack of dangerous unrest at the schools during the 1960s and 1970s – in sharp contrast to the age of revolution of the late eighteenth and early nineteenth centuries. They responded astutely by giving in over practices that had become so divorced from wider society that they could no longer be defended, including compulsory CCF and daily chapel, and by adopting a flexible approach to youthful experimentation while drawing a clear line beyond which pupils could not go. At Fettes, Eric Anderson, a future headmaster of Eton and avid fan of Sir Walter Scott, decreed that any boy in his house with hair longer than the bust of Scott in his hall must have his hair cut – a fairly liberal policy, since Sir Walter was by no means a short-back-and-sides man. His most famous charge, Tony Blair, fell foul of this rule and was frog-marched into a nearby barber's by Ian McIntosh, the headmaster at the time, after a chance encounter in the street.[42]

By increasing spending on education, the state increased pressure on public schools to do better for the bulk of their pupils; state spending also put pressure on the public schools to improve their facilities. This had fatal consequences.

Presiding over a 1956 meeting of the Independent Schools Association, Sir Harold Webber, MP, warned that owing to the 'quite fantastic' level of facilities at local state schools – with which independent schools must keep up – the time might come when independent schools would 'go down, one after the other'.[43] In the ten years after the Second World War a thousand new laboratories were built in state schools.[44] In addition to this indirect pressure, there was considerable direct pressure. From 1957 all public schools were forced to register with the government, which sent inspectors to make sure they were meeting minimum standards for the quality of facilities.

Many schools did indeed go down, as Sir Harold had predicted. Many more would have gone down without the aid of corporate

Britain, which was anxious for the public schools to produce more scientists: from 1957 more than a hundred companies provided millions of pounds to public schools to build science labs through the Industrial Fund for the Advancement of the Teaching of Science in Schools.[45] In addition to the financial pressure to upgrade facilities, public schools also needed to keep up with the rising salaries of state school teachers, manifested most spectacularly after the Houghton Committee on teachers' pay, which in 1974 prescribed a 30 per cent rise that had to be matched by the public schools in order to keep staff. In a drastic response, the headmaster of Fettes cancelled Founder's Day to economize.[46]

A steady drip-drip of declining rolls and eventual closures of some of the lesser-known schools from the 1950s to the 1970s brought the total number of public school children in England and Wales down from 510,000 in 1955 to a low of 403,000 in 1978 – a fall from 6.7 to 4.5 per cent of the school population.[47]† The headmistress of St Mary's Convent School in Lowestoft, which shut in 1972, cited an all-too-familiar reason: 'We feel, with modern trends in education demanding so much, that in future we should not be able to provide the facilities necessary to compare with those in state schools.'[48] St Mary's was one among many schools to close during the financial crisis of the early 1970s – a time when inflation raced upwards, forcing schools to raise fees every term. Perhaps the highest-profile closure was Sebright, a Worcestershire school qualifying for the elite HMC,

---

† Public school numbers quoted in this and the next chapter refer to pupils of all ages, including those of prep school age. They include the many pupils at prep schools attached to public schools, an increasingly common phenomenon in the twentieth century. They also include those at prep schools which are not part of public schools in the strict sense of the word, namely, schools for older children aiming for university entrance. This reflects the impossibility of separating the different groups from each other. The pupil number trends for older children alone since the mid-twentieth century, however, show a very similar picture to that for all ages combined.

which shut its doors in 1970.[49] On the one hand, public school parents' wages tended to rise with or above inflation. Moreover, inflation greatly reduced the real value of debts incurred by public schools in building facilities. On the other hand, high inflation tends to damage institutions with weak bargaining power, which find themselves unable to raise charges in line with high price rises without losing customers; this was an apt description of many of the less prestigious public schools. The combination of high inflation and low economic growth also wiped millions of pounds off the assets of public school parents, by hitting the stock market. All in all, the combination of increased competition from the state and economic turbulence made it hard for many schools to hold on to their customers.

One way for a business to make up for the loss of customers is to poach new ones from rivals. It was a tactic at which the more famous boys' public schools proved adept. A landmark event was Marlborough College's decision to admit fifteen girls into the sixth form in 1968. It was the first of the leading conventional schools to do so, though some self-styled 'progressive' schools, as well as Quaker institutions, had already welcomed girls for decades. These included Bedales, the secular Hampshire school patronized by the Huxleys, Trevelyans, Darwins, Stracheys and other great liberal intellectual dynasties. It had admitted girls since 1898, though the founder and first head, John Badley, insisted on addressing every pupil as 'Man' regardless of sex, as if he were still at his alma mater, Rugby.[50]

Other schools, including Wellington College, Charterhouse and St Edmund's, soon followed Marlborough's example. By the mid-1980s two-thirds of boys' public schools had female pupils, in some cases of all ages rather than just sixth-formers. Peter Watkinson, the headmaster of Rydal School (now Rydal Penrhos School) in Wales, freely admitted in the 1980s that it had been 'a survival tactic' for boys' schools: 'It has enabled a large number of boys' schools to ride in style the rough waves of unprecedented inflation and political hostility.'[51] It even enabled some schools to expand spectacularly –

allowing Bryanston, for example, to grow from an all-male roll of 420 to a co-ed roll of 600.[52]

The arrival of co-education caused perhaps the most bitter battle between public schools that has ever been seen. The headmaster of Merchant Taylors', a boys' school which refused to admit girls, blamed the policy for 'decapitating our sister schools'.[53] 'Decapitation' was a well-chosen word. The boys' schools tended to take the brightest among the older girls, the academic apex of the school, which provided a role model for the less bright and the younger to emulate. 'If the top of the school cannot keep up its standard, the standard throughout the school and consequently the calibre of teachers who can be recruited will fall', complained the (female) chairman of the Association of Governing Bodies of Girls' Public Schools in 1975. 'Therefore it is not too strong to say that the continuation of increase in the action of HMC schools in taking in sixth form girls is going to destroy both in quality and numbers the first-class girls' schools which have been doing such a great job for girls' education.'[54] The trend set in train a long period – still continuing – of girls' school closures. Even now girls' schools still account for a disproportionately large share of public school shutdowns.

The girls' schools had left themselves open to desertion by not being good enough. Facilities were often poor; Fettes actually took on its first girls in 1969 at the request of a local girls' school, Lansdowne House, since three pupils wanted to take science A levels, which Lansdowne House did not offer.[55] That budding scientists should find Fettes more suitable than their own school is not a good reflection on the latter, given Fettes's hitherto amateurish record in the field. Academic results were not always the focal point of the girls' schools, which responded in part to the priorities set by the more traditional parents. 'I just want her to be as enchanting as my wife and just as useful', said a father putting his daughter down for Heathfield School, Ascot, in the 1960s.[56] 'The curriculum is planned to enable girls to qualify for a career, and at the same time to stimulate in them interests which will enable them to live a full and useful life at home', asserted Benenden School when setting out its stall rather ambivalently in the Girls' School Year Book as late as 1970. 'Time given to music, drawing and handwork', it added. The quality of teaching at her convent school in the early 1980s was 'pretty patchy', remembers Emma Taylor, current headmistress of Christ College, Brecon. 'If you were good at academic things, well bully for you, but it wasn't absolutely essential.'[57] A 1978 survey of Marlborough girls found that 79 per cent felt teaching at Marlborough was better than at their former school.[58]

The lack of academic focus is reflected in the hard statistics of university entrance. In 1961 only 9 per cent of girls at 'efficient' independent schools, which included the bulk of the more academic schools, went to university. This was one-third of the proportion for boys at independents, and only half of the 18 per cent for girls at direct grant grammars. Nine years later, the proportion of girls going to university from efficient independents had risen only to 11 per cent, while the proportion of direct grant girls had jumped to 27 per cent.[59]

The arrival of girls in the boys' public schools proceeded fairly smoothly, despite some teething troubles. Louise Denison, one of the first five girls to arrive at St Peter's School, York, in 1976, recounted that on singing her first hymn in chapel, she was shocked to find her voice soaring far above those of the boys and men before she adjusted her pitch to a lower register. She also recalled 'members of staff who were concerned that we might cry if we were told off and were unsure how they would cope if this happened'.[60] After these initial shocks to the system, however, it was revealed that over the course of time girls improved boys' schools. They boosted academic results, since the boys' schools tended to pick the academically most distinguished girls. They also changed the culture of the boys' schools for ever, particularly the boarding schools: they diluted the rather juvenile nature of life – the cheering when a boy dropped a tray in the lunch queue, and the playing of pranks that could easily pass from jollity to cruelty – and they banished from boys' bosoms the sense of half-suppressed homosexuality.

In his first term at Sherborne in the 1920s, a generation or two before the arrival of girls at the boarding schools, John Le Mesurier, the actor, had been forced, along with other novitiates, to perform a recitation or song before the entire house by way of ritual humiliation. Le Mesurier skilfully recited by heart a monologue by the British comic actor Jack Hulbert. Far from being jeered or pelted with missiles, he found that 'my efforts were greeted with near total silence. Nobody shouted, nobody threw anything. Two boys started clapping but they were quickly reprimanded by the house master, who ordered the next victim forward.' It is hard to see a housemaster getting away with anything approaching such behaviour at a co-educational boarding school.[61] E. M. George, who has experienced Durham School as a co-ed institution in his role as its current headmaster, and as a single-sex school when a schoolboy in the 1970s, believes that 'girls coming in has fundamentally changed schools for the better. Suddenly the less macho subjects – art, music, drama – are considered to be really cool.'[62]

' "Oh no!" One senior would clutch another as they caught sight of a comely new boy, "I'm in love. Save me from myself"', recalled the humorist Stephen Fry of his time at the boys' school Uppingham in the 1970s.[63] By this time, however, most Marlborough boys would have been more likely to be taking a lecherous interest in the new girls. Quoting one of his male pupils, John Dancy, the headmaster who introduced girls to Marlborough, found that 'homosexual talk' among the boys virtually died out as soon as the girls came.[64]

The civilizing influence of girls was an important motive for co-education for some schools. In the discussion that led to the admittance of girls at St George's College, Weybridge, a Catholic school in Surrey, it was suggested that the presence of girls would encourage 'social manners and graces.'[65] If by this the college's advocates of co-education meant the end of predatory homosexuality and an approach to culture which sometimes made Hermann Goering seem like a fan of the fine arts in comparison, they were proved right.

The growth of co-education is one facet of a general feminization of the public schools. Even the remaining all-boys' schools have made much more of an effort to consider their pupils' feelings and emotional problems. How could they not when their pupils' parents have seen such advances in pastoral care for their daughters? Stamford School in Lincolnshire currently hosts what the head, William Phelan, describes as 'sex and drugs and sausage rolls evenings', at which parents discuss with each other what their sons might be up to, after hearing talks from visiting speakers on alcohol problems, internet safety, and so on.[66]

This greater openness about sensitive issues is the best way of combating the sad predilection for a tiny minority of public school teachers to abuse their pupils. Public schools have not eradicated the issue of sexual abuse, though it is almost certainly less prevalent than a century ago when there were many fewer checks and balances on masters and pupils. In 2014 images of pupils from Southbank International School in London were found on the computer of William Vahey, a convicted paedophile who had taught there.[67] In May 2014 the BBC reported that sexual abuse allegations relating to St Paul's School were being investigated by the Metropolitan Police.[68] As allegations and revelations of child abuse across many different kinds of institutions continued to shock the nation in 2014, the NSPCC child protection charity said boarding schools and other public institutions where children stayed should have a mandatory duty to report abuse.[69] This may reduce abuse still further. In 2005 the *Guardian* published a story citing claims by the police that they had discovered clear evidence that Cardinal Basil Hume, the deceased head of the Catholic Church in England and Wales, had become aware of the sexual abuse of pupils at Ampleforth College, where he was abbot, as early as 1975, but chose not to contact the police or social services. The *Guardian* added that police believed the subsequent two decades of assaults on pupils at Ampleforth and its prep school might have been avoided if Cardinal Hume had alerted outside authorities.[70]

Life in the decades after the Second World War was tough for the public schools. However, when the Conservatives were in power, public school heads could console themselves with the thought that although economic and social conditions appeared to conspire against them, at least no government minister wished them any ill will. During many of the periods of Labour rule, however, no such consolation was possible. Even when the state wished the public schools no harm, life was hard enough. When the state did harbour malicious thoughts towards the public schools, life threatened to get very nasty indeed.

Labour politicians and thinkers had long criticized the public schools on two main grounds: that the method by which public school children gained access to senior roles within government and business was unfair, and that the education of a group of boys mainly within their own social caste reinforced the class divisions that already existed in society. Anthony Crosland, Labour politician, Wykehamist and education secretary from 1965 to 1967, saw the public schools as 'the strongest remaining bastion of class privilege'.[71] Critics of the schools complained that even when working-class children went to public school, through scholarships or government-funded free places, they were often oppressed, and forced to join a new social class rather than keep to their old one. At Mill Hill School, one boy supported by a local government grant was sanctioned for 'speaking Cockney, after warning'.[72] It is, however, striking that all the talk of Labour politicians resulted in only one implemented policy to increase the state's control over education. It is ironic that this policy more or less had the opposite effect to its original intention.

In 1964 a Labour government finally acted on the party's hostility to public schools, by appointing a Public Schools Commission and instructing it to seek ways to integrate the public schools into the state system. The initial recommendation, made in 1968, was ignored by the government for the very understandable reason that, if implemented, it would have cost the government a huge amount of money. The commission proposed that the boarding schools should be used to fulfil unmet 'boarding need' among the wider community that lay outside their present client base. In other words, 30,000 expensive boarding places currently being paid for by parents should now be funded by government – at a much greater cost per place than existing places at state day schools.[73] In the 1970s the Labour Party's opposition hardened: it pledged to remove public schools' charitable status before ultimately abolishing them by prohibiting the charging of fees for full-time schooling. In September 1973 Roy Hattersley, shadow education minister, told a conference of public school heads: 'I must, above all else, leave you with no doubts about our serious intention initially to reduce and eventually to abolish private education in this country.'[74] Once in office, however, Labour proved singularly inept at curtailing the public schools, declaring in 1977 that it could not find a way of ending their charitable status without depriving Oxfam and other anti-poverty charities of the same privilege. This firmly suggested a lack of strength of will. Labour ministers were doubtless rendered less bold by regular Gallup polls showing large majorities of the general public approving of public schools.[75]

However, a proposal made in the second report of the Public Schools Commission, published in 1970, flew: that direct grant schools, which held a nebulous position somewhere between the full public schools and the state schools, must abandon their in-between territory and become entirely a part of the state or public school system. To put it more starkly, if they refused to become comprehensives, they had to rely entirely on parental fees. After returning to power, Labour put this proposal into action in 1976. As a result, by 1978 only 60 – most of them Roman Catholic grammars – had chosen the comprehensive route, while the remaining 118 became public schools. The government had foreseen the likely increase in public school numbers as direct grant schools chose this route. However, at the time of the decision ministers believed this would be temporary; in due course it was reckoned that public schools would be eradicated by further legislation. This did not, however, happen – and courtesy of this unfinished journey, the public school sector abruptly swelled with more than a hundred generally large, academically selective, and high-performing schools, including such famous names as Manchester and Bristol Grammar Schools.[76] Largely as a result, the public schools' share of the school population rose from a 1977 trough of 4.4 per cent to 6.2 per cent in 1981 – in absolute terms, a 114,000 increase to 516,000 pupils.[77]

The entry of the direct grant schools into the public school sector increased competition: from now on the bulk of the direct grant schools' places had to be filled by parents who could afford the fees. On balance, however, these new public school rivals did more good than harm to the public school sector as a whole. Kenneth Durham, a future headmaster of University College School, was teaching at the time at St Alban's School, a direct grant that became a public school, before going on to teach at London day schools that had always been public schools. 'Suddenly the independent schools' – a name increasingly given to the public schools after the accession of the direct grants, though we will retain the original term in this book – 'became associated with higher standards', he says. 'Prior to that the drive behind academic education was more social, to do with character building and all that sort of tosh rather than the straightforward idea that they did better.'[78] This perception of a clear divide between public and state school standards was hastened by the decline in the bulk of grammars that were not direct grant. This process had begun when Crosland, as education secretary, had issued his famous Circular 10/65 requesting local authorities to begin converting their secondary schools to comprehensives, and ended when Margaret Thatcher's Conservative government came to power in 1979 and removed the pressure on local authorities to keep doing this.[79] By this point only about a third of England still had a secondary–grammar split. Because of the decline of the grammars, the number of academically elite state schools was reduced to a mere rump – with the vast bulk of them now in the public school world.

The public schools had won a spectacular victory, through an inept own goal by opponents of independent education. However, the original public schools – those which had not been direct grant grammars – could not subsist on a mere vague popular sense that they offered high standards. They actually had to prove that they could offer high standards, both for the brightest pupils and for average children. At the end of the 1970s, however, many of them still did not do so, despite a general improvement in the sector.

It would be churlish to deny that in the generation after the Second World War the public schools had come an enormously long way.

'The new approach to feeding has undoubtedly benefited the present generation of boys, who are better fed and bigger than their predecessors', wrote a distinguished doctor of his charges. 'This can be borne out by records of weight and heights carefully kept over the past seven years.' This is not the record of working-class boys in a Victorian workhouse, their growth stunted by inadequate provision. It is, rather, the 1961 report by Winchester's most senior doctor, Dr Heatley, on the condition of boys in one of the country's most elite public schools. The doctor listed a host of other medical problems eradicated in the previous fifteen years following the modernization of the school facil-ities, including scalds borne by junior boys carrying hot water upstairs to the older boys, and 'headaches and associated visual defects' caused by poor lighting.[80] Given both this testimony and the rapid move within the Winchester syllabus away from the dominance of the Classics, one can almost say that in the post-war period the college abruptly leapt from a mediaeval to a modern school.

Winchester was not, to be fair, the only school which, before the modernization of facilities, seemed stuck in an ancient past. 'The lack of heating in dormitories, classrooms and dayrooms cannot be forgotten – we were chilled to the marrow', remembered two brothers who still shivered at their memory of Ardingly College in the 1940s. The toilets 'were open to the sky and there were no doors to the cubi-cles and no seats (except for one reserved for prefects which had a half door)'.[81]

In the post-war era, feeding and facilities were improved at Winchester and other schools. However, there was still a great deal more for the schools to do before the sector as a whole could be consid-ered to have reached excellence.

'I'm often asked to think of a teacher who inspired me', says Richard Cairns, headmaster of Brighton College at the time of writing. 'I can't think of a single one.' So much for the sacred and treasured relationship between master and grateful pupil, spun in an unbroken thread over the centuries. 'Teachers were late, they often seemed to teach the wrong things, and results didn't really matter', recalls Cairns of his time at the Catholic boarding school which he left in 1984. 'For Latin set texts we often seemed to be doing the wrong one. At the last minute there would be a panic, and then we'd do the right book of the *Aeneid*.' The syllabus was not exactly crafted according to scientific principles: 'We started off doing Greek, and then the Greek master died, so the headmaster announced we had to do geography instead.' There were, moreover, 'people who were very badly bullied'.[82]

Cairns's damning description of life at a British public school at this time is echoed at least in part by other current heads. From the point of view of the boys, public schools were, despite their immense progress from the low point of the early nineteenth century, still far from a golden age. Alongside 'pockets of brilliance' in the common room sat 'a few old veterans of the Second World War, probably shell-shocked, or with some sort of hang-up, who led groups of boys to exam failure year in year out without ever being challenged', says Mark Turner, headmaster of Shrewsbury at the time of writing, of his time at the Lancashire boarding school which he left in 1980.[83] Tony Little of Eton recalls the comic incompetence of science teaching during his time as a pupil at the same school, amid a general picture of 'really variable' teaching as a whole within its gates. For one science teacher, 'I don't recall one experiment ever working'. It was, moreover, 'unfathomable what he was talking about'. Life at Tonbridge School, the Kent day-cum-boarding school whose teaching staff he joined in 1977, revealed an equal 'patchiness' in the quality of education.[84]

At other schools, as at Eton, the quality of education often varied according to the subject. Emma Taylor, current head of Christ College, remembers that at her girls' school, 'if you were going to do well academically you had to be good at French and be a modern linguist', in obeisance to the long tradition of girls' private schools. 'If you were good at maths, physics and Latin, as I was, it was bad news.'[85] Often the lighter patches of public school teaching were in the provision for the Oxbridge candidates. The darker patches were correspondingly more likely to be found for the middling or mediocre pupils, despite considerable progress for this group compared with a generation previously. 'The best boys get the best masters, the worst boys get the worst', lamented a sixteen-year-old boy at a boarding school. 'If you're not bright here, you have had it.'[86] In the closing months of the 1970s, John Rae at Westminster confessed to his diary that 'we do not do well enough by the 50 per cent who are not potential Oxbridge candidates. Boys who are not well motivated are not pushed hard enough, which opens us to the charge that we are only interested in the scholars.' Rae resolved: 'I must make the common room face up to this problem.'[87]

A weakness that constantly recurs, in the memory of current heads educated at this time, is the lack of accountability – particularly for boarding pupils, whose parents were kept in the dark about their children's lives. If children were at boarding school, parents had little to do with the school for the entire year. Parents put up with the bad education because 'they didn't know about it', recalls Turner of his time at Rossall.[88] At some schools this was changing. 'I remember that twenty years ago my parents were discouraged from visiting me at School', wrote John Vallins, housemaster of Cranleigh School. 'They stooped, on occasion, to furtive meetings in coffee-shops, thus tacitly joining with me in league to evade the authority of the School and Housemaster.' It was, he claimed, very different now at his school – but many other schools still frowned on excessive parental interference.[89]

At both day and boarding schools, modern concepts such as line management and teaching observations were unheard of. If teaching was bad, all too often nothing was done about it. Even when he began teaching in the 1980s, 'there were far too many very bad teachers', says one current public school headmaster. 'I can think of tens and tens of teachers alongside whom I taught in those days who were not fit to be in the classroom. Some were academically hopeless. Others had lost their energy. Some had never been good teachers.'[90] This could, however, be swept under the carpet, because parents said little of it and senior masters less still. No master ever formally observed the lesson of another, so incompetence, even if suspected, was rarely challenged by senior staff. Andrew Halls, current headmaster of King's College School, did not have a lesson observed by another teacher until 1997, sixteen years into Halls' career – and the experience of other masters of the time is similar.

This would all change, however, with the advent in the 1980s of the age of accountability.

CHAPTER EIGHT

A Golden Age At Last

1980–2014

IN the first month of the new decade, Basil Cridland, a chemistry teacher at Dulwich College, made some dire predictions about the school's future in the 1980s. In a special report submitted to the college board, he forecast a sharp decline of 14 per cent in the roll over the following five years. Cridland cited a combination of causes, including a fall in the overall secondary school population and the phasing out of places previously paid for by local authorities; peculiarly for a public school, at their peak, local authority scholarships funded 85 per cent of Dulwich pupils.[1] The Dulwich College committee's rejection of various remedies reinforces the impression that public schools felt in a weak position. Raising fees was attacked on the grounds that it would hit academic standards by restricting the eligible pool of bright boys. Filling up the school by offering places to less academic boys was also criticized on the basis that the school had already compromised too much in this respect, to the point where 'some of the boys concerned are finding great difficulty with the curriculum'. The committee resolved 'to underline to the Board that some reduction in both numbers and standards seems inevitable unless girls are admitted at sixth form level' – and even that could not have made up the entire 14 per cent shortfall.[2]

A year later Cridland was forced to eat his words. He admitted that his figures were now 'out of date', adding, 'My tentative conclusion, is that the roll is likely now to be stabilised in the region of 1,430 to 1,450 boys in the next three or four years unless further new influences intervene.' Cridland blamed his mistake – or credited it, perhaps, given the happy nature of his error – on three factors. The third and final one was the decision to start taking younger boys into the college, but the top two were both related to the state. The very top one was negative: 'Dissatisfaction with the maintained sector in Education in 1980 which, in spite of the economic recession, resulted in a significant change by many parents to the choices of fee-paying independent schools.' The second was positive: the implementation from September 1981 of the government's Assisted Places Scheme, which paid partly, or entirely, for the public school education of poorer boys.[3] The state had, after decades of making life harder for the public schools, at last lent them a helping hand.

Signs of disquiet with the direction of travel of state education had begun to emerge in the mid–1970s, with high-profile media assaults on both the comprehensive system and some of the wilder experimental methods of state primaries. Greater dissatisfaction was to come under the Conservatives, however. In 1979 the new Tory government announced cuts in education, as part of its project to trim public expenditure in general. Two years later it unveiled plans for a reduction of 7 per cent, including a swingeing 30 per cent drop in capital spending. Between 1980–1 and 1985–6, spending on education dropped from 5.5 to 4.8 per cent of gross domestic product. As a result, by 1985 a picture of day-to-day teaching harmed by poor accommodation and a shortage even of books was painted by the annual report on local authority education provision by Her Majesty's Inspectorate for schools. Perhaps most damaging of all was the teachers' industrial action of 1985–7, prompted by dissatisfaction over pay in an environment of cost-cutting. Parents who could afford public school education regarded it in a much more positive light after seeing their children kept at home because of striking teachers in the state system. Thatcher had already given her own excoriating verdict when asked at a 1983 press conference what she was going to do about problems in state education. 'It's a disaster', she replied.[4]

The troubles faced by the state schools greatly benefited the public schools. A survey of parents of public school boys by Irene Fox, published in 1985, is peppered with complaints about the state-funded alternative, particularly, so Fox found, among grammar school-educated fathers who were pained by the progressive loss of this strand of state education. 'State schools in this area are appalling', wrote one mother. 'They really are blackboard jungles.' One father claimed: 'Many of the schools that I come into contact with as a policeman should be closed down.'[5] There was, certainly, media exaggeration of the state schools' problems. Advocates of state education could also argue, with some justice, that if the state system was failing, it was because the Conservative government was neglecting it. That point, however, cut no ice with parents faced with failing schools: it did not, after all, matter to parents why these schools were failing when they were making decisions about their children's education.[6]

The progressive dilapidation of state school buildings during the 1980s and most of the 1990s – until the Labour government headed by Tony Blair introduced a massive works programme – stood in sharp contrast to the high spending of public schools, paid for by large, inflation-busting fee increases. The 1980s saw the first round of what would become known as 'the facilities arms race' – a dash by schools to spend more than each other on gleaming new buildings and equipment, in a bid to attract pupils. Spending on this at public schools rose, in 2012 prices, from only £601 per pupil per year in 1982 to £1,151 in the last year of that decade: a 91 per cent increase.[7] In 1987 Fettes finally transformed the quality of the boarding accommodation, responding to the combined pressure of anxious mothers and those governors who, having not endured the school as old boys, looked askance at its condition.[8] Heather Brigstocke, high mistress of St Paul's Girls' from 1974 to 1989, supervised the construction of a new pool, theatre, computer centre and engineering workshop, much of it funded, as at many of the more established schools, by an ambitious appeal which exceeded its £1 million target. 'You should always have a building on the go, like your knitting', she advised the bursar, like an intemperate sinner teasing a self-denying priest.[9]

In addition to the sharp cuts in spending, the Assisted Places Scheme was another way in which the Conservative government showed its dislike of the state sector. Introduced in 1980, it was regarded as a replacement, for secondary school age children deemed to be intellectually able, for the state-funded places which had disappeared with the end of the direct grant system. The scheme was accompanied, however, by many fewer demands for state control, in return for the funding, than under the direct grant scheme. It required that at least 60 per cent of places should be offered to pupils previously at state schools, though the number of places taken by children from manual working-class families was low. Children from families below a certain income received a free place, with others from slightly better-off families paying lower fees. By 1997, its final year, 37,183 children, or 7.9 per cent of all pupils, held Assisted Places at Independent Schools Council (ISC) institutions – institutions which make up the bulk of the public school sector.‡ Most of the children were of secondary school age, though in 1996 the government had also opened the scheme to children of prep school age.[10] If not quite a decapitation of those state schools which relied on the academic example set by the brighter children to filter down to the rest of the school, it was, at least, a blow to the head.

‡ The Independent Schools Council, originally known as the Independent Schools Joint Council, set up in 1974, is an umbrella body for various associations representing the heads of public schools. The schools run by these heads include the vast bulk of pupils educated at fee-paying schools, and virtually all of what we would think of as public schools in this book's definition. Figures from the ISC are, therefore, from now on sometimes used as a convenient proxy for the public school sector as a whole.

Assisted Places also lifted the burden from the shoulders of many public schools – in particular those which had newly entered, or re-entered, the sector after decades as direct grant schools. At one point 44 schools drew more than 40 per cent of their pupils from the scheme, and even the average participating school had 118. Assisted Places pupils also boosted public schools' academic results – hence the gap in exam success between public and state schools, since the scheme's pupils were, on average, subject to more rigorous selection than fee-paying pupils. As a result they were more likely to go to university than other pupils.[11] In doing so, they contributed to the emerging middle-class consciousness that the brightest children went to public schools, and that their children should go there too.

Assisted Places also proved an effective way of raising children from poorer backgrounds into the broad elite. A study of 347 state school pupils identified at primary school in the 1980s as high fliers showed that those who went on to a public school on an Assisted Place were more than twice as likely to go to a top university than those who stayed at state school. It was not always an easy road. A *Times Educational Supplement* piece on this study quoted Tom, a working-class Assisted Place boy who had felt 'embarrassed' by his humble home, had 'lacked confidence', and had decided he would not send his own children to public school. On the other hand, he earned three As at A level and went on to Bristol University, an elite institution.[12]

Assisted Places certainly gave some impetus to the success of the public schools from the 1980s. 'Many schools will be sick if the APS is withdrawn – sick financially and in terms of the loss of children of ability', Richard Wilkinson, the headmaster of King Edward's School, Witley, declared in 1986.[13] By 1997 Assisted Places accounted for almost one in seven children at HMC schools, the academic cream of the public school sector.[14] This was not a high enough percentage, however, to account for anything like the entire improvement in public schools' record in getting pupils into university during this period, a proportion which rose heavily even at schools which did not take part in the scheme. Moreover, the years after the end of

Assisted Places – jettisoned by the new Labour government – actually saw a modest rise in total pupil numbers for public schools as a whole. The sector was not plunged into academic or financial sickness when the scheme expired, despite Wilkinson's warning.

The end of Assisted Places was, moreover, mitigated by the public schools' scramble to find a replacement. The solution – to raise funds from current parents and alumni – proved surprisingly effective. In 1991 public schools gave £63 million (£115 million in 2012 money) in fee assistance – 4 per cent of fee income – of which 58 per cent was spent on merit-based scholarships, leaving well under half for bursaries based on families' financial need. A decade later, fee assistance had jumped to £215 million (£301 million), or 6.2 per cent of fee income, of which just under half was in scholarships.[15] Manchester Grammar, a school with a large number of successful and wealthy alumni, succeeded in raising more than £8 million for bursaries. The move towards bursaries was given further impetus by the 2006 Charities Act, a child of the Blair government. In the strict interpretation of the Charity Commission, this Act obliged public schools to show they were acting for 'public benefit' by providing education to low-income families as well as the wealthy. (The demand had not existed in previous charity law – the Charitable Uses Act of 1601, which established the general principles of charity law for the next four centuries, described the broad category of 'Schools of Learninge' as valid recipients of charity, without reference to the poverty of their students.[16]) By 2010, fee assistance had risen to 8.8 per cent of fee income, of which 4.3 per cent was devoted to bursaries, a higher figure than in 2001.[17] The Charity Commission's strict interpretation of public benefit was, in 2011, overturned by the courts, but not before public schools had spent five years aggressively building up their bursary provision to meet the test.[18]

The New Labour regime that came to power in 1997 had a much more positive attitude towards state education than the Conservative regime which it replaced. Moreover, spending on state education rose sharply during the Blair-Brown era of 1997–2010. However, the regime of rule by numbers, which the Blair government saw as its solution to unsatisfactory public services, proved totally unsuited to the education sector. The regime soon turned into a tyranny that led to a system of perverse incentives. State school heads, aware that they would be judged by the government on their numerical results – and all judged equally, without any regard for the subjects behind these results – had an incentive to pick easier subjects. Research in 2011 found that 9.9 per cent of comprehensive school pupils sat media studies at A level, compared with only 1.5 per cent of public school teenagers. Even at state grammars, filled with some of the brightest children who in a more pupil-centred system should have been guided towards the harder subjects, pupils were more than twice as likely as public school children to take this subject.[19]

The danger of the drift towards academically easier disciplines was highlighted in 2010, when it was revealed that some leading universities were rejecting applicants who had taken more than one A level from a menu of less academic subjects, including media studies.[20] The systemic bias created towards easier subjects explains the popularity – at state rather than public schools – of the general science GCSE, introduced in the 1990s as an alternative to separate papers in physics, chemistry and biology, to the consternation of the Campaign for Science and Engineering, a lobby group supported by universities and academic associations.[21] The organisation's criticisms were given implicit official confirmation in 2010 when the Office of Qualifications and Examinations Regulation (Ofqual), the exams watchdog, decreed that the general science papers needed tougher questions.[22] The same incentive to drift towards easier subjects contributed to the drastic drop in pupils sitting modern languages GCSEs after the government removed the requirement for teenagers at state schools to take at least one of them in 2004.[23]

The higher spending should have sharpened state schools' competitive advantage versus the public schools. However, the government's series of own goals instead blunted their ability to compete.

In 1992 Britain's boarding schools passed a grisly milestone: the number of boarders at the mainstream public schools fell below 100,000, little more than a fifth of the total number of public school pupils.[24] It was a far cry from the early twentieth century when boarding had thrived while some day schools struggled.

One reason for this diminution in numbers is practical. The number of international schools in the world, able to provide a good education to the children of business people and diplomats, grew from a mere 50 in 1964 to 5,500 in 2010.[25] By removing the necessity for children to be sent back to Britain for their education, this destroyed one of the staple former markets of boarding schools.

Probably the bigger problem, however, was an active turning away from boarding school education by parents who felt that it had not been a happy experience for them. The litany of complaints about the quality of boarding school life, even among pupils who attended as late as the 1970s and 1980s, did not bode well for this sub-sector of the public schools. Boarding schools had taken too long to reform themselves.

There are undoubted virtues in boarding school life – when the institutions are run well. The virtues lie partly in the opportunities for sport: the facilities are often good, and the pupils have the time to play it, since they are not at home, and for study: there are set times for homework, supervised by the school, which create a helpful scholastic routine. 'They put me in a study with people who worked hard – quite wisely, because I don't think I was a naturally hard worker', says Angus McPhail, who went on from Abingdon School in Oxfordshire to read Politics, Philosophy and Economics at Oxford, before eventually becoming warden of Radley College. 'There was an element of taught behaviour which was quite helpful for me.'[26] The most important opportunities, however, are in human relations: the opportunities for forming close friendships, for learning how to get on with people who are not your friends, and, for heads of house, for governing your house in such a way that the differences between children who do not get on with each other stop short of creating discord or worse.

The opportunity perhaps most treasured by children who have enjoyed boarding school is, to put it in its most elemental way, the chance for sheer fun. Frederic Farrar, the Harrow schoolmaster, recalled this vividly in his best-selling 1858 novel *Eric, Or Little By Little*, based on his own schooldays at King William's College on the Isle of Man. The boys in the dormitory indulge in harmless horseplay such as leapfrog and ham acting, activities which entail a good deal of shifting about of objects in the dorm. When the master returns to check on them, the boys all appear to be asleep, but the circumstances are highly suspicious. 'The beds in all the adjoining rooms were in the strangest positions', though all is quiet. 'He heard nothing but the deep snores of Duncan, and instantly fixed on him as a chief culprit. "Duncan!" No reply; but calm stertorous music from Duncan's bed.' It is a scene which all parents have witnessed, on a smaller scale, with their own children.[27]

However, what happened if the boys in the dorm did not get on? Advocates for boarding schools believed that learning what to do in such cases provided excellent training for leadership. It was better, so the thinking ran, for a future servant of the empire to learn how to create a cohesive group of males while at boarding school than in the officers' mess at a besieged hill fort in Rajasthan, when a falling out might lead to military disaster and death. 'It is the custom nowadays to disparage the educational methods of the English public-school and to maintain that they are not practical and of a kind to fit the growing boy for the problems of after-life', wrote P. G. Wodehouse, an ex-Dulwich College boarder, in *Mr Mulliner Speaking*, his 1929 collection of humorous short stories. 'But you do learn one thing at a public-school, and that is how to act when somebody starts snoring. You jolly well grab a cake of soap and pop in and stuff it down the blighter's throat.'[28] Such japes cause no harm if done in a humorous and gentle spirit to a friend, but the testimony of boarding school boys over the centuries shows that this was often not the case.

A more subtle problem was the repression of the natural feelings of boarding school children. To survive, children needed to become emotionally detached from families. Some degree of detachment from one's family is natural, as one grows up. However, for children who go to boarding school the process of detachment is abrupt. It must, therefore, be managed well, by allowing children to know that they can phone home frequently without feeling any sense of shame about this. It was, in reality, managed badly all too often. A former Winchester College schoolboy of the 1980s recalls the plight of a bursary boy who, after arriving at the school, was constantly on the phone to his family. Repeatedly teased as 'Telephone Man' by other pupils, the victimized boy soon left.[29]

Even for children who are not teased, the process of detachment is sometimes tough. It can be traced through the letters sent home by Charles Wright, a boarder at St Peter's School, York, in the 1850s. 'I do not know how it is but I cannot help crying; it seems a week or more since I saw you last although it was only last night', he writes as a young boy. Three years later, however, he is considerably more relaxed – to the point of coldness, writing: 'I might as well give you a scribble although I don't know of what it will be concocted.'[30]

The consequences of such detachment were not entirely healthy. A 1953 study comparing young men and women who had been to public boarding schools with young adults from a London slum found some striking similarities, both in their early environments and in later character traits which were a reaction to their childhood experiences. 'In neither group do children appear to grow up in an atmosphere of emotional warmth', it concluded. Even after reaching adulthood, both groups found difficulty in 'the establishment of close, warmly affectionate personal relations'. In addition, 'both groups have insecurity feelings and anxiety; both attempt to keep a tight control of themselves and in emotional situations both at times burst through this control.' There were also many differences. The boarding school subject 'has a spontaneous, rich, and creative fantasy and good powers of intellectual discrimination'. Surprisingly, perhaps, the researcher did not find any homosexual tendencies among the boarding school group, but did among the adults brought up in slum environments.[31] Despite these differences, the fact that boarding schools and slums produced many of the same emotional outcomes was rather shocking.

Boarding school heads have, however, made great strides in creating a happier environment for their charges. The modification of the traditional tor climb at Kelly College (now Mount Kelly, following a recent merger), bordering on the austere beauty of Dartmoor National Park, encapsulates the changes in life at the British boarding school over the past generation or so. Old boys of the school from the 1970s remember the days when the ascent of Cox Tor, a local hill, cropped close by local Dartmoor ponies and topped with a granite summit the colour of rusty steel, was a tough race run only by the new boys in the first few days of school, 'gently encouraged by the prefects with the aid of twigs and branches', in the words of the head, Graham Hawley. These days it is no longer a tough initiation rite for boys who will spend the rest of term secluded in the intense atmosphere of an isolated boarding school: everyone in the school joins in, including the many girls and day pupils who now attend the school. Indeed, even parents and family dogs are encouraged to participate, and the head arranges that a local ice cream van is placed somewhere towards the top. It is all a far cry from the old days of physical chastisement, strict pupil hierarchies, monastic isolation and gastronomic privation.[32]

Hawley also emphasizes the school's painstaking approach to ensure that pupils are kept happy in their dormitories. The children in the first two years are kept in a separate boarding house, which, he says, reduces the chances of ill-treatment by older against younger children. This house is supervised by a housemistress, 'a mother-like figure' whose job is to look after the children full-time. These days an adult feminine presence is regarded as an asset, rather than an encumbrance, to boarding schools. For example, the current master of Wellington, Anthony Seldon, hosts a hundred lunches and dinners a year at which he and his wife meet every student in the school, in an attempt to create a family atmosphere, receiving them at the master's house.[33]

The first weeks and months of a child's time at a boarding school are crucial to their happiness within it. Anecdotal evidence from people educated over the past generation suggests that the number of housemasters who are vicious martinets has fallen, and the number who aspire to be kindly uncles, aunts or even parents has risen. A boy who greatly enjoyed his boarding experience at Charterhouse School in the 2000s remembers the 'caring and calm way' in which his housemaster dealt with a problem which emerged in his first few weeks at the school. The boy went to the man in tears, after realizing that he had signed up to a sub-aqua club without considering what his parents might think of the expense. 'He said, "no worries, I'll sort this out for you"' – and persuaded the club to take back the unused equipment and cancel the club membership. It might seem a trivial issue, but 'to me, then, it was a big deal'.[34]

But despite these positive changes, too many parents remember much less caring environments than this, and many of them have instead opted for day schools. One response to this trend is for boarding schools to recant the habit of earlier public school masters to treat day pupils as second-class citizens, accepted under sufferance merely to pacify the locals for whom the school was originally set up. The switch from boarding to day was, in some cases, total: by 1990 Northwood College in north-east London, established in the 1860s exclusively to provide a residential education for girls, had switched entirely to day pupils.[35]

Another solution is to look overseas for boarders – and by 1992 this strategy was well in hand. In 1975 British boarding schools had fewer than 9,000 foreign pupils whose parents lived overseas, but by the end of the 1980s there were almost 12,000, or one in every nine boarders. By 2014 this had climbed to 24,391 – 36 per cent of a much smaller total of 68,453. This included 9,085 from Hong Kong and mainland China, and 2,007 from Germany. These pupils are drawn, say heads, by the desire for an Anglophone education.[36] 'They have come to Shrewsbury partly on the back of its historical reputation', says Mark Turner, Shrewsbury's current head. 'They also know that if you can get a good education in English and good British university degrees, it is a passport to great success in their own country.'[37] Graham Hawley, headmaster of Kelly College, admitted that his school could not survive without its overseas boarders.[38]

This has proved a more long-lasting trend than the beneficial effect of the Harry Potter phenomenon on boarding school numbers – if there ever was such an effect in the first place. The worldwide success of the best-selling series of books about a boy at a boarding school for wizards and witches had helped reinvent the image of boarding schools, the Boarding Education Alliance said in 1999; in 2004, however, an official at the Independent Schools Council declared, after an annual fall in boarding school numbers, 'I think we've probably seen the peak of Harry's influence.'[39]

Several public schools have set up satellite branches overseas, to capitalize on growing foreign demand. Dulwich College's international empire has become positively huge: it has three schools in China, and one each in South Korea and Singapore. If all grow to the 1,000-strong rolls already established in Beijing and Shanghai, there will eventually be about 6,500 Dulwich pupils around the world, making it the size of a small university rather than a typical school.[40] Public school satellites have been set up in exotic locations as diverse as Almaty in Kazakhstan (Haileybury), Dubai (Repton) and Bangkok (Harrow) – part of a total of twenty-nine overseas schools run by Independent Schools Council members.[41] The heads of most of the academic premier league, however, have been wary of expanding overseas – though North London Collegiate, which has a Seoul school, is an exception. Most of the schools have a considerably more tenuous link with the mother ship than their use of the original school names suggests, since they are, like many of the branches of international hotel chains, franchises rather than directly run subsidiaries. The operator of the foreign branch pays a fee to the mother school, which does not become involved in its day-to-day running, although the mother school does tend to have a say in important issues such as the appointment of the head. The public schools have entered the realm of international brand management, with all its associated hazards to their reputation. Foreign daughter schools were, warned the high master of St Paul's, Martin Stephen, 'a risk to your brand image'.[42]

Boarding schools' enthusiastic embrace of foreign pupils of all races represents a transformation from their earlier history. For centuries the public schools had taken in British children while their parents were governing or guarding far-flung parts of the empire, but children of different nationalities were considerably more unusual, and children of different races rarer still. Perhaps the first overseas pupils of all were the four Russian boys who arrived in England in 1602 to learn English, visiting Eton, Winchester, Oxford and Cambridge, with the aid of Giles Fletcher, England's erstwhile ambassador to Moscow and an Old Etonian.[43] Another early exception to the predominant Britishness of the pupil rolls was Liverpool College, which as early as the 1860s taught Greeks, Armenians, Americans and black Africans, including the son of a Nigerian trader.[44] Downside School also has a long tradition of educating members of Poland's Catholic aristocracy, including the Zamoyskis and Sapiehas.[45]

In part, the dearth of foreign pupils reflected the less globalized nature of society – people think nothing these days of jetting halfway across the world for a holiday, but half a century ago this would not have been conceivable. At some schools, however, there was clearly out-and-out racism – or, at least, a passive acceptance that pupils' parents were racist and that this discrimination should be respected. J. F. Roxburgh, Stowe's headmaster, refused to admit the sons of a maharajah in 1928 on the grounds that 'schools which have open dormitories . . . ought not in my opinion to receive coloured boys', an enigmatic statement which may have reflected a prevailing view that homosexuality was more prevalent in India.[46] A year later a black boy from Sierra Leone was barred from Edinburgh Academy after the objection of governors, who feared that other parents might complain – though the rector (headmaster) had, to his credit, supported the application. No exception was necessarily made, even for the sons of emperors: in 1944 the school considered whether to accept an application from

Haile Selassie of Ethiopia's son and grandson, 'having in view an earlier decision against acceptance of pupils of coloured races'. The boys were turned down, though this may have been because of the school's concerns over security.[47] Even schools which welcomed foreigners were not necessarily more enlightened. When asked by the head boy why Brighton College admitted foreigners, William Dawson, headmaster from 1906 to 1933, explained his logic: 'I take them on my own terms: two years' fees in advance as surety for good behaviour. They're all highly sexed, and it's only a matter of months before they sleep with a house maid. Then out they go.'[48]

To their credit, however, both Winchester and several Girls' Public Day School Trust schools accepted refugees from Europe before the Second World War. In 1938 the headmaster of Winchester offered five places 'to the sons of persons expelled or about to be expelled from their homes in Central Europe on political or racial grounds'. These included sixteen-year-old Georg Grun, an Austrian Jew who had been in a concentration camp, billeted during the holidays with a touching show of humanity with the brother of the second master. The head criticized the decision of 'a few Wykehamists' to 'protest against the admission of Jewish boys to a Christian School'.[49] Jewish boys had, in fact, been accepted in considerable numbers to British public schools since the nineteenth century. At Clifton College John Percival, a future bishop, had set up an exclusively Jewish house in 1878, which was excused from the requirements of Christian worship. Girls admitted to the Girls' Public Day School Trust in its early years seem to have been treated well. In 1882 pupils at its Paddington and Maida Vale High School, who had Jewish classmates, asked to be given another piece to learn instead of a speech from Shakespeare's *Richard II* containing words 'repugnant to Jewish feeling'.[50]

Meanwhile, Eton played its own small part in snubbing the Nazis, though possibly by accident. In 1936 the headmaster rejected the son of Joachim von Ribbentrop, a key foreign policy aide to Hitler and his future foreign minister. The reasons given were that the boy was over the maximum permissible age of fourteen for entry to the school, and he was a late entry, compared with the many boys whose names had been put down many years before in a school with far more applications than places.[51] It is impossible, now, to know whether these reasons were an excuse that masked a more idealistic objection.

The arrival of large numbers of overseas pupils did not, after all, generate an outbreak of orgiastic sexual activity. Instead there was a fair amount of initial culture shock. On arriving at Cheltenham Ladies' College in 1985, an American girl thought to herself: 'I'd never written with an ink-pen in my life – didn't they use those in Little House on the Prairie?'[52] Looking to the long term, the decision to go international is gradually altering the very essence of the boarding schools.

On the debit side, heads of schools who have not aggressively tried to attract overseas pupils argue that this internationalization changes the institution's entire ethos. They say that a school peopled primarily by foreign pupils, as some are, would find it hard to form a rugby team, or teach English literature and history to pupils outside these traditions' cultural hinterlands. Overseas pupils predominantly do maths and science at A level, say heads. They add that Asian children are, because of the more hierarchical teacher–pupil relationship in their own culture, much less willing to engage in class discussion than European children.[53] In short, such schools might be very good schools. They might also, by educating future elites from around the world together, play their own small part in world peace; Lord Grey's wish that all foreign statesmen could have gone to public school is apposite here. One would have to question, however, whether they would still be British public schools.

In August 1991 the *Daily Telegraph* exploded a stick of dynamite under the public schools' foundations by introducing league tables that compared public schools' exam performance. Attempts at comparisons had been made before, such as *The Times*' 1964 foray. The tables compiled by John Clare, the *Telegraph's* education editor, were, however, more comprehensive. Clare compiled, in imitation of the rankings of football clubs, a Premier League, followed by First, Second and Third

Divisions – all based on the percentage of As and Bs at A level, since these were the requisite grades for entry to a selective university. The greatest surprise of the table, though perhaps only to men, was the stellar performance of girls' schools: Portsmouth High was top, and four of the others in the Premier League of ten schools were also single-sex girls' schools, as well as sixteen of twenty-nine in the First Division. Many of the schools excoriated by the nineteenth-century Clarendon Commission also came out well, confirming their progress over the past century or so; although only St Paul's was in the Premier League, Eton, Charterhouse, Westminster and Shrewsbury were in the First Division, the first two in sharp contrast to their poor performance in *The Times'* earlier ur-league table. Another striking fact was the poor performance of boarding compared with day schools, although there were exceptions. Well-known boarding schools such as Stonyhurst, Uppingham and Lancing were exposed as the public school equivalents of Torquay United, languishing in the lower ranks of the Third Division.[54]

The *Telegraph's* publication provoked many a snide comment from schools – one, in conversation with John Clare, likened it to 'industrial espionage'.[55] For all the schools' sniffiness, however, those who doubt that the league tables made a great deal of difference to the way schools ran themselves should consider the opinion of Alice Wilkes. Alice was the wife of Peter, who was sacked in 1996 for letting Cheltenham College fall into division three of the *Telegraph's* public school table during his tenure as head, according to his very publicly angry wife, though Peter himself was bound by a gagging clause not to raise the issue. Mrs Wilkes attacked the governors for their shallowness, likening their motivation to 'the embarrassment at a cocktail party or whatever of having to confess that your team hasn't done as well as you expected'.[56] The importance of the league tables is echoed by current heads who were young teachers at the time. When Joseph Spence, future master of Dulwich College, began teaching at Eton in the 1980s, parents were 'less anxious about results. They believed there were a lot of thoroughly good universities – and that, almost like oil and water, through a natural process of separation people would find themselves at the right sorts of places.' However, 'things began to tighten as people became obsessed with league tables. . . . There was a sense that it was the schools' responsibility to get the boy to where he should go.'[57]

The pressure on schools to perform better had, in fact, been growing before the arrival of league tables. It had already begun at Cheltenham itself, creating a pre-existing pressure for results that made league table underperformance all the more heinous when it happened. The key moment came in 1978, when Richard Morgan arrived at the school as its ambitious new head. His decision to intro-duce exam targets – initially for 40 per cent of A level grades to be As and Bs, though this was ramped up a year later – provoked the deri-sion and ire of the older members of staff. Masters who regarded these targets as impossible to achieve left in droves, to be replaced by new masters appointed by Morgan. The impossible was accom-plished, through a regime of detailed monitoring previously unseen at the school, with a report on each boy every two and a half weeks and meetings of the entire common room at which every boy was discussed in detail by a range of masters. The arrival of computers enabled even closer monitoring, with boys' marks set down and analysed for signs of progress or the lack of it. Complaining pupils might have found consolation in the thought that their masters had also begun to be monitored more closely, through a system of performance appraisals borrowed from the business world.[58]

The brighter boys, at least, had always been under pressure to succeed, and newspapers had, for many decades before the A level league tables, published league tables for Oxbridge scholarship results which gave a rank order to schools. The A level league tables were dependent, however, on the performance not merely of the top pupils, but of all those in the final year of sixth form. University attendance was steadily rising, and graduate status was becoming a *sine qua non* for good jobs – which came, indeed, to be known as 'graduate jobs'. A levels were the crucial exams, dictating entry or exclusion from university in this new era of more widespread higher education. This made A level league tables extremely popular among parents.

The average child, who was now aiming for university, had finally exacted his or her statistical revenge for centuries of neglect, but only up to a point; the average child was not always a winner. The more academic public schools responded to league tables by becoming progressively more ruthless about ejecting or refusing entry to children who were academically merely middling – though there were always other public schools willing to take these scholastically undistinguished customers. The progressively greater fussiness about pupils had begun with the invention of Common Entrance, the standardized exam for many public schools, in 1910. The days when a boy could get into one of the leading schools without answering a single exam question, as Winston Churchill had discovered at Harrow, were but a dim and distant memory in the age of league tables.[59]

Newspaper league tables were not the only source of pressure on heads and masters. Parental interest in results was also growing. Since the beginning of the day schools' history, the parents of day pupils had always kept closer tabs on their pupils' week-by-week results than had boarding school parents, and the relative importance of this demanding group was increased by a progressive decline in boarders as a share of total public school pupils from the 1980s. However, boarders' parents were also able to keep a more watchful eye on schools, thanks to changes in families' boarding preferences: the number of truly national boarding schools taking large numbers of pupils from different parts of the country declined as schools became regional hubs for boarding instead. The idea that parents should really try to visit their child's school once a year but no more began to die. In any case, parents did not even have to visit the schools to know how well their children were doing: they could keep tabs on a weekly basis by interrogating their children after the change to regional boarding left most schools as ghost towns at weekends while pupils returned home.[60]

Parents' sense that schools should be held accountable for their obligation to furnish their child with good A levels was heightened from the 1980s onwards by large fee increases that were well above inflation, and by the advent of Thatcherism, a creed which held that established institutions should constantly be compelled to justify their existence. As Andrew Halls of King's College School, puts it: 'League tables came during the Thatcherite era of meritocracy, with a focus on achievable and measurable outcomes. Notions like "it's been around for two hundred years, it's got lovely grounds", mattered a lot less than how many As it got per kid.'[61] 'I think that we are too examination-ridden – it's difficult to get away from it, but we're now an examination mill', complained one master in the mid-1980s. Parents' 'unreasonable' expectations were, however, 'quite understandable when parents are paying our high fees. If the father's a businessman, he regards it as an investment and he wants the dividend in success for his boy.'[62] The increasingly widespread nature of inspections created further impetus for improvement – the HMC announced in 1993 that it would inspect all its members' schools.[63]

The principle of accountability would, over the succeeding decades, progress even further. In the 2000s, the spread of email communication enabled a constant interchange between parents and masters; there might, nowadays, be twenty to forty items of correspondence between school and parents per term, and more if there were a problem.[64] Mobile phones make accountability even more rapid-response. At Shrewsbury, if a master is ten minutes late 'there are probably fifteen phone calls going home during the gap and the headmaster's switchboard is buzzing with what's going on', says Mark Turner, its headmaster.[65] Performance management of masters – now standard at public schools – has, meanwhile, reached its logical, if extreme, conclusion at Brighton College. Since 2006, every master and mistress receives an appraisal from every child whom they have taught – a form of consumer feedback which prompted the departure of many staff.[66] Stamford School in Lincolnshire has, in the ultimate sign of a parent-led school, even borrowed from the world of marketing by setting up focus groups to canvas parent opinion. Its focus groups are the logical conclusion to the attempts by the nineteenth-century public schools to save themselves from extinction by listening to parental demands to modernize the curriculum.[67]

Critics think accountability has gone too far, to the point where it is harming education. One ex-teacher has compared his time at a Midlands public school before email to his email-era experience at the overseas branch of another public school. In the old days, 'there was more trust: you paid your fees and trusted the school to take care of your kids'. When email took root, his inbox was filled with messages disputing a child's score in tests, complaining about unfair punishments, and so on. 'I was distracted a lot by that', he says. 'I got emails saying, "I believe you put my kid in the wrong Spanish set, I believe my kid's better than that." That's partly why I gave up teaching.'[68]

Public schools' improved performance, generated largely by this greater pressure from the outside world, has been borne out by a number of very different measures. In 1979 only 48 per cent of boys even from HMC schools went on to university. Fifteen years later this had soared to 84 per cent. The figures for the Girls' Schools Association – the biggest body for girls' public schools – very nearly tripled during the same period, from 28 per cent to 83 per cent. By 2013, 90.1 per cent of pupils leaving Independent Schools Council schools at the age of eighteen went on to university. The highest percentage of all – more than boys' schools or co-ed schools – was achieved by girls' schools, at 92.3 per cent.[69] These numbers show that at the girls' schools, the notion that education was about making daughters 'enchanting', to use the phrase of the 1960s parent in Chapter Seven, has been eradicated, at least among the pupils and teachers. Since the departure of Frances Gray, the high mistress of St Paul's Girls' who placed the role of home maker at the top of womanhood's moral hierarchy, St Paul's Girls' has educated the politicians Harriet Harman and Shirley Williams, the philosopher Onora O'Neill and a smattering of film stars, including Rachel Weisz, and Natasha and Joely Richardson.

Another method of measuring public schools' success, the earnings premium, which compares the earnings of one group of people with another, also shows public schools' improvement, although extremely up-to-date figures are not available. A study by the London School of Economics found that thirty-year-old ex-public school pupils born in 1970 – who would have been at public school in the mid-to-late 1980s – earned £5,000 a year more than people of otherwise identical backgrounds. This margin – slightly higher for men than for women, though not greatly so – had, strikingly, increased in comparison with the differential for ex-public school children born twelve years previously. The LSE study found that the extra earnings were because public school children gained better academic qualifications.[70] Intriguingly, a 1998 study on the earnings premium from Warwick University found that graduates who had attended public school earned 2.5 per cent more than state school colleagues with identical degrees from the same universities.[71]

Exam results also underline public school achievement. In 1961 'efficient independent schools' – in other words the better ones – achieved an overall A level pass rate of 75 per cent – 1 percentage point lower than the overall national average, and a full 7 percentage points lower than for direct grant grammar schools. Merely passing an A level had, by 2012, become sufficiently easy to make any direct comparison bogus, but analysis of A* grades for 2012 showed that 17.4 per cent of public school pupils achieved this level, compared with only 11.6 per cent for children at state grammar schools, even though state grammars are, on average, more academically selective.[72] Finally, 2006 research by Durham University's Curriculum Evaluation and Management Centre shows that public schools' belated attempts to help the less talented have borne fruit. On average, pupils at public schools achieved a grade higher in each GCSE subject than state school pupils of similar ability. The difference was higher still for children who, by public-school standards, were of below-average ability.[73]

British public schools' most striking academic achievement is in the absolute reversal of their earlier neglect of science and maths.

Sir Humphrey Appleby, the fictional civil service mandarin in *Yes Minister* whose adventures illustrate so artfully Britain's establishment in the 1980s, had been a public schoolboy, educated probably in the late 1940s and early 1950s. Unable to elucidate for his ministerial boss, Jim Hacker, the meaning of the scientific term 'inert' during a discussion about a politically sensitive chemical factory, he explains proudly that he has, 'of course', no knowledge of chemistry: 'I was in the Scholarship form.'[74] § By the time he spoke this, however, the days of scientific ignorance at the public schools were over. As early as 1961, the public schools outperformed the national average in chemistry and maths – and in maths, public school pupils did as well as direct grant pupils. By 2011 their triumph in science was complete. Public schools accounted for only 14.3 per cent of A level entries, but 41.9 per cent of A*s in further maths, 36.6 per cent in physics, 33.7 per cent in chemistry and 32.8 per cent in biology.[75] The public schools were doing more than their fair share of avoiding the doom-laden scenario so memorably described in 2008 by Richard Lambert, director-general of the CBI employers' organisation. He had feared that Britons might be left to 'pour the concrete' while skilled foreigners conducted the more complicated work of Britain's potential 'industrial renaissance'.[76]

Increasing parental involvement in school affairs finally dealt the death blow to any lingering concept of the primacy of the Classics, in favour of an emerging bias towards maths and science. This was driven, largely, by public school old boys and old girls who felt that they had not been steered enough towards these subjects during their own school days. One old boy who had done English, French and Latin at A level at King's College School in the 1980s acknowledged:

§ Elsewhere in the book version of *Yes Minister* Sir Humphrey is described as having attended Winchester. If so, he should in this era have done at least some science. It may well be, however, that, as the winner of a classical scholarship to the school, he did not bother to listen – leaving him unaware decades later that he had indeed sat through chemistry lessons.

'There's no question I had a great time. The education in those subjects was second to none.' He then went on to Cambridge University, 'but once I'd left it became very difficult to find a job'. In the light of this shock, when he looked back at his public school education, 'perhaps the only thing lacking was some sort of exposure to the wider world, and being made to think in a non-academic sense, "what are you going to do with this at the end of the day? What use will it be to you?" '[77] The City of London School – by now a public school charging high fees to a typical public school client base – had been strong in maths and science even in the nineteenth century, but by 2013 David Levin, the headmaster at the time, found that 'maths is the subject parents want their children to do. They get increasingly upset if there's a suggestion their child isn't good enough to do maths or shouldn't do maths.' This quite often applied, he said, even to the boy who 'struggles at maths' and preferred humanities.[78] This was echoed by Frances King, at the time headmistress of Roedean, who explained ruefully that her overseas parents in particular 'don't want the "namby-pamby subjects" that lead on to being a better citizen, such as philosophy. They want something that leads on to being a doctor or a lawyer. The more you invest in your child's education, the more you want results for it, if you're a typical parent.' Roedean's current most common A levels are maths, chemistry and biology, with history only fourth – though at girls' schools as a whole, pupils are slightly less likely to take physics, chemistry and biology at GCSE than at co-ed public schools.[79]

John Clark, headmaster of Birkenhead School at the time of writing, acknowledges that science is becoming the standard option. Pupils who like both humanities and science 'will end up doing science because it seems to point them in the direction of jobs'. However, Clark regrets the fact that humanities are being squeezed out: 'There's definitely a sense of education as being about getting to somewhere rather than becoming somebody. . . . Maybe there's a loss of the sense of the value of education in itself rather than education as a means to an end.'[80]

Today's public schools can only thrive, however, if they provide what parents want. Precisely because they have been responsive, they have indeed thrived over the past generation. The absorption of the direct grant schools into the private sector had already boosted total roll numbers at the beginning of the 1980s, but for the rest of the decade their share of the school population continued to rise, assisted by the troubles haunting the state sector as well as by the public schools' improving performance. This share peaked in 1990 at 7.6 per cent, or 540,000 pupils, though the absolute number continued to grow for most of the 1990s.[81]

Public schools' present vices arise largely from their new-found virtues. League tables, and the accountability revolution they helped to create, have certainly played a strong role in producing better exam results. Many public school teachers argue, however, that something valuable has been lost. Graham Lacey, senior master at Sevenoaks School in Kent, was an early critic of the tables. In an articulate 1997 tirade in the *Times Educational Supplement*, he warned that the public schools were neglecting the extra-curricular activities which had made them distinctive. This presented them with a danger. 'The new national obsession with exam results' had removed the difference between independent schools and their 'rivals in the state system', he claimed. 'The horns of the two sectors are now locked and the battle is being fought for the same prize' – a commanding position in the league tables. 'There is no guarantee that the independent schools will emerge victorious.'[82]

Lacey's point that league tables were becoming an unhealthy fixation at public schools is now made by many heads. Claire Oulton, headmistress of Benenden, the Kent girls' school, at the time of writing, believes that 'too many schools are slaves to chasing their way up the tables and are willing to sacrifice everything that lies in their path'.[83] Moreover, 2010 research commissioned by the HMC found that 'despite the desire to pursue broad educational aims and purposes', HMC teachers 'felt under pressure from parents and students to deliver the best possible examination results in a highly competitive market'. The result was 'a climate of instrumentalism and cynicism, in which they felt they were being turned into exam factories'.[84]

'I noticed a real change in the types of teacher during my time', says a pupil who boarded at Downe House School, a Berkshire girls' school, in the late 1990s and early 2000s. 'When I first started there were a lot of "old school" teachers who were very inspiring – maybe a bit more offbeat. They helped pass on a passion for the subject'. By the time she left there were many more who might have skulked in Lacey's nightmares, whose lessons were 'all about achieving targets and ticking the boxes on the syllabus'. On the side of the angels, she remembers, in particular, a history of art teacher who took the works of Salvador Dali as a mere starting-point for a journey into 1930s politics and culture, which included reading Ernest Hemingway to understand the Lost Generation that had been through the First World War.[85]

However, a pupil who was at Epsom College in Surrey in the late 1980s and early 1990s found the teaching both imaginative and rigorous. 'The history A-Level teaching was absolutely fantastic', he says. 'It taught me how to look at sources, and it gave me a love for history which I took into my life after school'. He remembers studying the picture in the National Portrait Gallery showing Richard III as a hunchback, and being told that it was part of the Tudors' attempt to legitimize their rule by showing the physical and, by implication, moral imperfections of the man they had deposed.[86]

Even if they sometimes succumb to league table mania, most current heads seem aware, at least, of the truth of Lacey's warning that public schools cannot compete purely on the basis of exam results. 'I don't think parents are looking primarily for academic results because while we're ahead of the grammar schools we're not that far ahead', says Clark of Birkenhead School, though like all public school heads, he emphasizes that good exam results are a necessary, but not a sufficient, condition for success: 'There must be something else that's making them want to spend £10,000'. Clark's explanation for what this 'something else' is harks back to many of the reasons seen in earlier chapters before the advent of league tables and emphasis on exam results. These include pupils' competition with their peers ('to some extent they're buying the other motivated children that surround their child'), and the close relationship that has existed, at best, between master and pupil over the centuries, though more in ideal than in practice for much of the history of public schools ('They ask particularly about what will happen if their child has difficulties. What's in place to support them?'). He gives the example of a boy in the school's upper sixth who did not take A level German – one of Clark's specialist subjects – because he wanted to be a dentist. Clark's personalized solution: 'We just sat and read a German book together. And he said this morning, "I so enjoyed that, what can we read next?" You've got to find ways of providing a broad education, rather than it being a natural part of the curriculum.'[87] It is touchingly similar to the scene in *Tom Brown's School Days* where Thomas Arnold works away with a chisel on a sailing boat, surrounded by enthusiastic boys.[88]

The same point is made by Tony Little, who ventures the opinion that parents 'do know there are cheaper ways of getting three A's at A-Level than coming to Eton. That's not really why they want their son here.' At the time of writing, in Little's ten years as the school's headmaster he had received only three letters from parents about Eton's position in league tables. All three came in the same week, following the news that Eton had been placed first in a national A level league table. All three were letters of complaint: if the school was coming top, they reasoned, Eton must be neglecting other important facets of an Eton education.[89]

The schools must, for their long-term health, find a happy medium between veering off the beaten track and sticking to the well-trodden path of the syllabus. At one end of the spectrum lies the alleged 'maths master' encountered by Roald Dahl, the children's author, at Repton in the 1920s. 'He was meant to teach us mathematics, but in truth he taught us nothing at all and that was the way he meant it to be', wrote Dahl. '"Let's have a look at the crossword puzzle in today's *Times*", he would say, fishing a crumpled newspaper out of his jacket pocket. "That'll be a lot more fun than fiddling around with figures. Figures are probably the dreariest things on this earth." [90] At the other end of the spectrum lie the dreary syllabus huggers.

The public schools have finally reached a point in their history at which they can be called impressive: impressive academically, scientifically, economically and pastorally. By the time of the Clarendon Commission in 1861 the boys' schools were already considerably more civilized institutions than when Arnold arrived at Rugby in 1828; by the beginning of the twentieth century they were much better at producing useful men for society, albeit in a narrow range; by the middle of the century they had veered off their narrow Classics track and broadened their education; in the 1960s the first of the mainstream boys' schools welcomed the civilizing influence of girls; by the end of the 1970s, in response to decades of pressure from state competition, they were on the cusp of being truly impressive institutions; after more than a century of being turned upside down and inside out but still managing to hold on to some of their timeless characteristics, their further improvement over the past generation may not seem such a leap. The girls' schools, meanwhile, had by this point become truly academic bodies, far less concerned with feminine graces than in the past. 'They weren't so strict on things like deportment, which is a shame because I'd like to have better posture', the Downe House pupil remembers. [91]

There are some bad teachers in the public schools, and indeed some bad schools. Bullying, narrow-mindedness and racism have not disappeared. However, these problems are far less prevalent than they were in previous ages. Despite new faults in the public school system, if there is a golden age of the public schools, it is now – but this may not last for long. The next chapter discusses the threats faced by these schools.

CHAPTER NINE

Beautiful Natures, Overpriced Products and Self-Destruction

SCHOOL fees are, in real terms, at their highest since the birth of the sector in the fourteenth century. This is a deeply worrying statistic for the public schools. The most troubling aspect of the problem is that fees have not, for the most part, risen because head teachers are trying to fleece gullible parents, or because they run their schools incompetently. If only it were that simple. Although fifty public schools, including Eton, Harrow and Westminster, were found guilty of organizing a fee-fixing cartel in 2005, the end of this practice brought no end to the rise in school fees.[1] This is because of the fundamental fact that fee increases are a response to very real upward pressures on schools' costs, arising from ever increasing expectations of what a public school should provide. It sometimes seems that these fee increases follow a grim and inevitable logic, with the same unstoppable momentum as Marx's prediction that capitalism would, by taking its inherent self-destructive qualities to a logical extreme, eventually destroy itself.

Before the mid-nineteenth century school fees were not standardized, but snippets from diaries, headmasters' papers, and so on, periodically give us an idea of what pupils were paying. The historical figures compare with the £28,788 a year average boarding fee for Independent Schools Council schools in January 2014 and the £12,723 in day fees.[2]

The earliest references of all to the fees paid by commoners in Winchester's first years show a range of different payments, of which the 14d a week (about £3 in annualized terms) paid by a Chelray of Berkshire was on the high side. This would be equivalent to about £3,150 a year in today's terms. The charges paid by different boys before the standardization of fees in the mid-nineteenth century were in almost all cases below today's, after adjusting for inflation. Even Con O'Neil, the son of an Irish rebel whose fees were paid by the king – not a benefactor likely to have picked the cheaper boarding options – paid only about £90 a year (£17,800 in today's terms) in 1616 and 1617. The very top of the range for Harrow fees in the second half of the eighteenth century would have been about £100 (£15,200) a year.[3] Converting into real terms the fees of six of the boarding schools covered by the Clarendon Commission in 1861, when fees were standardized, produces a range of between £10,080 and £21,160 (for Eton), with Merchant Taylors' day fees, at £1,008, veritable pin money compared with today's charges. Forty-nine years later, boarding fees for thirty-one boys' schools in the Public Schools Year Book (which covers HMC schools) range from £5,087 to £14,464 (Eton again), with an average of £9,595. Fluctuations over the following fifty-one years push average fees for the same schools to as low as £6,138 (1952) and as high as £13,548 (1938). When it comes to day school fees, charges for a range of HMC schools for 1910 to 1970 show fluctuations between an average of £1,037 in 1919 and £2,001 in 1952, before day fees begin a fairly steady rise to £3,750 in 1970. The girls' schools show a similar picture during this period.[4]

The huge real-term fee rises began in earnest at the start of the 1980s, at the same time as the boom in spending on facilities and the beginning of a period of much more aggressive reduction in pupil–teacher ratios than in the 1970s. Taking boys' and girls' education together, day fees leapt 76 per cent in real terms during the 1980s, to be followed by slightly less hefty (though still large) increases in the 1990s and 2000s. The peak of boarding school fee increases was the 1990s, when they rose by 66 per cent. Both day and boarding school fees have roughly tripled in real terms since 1980.[5]

Public schools argue that this large increase has made them better schools. Critics warn, however, that such large fee increases are financially unsustainable. The most obvious answer to this question is that, at least until now, they must have been sustainable: after a sharp rise in the 1980s and a fairly gentle fall in the early 1990s, the public schools' share of the school population has remained remarkably stable, at around 7 per cent, since that point. On the other hand, given the large growth in average income for most of that period – and, in particular, in the income per head of the top 10 per cent, who make up the public schools' core client base – it is not much of an achievement to have kept merely a stable share of the market. The public schools have soaked up a large amount of extra wealth in Britain mainly through charging pupils more, rather than through increasing the number of pupils who come to their schools by a sizeable amount (though absolute numbers have risen a little because of the growth in Britain's population).[6]

Another way of looking at whether the fee increases are financially sustainable is affordability – again concentrating on the top 10 per cent of the population. Dividing their average earnings by public school fees shows that fees have become progressively less affordable since 1980. Day school fees have risen from a little above an eighth of earnings for the top 10 per cent in that year to about a sixth in 1995, and to over a fifth in 2012. Boarding school fees have risen from a little under a quarter in 1980 to a half in 2012.[7]

These figures do not allow for the rise in the price of families' assets – houses, shares and so on – over the period. 'If you're trying to fund two or even three boys on full fees out of post-tax income, you need a colossal post-tax income', acknowledges Angus McPhail, warden at the time of Radley College, which currently charges £32,100 a year. Many parents need to fund school fees from rises in the price of property and other assets as well as one-off bonuses, rather than regular salaries, he says.[8] Eating into assets to pay for a public school education 'is, in a way, almost part of my plan', says one parent whose son is in the first year of prep school. When considering how much of a financial sacrifice he would be prepared to make, 'I'd go a long way', he says – remembering how his public school education, on a bursary, propelled him into a career in the civil service elite.[9]

So far, so good – until the crash of 2008, when the earnings of the wealthy stalled, their bonuses disappeared, and their house and share prices dropped like stones. Christopher Jonas, chairman of the governors at Roedean and City of London grandee, delivered a jeremiad to assembled heads at a public school conference the following year: the growth in private school fees over the past decade had 'outstripped the customer's underlying ability to pay them'. Jonas argued that parents had been able to afford the large increase in private school fees over the past ten years because of the happy combination of high salary bonuses, the sharp rise in house prices and low interest rates, which made borrowing cheap. He calculated that private schools had been big beneficiaries of a credit-driven boom, and that the conditions that created that boom had now disappeared.[10] Share and house prices have since recovered, but Britain's high public debt, accumulated during the global credit crunch, is likely to act as a drag on the economy for the next decade or so – making future increases in wealth and income far less sustained than over the decade and a half before the credit crunch.

In theory, public schools can simply pare their fee increases, but they may no longer be capable of doing this. Kenneth Durham, headmaster of University College School in London at the time of writing, chairman of the HMC in 2011–12, and a former economics master, is sceptical. 'Independent schools came to realize early on that they had to be highly competitive in an awful lot of areas, and price wasn't one of them', he notes. This competition included academic standards, class sizes and facilities. 'All of those factors rewarded expenditure. We realized we competed far better by spending than by saving money'. Moving to the present, 'we're stuck in a bind where we have to go on doing that, but our ability to do it by raising fees is going to become increasingly hobbled and hard to do'. In short, 'we've succeeded extremely well for the past twenty years or so by pushing

up fees faster than incomes have been rising, so that can't be continu-
ously sustainable'.[11] Durham's case is reinforced by the fact that since
Jonas's warning, public school affordability has actually fallen slightly
further.[12] His sentiment is echoed by David Levin, headmaster of
City of London School at the time of writing and Durham's prede-
cessor as chairman of the HMC: 'I think independent schools are
going to suffer because of the arms race in new buildings. They've
become an overpriced product.' Levin warns that outside the public
school heartlands of London and the south-east, 'a lot of independent
schools are really struggling'.[13]

In northern England, far from the large concentrations of wealth
in the south, this struggle is clearly already beginning to wound the
schools – sometimes mortally. A string of public schools in the region
have closed or have decided to go over to the maintained sector as
academies or free schools since the credit crunch, which hit the
earning power of parents. The 2010 closure of Southport School
in Lancashire was followed two years later by the declaration by
Queen Elizabeth's Grammar School, Blackburn, further to the east
within the same county, that it would become a free school. In 2013
Liverpool College converted into an academy, becoming perhaps
the most distinguished public school casualty in the movement's
history. 'There's no question that the market is tough', says E. M.
George, headmaster of Durham School. 'We haven't got the number
of affluent families in the north-east that London has.'[14]

Tempered by their harsh environment, northern schools have
striven more than southern schools to rein in fee increases. William
Phelan, headmaster at Stamford School, an all-boys day school in
Lincolnshire, north of the public school strongholds, insists that he's
'not keen on an arms race with other schools'. He has decided that
although the school has large sporting facilities and a new theatre,
Stamford School does not really need a specific room for the sport of
fencing.[15]

Public schools face a further problem: the bulk of them are small
compared with state schools. The average has only about 560 pupils.[16]

This makes them more expensive to run than the average state school because of the lack of economies of scale, says Jonathan Taylor, headmaster of Bootham, which has 480 or so pupils – much smaller than most comprehensives. 'Longer-term, who knows what the future holds? Will there be any independent schools with our sorts of numbers in the future? . . . In fifty years you'd have to have a question mark about it . . . The economic model is very difficult.' Like many smaller public schools, Bootham has chosen to meet the high staff costs of having tiny A level sets for minority subjects such as German and music, rather than discarding them. However, because of the great expense of catering to every academic need at Bootham and other schools, 'the local doctor and local solicitor, who used to be able to send children to the local independent school, can't afford it anymore.'[17]

At least those public schools which are left in the north have benefited by scooping up many of the children at former public schools that have gone down the academy route. Birkenhead School absorbed many girls from Birkenhead High when it became an academy in 2009. This gives the lie to initial fears that academies would force many public schools to close down because their semi-independent status would appeal to public school parents.[18] Academies, first established in 2002, are state schools free of local authority control, and with somewhat more autonomy from the state than other schools.

However, so many northern schools have closed that one wonders whether an annal of the sector written in twenty years' time will have to be referred to not as a history of Britain's public schools, but as a regional history of the public schools of the southern counties of England – much as one might write a history of the bards in Wales or of the Northern Soul movement. The 2014 Independent Schools Council annual survey showed a rise in pupil numbers in London and the south-east, but a fall everywhere else. One possible solution, an increasing reliance on foreign pupils, has its limits: with independent schools in the US, Canada, Australia and New Zealand all bidding for foreign pupils, competition is tough. Frances

King, former headmistress of Roedean, cites a sign of saturation. On a visit to Nigeria she visited Lagos' top private prep school, to be told she was the fourteenth UK head to have come that term.[19]

Optimists argue that most public schools will be able to step back from the brink of extinction by reforming their high-spending ways. Public schools have, however, in practice had an appalling record at doing so; many a public school history is the tale of a school that has, over the decades, lurched from one financial crisis to another, as it takes on debt to build new facilities designed to keep up with the competition, only to find that it cannot shoulder the burden. In 1894 Brighton College went bankrupt after an over-ambitious building spree that was followed by a fall in pupil numbers. For the next fifteen years it was controlled by its creditor, the Phoenix Fire Insurance Company.[20] This is merely one of the more spectacular cases of over-reach. One can sympathize with present-day schools which fall into similar traps: in an environment where new state-of-the-art facilities are normal, prospective parents come to see them as essential – and will take their children to a school that has them. There is short-term rationality for individual schools in obeying a model which is irrational in the longer term for the system as a whole. At £1,516 per pupil in 2013, capital spending on buildings, facilities and equipment was a little lower in real terms than its 2009 peak. This was not likely to remain the case for long, however; this 2013 figure was 17 per cent higher than in 2012.[21] The phenomenon of high spending will not push every public school into bankruptcy, but it will continue to produce casualties.

For public schools at the top of the academic hierarchy, money is not a problem. Sufficient numbers of parents will be prepared to pay virtually anything to increase the chances that their children can get into the top universities. These schools will, however, be in a difficult position if political changes remove this key selling point.

Attempts by the state to curb the power of the public schools through legislation and regulation have generally oscillated between mild and total incompetence. Much more powerful has been the competition provided by the state schools. The decision by the government to encroach on universities' historical autonomy in choosing their students may pose a much greater political danger to the public schools than the far more radical threats, in previous decades, to abolish them altogether.

Greater state interference in university admissions began when Tony Blair decided to give universities the right to charge considerably higher tuition fees than previously permitted. Blair was, however, forced to make major concessions to Labour MPs to secure a 'yes' vote for what he wanted in parliament in 2004. One of these concessions was the creation of the Office for Fair Access (Offa), which has the power to prevent a university from charging high fees if it cannot satisfy Offa that it is making strong efforts to admit children from poorer rather than richer families. The problem for the public schools was that the ready reckoner used to divide rich from poor is public school education. Universities agree with Offa on targets for the proportion of UK students to be admitted from state rather than independent schools, with a 2014–15 target for Cambridge of 61 to 63 per cent.[22] Little has happened, in practice, if universities miss these targets, but the pressure remains to go at least some way towards meeting them. In 2012 Professor Les Ebdon, the head of Offa, advocated that students from struggling comprehensives should be given less exacting A level offers than other students. This prompted Christopher Ray, the dourly humorous high master of Manchester Grammar, to cite 'Harrison Bergeron', the 1961 story by Kurt Vonnegut Jr in which the United States Handicapper General makes everyone equal in intelligence, speed and strength – with the naturally intelligent forced to wear earphones with deafening radio signals to impair their concentration.[23]

Only a minority of current public school heads think this has made it harder to get their pupils into the top universities, but some of them see how easily a target could be hardened into a quota, where universities would be barred by law from admitting more than a certain proportion of public school pupils.[24] It is unlikely that a Conservative or Conservative-dominated government would do this, but it seems credible that a Labour government might harden the requirement. Blair created a sword of Damocles for the public schools, which could fall at any point in the years to come.

Some argue that if this rule were imposed, public school students could easily switch to overseas universities, particularly to those in the US. The number of public school children doing this has already risen, but remains low: the proportion of public school pupils choosing an overseas over a UK university is still, in 2014, only 3.7 per cent.[25] Nonetheless, Joseph Spence, master of Dulwich College, thinks that government policy has started to make it harder for public school children to get in. On the other hand, 'international universities would welcome kids with the skills we're providing'. He thinks that overseas university education 'is about to take off' at the public schools. As well as Dulwich boys going to US universities – about 12 a year out of 200 leaving the sixth form – more of his pupils are going to European universities, such as an Indian boy doing his medical degree in English at Milan University.[26]

However, the high fees which the top US colleges charge present an obstacle. The total cost of an undergraduate degree at Harvard College without financial aid was $58,607 (about £37,000) for tuition, room, board and fees combined in 2014–15. Although 70 per cent of Harvard undergraduates receive some financial aid, richer families in the UK not eligible for this might decide that it would be cheaper and less complicated to circumvent the Offa rules by buying a house in a wealthy area with a middle-class comprehensive and paying for daily after-school tuition for their child.[27]

Britain could even see a partial return to the private tuition that was the primary education of many of the wealthy for several centuries before public schools started crowding them out – with pupils at state schools in the day and with private tutors in the evening and at weekends. Wealthy parents could, in this case, take a leaf out of the Blairs' book: it was reported that they paid for private tuition for their children from at least one Westminster School teacher while sending them, for political reasons, to state schools.[28]

There are other forms of slow death for public schools which future governments might devise, either on purpose or, like a boot crushing a spider, out of an indifference to the sector's fate. It is, in truth, impossible to know – and the impossibility of predicting this is in large part what poses the danger: if public schools are unable to predict the threat they cannot prepare for it. Emma Taylor, headmistress of Christ College, Brecon, which draws about half its pupils from outside Wales, furnishes an intriguing example of how destructive even a small change in policy might be: 'The thing that would kill us off would be if the Welsh government said we had to teach the Welsh language' – a current requirement for state schools but not public schools. 'About half our families wouldn't send their children here if they had to do Welsh', she claims. Taylor concludes that because of the hostility of the Welsh government to public schools, 'we live in an environment where we have to watch all the time what's coming out'.[29] If what is known cannot be feared, the opposite holds true as well.

One part of the public school movement is in clear and severe long-term decline, with little hope of its deterioration being arrested. The girls' schools have been losing pupils for decades. The figures from the Girls' Schools Association provide a rough overall picture, and it is not a pretty one: the number of girls educated at members of the GSA slumped by 25 per cent to 84,488 in the twenty years to 2014, and the decline steepened in the second decade.[30]

This slide has occurred even though the girls' schools have, perhaps more than any other part of the public school world, changed what they do in response to parental demands – reflecting the greatly different view which middle-class parents have of their daughters' future role in society. The vast bulk of girls from single-sex public schools go on to higher education. They also achieve better results than girls in co-ed public schools: 2008 research from the association showed that 57 per cent of girls' A level results at the association's schools were A grades, compared with only 49 per cent at co-ed public schools – with an even wider gap for the top two GCSE grades.[31] Research in 2009 by Durham University found that pupils in single-sex public schools – whether boys or girls – improved more on average in their academic work than pupils at co-ed schools between the ages of eleven and sixteen.[32]

The truth is that the decline in numbers at girls' schools has nothing to do with academic results, and everything to do with changes in society. Many parents now prefer their daughters to be educated in a less sheltered environment – and teenage girls are, for once, inclined to agree with their parents. Girls' schools do, even after centuries of change, retain a ghost of the old view, born in the convent schools, that their charges must be protected. 'Parents are rightly frightened by the forces that their daughters are subjected to from society', says Laura Hyde, headmistress of St James' Senior Girls' School in London. 'They're desperate to find a school that will protect and support the beautiful aspects of their daughters' natures', she enthuses – her assertion audibly supported by the sound of a girl at her piano lesson, audible from inside the headmistress's study from beginning to end of the interview. Mrs Hyde speaks of the necessity of the girls' 'moral protection'.[33] The girls' schools look set to survive as a much smaller niche within the overall public school movement; if they do live on, the ancient desire for moral protection of their pupils' 'beautiful aspects' will play an important part in their survival.

CHAPTER TEN

The Pauline and the Pasty

BRITAIN's public schools have, more or less, confounded all the critics who claimed that they provided a backward education, irrelevant to the modern age. However, the brickbats against which they must shield themselves in the twenty-first century are heavier and deadlier than ever. Opponents of the public schools say that their alumni hog the most important jobs in a way that is inefficient, divisive, dangerous and damaging.

It is inefficient because it confers a career advantage on people who are no more talented than the norm; this advantage makes it harder for more able people educated by the state to secure the highly skilled jobs for which Britain needs people of ability. In a pithily titled *Observer* article, 'Born poor? Bad luck, you have won last prize in the lottery of life', Will Hutton, an economist and writer, accuses the public schools of fostering 'bad capitalism', because they restrict the economic potential of others who lack the public school advantage.[1]

It is divisive because the many politicians who went to public school, including David Cameron, Nick Clegg and George Osborne, have little understanding of how ordinary people live. The segregation argument was put eloquently by R. H. Tawney, the economic historian, back in 1931. The public school system was 'educationally vicious, since to mix with companions from homes of different types is an important part of the education of the young', he wrote. 'It is socially disastrous, for it does more than any other single cause, except capitalism itself, to perpetuate the division of the nation into classes of which one is almost unintelligible to the other.'[2]

It is dangerous because pubic school independence from the state allows the schools to create unsatisfactory and even unsavoury worlds of their own. This means that the quality of public school education can be appalling, since there is no irreducible minimum enforced by the state in the daily management of schools.[3] Consequently, public schools are able to go off and do their own thing without the guidance of the benevolent hand of the state.[4]

It is damaging because public schools harm the quality of education for everyone in the state sector, by draining it of bright pupils from homes which value education. If much of the economic elite knows nothing of, and cares nothing for, state education, what chance does it have? It is in danger of becoming a Cinderella service. Thus say opponents of the public schools.

This is a serious charge sheet. This chapter looks at whether or not these accusations are well founded.

Public school alumni do not hog all the top jobs, but they do take a highly disproportionate share. In 2014 the Social Mobility and Child Poverty Commission published figures showing what proportion of the elite had attended public school. A striking chart showed the schools' triumph: seven in ten senior judges, six in ten senior officers in the armed forces, and more than half of the permanent secretaries, senior diplomats and leading media figures – the hundred most important editors and columnists – had been to one. The Commission did not have figures on leading medics and barristers, but 2009 research published by the Sutton Trust education charity showed that 51 per cent of the former and 68 per cent of the latter had been to public school.

Moreover, in several cases these proportions had fallen only slightly, or not at all, since the mid-1980s. The proportion of leading medics had remained unchanged at 51 per cent, and the proportion of leading media figures had actually tipped above half, rising from 47 per cent to 54 per cent. These two numbers showed the breadth of public school strength: they were holding their own in producing both scribblers and scientists. Separate research published in 2014 by the Sutton Trust found that 60 per cent of senior people in financial services, source of many of Britain's high-paid jobs, had been public school pupils.[5]

The public school background of these leaders of their professions varies. Many leading media figures come from the day schools. University College School, which has educated journalists as varied as the *Guardian* columnist Jonathan Freedland, the *Financial Times* columnist Martin Wolf, and the *Daily Mail* editor Paul Dacre, stands out in particular. Among female journalists, *Vogue* editor-in-chief Alexandra Shulman, former BBC economics editor Stephanie Flanders and *Prospect* magazine editor Bronwen Maddox were all at St Paul's Girls' School. A high proportion of the most senior judges, by contrast, have been at elite boarding schools such as Eton and Harrow.[6]

The public schools have recently even started to produce pop stars, after lagging in the field – they account for 22 per cent of them, according to the Social Mobility and Child Poverty Commission. King's College School, which has long been particularly strong in music, has educated – all within a few years of each other – Marcus Mumford and Ben Lovett from the folk rock group Mumford & Sons, the singer-songwriter Patrick Wolf, and Dan Smith, the front man of the band Bastille, whose 2012 song 'Pompeii', about the ancient Roman city buried by a volcano, is the most streamed song in British history (albeit a short history).[7] His old Classics masters must be rubbing their hands with glee: he had been listening after all.

The public schools' disproportionate share of society's top jobs looks set to continue for another generation. In 2013 the Social Mobility and Child Poverty Commission found that the proportion of public school-educated undergraduates at the top-tier Russell Group universities had actually risen rather than fallen since the early

2000s. To take the four most prestigious institutions in the country, they still supplied 42 per cent of new UK undergraduates at Oxford (in other words, 58 per cent were from state schools), the same percentage at Cambridge, 37 per cent at Imperial College London and 35 per cent at University College London.[8] This is crucial to future public school predominance: academic research from 2013 finds that ex-public school graduates are a third more likely to break into high-status occupations than state-educated graduates from similarly affluent families and neighbourhoods, largely because they are more likely to go to leading universities.[9] Furthermore, figures for 2004 showed that the younger partners at leading commercial law firms of solicitors were actually far more likely to be public school-educated than the older ones – 71 per cent of partners younger than thirty-nine were public school-educated, compared with 51 per cent of older partners.[10]

A key question is whether this is bad for the country. Critics say that the public schools' disproportionate share of undergraduate places at the most elite Russell Group universities is a bad thing, because this prevents bright state school pupils from using a degree at a top university as a launch pad for a glittering career. They point to an estimated 3,700 'missing' state-educated students who would get into Russell Group universities in England, if state school pupils with top A level grades were as likely to go to Russell Group universities as public school pupils.[11] However, many admissions tutors say that most of this 'missing' figure is explained by the inappropriate subjects – media studies and so on – which state school students are more likely to take. In 2009 Geoff Parks, director of admissions for the Cambridge colleges, said it would be difficult for state schools' share of undergraduate places to rise above 63 per cent – because state school students accounted for 63 per cent of the number of students achieving the three As at A level normally required for Cambridge entry, in subject combinations appropriate for Cambridge courses. (By 2012–13, after a large jump from the previous year, the state school proportion actually reached 63 per cent precisely.)[12]

Public school pupils are far more likely to go to university than state school pupils. Largely because of this, the charge is often made that the public schools get too many unimpressive candidates into university at the expense of better state-educated pupils. The numbers, however, rebut this. On the one hand, public school pupils do, on average, gain worse degrees than state-educated pupils with the same A level grades, suggesting that allowance should continue to be made for state school pupils who seem bright but have less than stellar A level results.[13] On the other hand, taking the raw figures as a whole, at 67 per cent the proportion of public school pupils who earn a 2.1 and above is higher than the overall graduate average of 63 per cent.[14] This is a powerful argument against excluding more public school pupils.

But despite these justifications, the public schools' disproportionately high share of the most important jobs cannot entirely be explained by their share of places at elite universities. Very roughly, they fill about 40 per cent of these at the moment. In the 1970s and first years of the 1980s, when many of the senior figures covered in the research above were at university, they filled 30 to 40 per cent of new Cambridge places (figures for the other top universities are unavailable).[15] However, in many fields public school pupils fill more than 50 per cent of the top jobs. This leaves a gap between academic achievement and career achievement.

Opponents of the public schools are likely to see a ready explanation in the role of sinister old boy, and now old girl, networks in boosting people's careers. However, the 2013 research showing that ex-public school graduates were more likely to break into high-status occupations than state-educated graduates looked at their use of personal networks, and found these networks played a relatively minor role.[16]

There are many other candidates for that special magic, beyond academic results, behind their extra share of the most important jobs. The prefect system gives public school pupils an advantage by training them for leadership; the large number of extra-curricular activities at public schools teaches pupils how to lead, organize and inspire; for some pupils, sport teaches resilience and other qualities that are also helpful in making it to the top. Given all this, it is healthy for public school pupils to fill 40 per cent of the top university places and 50 per cent or so of the top jobs in Britain.

However, when the percentage rises to 60 per cent or above – as it does for barristers, judges and younger partners at leading commercial law firms – the proportion has probably reached unhealthy levels, because it means that in this particular sector – the law – the door is less than half open to bright state school alumni. In particular, the 71 per cent public school figure for leading solicitors is worrying. It is higher than is safe, and continuing efforts by the profession to look into this should be welcomed. A word of caution, however, for all who probe the murky depths of this area: paying for a public school education is not the only way in which wealthy people give their children career advantages. Sometimes there are other, far better explanations. In the 1970s, barristers, who also accounted for the bulk of future judges, had to take unpaid pupillages after university, a system which favoured those with wealthy backgrounds. Moreover, public school children are sometimes able to use family connections that have nothing to do with their public school education. Simon Cowell, the music entrepreneur, went to Dover College, but this did not get him into the music industry; his first job in music was in the mail room of EMI Music Publishing where his father was an executive. Public schools educate people to a high level in useful subjects; they instil useful personal qualities; they cannot, however, explain every career success for their pupils.

Leaving aside the issue of public schools' share of places at elite universities, the public schools provide a broader benefit: they are good for the economy and society because they increase the total amount of education and knowledge in Britain. In this sense they are efficient. Any institution which increases the total amount of knowledge is not quite by definition a 'good' thing; however, if people want to say it is a 'bad' thing, the case against it has to be very strong indeed.

The best way of understanding this notion is by looking at the concept of human capital – borrowed from economics – and to liken Britain's economy to a huge pie. Economic growth, and hence wealth and well-being, depends on putting into the pie various forms of capital, including land, factory plant and so on. One of these sources of capital is human capital: the total stock of knowledge and ability of the entire workforce. Any increase in capital, including human capital, increases the size of the economy. The existence of the public schools greatly increases overall UK spending on education, and hence on human capital. Public schools spend more per pupil than state schools. Moreover, state spending per head would, in reality, have to fall to absorb the extra numbers if public school children left en masse for the state sector.[17]

The human capital justification for public schools is even greater, given the nature of education which public school children receive. The public schools are particularly prone to produce star students in the tougher, and more economically useful, sciences. In 2011 they also contributed more than half of the A*s in A level German, and above 40 per cent for Spanish and French – handy subjects for British exporters, and hence for British jobs.[18] This is a particularly valuable form of human capital. By increasing human capital, the public schools are providing more, and better, ingredients to make the pie.

Critics say that talk of public schools' contribution to society is beside the point. To many of them, what matters is fairness: the share of the pie rather than the size of the pie. Public schools certainly widen inequality of opportunity, because they educate some children to a high level but do not educate the bulk of the population. However, the average amount of pie per person is larger, and I consider that to be more important.

The acute sensitivity within the higher ranks of the Tory party to the class segregation criticism was revealed in dramatic but comic degree on that fateful day in March 2012 when a pasty put a Pauline in peril. George Osborne, chancellor of the exchequer and old boy of St Paul's, made the rash decision to impose value-added tax at 20 per cent on the heated pasty, an iconic snack of the working classes. Osborne was, in fact, rationally closing a rare working-class tax loophole, but this mattered not a jot. The main media focus came to rest on the pasty-eating habits, or lack thereof, of Osborne and Cameron, neither of whom could convincingly prove when they had last eaten the tasty snack. The issue might have seemed extraordinarily petty to a foreigner unschooled in Britain's intense interest in social class, but it generated a media storm. Now, at last, commentators could point to a specific issue that appeared to show that Cameron, Osborne and the rest of their clique were out of touch – and most articles on the subject referred to their public school background as proof of this otherworldliness.[19] The country was being run, argued pundits, by men who knew nothing of ordinary people's lives, and who had no idea of the big implications for ordinary people's budgets of a sudden 20 per cent price increase in a regular lunchtime food.[20] Following a partial U-turn, the working classes were able to continue consuming some (though not all) heated pasties at the same cost as before, and the chancellor was left eating humble pie.[21]

The public schools are now much less horizontally segregated than previously: in fact they are ethnically very mixed. In January 2012, 26.7 per cent of pupils at Independent Schools Council schools were from ethnic minorities, slightly higher than the figure of 25.4 per cent for state schools. Public school pupils are exposed to a variety of different cultures; the former problem of a lack of exposure to non-white British and foreign culture has disappeared.[22]

However, opponents attack the public schools for isolating their charges from native working-class culture.

Many of the public schools have tried to fight this segregation ever since the days of the Victorian missions, now replaced by various forms of afternoon community service. Moreover, the old implicit and explicit non-financial bars to working-class entry have gone. Even the mockery by boys from conventional public school backgrounds of fee-paying boys from 'trade' has become more muted: the boy already referred to in the previous chapter who entered Epsom College in the late 1980s, his fees paid by a working-class father who had built up a successful cleaning business, remembers only snippets of teasing about it. This was largely from the son of a lawyer who commented that his father 'picks up turds for a living' – to which his riposte was 'yes, he picked up your father'.[23]

In their defence against charges of segregation, the public schools point to their bursary programmes. Even if the bulk of Eton's pupils pay high fees, in absolute terms the number on some type of bursary now exceeds the original number of seventy scholars set out at its foundation. About one-fifth of Etonians are on bursaries, roughly 250, of whom about 50 pay nothing at all.[24] At Charterhouse, seventy pupils have bursaries, compared with a stipulation of only forty at the school's foundation – though only a dozen or so pay nothing.[25] At Winchester the total on bursaries is, at seventy-six, including two paying nothing, a smidgeon above the original number of seventy.[26] These figures are a rejoinder to the common call for the public schools to go back to their original mission of educating the poor, though in fact the majority of the public schools were never formally set up to do so.[27]

It would, however, be naïve to think that bursaries are exclusively, or even primarily, for the poor. Rather than aiding low-income parents, much bursary provision is actually a form of discounting in a competitive market to entice middle-class parents, some of whom could, at a pinch, afford the fees of their chosen public school or another slightly cheaper one. Figures for 2010 from Staffordshire University show an ascending scale of bursary provision as one moves down school league tables, moving away from the academically selective, oversubscribed schools to those parts of the tables inhabited by academically weaker schools with a correspondingly weaker competitive position when bargaining with parents over fees. Schools below the 280th place in *The Times* league table of independent schools awarded 4.2 per cent of school income as bursaries. Schools whose placing in the top seventy rewards them with a long line of potential pupils whose parents could pay the full fees, awarded only 2.2 per cent in bursaries.[28] Further proof that most bursaries are not for the genuinely poor is shown by the fact that of the 7.8 per cent of public school children on some kind of bursary, 60 per cent had less than half their fees remitted.[29] About a dozen Winchester boys out of the seventy-six on bursaries are from families with a net income below £21,788, though Winchester's calculation of income differs from that of the government.[30]

One solution to the low proportion of what one might call 'pure bursaries' – those available to anyone, rather than bursaries used in the bargaining process to attract middle-class families on the margin of being able to afford full fees – is for the schools to increase the level of full fees to create bursary funds. This would, however, jeopardize their own objective by restricting entry on full fees to a smaller pool of families. Public schools would become both less and more exclusive at the same time.

In theory, at least, this segregation matters, because if a country's future leaders have little contact with poorer people, they might make bad decisions about them – decisions that are callous, unfair, ineffective, or all three. One of the best illustrations in British history of how a segregated political class can, through sheer ignorance of how other classes live, preside over bad policy, remains the shock over Boer War recruitment described in Chapter Five.

The accusations of class segregation have, in the later stages of the 2010–15 coalition government, centred largely on Cameron's inner circle. At the time of writing Cameron was supported by several Old Etonian aides, including Jo Johnson, head of the Number Ten policy board, and Ed Llewellyn, Cameron's chief of staff. In response, some Conservative MPs in northern and marginal seats complained that Cameron was isolated from the concerns of ordinary people by the background of his inner circle. 'There are six people writing the manifesto and five of them went to Eton; the other went to St Paul's', one Conservative MP in a marginal constituency complained in 2014 (the sole Pauline was Osborne).[31] Even Michael Gove, the education secretary and ex-public schoolboy (Robert Gordon's College), described the concentration of Old Etonians in Cameron's inner circle as 'ridiculous', though he did not conclude that this put Cameron out of touch.[32]

However, the case that coalition policies are flawed by a lack of understanding of ordinary people is weak. Any administration, whether Conservative-dominated or Labour, would have found it difficult to keep benefits as they were during the current age of austerity. Furthermore, whether one agrees or disagrees with the cut in the top rate of income tax, there is a respectable intellectual argument for it: the historical experience that when income tax for the highest income rises above a certain level, the amount collected tends to fall. It is outside the scope of this book to take a view on whether Cameron and Osborne are right, but we should nevertheless give them the credit for having an evidence-based case for the policies they pursue that goes beyond mere 'let them eat cake' callousness. There is maths behind their method. Even the furore over the pasty tax does not suggest that they are out of touch; the decision to levy VAT was simply the latest foray by the Treasury in a long history of battles over correct VAT rates on heated food.[33] Ironically, it was probably the elevated social background of Cameron and Osborne which derailed the tax change in the end; other politicians from more plebeian backgrounds would have felt less politically exposed over the issue.

The Boer War did indeed reveal a shocking ignorance of how ordinary people lived. However, only forty years after the end of that war it was a public schoolboy, the Old Carthusian William Beveridge, who devised the theoretical blueprint for the welfare state after observing precisely what everyday life for other classes was like. It was an Old Haileyburian prime minister, Attlee, who implemented the Beveridge Report's recommendations. Admittedly, Beveridge did not experience some dramatic awakening to social problems while at Charterhouse. 'I can't trace anything which I particularly value in myself of mental or moral development to Charterhouse', he recalled. On the other hand, his biographer traces his 'habits of hard work, early rising and meticulous accuracy' – at least two of which helped to give the report the crucial intellectual heft – to his time at the school.[34] He had a good education, and he used it well, for the good of humanity.

A more recent Charterhouse pupil, who taught at the school in the 2000s, admits that when he became an English teacher at an inner-city Midlands state school, 'it was very difficult to adapt ... It has been difficult understanding the pressures pupils face.' However, although he did not encounter pupils with such backgrounds at Charterhouse, 'at the same time I feel my Charterhouse education has really been valuable here because I've been able to get involved with the sport, and my subject knowledge is very strong'. He also finds that his fellow ex-Carthusians have shown 'an amazing level of sympathy, without any direct contact with the pupils'. He attributes this partly to the good teaching they imbibed in history, geography and politics. A good public school education can create empathy with other classes.[35]

In any case, the Conservative party is actually becoming less rather than more public school – more rather than less broadly based in terms of class. The proportion of Conservative MPs educated privately fell from 70 per cent in 1983 to 54 per cent in 2010 – hardly pointing to a continuing dominance of public school old boys. The fall in the Tory proportion helped to bring down the overall public school proportion for the three main parties in the House of Commons from 51 per cent to 37 per cent over the same period, making politics far less public school-dominated than most professions.[36] Cameron may have several Old Etonians around him, and Eton and other public schools continue to provide a good political education; however, much of his parliamentary rank-and-file and most senior appointments at the time of writing, including foreign secretary Philip Hammond and home secretary Theresa May, were entirely, or primarily, state-educated.

Moreover, a large public school presence in politics is no bar to a meritocratic political system. Reaching the commanding heights of British politics is considerably more meritocratic than in the many countries where political dynasties exist. The US, Japan, China, India,

Pakistan and Greece all have a strongly dynastic element in the very top ranks of their politicians: prime ministers, party leaders and so on. Since the early twentieth century Britain has not. Critics might argue that as an Etonian Cameron had a head start in becoming an MP and eventual party leader. Perhaps so, but he had to compete within a large pool of other bright young men. For supporters of meritocracy, a far more worrying rise to power was the 2007 accession of Bilawal Bhutto Zardari, son of a president and prime minister, to the chairmanship of the powerful Pakistan People's Party, run by his family, at the tender age of nineteen.

Cameron and other Eton boys were, moreover, given a good political education at a school with a long tradition of educating politicians. Boys applying for an Eton scholarship in 2013 were asked to imagine that they, as a prime minister following in the long line of Eton premiers since Walpole, must write the script for a speech justifying the use of the army against violent protestors during an oil crisis in 2040.[37] It is a difficult question requiring a difficult answer – one that rejects black-and-white thinking in favour of an understanding of shades of grey. This highly nuanced education in political thought can be traced back, at Britain's public schools, to Sumner at Harrow in the eighteenth century, and to the debates in which Gladstone took part at Eton in the early years of the nineteenth. Cameron was trained for the job.

Winchester College maintained, for half a century, a rather wary attitude towards the A level, even after coming reluctantly to accept that, for the sake of university entrance and future career, it was a necessary evil. One might compare the relationship between the old institution and the upstart qualification to the unpleasant obligation of an annual visit to the dentist. 'There are disadvantages in this increasing use of A-level, in that it reduces the flexibility which the absence of examination makes possible', wrote the school's headmaster in his 1957 annual report to the warden and fellows, 'but with boys of the ability we have here it ought to be possible to prepare them for any examinations and educate them at the same time'.[38] It was therefore not entirely surprising that in the 2000s Winchester took a leading role, along with a small number of other public schools, in developing the Cambridge Pre-U (short for Pre-University), a highly academic qualification designed to be more rigorous than the A level.[39] Schools began teaching it in 2008.

The Pre-U was one among several competing qualifications adopted by the public schools during this period. In 2008 when the Pre-U was launched, the number of GCSEs sat dropped by 158,242 to 5,669,077. Examiners blamed this on the growing popularity of the International GCSE, a harder version of the standard GCSE that was proving increasing popular with the public schools. At this stage, however, almost no state school offered it because Whitehall refused to fund it.[40] St Paul's had already made the switch to science IGCSEs, which the more academic public schools were beginning to adopt in droves, because it believed GCSEs were not rigorous enough. In 2009 Ofqual said it had 'significant causes for concern' about GCSE science. It demanded an 'improved quality of questions, to stretch and challenge all students'.[41] By this stage some of the more academic public schools, including two girls' schools, North London Collegiate and Godolphin and Latymer, and the co-ed school Sevenoaks, had switched in whole or in part away from A levels and towards the International Baccalaureate for sixth-form students, prompted by the same concerns about A levels that had propelled public schools towards the Pre-U. By 2012, 65 per cent of public schools supplying data to the ISC were offering IGCSEs, that is, 571 schools. One in eleven offered the Pre-U, and one in eight the IB.[42]

Where public schools led the way, state schools followed. By 2014, 78 of the 168 schools offering the Pre-U were in the maintained sector.[43] By 2012, more than half of the 200 schools offering the International Baccalaureate in Britain were state schools. Moreover, in 2010 Whitehall relented in its initial opposition, to allow state funding of IGCSE syllabuses.[44] In addition, the public schools' switch to the Pre-U increased the pressure on the government to toughen A levels, a process under way in 2014, under Michael Gove the education secretary, though public schools and universities did not agree with all of the reforms.[45]

It is hard to see that any of these rival qualifications to the A level and GCSE norm would have taken off in British state schools had the public schools not existed. The public schools were able to pioneer these exams in a way that state school heads found much harder to do, because of the uniform exam system which the state, like most states around the world, has a tendency to impose. This uniformity is understandable, because the modern state is in a condition of constant hyper-accountability. When the National Health Service was founded in 1948, Aneurin Bevan warned perceptively: 'Every time a maid kicks over a bucket of slops in a ward, an agonised wail will go through Whitehall.' The apparatus of the state is slow and unwieldy: the kind of experimentation in which individual public schools are free to engage is a very difficult thing for the state sector to achieve.

It is also easier for public schools to educate in a way that is appropriate to their pupils' background and cultural values. James Whitehead, headmaster of Downside School, a Catholic school in Somerset, plans to veer off the narrow, well-trodden road of the A level English syllabus when he combines his headship duties with some teaching in the future. This may involve using the set texts of Christina Rossetti's poetry, for example, as a starting point for an exploration of the pre-Raphaelite movement in general, including the 'recurring religious symbolism' in pre-Raphaelite images, both pictorial and poetic. He may also look at the poetry of Manley Hopkins, a Catholic convert who knew Rossetti, an Anglo-Catholic. It will be a distinctively Downside approach to the syllabus, steeped in a rich understanding of Rossetti's world – if done well.[46]

Bootham School provides an equally distinctive education, poles apart from that of Downside or most other public schools. While boys from King's College School have kept alive the martial spirit of the public schools by re-enacting the Battle of Hastings every year in battle dress and armour, the traditional outing of Bootham children has been a protest visit to the radomes of nearby Menwith Hill, site of a sprawling US missile warning and monitoring system.[47] Jonathan Taylor, the current head, recalls organizing a coach trip up to the G8 summit in Edinburgh in 2005, where pupils protested about the failure of rich nations to help poor ones. He thinks this would have been much harder at the state school at which he used to teach: 'We would probably have had all sorts of hoops to go through and forms to fill and risk assessments to make, and that sort of stuff which is a bit easier in a small independent school.'[48]

Even a cursory probe into the outer regions of the public school movement unearths, however, at least some respectable arguments in favour of uniformity. In 2012, the Office for Standards in Education, Children's Services and Skills (Ofsted), the government schools inspectorate, concluded that the teaching in many of the more than 1,000 independent schools which it inspected was rarely better than 'competent', and that across the range it was 'seldom inspiring'. In one-third it was not good enough, and in only 7 per cent was it 'outstanding'. Ofsted responded by pledging a tougher inspection regime.[49]

However, the schools which Ofsted criticizes are generally small, cheap and far removed from the large, well-established public schools covered by this history book. They are more akin to the old-fashioned, precarious private schools discussed in earlier chapters. They also educate only a small proportion of total public/private/independent school pupils, depending on one's preferred term. Virtually all the larger schools are excluded from Ofsted's damning verdict: they are members of the Independent Schools Council, which puts them under the regime of the Independent Schools Inspectorate rather than Ofsted. It is, however, hard to see how one can avoid some bad schools springing up in the private sector unless the state imposes strict uniformity on independent schools as a whole. Variability of quality is the price of freedom. It is a price worth paying, given the overall benefits which independent education brings. There is, in any case, a huge variation in results within the state sector too, even between different schools serving pupils of similar background; there are some very bad state schools.

The uniformity to which the state system is prone is also largely responsible for a key disadvantage: their flawed approach to talented children. The public schools have always, even during their darkest periods, shown some capacity for educating the most able; their role in schooling future leaders has been one of the most enduring themes of their history, even over the past seven decades or so during which their ability to educate the average child has also greatly improved. From 1999 the Blair–Brown Labour government gamely tried to improve provision for able state school children through its Gifted and Talented programme, which served pupils selected by schools as meeting these criteria. The scheme never dug deep roots inside the state system, however, because it was hindered by constant changes made by central government. Initially, a National Academy for Gifted and Talented Youth provided out-of-school activities for five years. Then came three years when the programme was based on an interactive website, followed by a year as part of the government's much broader National Strategies programme. In 2011 the new Conservative–Liberal Democrat government abandoned it altogether. In the same year the Chief Inspector of Schools complained, about state schools in general, that 'the level of challenge for more able pupils is a particular issue'.[50] The point was repeated two years later, when Ofsted lamented that thousands of bright children were being 'systematically failed' by non-selective secondaries.[51]

This policy foundered, largely because of an underlying incentive structure which rewarded schools for improving the results of children of middling ability rather than those higher up the scale. Whitehall focused on schools' relative success in achieving, or failing to achieve, the government's demand that at least 30 per cent of pupils achieve 'good' grades (A* to C) at GCSE. Gordon Brown pledged, shortly after becoming premier in 2007, to have schools that missed this benchmark closed or taken over.[52]

A further problem was the reluctance of state school teachers to separate the talented from the general pool of students. 'The school is reluctant to use the term ... gifted and talented', complained one comprehensive school teacher. 'If you are dealing with students who are G&T [one of the more comical pieces of jargon of the education sector] does that mean the rest are not? We don't actually like the term "more able" either because that again implies that others are less able.' Another comprehensive teacher reported 'issues with labelling', including the need for trying not to 'make the label sound elitist'. One might argue that this was not the spirit in which the public and grammar schools had produced Oxbridge scholarship pupils, but, to be fair to the schools, the government's one-size-fits-all approach did not help them in making their choice. It asked all schools to select 5 to 10 per cent of their pupils, regardless of the social and economic characteristics of their catchment areas. Some schools responded by choosing none of their pupils, or all of them – in effect boycotting a policy which was, in any case, woefully under-resourced throughout its pitiful existence.[53] Any impression that the state was bringing out the talents of the able was not supported by 2008 figures, which showed that one in seven pupils selected as Gifted and Talented failed to gain five good GCSEs.[54] The obstructive attitude of some state school heads towards the programme chimes with the comment by Roderick MacKinnon, headmaster of a state school before taking up the headship of Bristol Grammar School, the ex-direct grant grammar, that 'the emphasis in the state system is "one person can't do something so everybody must stop" '.[55] With programmes such as these, it is not surprising that many parents with children whom they deemed talented have opted for the public schools, which see no shame in the concept of an elite.

The tendency for the state system to impose uniformity is underlined by the grisly sequel to the state's adoption of IGCSEs. The flowers that bloomed belatedly are now dying. In July 2014 it emerged that IGCSEs would be axed from school league tables – in effect preventing schools from offering them since the government judges them by their league table performance. It was reported that they could be reintroduced at a later date, if their design were changed to become more like that of the new GCSEs. However, the news bequeaths IGCSEs with a future that looks uncertain at best.[56]

'All for one, one for all', say the three musketeers (plus d'Artagnan, the newcomer) in Alexandre Dumas's 1844 novel of the same name. These feisty warriors doubtless did not consider that this maxim could be applied to maintaining the quality of public services. However, many thinkers see it as providing a good philosophy for Britain's state schools: on the one hand, if everyone remains equally committed to maintaining the quality of a system, the system will remain strong. On the other hand, if state schools are cursed by the disappearance of many parents with a particularly strong interest in the education which their children are receiving in class, and with the resources and articulacy to be able to maintain the quality of that class's education, state school education suffers because these parents lack the personal interest in improving state education. In other words, the enemies of public schools argue that they weaken state education by leeching talent and motivated parents away from it. State schools will benefit if these parents are forced to return their children to state schools – or so this thinking runs.

There is validity in the view that if an entire society, including the wealthy, has no choice but to use a particular public service, the public impetus to keep that service high quality is increased. On the other hand, this is no guarantee of quality. London's train and underground services are used by thousands of affluent bankers fighting their way every day into London's financial district, but these services are still considered by expatriates to be poor in comparison with other inter-national cities. Sometimes well-connected people complain about a public service and make it better; sometimes they have no power to do so, and it simply gets worse.

This said, there is no doubt that if a hundred children from wealthy homes were suddenly put into an inner-city comprehensive in London, there would suddenly be no shortage of school governors (as there are in many inner-city schools), of reading help, of strings pulled, doors unlocked and wallets emptied to secure extra help for the school. Parents can do more about their child's school than their transport system.

That is not, however, where children of wealthy parents would go if public schools disappeared tomorrow. If they kept their children in British education at all, rather than sending them abroad, such parents would ensure they would attend the best-performing comprehensives, which are generally in upper middle-class areas. Research by the Sutton Trust found that the country's top 164 comprehensive schools took only 9.2 per cent of their children from deprived homes.[57] These schools are less segregated than public schools. However, the fact remains that in any state school system, the rich will generally be schooled with the rich and the poor with the poor – whether in Britain, or in Finland or Sweden, countries used by the left and the right, respectively, as models of a good state school system to which to aspire.[58] Let us imagine that the three musketeers plus d'Artagnan were all modern-day Londoners with children of school age, spawned by nocturnal dalliances after a day's fighting. It is doubtful that d'Artagnan, a poor Gascon though of a noble family, could have found a house in as wealthy an area as the other three musketeers (and in any case he might have missed the strict deadline for local school applications, given his recent move from the countryside to the school catchment area). The musketeers would be divided by their economic circum-stances.

In Britain, this class divide within the state sector can be mitigated by reforming admissions policies to reduce the ability of upper middle-class parents to manipulate the system to get their children into their preferred school. As proof that such manipulation exists, the Sutton Trust research found that about 20 per cent of children in the average catchment area of the country's top comprehensives came from deprived homes – double the percentage of children actually admitted who were from deprived homes. Admission policies to deal with manipulation are a less than perfect answer, however. This is in part because regular attempts to reform it are never entirely successful, and in part because even without manipulation, a school will only be as socially mixed as its catchment area. Fiona Millar, an education campaigner, suggests that for some urban districts, a suitable solution to social segregation is a return to the banding system run by the defunct Inner London Education Authority, under which local secondaries took a certain proportion of children from each ability level.[59] However, such policies will always face the practical problem that children generally have to be able to go to a nearby school and that families will pay large sums to ensure that they are living near a good local state school.

It is hard for a government to create a schooling system without some degree of social segregation. Moreover, the degree to which private schools increase segregation is a complex issue. They separate the wealthiest part of the upper and upper-middle class, the top 5 per cent or so of families by income who form the inner core of the private school market, from the rest of society. If they make house prices near top state schools less expensive, however, they may possibly reduce segregation among the remaining 95 per cent. The findings of one relevant study, albeit of Paris rather than an English location, found that local private schools reduced the house price premium which houses near good state schools enjoy – the premium which is the biggest cause of social segregation in the state sector.[60]

Any damage which public schools might cause to the state system is, in theory, mitigated by the increasing tendency for public schools to 'sponsor' academies – although 'sponsor', in the newspeak New Labour lexicon, does not necessarily mean what you or I understand by it. From 2007 the government made it clear that it was interested in public schools' time and expertise rather than their money – building on the strong record of many of them in lending specialist teachers to give extra lessons to local state schools. 'It is your educational DNA we are seeking, not your fee income', Lord Adonis, minister responsible for academies, told public school heads.[61] Individual schools that have acted as academy sponsors include Wellington and Dulwich Colleges. It is not clear, however, that public school leaders are any better than anyone else at running tough state schools with poor results – the initial requirements for academy status, though in 2010 Michael Gove announced that any school could seek to become an academy. In 2009 the United Learning Trust, set up by the United Church Schools Trust public school group to run academies, was barred by Whitehall from taking on any more than the nineteen it had been allocated after two of these were judged 'inadequate' by Ofsted – though they were later found to have improved, allowing the Trust to assume control of further schools.[62] In 2012 the Sir Robert Woodard Academy in Lancing, West Sussex, run by the public school charity Woodard Schools, was described as 'inadequate' in an Ofsted report after a slide in GCSE results. 'If this is an example of the DNA of the private sector being injected into the state system, then I think we could do without it', quipped a former teacher at the school with a fine sense of irony.[63]

There is, however, a broader counter-argument to the claim that public schools are fated always to damage the state system from which they are separated. The example set by the public schools is constantly spurring the state to do better by its schools, whether in exam reform, school freedom or sport. In 2014 Sir Michael Wilshaw, head of Ofsted, declared that 'it's really not good enough' that about a third of top sports men and women came from independent schools (37.5 per cent of Team GB medal winners at the London Olympics in 2012 were educated at public school).[64] State sector head teachers needed to stop treating competitive sport as an 'optional extra', he concluded.[65]

At many times over the past century, however, the state schools have, by taking the lead, spurred the public schools into improvement. It is often said that the public schools have shown a remarkable ability to adapt over their long history. In truth, for much of this time their adaptation has been remarkably slow – but it sped up noticeably when state schools started posing serious competition.

Public schools in their present form do more good than harm. On the debit side, they increase social (though not racial) segregation, but not to the point where this interferes with the effective running of the country; they also widen inequality of opportunity. On the credit side, their existence increases the total amount of education, knowledge and hence opportunity in Britain; they are particularly strong in useful, modern subjects – a spectacular historical turnaround. Their greatest virtue of all, however, is that they provide a necessary diversity of approach to how to educate children. In any field, diversity of method is ultimately beneficial, because it increases the chances that someone, somewhere, will find the best way of achieving success. That is true in government, business and education.

The state and public school systems need each other to avoid falling into complacency, mediocrity and narrow-mindedness. If public schools succeed in skirting around these traps with the unwitting help of the state sector, they might survive for another six centuries.

Epilogue

THE roof of Westminster School's Busby library was destroyed one night during the Blitz, but after the Second World War ended the wreath that had adorned the ceiling was carved in exactly the same way as before – with one small change. Several figures of the Black Redstart, a sombre-looking bird which multiplied during the conflict owing to its predilection for nesting in bomb sites, were added to the new work of art.

It sounds the perfect metaphor for the public schools' ability to survive through constant adaptation while retaining age-old features, but is it an accurate picture of reality?

The public school movement began with William of Wykeham's foundation for seventy poor scholars at Winchester College. However, on dining in the scholars' house in the present day one is struck, as one spreads the obligatory germ-killing hand gel across one's hands before sitting next to two boys talking in Korean, by the differences not merely compared with what one imagines of six centuries ago, but even those of a generation ago. The 1950s college doctor's triumphant report on the end of starvation rations and other barbarities seems an aeon away, as do the 1930s complaints by old boys about the presence of Jewish refugees. When the food arrives, however, it is almost a relief to find that it is not very good – a point made, to a degree, in the inspectors' latest report on the school.[1] Thank God that one tradition remains.

The primacy of the Classics has long since gone from the public schools, in favour of a dominance, at least in some of these schools, of those science subjects that had been derided by them for centuries; the old system of government by boys has been greatly weakened; the cult of sport has come and gone. It is fair to ask if the public schools have really survived. A philosopher casting a look at them might argue that Winchester, Eton, Westminster and all the older schools are in fact relatively new institutions, which have gradually but totally replaced their ancient forebears over the past century and a half of reform. Ralph Townsend, current headmaster of Winchester, the most venerable of them all, admits that it is hard to find 'an unbroken thread' of continuity from the fourteenth to the twenty-first century.[2]

Since the early nineteenth century, however, a continuous theme in public school history is, paradoxically, their ability to cast off the shackles of historical tradition. This is not a quality with which they have been blessed ever since the phenomenon began; after starting off by providing a fairly good education, they failed to move with the times and began to look dangerously backward. This was partly because of the incestuous nature of public school leadership. Many of the heads were old boys of the schools they led; those who were not were often from another public school with similar ideas of education. The desire among headmasters for continuity loomed too large for many centuries, as shown in Joseph Drury's 1805 comment that his successor as headmaster of Harrow must be from one of six public schools at the very most. However, within a decade or two after Drury's words, new schools were being founded and run by men who realized the need for the public schools to change – and, even more importantly, to realize that they needed to keep changing to meet the demands of parents and of society.

The greatest public school advances of the following century were to widen the syllabus beyond the Classics and some maths to include science, modern languages and more contemporary history and literature, to introduce sport as a successful solution to bullying and rioting, and to improve the quality of the relationship between master and pupil. The improvements in the curriculum made the upper class a much more effective warrior class than before. They did so in time for the much more challenging martial environment that followed the post-Waterloo century of fighting dervishes, Boxers, and other men who, whatever their virtues, could never hope to win against a European army with modern weapons. In the twentieth century public school boffins and leaders of men invented the tank and worked out how to use it strategically, improved the hand grenade and won the Battle of Britain. They were, at their best, a bunch of very modern major-generals, to borrow the phrase from Gilbert and Sullivan. The introduction of organized sport, meanwhile, probably saved the public schools from extinction by preventing them from sinking into total anarchy.

These changes were made by men who saw that if public schools clung to the old traditions of learning and school government, the history of public schools would come to a sad end. To reformers, however, the pace of public school change in the nineteenth century must at times have seemed as agonizingly slow as a double Classics lesson on a Friday afternoon in summer. The twentieth century saw the public schools change much faster, because they had to, in response to competition from state schools. The great achievements of this century were the successful attempts to start providing a good academic education for the average boy, which went hand in hand with an improvement in the quality of teaching, the improvement in the welfare and happiness of public school children, and the revolution in the public school education of girls. The feminine arts were downgraded and replaced by the same emphasis on exams and university entrance as for boys' education. The long historical shadow cast by mediaeval convent schooling was at last dissipated by the sunlight of modern, academic female education. For the boys' schools, the biggest breaks with their past were twofold. These were the end of the system of strict hierarchies – which placed older boys far above younger, classicists above scientists, and the First XV above everyone else save the masters – and the removal of the last vestiges of the monastic life first established by William of Wykeham, which had excluded girls and even women teachers, and had justified austerity and outright privation.

Despite this willingness to jettison historical practice, what remain are the memories and marks of pupils from past ages. These derive in part from the buildings. Eton claims the oldest classroom in continuous use in the country, a fifteenth-century edifice now employed, among other things, for Japanese lessons.[3] At some schools customs remain strong. 'Notions' is kept up even by the younger boys dining in Winchester College, to the point where sentences become indecipherable to the non-Wykehamist guest. Most powerful of all is the awareness of the distinguished old boys who have come and gone. It does not matter whether they owed their future success to the school in any way: despite Charles Darwin's contempt for his alma mater, Shrewsbury School, it has erected a statue of him and makes great play of the man in its marketing.[4] History does not have to be accurate to be powerful.

This air of history reinforces the centuries-old sense among public schools that they are educating leaders from among the country's elite. Although they would recoil from using such open language these days, this has been a consistent theme for centuries, which both fuels, and is fuelled by, the schools' sense of history. 'If you know that some interesting people have gone on to do some interesting things, whether it's George Orwell or the Duke of Wellington', says Tony Little, current headmaster of Eton, with some understatement, 'that does implicitly ask the question, why not you?'[5] Sometimes the question is explicit. At the time when Boris Johnson arrived at Eton as one of the new scholars, the provost was in the habit of haranguing them with an introductory speech about their role as the nation's future leaders.[6]

To put it another way, Etonian prime ministers beget Etonian prime ministers. David Cameron is the school's nineteenth, but he certainly will not be the last, even if Boris fails to succeed Cameron and emulate the example of fellow Eton scholar Robert Walpole, the very first. There is life in the old boys yet.

I started this book with Ed Miliband's reference to Flashman, the villain who marred Tom Brown's school days. A hardened reprobate like Flashman would probably not have been turned into a better person by today's more gentle, feminized and academically demanding public schools. However, his cronies in the book, who are portrayed as boys who are more easily led into good or bad ways, might be very different. They would be acutely aware of the need to go to a good, highly competitive university to preserve their privileged lifestyle, and today's public school is able to help them realize that need. They would be cognizant of the fact that roasting boys was not something that was morally acceptable, or something that they could now get away with. They would probably be more aware of how boys of other classes and nationalities, and girls of whatever background, lived and thought and felt. As a class, these boys from the upper and upper middle classes have learnt to embrace and master the modern world. The public schools deserve much of the credit for this achievement.

Notes

Chapter One: An Idealistic Cynic and the Birth of a System 1382–1603

1. *Oxford Dictionary of National Biography* (*ODNB*). Throughout the book, '*ODNB*' refers to the entry for the named person in the 1992–2004 edition.
2. Virginia Davis, *William Wykeham: A Life*, London: Hambledon Continuum, 2007, p. 34.
3. Ibid., pp. 111, 87.
4. Ibid., p. 8.
5. Ibid., pp. 4, 8.
6. John Lawson and Harold Silver, *A Social History of Education in England*, London: Methuen, 1973, p. 112.
7. Nicholas Orme, *Medieval Schools*, New Haven, CT, London: Yale University Press, 2006, p. 136.
8. Hugh Cunningham, *The Invention of Childhood*, London: BBC Books, 2006, p. 52.
9. For example, Orme, *Medieval Schools*, p. 112.
10. Davis, *William Wykeham*, p. 146.
11. Arthur Francis Leach, *A History of Winchester College*, London: Duckworth & Co., 1899, p. 65; see also http://www.new.ox.ac.uk/history-of-new-college-oxford (accessed 26 June 2013).
12. Leach, *A History of Winchester College*, p. 129.
13. Winchester College 1400 Statutes, Rubrics 2, 45.
14. Orme, *Medieval Schools*, p. 138.
15. Leach, *A History of Winchester College*, p. 368.
16. Orme, *Medieval Schools*, p. 130.
17. Ibid., pp. 139–41.
18. Leach, *A History of Winchester College*, pp. 202, 198, 217; email communication with Winchester College archivist, 22 May 2013.
19. Winchester College Founder's Charter.
20. Leach, *A History of Winchester College*, p. 93; Winchester College 1400 Statutes, Rubric 2.
21. Leach, *A History of Winchester College*, p. 142.

22. Winchester College 1400 Statutes, Rubric 16; for an example of the prevailing view that this began the public school system, see *Report of the Committee on Public Schools appointed by the President of the Board of Education in July* 1942, 1944, p. 7.
23. Leach, *A History of Winchester College*, pp. 100, 191, 187.
24. Ibid., p. 158.
25. Guy Fitch Lytle, 'Patronage and the Election of Winchester Scholars', *Winchester College Sixth-Centenary Essays*, ed. Roger Custance, Oxford: Oxford University Press, 1982, p. 174; Davis, *William Wykeham*, pp. 155–9.
26. Lytle, 'Patronage and the Election of Winchester Scholars', p. 174.
27. Winchester College 1400 Statutes, Rubric 1.
28. Sir H. C. Maxwell-Lyte, *A History of Eton College*, 4th edn, London: Macmillan, 1911, pp. 14–15.
29. Tim Card, *Eton Established: A History from 1440 to 1860*, London: John Murray, 2001, pp. 10–16.
30. Leach, *A History of Winchester College*, p. 175.
31. Information provided by official Eton College guide, an ex-master, on author's visit to College.
32. Card, *Eton Established*, p. 13; Maxwell-Lyte, *Eton College*, p. 20.
33. *Eton College Register 1441–1698*, Eton: Spottiswoode, Ballantyne, 1943.
34. Maxwell-Lyte, *Eton College*, pp. 59, 199, 28.
35. Orme, *Medieval Schools*, p. 152.
36. Ibid., p. 221.
37. Maxwell-Lyte, *Eton College*, pp. 157–8.
38. http://www.etoncollege.com/TheChapel.aspx (accessed 15 May 2013).
39. Maxwell-Lyte, *Eton College*, p. 63.
40. Ibid., pp. 65, 72–81.
41. Ibid., p. 140.
42. Orme, *Medieval Schools*, p. 146; Winchester College 1400 Statutes, Rubric 12.
43. William Horman, *Vulgaria Puerorum*, 1519. Reprinted Oxford: Roxburghe Club, 1926, pp. 24, 41, 373, see Introduction for Ascham's criticism.
44. Card, *Eton Established*, p. 33.
45. A. H. Mead, *A Miraculous Draught of Fishes: A History of St. Paul's School*, London: James & James, 1990, pp. 14–15, 31, 32.
46. Michael J. F. McDonnell, *A History of St Paul's School*, London: Chapman and Hall, 1909, p. 41.
47. Mead, *St. Paul's School, passim*, for example p. 32.
48. Ibid., pp. 17–18.
49. Ibid., p. 21.
50. See Statutes IV to IV, in F. W. M. Draper, *Four Centuries of Merchant Taylors' School, 1561–1961*, Oxford: Oxford University Press, 1962, p. 242.
51. For a list of high masters, see Mead, *St. Paul's School*, pp. 137–8.
52. Ibid., p. 23.
53. Richard L. DeMolen, *Richard Mulcaster and Education Reform in the Renaissance*, Nieuwkoop: De Graaf, 1991, pp. 43–51.
54. Lawson and Silver, *Social History of Education*, pp. 76–7.
55. Maxwell-Lyte, *Eton College*, p. 143.
56. DeMolen, *Mulcaster*, p. 57.
57. Richard Mulcaster, *Elementarie*, ed. E. T. Campagnac, Oxford: Clarendon Press, 1925, pp. 23, 28.

58. John Field, *The King's Nurseries*, London: James & James, 1987, p. 25.
59. Draper, *Merchant Taylors' School*, p. 28.
60. William Barker, entry for Mulcaster, *ODNB*, Vol. 39, pp. 697–9.
61. I am indebted to the Winchester Collegers for their scholarly enthusiasm for Notions during my lunch in College, 5 March 2013.
62. Charles Stevens, *The English Dialect of Winchester College*, London and New Brunswick, NJ: Athlone Press, 1998, various entries.
63. DeMolen, *Mulcaster*, pp. 4, 13–31.
64. Ibid., p. 14.
65. George Fisher Russell Barker, *Memoir of Richard Busby*, London: Lawrence & Bullen, 1895, p. 100.
66. C. H. Firth, Revd Sean Kelsey, entry for Sidney in *ODNB*, Vol. 50, pp. 556–69; John Gouwes, entry for Greville in *ODNB*, Vol. 23, pp. 786–90; entries for Sidney and Greville in *ODNB*.
67. Westminster School archives: A0002/24, Statutes of the Collegiate Church of St Peter, Items 27, 30.
68. Westminster School archives: A0002/24, Statutes of the Collegiate Church of St Peter, Item 27.
69. Mary Cathcart Borer, *Willingly to School: A History of Women's Education*, Guildford and London: Lutterworth Press, 1976, pp. 34, 48, 71–2.
70. John Knox, *The First Blast of the Trumpet Against the Monstrous Regiment of Women*, Raleigh, NC: Lulu.com, p. 25.
71. P. Botley, N. G. Wilson, entry in *ODNB*, Vol. 25, pp. 337–8.
72. DeMolen, *Mulcaster*, p. 37.
73. Leach, *A History of Winchester College*, p. 292.
74. Michael J. F. McDonnell, *Registers of St Paul's School 1509–1748*, printed by the school, 1977.
75. Bootham School, *Bootham School, 1823–1923*, London, Toronto: J. M. Dent & Co., 1926, p. 22.
76. G. F. R. Barker, Revd Matthew Kilburn, entry in *ODNB*, Vol. 41, pp. 84–8.
77. McDonnell, *St Paul's School*, p. 79, for their Pauline education.
78. Patrick Humphries, entry for Denny in *ODNB*, Vol. 15, p. 831; Sybil M. Jack, entry for Paget in *ODNB*, Vol. 42, p. 376.
79. See boys' entries in *Eton College Register 1441–1698*.
80. Firth, Kelsey, entry for Sidney in *ODNB*, Vol 50, p. 557.
81. It is not clear whether he was a scholar at any point, or a town boy (non-scholar) throughout his time at Westminster. His chequered academic career perhaps suggests the latter. See his entry in *The Record of Old Westminsters*, compiled by G. F. Russell Barker and Allan H. Stenning, London: Chiswick Press, 1928, Vol. 2, p. 685.
82. John Aubrey, *Brief Lives*, ed. Richard Barber, London: Folio Society, 1975, p. 79.
83. G. F. R. Barker, Revd Matthew Kilburn, entry in *ODNB*, Vol. 41, pp. 84–8.
84. Karl Toepfer, entry for Jonson in *ODNB*, Vol. 30, p. 682.
85. Field, *King's Nurseries*, p. 28.
86. McDonnell, *St Paul's School*, Introduction.
87. Toepfer, entry for Jonson in *ODNB*, Vol. 30, p. 682.
88. Orme, *Medieval Schools*, p. 132.
89. Firth, Kelsey, entry for Sidney in *ODNB*, Vol. 50, p. 557.
90. 'W.H.H.', entry for Neile in *Dictionary of National Biography* (*DNB*), Oxford: Oxford University Press, 1894–5, Vol. 14, p. 171.

91. P. R. N. Carter, entry for Wingfield in *ODNB*, Vol. 59, p. 729.
92. Lawson and Silver, *Social History of Education*, p. 126.
93. Robert Tittler, *Nicholas Bacon: The Making of a Tudor Statesman*, London: Cape, 1976, p. 59.
94. Nicholas Orme, entry for Horman in *ODNB*, Vol. 28, p. 113.
95. T. W. Bamford, *The Rise of the Public Schools*, London: Nelson, 1967, p. 148.
96. Edward Mack, *Public Schools and British Opinion 1780-1860*, Westport, CT: Greenwood Press, 1973, p. 60.
97. Mead, *St Paul's School*, p. 19.
98. Edward Creasy, *Memoirs of Eminent Etonians*, London: Richard Bentley, 1850, p. 6.

Chapter Two: Earls and Shoemakers 1611-1767

1. Anthony Quick, *Charterhouse: A History of the School*, London: James & James, 1990, pp. 4–12.
2. Ibid., pp. 33–5.
3. Guy Fitch Lytle, 'Patronage and the Election of Winchester Scholars', *Winchester College Sixth-Centenary Essays*, ed. Roger Custance, Oxford: Oxford University Press, 1982, p. 174.
4. Quick, *Charterhouse*, p. 34.
5. For a discussion of famous Old Carthusians, including Addison and Steele, ibid., pp. 34–40.
6. John Field, *The King's Nurseries*, London: James & James, 1987, p. 44.
7. Ibid., p. 39.
8. George Fisher Russell Barker, *Memoir of Richard Busby*, London: Lawrence & Bullen, 1895, p. 3.
9. John Sargeaunt, *Annals of Westminster School*, London: Methuen, 1898, p. 122.
10. Stuart Handley, entry for Montagu in *ODNB*, Vol. 38, p. 692.
11. Barker, *Richard Busby*, p. 125.
12. Field, *King's Nurseries*, p. 37; C. S. Knighton, entry for Busby in *ODNB*, Vol. 9, p. 78.
13. Field, *King's Nurseries*, p. 37; visit to Busby's library, 5 February 2013; information supplied by the school archivist, 5 February 2013.
14. For a list of distinguished Old Westminsters, see Field, *King's Nurseries*, pp. 129–39.
15. Information supplied by the school archivist, 5 February 2013.
16. Barker, *Richard Busby*, p. 51.
17. Knighton, entry for Busby in *ODNB*, Vol. 9, p. 77.
18. Lawrence Tanner, *Westminster School*, London: *Country Life*, 1934, Vol. 1, p. 15.
19. Diary of Thomas Burton: http://www.british-history.ac.uk/report.aspx?compid=36889#s2 (accessed 10 March 2014).
20. Knighton, entry for Busby in *ODNB*, Vol. 9, p. 77.
21. Tanner, *Westminster School*, p. 32.
22. Field, *King's Nurseries*, pp. 128–38; Stephen Wright, entry for Burgess in *ODNB*, Vol. 8, p. 765; Mordechai Feingold, entry for Stubbe in *ODNB*, Vol. 53, pp. 199–201.
23. Lytle, 'Patronage and the Election of Winchester Scholars', p. 182.
24. Handley, entry for Montagu in *ODNB*, Vol. 38, p. 692.
25. Field, *King's Nurseries*, pp. 129–39.
26. Harold Love, entry for Charles Sackville, 6th Earl of Dorset, in *ODNB*, Vol. 48, pp. 528–9.
27. Knighton, entry for Busby in *ODNB*, Vol. 9, p. 78.

28. Field, *King's Nurseries*, pp. 43, 36.
29. Sargeaunt, *Westminster School*, p. 101.
30. Ibid., p. 101; Field, *King's Nurseries*, p. 43.
31. John Carleton, *Westminster School*, London: Rupert Hart-Davis, 1965, p. 16.
32. Barker, *Richard Busby*, p. 100.
33. Sir H. C. Maxwell-Lyte, *A History of Eton College*, 4th edn, London: Macmillan, 1911, p. 260.
34. Arthur Francis Leach, *A History of Winchester College*, London: Duckworth & Co., 1899, pp. 206ff.
35. Christopher Tyerman, *A History of Harrow School*, Oxford, New York: Oxford University Press, 2000, pp. 40, 61.
36. W. H. D. Rouse, *A History of Rugby School*, London: Duckworth & Co., 1898, pp. 24, 85, 90.
37. Ibid., pp. 60–3, 102.
38. Tyerman, *History of Harrow School*, p. 73.
39. Ibid., p. 101.
40. Ibid., p. 100.
41. Ibid., p. 81.
42. Ibid., p. 115.
43. Analysis of figures provided by Tyerman, *History of Harrow School*, p. 110ff; Jeffrey Williamson, 'Structure of Pay in Britain 1710–1911', *Research in Economic History*, Vol. 7, 1982, p. 48.
44. Tyerman, *History of Harrow School*, p. 128.
45. John Lawson and Harold Silver, *A Social History of Education in England*, London: Methuen, 1973, p. 156.
46. A. H. Mead, *A Miraculous Draught of Fishes: A History of St. Paul's School*, London: James & James, 1990, p. 18.
47. Field, *King's Nurseries*, p. 40.
48. Lawson and Silver, *Social History of Education*, p. 125.
49. Richard Ollard, *Pepys: A Biography*, London: Hodder and Stoughton, 1974, p. 23.
50. For a discussion of ratios, see Chapter Three.
51. Ibid., pp. 198, 199.
52. Ibid., p. 222.
53. Ibid., p. 221; Tim Card, *Eton Established: A History from 1440 to 1860*, London: John Murray, 2001, p. 57.
54. Maxwell-Lyte, *Eton College*, p. 217.
55. Ibid., p. 214.
56. Frances Mayhew Rippy, entry for Prior in *ODNB*, Vol. 45, p. 417.
57. Leach, *History of Winchester College*, p. 388.
58. *Eton College Register 1441–1698*, Eton: Spottiswoode, Ballantyne, 1943.
59. Colin Haydon, entry for Sherlock in *ODNB*, Vol. 50, pp. 322–4.
60. See, for example, Harrow School archives: Governors' minutes, 11 July 1836.
61. Leach, *History of Winchester College*, p. 375; Williamson, 'Structure of Pay in Britain 1710–1911', p. 48.
62. See, for example, the registers quoted in the Bibliography.
63. James McDermott, entry for Farnaby in *ODNB*, Vol. 19, pp. 68–70; Vivian Ogilvie, *The English Public School*, London: B.T. Batsford, 1957, p. 77.
64. Lawson and Silver, *Social History of Education*, p. 172.

65. Edward Mack, *Public Schools and British Opinion 1780–1860*, Westport, CT: Greenwood Press, 1973, p. 21.
66. George Charles Brauer, *The Education of a Gentleman*, New York: Bookman Associates, 1959, p. 198.
67. Ibid., p. 205.
68. Ibid., p. 206.
69. Ibid., p. 207.
70. Tyerman, *History of Harrow School*, p. 111.
71. Mead, *St. Paul's School*, pp. 46, 39.
72. Mary Cathcart, *Willingly to School. A History of Women's Education*, Guildford and London: Lutterworth Press, 1976, p. 97.
73. Ibid., pp. 7, 84–5, 98.
74. Lawson and Silver, *Social History of Education*, p. 122.
75. Borer, *Willingly to School*, p. 171.
76. Mead, *St. Paul's School*, p. 46; Ogilvie, *English Public School*, p. 97.
77. John Cannon, *Aristocratic Century*, Cambridge: Cambridge University Press, 1984, p. 41.

Chapter Three: Of Frogs and Men 1768–1827

1. *Eton College Register 1753–90*, Eton: Spottiswoode, Ballantyne & Co., 1921.
2. Sir H. C. Maxwell-Lyte, *A History of Eton College*, 4th edn, London: Macmillan, 1911, p. 342.
3. Roger Custance, 'Warden Nicholas and the Mutiny at Winchester College', in Roger Custance (ed.), *Winchester College: Sixth Centenary Essays*, Oxford: Oxford University Press, 1982, p. 337.
4. James Bentley, *Dare to be Wise: a History of the Manchester Grammar School*, London: James & James, 1990, p. 32.
5. Various sources, including Vivian Ogilvie, *The English Public School*, London: B.T. Batsford, 1957, p. 111; Arthur Francis Leach, *A History of Winchester College*, London: Duckworth & Co., 1899, p. 426.
6. W. H. D. Rouse, *A History of Rugby School*, London: Duckworth & Co., 1898, p. 177.
7. John D'Ewes Evelyn Firth, *A History of Winchester College*, London, Glasgow: Blackie & Son, 1936, p. 90.
8. Samuel Butler, *The Life and Letters of Dr Samuel Butler*, London: John Murray, 1896, Vol. 1, p. 158: letter from Henry Dyson Gabell, headmaster of Winchester, to Samuel Butler, headmaster of Shrewsbury.
9. Ibid., Vol. 1, p. 158: letter from John Keate, headmaster of Eton, to Samuel Butler, headmaster of Shrewsbury.
10. Thomas Hinde, *Paths of Progress: A History of Marlborough College*, London: James & James, 1992, pp. 40–51.
11. Frank Miles and Graeme Cranch, *King's College School: The First 150 Years*, Wimbledon: King's College School, 1979, p. 54.
12. John Field, *The King's Nurseries*, London: James & James, 1987, p. 62.
13. Firth, *History of Winchester College*, p. 90; F. W. M. Draper, *Four Centuries of Merchant Taylors' School, 1561–1961*, Oxford: Oxford University Press, 1962, p. 114.
14. George Thomas, Earl of Albemarle, *Fifty Years of My Life*, London: Macmillan, 1876, Vol. 1, pp. 257–8.

15. Edward Mack, *Public Schools and British Opinion 1780–1860*, Westport, CT: Greenwood Press, 1973, p. 158.
16. Rouse, *History of Rugby School*, p. 294.
17. Maxwell-Lyte, *History of Eton College*, p. 160.
18. Mack, *Public Schools and British Opinion 1780–1860*, p. 80.
19. Ibid., p. 80.
20. Raymond Flower, *Oundle and the English Public School*, London: Stacey, 1989, p. 51.
21. Martin Tupper, *My Life as an Author*, Edinburgh, London: Ballantyne, Hanson and Co., 1886, p. 17.
22. Christopher Tyerman, *A History of Harrow School*, Oxford, New York: Oxford University Press, 2000, pp. 102, 275–6.
23. Mack, *Public Schools and British Opinion 1780–1860*, p. 77.
24. Tyerman, *History of Harrow School*, p. 194.
25. E. W. Howson and G. T. Warner, *Harrow School*, London: Edward Arnold, 1898, p. 98.
26. Maxwell-Lyte, *History of Eton College*, p. 351.
27. Ian Gilmour, *The Making of the Poets: Byron and Shelley in Their Time*, London: Chatto & Windus, 2002, pp. 96–7.
28. Field, *King's Nurseries*, p. 70.
29. Tyerman, *History of Harrow School*, p. 152.
30. Harrow School Archives: HM/D/33, 34.
31. Harrow School Archives: Pouchée diaries, p. 25.
32. Mack, *Public Schools and British Opinion 1780–1860*, p. 63, quoting Ruville, *Life of Pitt*, London: William Heinemann, 1907, Vol. 1, p. 73.
33. Flower, *Oundle and the English Public School*, p. 49.
34. Field, *King's Nurseries*, p. 70.
35. Tupper, *My Life as an Author*, p. 14.
36. John Timbs, *School-Days of Eminent Men*, London: Lockwood & Co., 1862, p. 270.
37. Mack, *Public Schools and British Opinion 1780–1860*, p. 154.
38. Harrow School Archives: Pouchée diaries, *passim*.
39. Tyerman, *History of Harrow School*, p. 212.
40. 'Gregory Griffin', *The Microcosm*, Windsor: privately printed, p. 30.
41. Maxwell-Lyte, *History of Eton College*, p. 317; *Eton College Register 1753–90*, Eton: Spottiswoode, Ballantyne & Co., 1921.
42. George Charles Brauer, *The Education of a Gentleman*, New York: Bookman Associates, 1959, p. 203.
43. Tyerman, *History of Harrow School*, p. 202.
44. Anthony Quick, *Charterhouse: A History of the School*, London: James & James, 1990, p. 47.
45. A. H. Mead, *A Miraculous Draught of Fishes: A History of St. Paul's School*, London: James & James, 1990, p. 58.
46. Hugh Cunningham, *The Invention of Childhood*, London: BBC Books, 2006, p. 117.
47. Field, *King's Nurseries*, p. 65.
48. James Basil Oldham, *A History of Shrewsbury School, 1552–1952*, Oxford: Basil Blackwell, 1952, pp. 76–7.
49. Butler, *Butler*, Vol. 1, p. 334.
50. Oldham, *A History of Shrewsbury School, 1552–1952*, p. 98.

51. Ibid., p. 98.
52. Butler, *Butler*, Vol. 2, p. 63.
53. Oldham, *History of Shrewsbury School*, p. 97.
54. Butler, *Butler*, vol. 2, p. 134.
55. Ibid., p. 13.
56. Oldham, *History of Shrewsbury School*, p. 193.
57. See, for example, the diary entry for 21 December 1975, in John Rae, *The Old Boys' Network: A Headmaster's Diaries 1972–1986*, London: Short, 2010.
58. Oldham, *History of Shrewsbury School*, p. 91.
59. Ibid., p. 96.
60. Ibid., pp. 95–66.
61. Ibid., p. 77.
62. Mack, *Public Schools and British Opinion 1780–1860*, p. 143.
63. Oldham, *History of Shrewsbury School*, p. 195.
64. Ibid., pp. 101, 92.
65. Butler, *Butler*, Vol. 2, p. 135.
66. Anonymous, *A History of Shrewsbury School*, Shrewsbury: Adnitt and Naunton, 1889, p. 141; *Antigone, Oedipus the King, Electra*, trans. H. D. F. Kitto, Oxford: Oxford University Press, 1994, p. 64, lines 483–4.
67. Oldham, *History of Shrewsbury School*, pp. 108–10.
68. Draper, *Four Centuries of Merchant Taylors' School*, pp. 102–5.
69. T. W. Bamford, *The Rise of the Public Schools*, London: Nelson, 1967, p. 62.
70. Mead, *A History of St. Paul's School*, p. 57.
71. Mack, *Public Schools and British Opinion 1780–1860*, p. 144.
72. Firth, *History of Winchester College*, p. 107.
73. Maxwell-Lyte, *Eton College*, p. 383.
74. Hinde, *History of Marlborough College*, p. 11.
75. Maxwell-Lyte, *Eton College*, p. 382.
76. Mack, *Public Schools and British Opinion 1780–1860*, p. 192.
77. Ibid., pp. 143–7.
78. Tyerman, *History of Harrow School*, p. 82.
79. Mack, *Public Schools and British Opinion 1780–1860*, p. 143.
80. Mead, *A History of St Paul's School*, p. 57.
81. *Report of Her Majesty's commissioners appointed to inquire into the revenues and management of certain colleges and schools, and the studies pursued and instruction given therein*, 1864, Vol. 1, p. 75. Hereafter Clarendon Commission.
82. Maxwell-Lyte, *Eton College*, p. 437.
83. Quick, *Charterhouse: A History of the School*, p. 43.
84. Bentley, *Dare to be Wise*, p. 46.
85. Joel Mokyr, *The Enlightened Economy, An Economic History of Britain 1700–1850*, New Haven, CT, London: Yale University Press, 2009, p. 232.
86. Flower, *Oundle and the English Public School*, p. 47.
87. Peter Hill, *The History of Bristol Grammar School*, London: Sir Isaac Pitman & Sons, 1951, pp. 67, 54.
88. Bernard Knight, *The Story of Christ College, Brecon*, Brecon: The Society of Friends of Christ College, Brecon, 1978, pp. 34–6.
89. Mokyr, *Enlightened Economy*, p. 239; see also Bamford, *Rise of the Public Schools*, p. 100.
90. Robert E. Schofield, entry for Priestley in *ODNB*, Vol. 45, p. 353.

91. Frank Greenaway, entry for Dalton in *ODNB*, Vol. 14, p. 1015.

92. Simon Schaffter, entry for Cavendish in *ODNB*, Vol. 10, p. 621; Frank Greenaway, entry for Henry *ODNB*, Vol. 26, p. 596; Michael Hoskin, entry for Goodricke in *ODNB*, Vol. 22, p. 808; Mokyr, *Enlightened Economy*, pp. 233–4.

93. A. D. Morrison-Low, entry on Brewster in *ODNB*, Vol. 7, p. 524.

94. François Crouzet, *The First Industrialists: The Problem of Origins*, Cambridge: Cambridge University Press, 1985, for example pp. 68 and 99.

95. Ackworth School, *So Numerous a Family: 200 Years of Quaker Education at Ackworth, 1779–1979*, Pontefract, W. Yorkshire: Ackworth School, 1979, p. 2.

96. Bootham School, *Bootham School, 1823–1923*, London, Toronto: J. M. Dent & Co., 1926, p. 22.

97. Roderick Braithwaite, *Strikingly Alive: The History of the Mill Hill School Foundation, 1807–2007*, Chichester: Phillimore & Co. Ltd., 2006, p. 45.

98. Ackworth School, *So Numerous a Family*, p. 22.

99. Braithwaite, *History of the Mill Hill School Foundation*, pp. 48, 75.

100. Bootham School, *Bootham School*, p. 28.

101. Ruth Dudley-Edwards, entry for Wilson in *ODNB*, Vol. 59, p. 582.

102. Miles Taylor, entry for Bright in *ODNB*, Vol. 7, p. 626.

103. Anthony Marett-Crosby, *A School of the Lord's Service: A History of Ampleforth*, London: James & James, 2002, pp. 14, 26.

104. T. E. Muir, *Stonyhurst College, 1593–1993*, London: James & James, 1992, p. 80.

105. At Cambridge, all those proceeding to degrees in any subject except for divinity were no longer required to subscribe to the tenets of the Church of England from 1856. See Elisabeth Leedham-Green, *A Concise History of the University of Cambridge*, Cambridge: Cambridge University Press, 1996, p. 159.

106. Muir, *Stonyhurst College*, pp. 80, 89.

107. Ibid., p. 210.

108. Augustus J. C. Hare, *Memorials of a Quiet Life*, Vol. 1, London: Strahan and Co., 1872, pp. 161–2.

109. G. F. R. Barker, Revd H. C. G. Matthew, entry for Frere in *ODNB*, Vol. 20, pp. 986–7; H.M. Stephens, Revd H. C. G. Matthew, entry for Ellis in *ODNB*, Vol. 18, p. 215.

110. Mack, *Public Schools and British Opinion 1780–1860*, p. 176.

111. Ibid., p. 174.

112. W. A. C. Stewart and W. P. McCann, *The Educational Innovators. Progressive Schools, 1881–1967*, Basingstoke: Macmillan, 2000, Vol. 1, pp. 184, 189.

113. William Gladstone (under the pseudonym of Bartholomew Bouverie), *The Eton Miscellany*, Eton, 1827, p. 14.

114. H. C. G. Matthew, entry for Gladstone in *ODNB*, Vol. 22, p. 384.

115. Malcolm Falkus, 'Fagging and Boy Government', in *The World of the Public School*, London: Weidenfeld & Nicolson, 1977, p. 62.

116. W. C. Macready, *Macready's Reminiscences*, ed. Sir Frederick Pollock, London: Macmillan, 1875, p. 12.

117. Leach, *A History of Winchester College*, p. 364.

118. Richard Holmes, *Wellington: The Iron Duke*, London: HarperCollins, 1996, p. 288.

119. http://www.egs.edu/library/bertrand-russell/articles/mysticism-and-logic-and-other-essays/the-place-of-science-in-a-liberal-education/ (accessed 14 July 2014).

120. Quoted in Mack, *Public Schools and British Opinion 1780–1860*, p. 60.

121. Tyerman, *History of Harrow School*, p. 120.

122. Ibid., pp. 120–31.
123. Mack, *Public Schools and British Opinion 1780–1860*, p. 187.
124. Mary Cathcart Borer, *Willingly to School: A History of Women's Education*, Guildford and London: Lutterworth Press, 1976, p. 184.
125. John Lawson and Harold Silver, *A Social History of Education in England*, London: Methuen, 1973, p. 208.
126. Borer, *Willingly to School*, pp. 231–4.
127. Ibid., pp. 187–9.
128. Bamford, *Rise of the Public Schools*, p. 4.
129. Vivian Ogilvie, *The English Public School*, London: B.T. Batsford, 1957, p. 129.
130. Rouse, *History of Rugby School*, p. 181.
131. Field, *King's Nurseries*, p. 62; Ogilvie, *English Public School*, p. 129.
132. Harrow School archives: HM/W/FSD, letter from governors to Wordsworth; Tyerman, *History of Harrow School*, p. 167.
133. Tyerman, *History of Harrow School*, pp. 227, 229, 250.
134. Ibid., p. 143.
135. Butler, *Butler*, Vol. 2, p. 139. Drury did not, in fact, get his wish, but the next five men after his successor, George Butler (no relation to Samuel), would have met with his approval.
136. Field, *King's Nurseries*, p. 66.
137. Mack, *Public Schools and British Opinion 1780–1860*, p. 14.
138. Flower, *Oundle and the English Public School*, p. 48.

Chapter Four: 'First-Character. Second-Physique. Third-Intelligence.' 1828–1869

1. David Henry Edward Wainwright, *Liverpool Gentlemen. A History of Liverpool College, an Independent Day School, from 1840*, London: Faber and Faber, 1960, p. 41. Liverpool College was originally known as the Upper School of the Liverpool Collegiate Institution.
2. Christopher Tyerman, *A History of Harrow School*, Oxford, New York: Oxford University Press, 2000, p. 227.
3. M. C. Morgan, *Cheltenham College: The First Hundred Years*, Chalfont St. Giles: published for the Cheltonian Society by Richard Sadler, 1968, p. 46.
4. Martin D. W. Jones, *Brighton College 1845–1995*, Chichester, West Sussex: Phillimore, 1995, p. 73.
5. T. W. Bamford, *The Rise of the Public Schools*, London: Nelson, 1967, p. 18.
6. C. H. Lee, *The British Economy Since 1700*, Cambridge: Cambridge University Press, 1986, p. 29.
7. Sheldon Rothblatt, *The Revolution of the Dons*, London: Faber and Faber, 1968, p. 60.
8. Morgan, *Cheltenham College*, p. 5.
9. W. H. D. Rouse, *A History of Rugby School*, London: Duckworth & Co., 1898, p. 276; Tyerman, *History of Harrow School*, p. 226.
10. Terence Copley, *Black Tom: Arnold of Rugby: The Myth and the Man*, London: Continuum, 2002, p. 26.
11. Edward Mack, *Public Schools and British Opinion 1780–1860*, Westport, CT: Greenwood Press, 1973, p. 158.
12. Thomas Hughes, *Tom Brown's School Days*, Cambridge: Macmillan, 1857, p. 157.
13. Copley, *Black Tom*, p. 122.
14. Ibid., pp. 134, 128.

15. Ibid., pp. 129, 100.
16. Ibid., p. 178ff.
17. Vivian Ogilvie, *The English Public School*, London: B.T. Batsford, 1957, p. 147.
18. Ibid., p. 122.
19. Rouse, *History of Rugby School*, p. 294.
20. Mack, *Public Schools and British Opinion 1780–1860*, p. 379.
21. Robert Philp, *A Keen Wind Blows: The Story of Fettes College*, London: James & James, 1998, p. 24.
22. Morgan, *Cheltenham College*, pp. 35, 73.
23. T. E. Muir, *Stonyhurst College, 1593–1993*, London: James & James, 1992, p. 98.
24. M. H. Port, entry for Blore in *ODNB*, Vol. 6, pp. 283–7; Geoffrey Tyack, entry for Nash in *ODNB*, Vol. 40, p. 217.
25. Thomas Hinde, *Paths of Progress: A History of Marlborough College*, London: James & James, 1992, p. 19.
26. Ibid., pp. 33–48.
27. Ibid., p. 51.
28. J. A. Mangan, *Athleticism in the Victorian and Edwardian Public School: The Emergence and Consolidation of the Educational Ideology*, Cambridge: Cambridge University Press, 1981, p. 22.
29. Hugh Cunningham, *The Invention of Childhood*, London: BBC Books, 2006, p. 145.
30. Ogilvie, *The English Public School*, p. 113.
31. Mangan, *Athleticism*, p. 83.
32. Ibid., p. 196; McC. Christison (ed.), *Dulwich College War Record 1914–1919*, London: Dulwich College, 1923.
33. Clive Ellis, *The Life of Charles Burgess Fry*, London: J.M. Dent, pp. 197–8.
34. See Sir H. C. Maxwell-Lyte, *A History of Eton College*, 4th edn, London: Macmillan, 1911, p. 344.
35. Gordon Ross, 'Breathless Hush in the Close', in *The World of the Public School*, London: Weidenfeld & Nicolson, 1977, p. 61.
36. Graeme Paton, 'Children's behaviour improved by school sport', *Daily Telegraph*, 6 June 2007.
37. Telephone interview, 10 July 2014.
38. Hinde, *History of Marlborough College*, p. 105.
39. Mangan, *Athleticism*, p. 196.
40. Muir, *Stonyhurst College*, p. 126.
41. Kenneth Harris, *Attlee*, London: Weidenfeld & Nicolson, 1982, p. 9.
42. Mangan, *Athleticism*, p. 55.
43. Christine Heward, *Making a Man of Him: Parents and Their Sons' Education at an English Public School 1929–50*, London: Routledge, 1988, p. 138.
44. Jones, *Brighton College*, p. 153.
45. Philp, *Fettes College*, p. 38.
46. Mangan, *Athleticism*, p. 27.
47. Ibid., pp. 27, 202.
48. Ian Hay, *The Lighter Side of School Life*, London, Edinburgh, Boston: T.N. Foulis, 1924, pp. 94–5.
49. Matthew Davenport Hill, *Eton and Elsewhere*, London: John Murray, 1928, pp. 140, 205.
50. Tyerman, *History of Harrow School*, p. 159.
51. Ibid., p. 191.
52. Telephone interview, 18 June 2013.

53. Geoffrey Hoyland, *The Man Who Made a School: Thring of Uppingham*, London: S.C.M. Press, 1946, pp. 48–9.
54. Tyerman, *History of Harrow School*, p. 253.
55. For a discussion of the evidence and its credibility, see John Roach, entry for Vaughan in *ODNB*, Vol. 56, p. 161.
56. Tyerman, *History of Harrow School*, p. 254.
57. Governors' minutes, 28 May 1853; see also Stephen Wood, *A History of London*, London and Basingstoke: Macmillan, 1998, pp. 423–5.
58. V. M. Allom, *Ex Oriente Salus: A Centenary History of Eastbourne College*, Eastbourne: Eastbourne College, 1967, p. 2.
59. Maxwell-Lyte, *History of Eton College*, p. 458. The incident is cited by his son.
60. Hoyland, *Thring of Uppingham*, p. 19.
61. Maxwell-Lyte, *History of Eton College*, pp. 458–9.
62. Ibid., pp. 461, 483.
63. Leonard W. Cowie, *That One Idea: Nathaniel Woodard and His Schools*, Rugeley, Staffordshire: Woodard Corporation, 1991, p. 46.
64. Tyerman, *History of Harrow School*, pp. 256–65.
65. Ibid., p. 256.
66. Morgan, *Cheltenham College*, p. 11.
67. Rouse, *History of Rugby School*, p. 177.
68. Based on entries in Debrett's. The calculation excludes Prince Charles.
69. John Roach, *Public Examinations in England 1850–1900*, Cambridge: Cambridge University Press, 2008, pp. 4–6, 216.
70. Frank Miles and Graeme Cranch, *King's College School: The First 150 Years*, Wimbledon: King's College School, 1979, pp. 36, 47.
71. O. F. Christie, *A History of Clifton College, 1860–1934*, Bristol: J.W. Arrowsmith, 1935, p. 38.
72. Wainwright, *Liverpool Gentlemen*, p. 147.
73. Miles and Cranch, *King's College School*, p. 38.
74. Arthur Francis Leach, *A History of Winchester College*, London, Duckworth & Co., 1899, p. 467.
75. Hinde, *History of Marlborough College*, p. 61.
76. Magnus Magnusson, *The Clacken and the Slate. The Story of the Edinburgh Academy 1824–1974*, London: Collins, 1974, p. 193.
77. Wainwright, *Liverpool Gentlemen*, p. 127.
78. Ibid., pp. 127, 150.
79. Miles and Cranch, *King's College School*, p. 36.
80. Wainwright, *Liverpool Gentlemen*, pp. 100, 147, 156.
81. Magnusson, *Edinburgh Academy*, pp. 62–4, 109, 130–4, 159.
82. Tyerman, *History of Harrow School*, p. 250.
83. David Newsome, *A History of Wellington College, 1859–1959*, London: John Murray, 1959, p. 14.
84. Miles and Cranch, *King's College School*, pp. 19, 85.
85. Wainwright, *Liverpool Gentlemen*, p. 57.
86. Magnusson, *Edinburgh Academy*, p. 87.
87. Hinde, *History of Marlborough College*, p. 61.
88. Magnusson, *Edinburgh Academy*, p. 193.
89. Morgan, *Cheltenham College*, p. 34.
90. Bamford, *Rise of the Public Schools*, p. 106.

91. G. G. H. Page (ed.), *An Angel Without Wings: The History of University College School 1830–1980*, London: University College School, 1981, p. 13.

92. Magnusson, *Edinburgh Academy*, pp. 113–19.

93. Morgan, *Cheltenham College*, p. 3; Jones, *Brighton College*, p. 14.

94. Jones, *Brighton College*, pp. 9, 14.

95. William Makepeace Thackeray, *The Newcomes: Memoirs of a Respectable Family*, New York: Harper & Brothers, 1855, Vol. 1, p. 39.

96. Bamford, *Rise of the Public Schools*, p. 119.

97. *Report of Her Majesty's commissioners appointed to inquire into the revenues and management of certain colleges and schools, and the studies pursued and instruction given therein*, 1864, Vol. 2, p. 219. (Hereafter Clarendon Commission.)

98. Ibid., Vol. 2, p. 69.

99. Ibid., Vol. 1, pp. 33, 24.

100. Ibid., Vol. 1, p. 42.

101. Ibid., Vol. I, p. 42.

102. Cited in Philip Mason, *The English Gentleman: The Rise and Fall of an Ideal*, London: André Deutsch, 1982, p. 127.

103. *Report to the commissioners appointed by Her Majesty to inquire into the education given in schools in England not comprised within Her Majesty's two recent commissions, and to the commissioners appointed by Her Majesty to inquire into the schools in Scotland, on the common school systems of the United States and of the provinces of Upper and Lower Canada*, 1868, Vol. 1, p. 36. (Hereafter Taunton Commission.)

104. For more on grammar schools' journey to public schools, see, for example, Raymond Flower, *Oundle and the English Public School*, London: Stacey, 1989, pp. 69–78.

105. Dorothea Beale's *Education of Girls*, officially sanctioned by the Taunton Commission, contains edited versions of all the material relating to girls' schools, plus an introduction by Beale: D. Beale, *Reports issued by the Schools' Inquiry Commission, on the Education of Girls. Reprinted . . . with extracts from the evidence and a preface*, London: David Nutt, 1869, p. 3.

106. Ibid., p. 1.

107. Ibid., pp. 123. XV.

108. Ibid., pp. 124, 123, 125.

109. Ibid., pp. 121–2.

110. Ibid., p. 13.

111. Ibid., p. 126.

112. Nigel Watson, *And Their Works Do Follow Them: The Story of North London Collegiate School*, London: James & James, 2000, pp. 14–17.

113. Gillian Avery, *Cheltenham Ladies: A History of the Cheltenham Ladies' College*, London: James & James, 2003, pp. 13, 71, 92. See also the college entries in the *Girls' School Year Book*.

114. Beale, *Education of Girls*, p. v.

115. Avery, *Cheltenham Ladies' College*, pp. 14–20, 7, 40.

116. Elizabeth Raikes, *Dorothea Beale of Cheltenham*, London: Archibald Constable & Co., 1908, p. 259.

117. Ibid., p. 260.

118. Avery, *Cheltenham Ladies' College*, pp. 39, 69–70, 64.

119. Ibid., p. 44.

120. Beale, *Education of Girls*, p. 25.

121. Christie, *History of Clifton College*, p. 39.
122. James Sabben-Clare, *Winchester College. After 600 Years, 1382–1988*, Winchester: P. & G. Wells, 1989, p. 64.
123. Hinde, *History of Marlborough College*, p. 74.
124. Ibid., p. 69.
125. Anthony David Edwards, *The Role of International Exhibitions in Britain, 1850–1910: Perceptions of Economic Decline and the Technical Education Issue*, Amherst, NY: Cambria Press, 2008, p. 63.
126. Morgan, *Cheltenham College*, p. 70.
127. James Bentley, *Dare to be Wise: A History of the Manchester Grammar School*, London: James & James, 1990, pp. 57–62.
128. Thomas Hinde, *Carpenter's Children: The Story of the City of London School*, London: James & James, 1995, p. 43. An 1865 survey of seventy-three boys showed that thirty-seven were the sons of professionals such as doctors and lawyers, with thirty-six from tradesmen's homes.
129. Clarendon Commission, Vol. 1, p. 12.
130. Taunton Commission, Vol. 1, p. 44.
131. Ibid., Vol. 1, p. 44.
132. G. G. H. Page (ed.), *The History of University College School*, p. 12.
133. Hinde, *City of London School*, p. 38. See also list of Old Boys in appendix.
134. Ogilvie, *The English Public School*, p. 111; Roach, *Public Examinations*, pp. 216–18.
135. Roach, *Public Examinations*, p. 211.
136. Ibid., pp. 196–218.
137. Ibid., p. 199.

Chapter Five: 'The Monastic System is Getting on My Nerves.' 1870–1902

1. Robert Philp, *A Keen Wind Blows: The Story of Fettes College*, London: James & James, 1998, p. 16.
2. Ibid., pp. 14–16.
3. With regard to the development of Fettes, including the move to boarding, ibid., pp. 16–24.
4. Magnus Magnusson, *The Clacken and the Slate. The Story of the Edinburgh Academy 1824–1974*, London: Collins, 1974, pp. 258, 224.
5. David Henry Edward Wainwright, *Liverpool Gentlemen. A History of Liverpool College, an Independent Day School, from 1840*, London: Faber and Faber, 1960, pp. 153–6.
6. Email communication with principal of Liverpool College, 16 October 2013.
7. Frank Miles and Graeme Cranch, *King's College School: The First 150 Years*, London: King's College School, 1979, pp. 146, 216, 262, 265.
8. Westminster School Governors' minutes, 28 February 1881: Memorial from the Masters.
9. Anthony Quick, *Charterhouse: A History of the School*, London: James & James, 1990, p. 225.
10. Miles and Cranch, *King's College School*, pp. 205, 240.
11. Wainwright, *Liverpool Gentlemen*, p. 93.
12. Donald Leinster-Mackay, *The Educational World of Edward Thring*, London: Falmer, 1987, p. 14.

13. J. R. de S. Honey, *Tom Brown's Universe: The Development of the Victorian Public School*, London: Millington, 1977, p. 245.
14. *The Year Book of Education*, London: Evans Bros, 1932, p. 225.
15. Telephone interview, 20 January 2014.
16. 'The Reform of the Public School', in Sir Cyril Norwood and Arthur Herbert Hope, (eds), *The Higher Education of Boys in England*, London: John Murray, 1909, p. 523.
17. S. P. B. Mais, *A Schoolmaster's Diary: Extracts from the Journal of Patrick Traherne, Sometime Assistant Master at Radchester and Marlton*, London: Grant Richards: 1918, pp. 22–5.
18. R. Gurner, *I Chose Teaching*, London: J.M. Dent and Sons, 1937, p. 55.
19. G. G. H. Page (ed.), *An Angel Without Wings: The History of University College School 1830–1980*, London: University College School, 1981, p. 37.
20. Ian Anstruther, *Oscar Browning: A Biography*, London: John Murray, 1983, p. 24.
21. Ibid., pp. 15, 23–4, 39–40, 51.
22. Ibid., p. 52; Alisdare Hickson, *The Poisoned Bowl: Sex, Repression and the Public School System*, London: Constable, 1995, p. 59.
23. Anstruther, *Browning*, pp. 44, 15.
24. For a flavour of Johnson's virtues and vices, see Tim Card, *Eton Renewed: A History from 1860 to the Present Day*, London: John Murray, 1994, pp. 59–66.
25. Matthew Davenport Hill, *Eton and Elsewhere*, London: John Murray, 1928, p. 114.
26. Leinster-Mackay, *Thring*, p. 68, 118.
27. Ibid., p. 69.
28. Ibid., p. 73.
29. George Parkin, *Edward Thring, Life, Diary and Letters*, London: Macmillan, 1898, pp. 74–7.
30. Geoffrey Hoyland, *The Man Who Made a School: Thring of Uppingham*, London: S.C.M. Press, 1946, p. 56.
31. Ibid., *passim*, for example p. 201.
32. Vivian Ogilvie, *The English Public School*, London: B.T. Batsford, 1957, p. 128; *Report of Her Majesty's commissioners appointed to inquire into the revenues and management of certain colleges and schools, and the studies pursued and instruction given therein*, 1864, Vol. 1, p. 26. (Hereafter Clarendon Commission.)
33. Leinster-Mackay, *Thring*, p. 143.
34. Anstruther, *Browning, passim*, but especially p. 77ff.; Card, *Eton Renewed*, p. 64; see also entries on Browning and Johnson in *ODNB*.
35. Sir H. C. Maxwell-Lyte, *A History of Eton College*, 4th edn, London: Macmillan, 1911, p. 114; Tim Card, *Eton Established: A History from 1440 to 1860*: London, John Murray, 2001, p. 38, quoting William Edgerton, Udall's biographer.
36. Havelock Ellis, *Studies in the Psychology of Sex*, Vol. 2, Philadelphia: F.A. Davis, 1924, p. 81.
37. Peregrine Worsthorne, 'Boy made Man', in George MacDonald Fraser (ed.), *The World of the Public School*, London: Weidenfeld & Nicolson, 1977, p. 90.
38. Anstruther, *Browning*, p. 55.
39. Card, *Eton Renewed*, p. 64.
40. Ellis, *Studies in the Psychology of Sex*, Vol. 2, p. 76.
41. Card, *Eton Renewed*, p. 66.
42. Thomas Hughes, *Tom Brown's School Days*, Cambridge: Macmillan, 1857, p. 257.
43. Frederic Harrison, *Autobiographic Memoirs*, London: Macmillan, 1911, Vol. 1, p. 35.

44. E. F. Benson, *David Blaize*, London: Hogarth Press, 1989, p. 184.
45. Ellis, *Studies in the Psychology of Sex*, Vol. 2, p. 76.
46. Martin D. W. Jones, *Brighton College 1845–1995*, Chichester, West Sussex: Phillimore, 1995, p. 95.
47. Anstruther, *Browning*, p. 61.
48. Richard Davenport-Hines, entry for Browning in *ODNB*, Vol. 8, p. 251.
49. Card, *Eton Renewed*, p. 62.
50. Alan Bennett, *Plays 1*, London and Boston: Faber and Faber, 1996, p. 34.
51. T. W. Bamford, *The Rise of the Public Schools*, London: Nelson, 1967, p. 82.
52. Card, *Eton Renewed*, p. 66.
53. O. F. Christie, *A History of Clifton College, 1860–1934*, Bristol: J.W. Arrowsmith, 1935, p. 35.
54. Bamford, *Rise of the Public Schools*, p. 72.
55. Anstruther, *Browning*, pp. 62–3.
56. Derek Verschoyle, 'Indian Innocence, Ltd', in Graham Greene (ed.), *The Old School*, London: Jonathan Cape, 1934, p. 210.
57. Harold Nicolson, 'Pity the Pedagogue', in Greene, *Old School*, p. 119.
58. Jones, *Brighton College*, p. 279.
59. Miles and Cranch, *King's College School*, p. 113.
60. Ibid., pp. 133, 143.
61. Josephine Kamm, *Indicative Past: A Hundred Years of The Girls' Public Day School Trust*, London: Allen & Unwin, 1971, pp. 46–7, 50.
62. Ibid., pp. 77–8.
63. Nigel Watson, *And Their Works Do Follow Them: The Story of North London Collegiate School*, London: James & James, 2000, p. 46.
64. Sara Delamont, entry on Agnata Butler in *ODNB*, Vol. 9, pp. 114–15.
65. Watson, *North London Collegiate School*, pp. 28, 47.
66. Kamm, *Indicative Past*, p. 15.
67. Gillian Avery, *Cheltenham Ladies: A History of the Cheltenham Ladies' College*, London: James & James, 2003, p. 247.
68. Dorothy De Zouche, *Roedean School, 1885–1955*, Brighton: Roedean School, 1955, p. 27.
69. Lorna Flint, *Wycombe Abbey School 1896–1986*, privately printed, 1989, p. 28.
70. Ibid., p. 23.
71. Avery, *Cheltenham Ladies' College*, p. 102.
72. Winifred Peck, *A Little Learning, or A Victorian Childhood*, London: Faber and Faber, 1952, p. 36.
73. Kamm, *Indicative Past*, p. 64.
74. Angela Brazil, *The Youngest Girl in the Fifth*, from *The Angela Brazil Omnibus Book*, London and Glasgow: Blackie & Son, 1937, p. 15.
75. Kamm, *Indicative Past*, p. 74.
76. Ibid., pp. 43, 47.
77. Ibid., p. 52; Jeffrey Williamson, 'Structure of Pay in Britain 1710–1911', *Research in Economic History*, vol. 7, 1982, p. 48. I have used two sisters, of ten and fifteen, to work out affordability.
78. Kamm, *Indicative Past*, p. 57.
79. Ibid., p. 77.
80. Ibid., p. 85.

81. Avery, *Cheltenham Ladies' College*, p. 255.
82. Kamm, *Indicative Past*, pp. 96–7, 126–7.
83. Edward Mack, *Public Schools and British Opinion Since 1860*, New York: Columbia University Press, 1941, p. 218.
84. *Report of the Committee Appointed to Consider the Education and Training of Officers of the Army*, Appendix XXXII. Chaired by Lord Akers-Douglas, London: HMSO, 1902.
85. Mack, *Public Schools and British Opinion Since 1860*, p. 284.
86. Geoffrey Searle, *The Quest for National Efficiency: A Study in British Politics and Political Thought, 1899–1914*, Oxford: Blackwell, 1971, p. 305.
87. Christie, *History of Clifton College*, p. 122; Mack, *Public Schools and British Opinion Since 1860*, p. 100; M. C. Morgan, *Cheltenham College: The First Hundred Years*, Chalfont St Giles: published for the Cheltonian Society by Richard Sadler, 1968, p. 128; Card, *Eton Renewed*, p. 131; email from Eton archivist, 1 May 2013.
88. Morgan, *Cheltenham College*, p. 128.
89. Kenneth Harris, *Attlee*, London: Weidenfeld & Nicolson, 1982, p. 17.
90. Henry Lowther Clarke and W. N. Weech, *History of Sedbergh School 1525–1925*, Sedbergh: Jackson and Son, 1925, p. 194. The authors say the boys were enthusiastic, but do not provide any quotes as evidence.
91. Quick, *Charterhouse*, p. 66.
92. J. B. Wainewright (ed.), *Winchester College, 1835–1906: A Register*, Winchester: P. & G. Wells, 1907.
93. Clarendon Commission, Vol. 1, p. 81.
94. W. D. Rubinstein, *Capitalism, Culture, and Decline in Britain, 1750–1990*, London: Routledge, 1993, pp. 113–19.
95. Office for National Statistic, http://www.ons.gov.uk/ons/rel/ctu/annual-abstract-of-statistics/no–146--2010-edition/annual-abstract-of-statistics.pdf (accessed 1 July 2013). The author's calculations assume a roughly equal distribution of ages within the ONS's specified age groups.
96. Honey, *Tom Brown's Universe*, pp. 263–6; Rubinstein, *Capitalism*, p. 119.
97. Bryan Maybee, *Pro Liberis, Independent Schools Association 1878–2010*, Woodbridge: John Catt Educational, 2010, p. 31.
98. John Lawson and Harold Silver, *A Social History of Education in England*, London: Methuen, 1973, pp. 337–8.
99. Frank Richards, *Billy Bunter of Greyfriars School*, London: Hawe Books, 1991, p. 21.

Chapter Six: Beware Greeks Bearing Gifts 1902–1945

1. John Lawson and Harold Silver, *A Social History of Education in England*, London: Methuen, 1973, p. 367ff.
2. Michael Sanderson, *Educational Opportunity and Social Change in England*, London: Faber and Faber, 1987, p. 29.
3. John Vaizey, *The Costs of Education*, London: Allen & Unwin, 1958, p. 98.
4. Lawson and Silver, *Social History of Education*, p. 372.
5. Sanderson, *Educational Opportunity*, p. 32. See also Sanderson's footnote.
6. Anthony Trott, *No Place for Fop or Idler: The Story of King Edward's School, Birmingham*, London: James & James, 1992, p. 94.

7. Frank Miles and Graeme Cranch, *King's College School: The First 150 Years*, London: King's College School, 1979, p. 240.
8. Nigel Watson, *And Their Works Do Follow Them: The Story of North London Collegiate School*, London: James & James, 2000, p. 57ff.
9. Josephine Kamm, *Indicative Past: A Hundred Years of The Girls' Public Day School Trust*, London: Allen & Unwin, 1971, pp. 119, 103.
10. Geoffrey Sherington, *English Education, Social Change and War, 1911–20*, Manchester: Manchester University Press, 1981, p. 146.
11. Martin W. Holdgate, *Arnold: The Story of a Blackpool School*, Kirkby Stephen: Hayloft Publishing, 2009, p. 55.
12. Watson, *And Their Works Do Follow Them*, p. 59.
13. Graham Greene (ed.), *The Old School*, London: Jonathan Cape, 1934, p. 190.
14. Board of Education, *Private Schools, and Other Schools Not in Receipt of Grants from Public Funds*, London, 1932, p. 27.
15. Frank Fletcher, *After Many Days. A Schoolmaster's Memories*, London: Robert Hale & Co., 1937, p. 272.
16. Miles and Cranch, *King's College School*, p. 240.
17. Ian Hay, *The Lighter Side of School Life*, London, Edinburgh, Boston: T.N. Foulis, 1924. Strictly speaking, the translation is 'I beware Greeks even when they bring gifts'.
18. A. H. H. Maclean, *Public Schools and the Great War, 1914–19*, London: Edward Stanford, 1923.
19. Edward Mack, *Public Schools and British Opinion Since 1860*, New York: Columbia University Press, 1941, p. 307; Tim Card, *Eton Renewed: A History from 1860 to the Present Day*, London: John Murray, 1994, pp. 143–4.
20. *Eton College Chronicle*, 8 February 1917, p. 168.
21. Maclean, *Public Schools and the Great War*.
22. http://www.englishverse.com/poems/the_soldier (accessed 17 June 2014).
23. Card, *Eton Renewed*, p. 301.
24. http://www.poemhunter.com/poem/land-of-hope-and-glory/ (accessed 17 June 2014).
25. Maclean, *Public Schools and the Great War*, p. 19.
26. Sherington, *English Education, Social Change and War*, pp. 44–53.
27. *Report of the Committee appointed by the Prime Minister to Enquire into the Position of Natural Science in the Educational System of Great Britain*, Parlt. Pprs. 1918, IX, Cd9011, Paragraphs 16, 19, 15.
28. Ibid., Paragraphs 10, 11.
29. *Report of the Committee appointed by the Prime Minister to Enquire into the Position of Modern Languages in the Educational System of Great Britain*, Parlt. Pprs. 1918, IX, Cd9036, Paragraph 132.
30. Robert Philp, *A Keen Wind Blows: The Story of Fettes College*, London: James & James, 1998, pp. 36, 43, 41.
31. T. C. Worsley, *Flannelled Fool*, London: Hogarth Press, 1985, p. 20.
32. *Girls' School Year Book*, London: A&C Black, 1930.
33. Girls' Day School Trust archives: GDS/17/7/2.
34. GDS/17/7/2 Memo by heads of GDST schools regarding their objection to Board of Education regulations for compulsory courses in feminine arts; DC/GDS13/11/7 Kensington High School 1914 prospectus.
35. *Girls' School Year Book*.

36. Howard Bailes, *St Paul's Girls' School*, London: James & James, 2000, p. 72.
37. Gillian Avery, *Cheltenham Ladies: A History of the Cheltenham Ladies' College*, London: James & James, 2003, p. 139.
38. See individual school entries in *Public Schools Year Book*, London, for the appropriate years.
39. Andrew Hodges, *Alan Turing: The Enigma*, London: Vintage, 1992, p. 26.
40. Entries in *Public Schools Year Book*, 1938.
41. P. G. Wodehouse, *Tales of St Austin's*, Harmondsworth: Puffin Books, 1972, p. 15.
42. Francis R. G. Duckworth, *From a Pedagogue's Sketch-Book*, London and Leipzig: T. Fisher Unwin, 1912, pp. 156–7.
43. Figures taken from *Public Schools Year Book*, 1938.
44. Cyril Norwood, *The English Tradition of Education*, London: John Murray, 1931, p. 129.
45. Ibid., p. 130.
46. Christine Heward, *Making a Man of Him: Parents and Their Sons' Education at an English Public School 1929–50*, London: Routledge, 1988, p. 60.
47. Cited by Mack, *Public Schools and British Opinion Since 1860*, p. 300.
48. Anthony Marett-Crosby, *A School of the Lord's Service: A History of Ampleforth*, London, James & James, 2002, pp. 52–3.
49. Norwood, *English Tradition of Education*, pp. 130–1.
50. Brian Rees, *Stowe: The History of a Public School 1923–1989*, London, 2008, p. 57.
51. Jan Piggott, *Dulwich College: A History, 1616–2008*, Dulwich: Dulwich College Enterprises Ltd, 2008, p. 242.
52. H. A. Vachell, *The Hill*, London: George Newnes, 1905, p. 16.
53. Jason Tomes, entry for Bracken in *ODNB*, Vol. 7, pp. 145–6; email communication with Sedbergh School archivist, 20 June 2013. C. E. Lysaght, *Brendan Bracken*, London: Allen Lane, 1979, pp. 306–7.
54. Evelyn Waugh, *Decline and Fall*, London: Chapman & Hall, 1935, p. 29.
55. Mack, *Public Schools and British Opinion Since 1860*, p. 405.
56. T. W. Bamford, *The Rise of the Public Schools*, London: Nelson, 1967, p. 321.
57. Fred Clarke, 'Recruitment of the Nation's Leaders', *Sociological Review*, 1936, p. 343.
58. Keith Robbins, entry for Grey in *ODNB*, Vol. 23, p. 826.
59. T. J. H. Bishop and Rupert Wilkinson, *Winchester and the Public School Elite*, London: Faber and Faber, 1967, pp. 164–71.
60. Kenneth Harris, *Attlee*, London: Weidenfeld & Nicolson, 1982, pp. 406, 33.
61. Dulwich College Governors' minutes, October 1932, p. 40.
62. Bishop and Wilkinson, *Winchester*, p. 223.
63. J. R. de S. Honey, *Tom Brown's Universe: The Development of the Victorian Public School*, London: Millington, 1977, p. 161.
64. Heward, *Making a Man of Him*, p. 76.
65. Rudyard Kipling, *Stalky and Co.*, London: Macmillan, 1929, pp. 10–13.
66. Rupert Wilkinson, *The Prefects. British Leadership and the Public School Tradition. A Comparative Study in the Making of Rulers*, London: Oxford University Press, 1964, pp. 3, 49.
67. David Boyd, *Elites and their Education*, Windsor: National Foundation for Educational Research, 1973, pp. 80, 83, 84.
68. Brian Simon, *Education and the Social Order 1940–1990*, London: Lawrence & Wishart, 2010 edition, p. 38.

69. Moberly Bell, *A History of the Church Schools Company*, London: Society for Promoting Christian Knowledge, 1958, p. 71.
70. Richard Drysdale (ed.), *Over Ancient Ways: A Portrait of St Peter's School, York*, London: Third Millennium Publishing, 2007, p. 33.
71. *Public Schools Year Book*, 1919, 1930 and 1938.
72. Bell, *History of the Church Schools Company*, p. 71.
73. C. H. Lee, *The British Economy Since 1700*, Cambridge: Cambridge University Press, 1986, pp. 29, 147.
74. James Basil Oldham, *A History of Shrewsbury School, 1552–1952*, Oxford: Basil Blackwell, 1952, p. 279; Card, *Eton Renewed*, p. 191.
75. http://www.ons.gov.uk/ons/publications/re-reference-tables.html?edition=tcm%3A77-262743 (accessed 7 December 2012).
76. Nigel Watson, *A Tradition for Freedom: The Story of University College School*, London: James & James, 2007, pp. 45–57; Christopher Tyerman, *A History of Harrow School*, Oxford, New York: Oxford University Press, 2000, p. 410.
77. Watson, *University College School*, p. 107.
78. Card, *Eton Renewed*, p. 190.
79. Andrew Thorpe, 'Essay on Britain', in Jeremy Noakes (ed.), *The Civilian in War*, Exeter: University of Exeter Press, 1997, p. 21.
80. Thomas Hinde, *Carpenter's Children: The Story of the City of London School*, London: James & James, 1995, p. 99.
81. http://www.bbc.co.uk/history/ww2peopleswar/stories/78/a6873078.shtml (accessed 30 June 2014).
82. Roderick Braithwaite, *Strikingly Alive: The History of the Mill Hill School Foundation, 1807–2007*, Chichester: Published for the Mill Hill School Foundation by Phillimore, 2006, p. 228; David Henry Edward Wainwright, *Liverpool Gentlemen: A History of Liverpool College, An Independent Day School from 1840*, London: Faber and Faber, 1960, p. 248; John Field, *The King's Nurseries*, London: James & James, 1987, p. 96.
83. Kamm, *Indicative Past*, p. 77.
84. Simon, *Education and the Social Order*, p. 41.
85. George Orwell, *The Lion and the Unicorn*, London: Secker & Warburg, 1941, Part IV.
86. Boyd, *Elites and their Education*, pp. 41, 82.
87. Anthony Quick, *Charterhouse: A History of the School*, London: James & James, 1990, p. 27.
88. Ibid., p. 82. The definition of public schools excludes, in this case, Dartmouth Naval College. Until 1941, although parents paid fees for boys at Dartmouth, as they did for public schools, Dartmouth was always a vocational training college rather than a true public school.
89. Bamford, *Rise of the Public Schools*, p. 239.
90. The task of preparing men for colonial and imperial life was a major concern of some of the heads of the new public schools set up at the end of the nineteenth century and in the early twentieth century (though it is harder to find reference to this at many of the older schools). Badley, the founder of Bedales, declared that a young man able to perform the various manual tasks performed at his school, including the ability to 'handle an axe as well as a bat', and to 'mend his own clothes like a sailor', was 'obviously the ideal colonist' (Roy Wake and Pennie Denton, *Bedales School: The First Hundred Years*, London: Haggerston Press, 1993, p. 28).

91. Bell, *History of the Church Schools Company*, p. 77.
92. Girls' Day School Trust archives: DC/GDS/5/1.
93. *Report of the Committee on Public Schools Appointed by the President of the Board of Education in July 1942*, 1944, p. 101. (Hereafter known as Fleming Report.)
94. R. A. Butler, *The Art of the Possible*, London: Hamilton, 1971, p. 120.
95. Fleming Report, pp. 100–5.

Chapter Seven: Embracing the Examination Incubus 1945–1979

1. Winchester College Archives: A3/6, Canon Leeson's reports, 1945, p. 6.
2. John Vaizey, *The Costs of Education*, London: Allen & Unwin, 1958, p. 100.
3. Brian Simon, *Education and the Social Order 1940–1990*, London: Lawrence & Wishart, 2010 edn, p. 601.
4. Eton College archives: 60/8/2/1/24, Provost and Fellows Agenda Papers, 1960, letter from head to provost, 21 January 1960.
5. Christopher Hibbert, *No Ordinary Place: Radley College and the Public School System, 1847–1997*, London: John Murray, 1997, p. 241.
6. Eton College archives: 60/8/2/1/24, Provost and Fellows Agenda Papers, 1960, 12 January letter to provost.
7. Westminster School archives: D63S1 Timetable Committee 1963–65, p. 2 of 25 October 1963 document on 'The Time-table'.
8. Ibid., p. 6.
9. Simon Batten, *A Shining Light: 150 Years of Bloxham School*, London: James & James, 2010, pp. 74–84.
10. John Vallins, 'Fortnightly Boarding', *Conference* (the HMC magazine), June 1970, p. 11.
11. 'Public Schools' Difference in Standards', *The Times*, 17 February 1964.
12. Simon, *Education and the Social Order*, pp. 597–8.
13. Robert Philp, *A Keen Wind Blows: The Story of Fettes College*, London: James & James, 1998, pp. 67–8.
14. Ibid., p. 68.
15. Eton archives: 60/8/2/1/24, Provost and Fellows Agenda Papers, 1960, letter by Lord John Hope.
16. John Rae, *The Old Boys' Network: A Headmaster's Diaries 1972–1986*, London: Short, 2010, diary entry for 29 November 1979.
17. Nigel Watson, *A Tradition for Freedom: The Story of University College School*, London: James & James, 2007, pp. 88–9.
18. Richard Sachs, 'Small Hurricane at Shrewsbury: Many Myths Dead', *The Times*, 27 January 1978.
19. Department of Education annual statistics, 1976, p. 1.
20. Raymond Flower, *Oundle and the English Public School*, London: Stacey, 1989, p. 153; Oundle School magazine, July 1958.
21. J. R. de S. Honey, *Tom Brown's Universe: The Development of the Victorian Public School*, London: Millington, 1977, p. 45.
22. Rae, *Old Boys' Network*, diary entry for 23 June 1977.
23. Royston Lambert and Spencer Millham, *The Hothouse Society*, Harmondsworth: Penguin, 1974, p. 175.
24. Report of the Headmasters' Conference, 1969, p. 18.

25. Guy Kendall, *A Headmaster Reflects*, London, Edinburgh, Glasgow: William Hodge & Company, 1937, pp. 197–8.
26. Alec Waugh, *The Loom of Youth*, London: Methuen, 1984, pp. 91–2.
27. Robert Graves, *Goodbye to All That*, London: The Folio Society, 1981, p. 50.
28. James Cobban, 'Looking Back', *Conference* (the HMC magazine), February 1972, p. 21.
29. Report of the Headmasters' Conference, 1969, p. 18.
30. J. M. Peterson, 'The Place of Traditional Games', *Conference*, December 1965, p. 41.
31. Richard Branson, *Sir Richard Branson: The Autobiography*, Harlow: Pearson Education, 2002, p. 37.
32. 'Youth's Appeal to Tribunal', *The Times*, 9 February 1954.
33. Colin Leach, *A School at Shrewsbury: The Four Foundations*, London, James & James, 1990, p. 103.
34. Email communication with City of London School archivist, 16 July 2013.
35. Leach, *Shrewsbury*, p. 107.
36. Batten, *Bloxham School*, p. 127.
37. Email communication with Shrewsbury School archivist, 22 July 2013.
38. T. E. Muir, *Stonyhurst College, 1593–1993*, London: James & James, 1992, p. 135.
39. City of London School Chronicle, July 1972, p. 50.
40. Christopher Tyerman, *A History of Harrow School*, Oxford, New York: Oxford University Press, 2000, p. 477.
41. Hibbert, *Radley College*, p. 270.
42. Philp, *Fettes College*, p. 87.
43. 'Future of Independent Schools "Seriously Threatened"', *The Times*, 5 January 1956.
44. Kenneth Lindsay, 'Science in Schools', Letter to the Editor, *The Times*, 7 November 1955. The figure excludes labs built at direct grant grammars, which were only partly state-funded. Lindsay said he was quoting Sir David Eccles, the education secretary.
45. 'Making Scientists of Quality', *The Times*, 4 November 1957.
46. Philp, *Fettes College*, p. 104.
47. Based on Simon, *Education and the Social Order*, especially Tables 2a and 9.
48. 'Convent School to Close', *The Times*, 2 February 1972.
49. 'Parents Fail to Save School', *The Times*, 15 April 1970.
50. Roy Wake and Pennie Denton, *Bedales School: The First Hundred Years*, London: Haggerston Press, 1993, p. 37.
51. Lucy Hodges, 'Girls "Strengthen" Public Schools', *The Times*, 29 March 1984.
52. Ibid.
53. Francis Davey, head of Merchant Taylors', in a letter to *The Times*, 'Girls Admitted to Boys Schools', 22 September 1977.
54. Letter to *The Times*, 26 July 1975.
55. Philp, *Fettes College*, p. 93.
56. 'New Trends in Girls' Public Schools', *The Times*, 11 December 1963.
57. Telephone interview, 4 February 2013.
58. Thomas Hinde, *Paths of Progress: A History of Marlborough College*, London: James & James, 1992, p. 215.
59. Figures from annual statistics of Department of Education.
60. Richard Drysdale (ed.), *Over Ancient Ways: A Portrait of St Peter's School, York*, London: Third Millennium Publishing, 2007, p. 51.

61. John Le Mesurier, *A Jobbing Actor*, London: Elm Tree Books, 1984, p. 16.
62. Telephone interview, 4 February 2013.
63. Stephen Fry, *Moab is My Washpot*, London: Arrow, 1997, p. 249.
64. Report of the Headmasters' Conference, 1969, p. 69.
65. Anonymous, *St George's College Weybridge 1869–1969*, privately printed, p. 31.
66. Telephone interview, 9 June 2014.
67. http://www.theguardian.com/education/2014/jun/22/school-faces-claim-over-paedophile-teacher (accessed 3 July 2014).
68. http://www.bbc.co.uk/news/uk-england-london-27235785 (accessed 8 July 2014).
69. http://www.bbc.co.uk/news/uk-28213318 (accessed 9 July 2014).
70. http://www.theguardian.com/uk/2005/nov/19/publicschools.schools (accessed 9 July 2014).
71. Geoffrey Walford, *Privatisation and Privilege in Education*, London: Routledge, 1990, p. 29.
72. Roderick Braithwaite, *Strikingly Alive: The History of the Mill Hill School Foundation, 1807–2007*, Chichester: published for the Mill Hill School Foundation by Phillimore, 2006, p. 234.
73. Ibid., pp. 29–30; *The Public Schools Commission: First Report*, London: HMSO, 1968, p. 8.
74. John Rae, *The Public School Revolution*, London: Faber and Faber, 1981, p. 13.
75. Brian Harrison, *Finding a Role? The United Kingdom, 1970–1990*, Oxford: Clarendon, 2011, p. 389.
76. Walford, *Privatisation and Privilege*, pp. 30–2.
77. Figures based on tables already cited in Simon, *Education and the Social Order*, and statistics from the Department of Education.
78. Interview, University College School, 23 January 2013.
79. Simon, *Education and the Social Order*, pp. 280–1.
80. Winchester headmaster's report to warden and fellows, 1961.
81. David Gibb, *A School with a View: A History of Ardingly College 1858–2008*, London: James & James, 2008, p. 75.
82. Telephone interview, 1 February 2013.
83. Telephone interview, 22 February 2013.
84. Interview, Eton College, 4 February 2013.
85. Telephone interview, 4 February 2013.
86. Lambert and Millham, *Hothouse Society*, p. 102.
87. Rae, *Old Boys' Network*, diary entry for 9 September 1979.
88. Telephone interview with Mark Turner, headmaster of Shrewsbury, 22 February 2013.
89. John Vallins, 'Fortnightly Boarding', *Conference*, June 1970, p. 11.
90. Interview with Andrew Halls, King's College School, 26 March 2013.

Chapter Eight: A Golden Age At Last 1980–2014

1. Dulwich College Governors' minutes, 1976, p. 251.
2. Ibid., 1980, pp. 185–96.
3. Ibid., 1980, pp. 185–6; 1981, p. 41.
4. Brian Simon, *Education and the Social Order 1940–1990*, London: Lawrence & Wishart, 2010 edition, pp. 479–527.

5. Irene Fox, *Private Schools and Public Issues: The Parents' View*, London: Macmillan, 1985, pp. 140, 145.
6. Ibid., pp. 114, 140, 145.
7. Based on the analysis of Independent Schools Council annual surveys.
8. Fox, *Private Schools and Public Issues*, p. 114.
9. Howard Bailes, *St Paul's Girls' School*, London: James & James, 2000, p. 103.
10. Independent Schools Council Census.
11. Geoffrey Walford, *Privatisation and Privilege in Education*, London: Routledge, 1990, pp. 67-72.
12. Geraldine Hackett, 'Blue-collar Elite Best off in Private Schools', *Times Educational Supplement*, 27 March 1998. The article refers to *Education and the Middle Class*, a book by Sally Power, Tony Edwards, Valerie Wigfall and Geoff Whitty, Maidenhead: Open University Press, 2003.
13. Geoffrey Walford, *Private Education: Tradition and Diversity*, London: Continuum, 2006, p. 108.
14. Independent Schools Council Census.
15. Ibid.
16. http://www.hks.harvard.edu/fs/phall/01.%20Charitable%20uses.pdf (accessed 7 January 2014).
17. Peter Davies, John Noble, Kim Slack and Katy Vigurs, 'Fee Remissions and Bursaries in Independent Schools', Institute for Education Policy Research, on behalf of The Sutton Trust, July 2010, p. 15.
18. Chris Cook, 'Private Schools Win Review on Charitable Status', *Financial Times*, 14 October 2011.
19. Graeme Paton, 'State Pupils and "Worthless" A-levels', *Daily Telegraph*, 15 June 2011; see also the London School of Economics list of 'non-preferred subjects': http://www.lse.ac.uk/study/undergraduate/howtoapply/lseentryrequirements.aspx (accessed 9 January 2014).
20. Graeme Paton, 'Maths and Science Rise in Downturn', *Daily Telegraph*, 20 August 2010.
21. Email communication with the Campaign for Science and Engineering, 15 May 2013.
22. Jessica Shepherd, 'Students Sat "Easy" GCSE Science Exams', *Guardian*, 27 August 2010.
23. Graeme Paton, 'Pupils Taking French Drop by Half', *Daily Telegraph*, 28 August 2009.
24. Boarding figures taken from annual Independent Schools Council Census. Independent Schools Council schools are thought to account for virtually all boarding.
25. Mary Hayden and Geoff Thompson, *Taking the IB Diploma Programme Forward*, London: John Catt Educational, 2011, p. 145.
26. Telephone interview, 13 June 2014.
27. Ian Anstruther, *Dean Farrar and 'Eric'* (including the full text of the book), London: Haggerston Press, 2002, p. 40.
28. Quoted in Edward Mack, *Public Schools and British Opinion Since 1860*, New York: Columbia University Press, 1941, p. 329.
29. Discussion with an ex-Winchester College schoolboy from the 1980s, 15 June 2014.
30. Richard Drysdale (ed.), *Over Ancient Ways: A Portrait of St Peter's School, York*, London: Third Millennium Publishing, 2007, pp. 24-5.

31. B. M. Spinley, *The Deprived and the Privileged: Personality Development in English Society*, London: Routledge & Kegan Paul, 1953, pp. 129ff.

32. Telephone interview, 20 June 2014.

33. Telephone interview, 20 January 2014.

34. Telephone interview, 17 June 2014.

35. Amit Roy, 'Public Schools Pin their Hopes on Hong Kong Boarding', *Sunday Times*, 13 August 1989.

36. Figures taken from Independent Schools Council Censuses. The calculation is the author's own, based on spreadsheet analysis. The author's calculations assume that minimal numbers of non-British pupils with overseas parents were at day schools.

37. Telephone interview, 22 February 2013.

38. Telephone interview, 20 June 2014. Asked whether the college could survive without overseas boarders, who make up 18 per cent of total school numbers, Graham Hawley says: 'No. I don't think we could.'

39. http://news.bbc.co.uk/1/hi/education/563232.stm; http://www.independent.co.uk/news/education/education-news/boarding-schools-miss-their-harry-potter-magic–58153.html (both accessed 19 June 2014).

40. Figures supplied by master in interview, Dulwich College, 26 March 2013.

41. Independent Schools Council Census.

42. David Turner, 'On the Playing Fields of Bangkok', *Financial Times*, 25 November 2008.

43. Tim Card, *Eton Established: A History from 1440 to 1860*, London: John Murray, 2001, p. 51.

44. David Henry Edward Wainwright, *Liverpool Gentlemen. A History of Liverpool College, an Independent Day School, from 1840*, London: Faber and Faber, 1960, p. 125.

45. Telephone interview with James Whitehead, headmaster of Downside School, 20 June 2014.

46. Alisdare Hickson, *The Poisoned Bowl: Sex, Repression and the Public School System*, London: Constable, 1995, p. 43.

47. Magnus Magnusson, *The Clacken and the Slate. The Story of the Edinburgh Academy 1824–1974*, London: Collins, 1974, p. 369.

48. Martin D. W. Jones, *Brighton College 1845–1995*, Chichester, West Sussex: Phillimore, 1995, p. 167.

49. Winchester College archives: A3/6 Canon Leeson's reports, 1938.

50. Josephine Kamm, *Indicative Past: A Hundred Years of The Girls' Public Day School Trust*, London: Allen & Unwin, 1971, p. 74.

51. Email communication with Eton archivist, 1 May 2013.

52. Gillian Avery, *Cheltenham Ladies: A History of the Cheltenham Ladies' College*, London: James & James, 2003, p. 226.

53. Interviews with heads, including Richard Cairns of Brighton College.

54. John Clare, 'The A-Level Meritocracy'; 'Girls' School Comes Top in Telegraph A-Level Survey', *Daily Telegraph*, 29 August 1991.

55. Ibid.

56. Nicholas Pyke, 'Sacrificed to the Cocktail Party Factor', *Times Educational Supplement*, 25 October 1996.

57. Interview, Dulwich College, 26 March 2013.

58. Interview with David Levin, master at the school under Morgan, City of London School, 18 February 2013.

59. Sebastian Haffner, *Churchill*, London: Haus, 2003, p. 13.

60. Interviews with Richard Cairns and other public school heads.

61. Interview with Andrew Halls, King's College School, 26 March 2013.

62. Geoffrey Walford, *Private Education*, New York: Continuum, 2005, p. 55.

63. Ben Preston, 'Public Schools Plan Standards Monitors', *The Times*, 13 September 1993.

64. Various interviews with heads, including Andrew Halls.

65. Telephone interview with Mark Turner, headmaster of Shrewsbury, 22 February 2013.

66. Telephone interview, 1 February 2013.

67. Telephone interview, 9 June 2014.

68. Telephone interview, 16 June 2014.

69. Independent Schools Council Annual Censuses.

70. Graeme Paton, 'A Private Education Can Boost Earnings by a Fifth', *Daily Telegraph*, 11 January 2008.

71. Alison Goddard, 'Pay Reflects School Ties', *Times Educational Supplement*, 30 October 1998.

72. Figures supplied by Joint Council for Qualifications.

73. John Charnley, 'The GCSE Performance of Independent School Pupils: Gender and School Type Differences', Curriculum Evaluation and Management Centre, 2008, http://www.cem.org/publications–4 (accessed 15 May 2013).

74. Jonathan Lynn and Anthony Jay, *The Complete Yes Minister*, London: Harper and Row, 1984, p. 254.

75. Rudolf Eliott Lockhart, 'Independent Schools and Exam Performance in 2011', Independent Schools Council, 2011.

76. David Turner, 'More Students Take Science Degrees', *Financial Times*, 22 October 2008.

77. Telephone interview, 17 June 2014.

78. Interview with David Levin, master at the school under Morgan, City of London School, 18 February 2013.

79. Telephone interview, London, 14 May 2013; Charnley, 'GCSE Performance of Independent School Pupils'.

80. Telephone interview, 5 February 2013.

81. Based on Simon, *Education and the Social Order*, especially Tables 2a, 9.

82. Graham Lacey, 'Independents May Slip in Age of the League Table', *Times Educational Suppolement*, 17 January 1997.

83. Email communication with Claire Oulton, headmistress of Benenden, February 2013.

84. Graeme Paton, 'Parents "Obsessed with Exam Results"', *Daily Telegraph*, 29 September 2010.

85. Telephone interview, 6 June 2014.

86. Telephone interview, 27 June 2014.

87. Telephone interview, 5 February 2013.

88. Thomas Hughes, *Tom Brown's School Days*, Cambridge: Macmillan, 1857, p. 171.

89. Interview, Eton College, 4 February 2013.

90. Roald Dahl, *Boy: Tales of Childhood*, Harmondsworth: Penguin Books, 1986, p. 150.

91. Telephone interview, 6 June 2014.

Chapter Nine: Beautiful Natures, Overpriced Products and Self-Destruction

1. http://www.theguardian.com/uk/2006/feb/27/schools.publicschools (accessed 20 June 2014).
2. Independent Schools Council Census.
3. Arthur Francis Leach, *A History of Winchester College*, London: Duckworth & Co., 1899, p. 100; Tim Card, *Eton Renewed: A History from 1860 to the Present Day*, London: John Murray, 1994, pp. 48, 54; Christopher Tyerman, *A History of Harrow School*, Oxford, New York: Oxford University Press, 2000, p. 55. The sole reference which I have found in school histories to charges paid by boys which would be higher than today's rates – though not much higher – is to the ten noblemen mentioned in Chapter Two, living with the Winchester headmaster in 1730, who paid £200 (£37,000) each, compared with a standard fee of £33,750 for 2013.
4. M. C. Morgan, *Cheltenham College: The First Hundred Years*, Chalfont St Giles: published for the Cheltonian Society by Richard Sadler, 1968, p. 4; *Report of Her Majesty's commissioners appointed to inquire into the revenues and management of certain colleges and schools, and the studies pursued and instruction given therein*, 1864; appropriate years of *Public Schools Year Book*, *Girls' School Year Book*. For boys, the highest boarding fee fluctuates between £6,146 (1952) and £12,356 (1910), but with no clear trend. Day fees begin to rise in the 1950s, with the annual charge for the lowest rising from £1,170 in 1952 to £2,279 in 1970. For girls' schools, I have analysed eighteen schools for which fee figures are available throughout the period from 1910 to 1970.
5. Figures from the 1980s onwards are taken from Independent Schools Council Censuses. Exact comparisons are difficult because of the usual statistical inconsistencies that build up over the decades, but the overall trend is clear.
6. Based on Brian Simon, *Education and the Social Order 1940–1990*, London: Lawrence & Wishart, 2010 edition, especially Tables 2a, 9, and on Department of Education annual statistics.
7. Figures taken from the Office for National Statistics (formerly Central Statistical Office) annual earnings surveys, and from Independent Schools Council Censuses.
8. Telephone interview, 13 June 2014.
9. Telephone interview, 10 July 2014.
10. David Turner, 'Top Private School Governor Warns on Ability to Pay Fees', *Financial Times*, 3 June 2009.
11. Interview, University College School, 23 January 2013.
12. Figures taken from Office for National Statistics (formerly Central Statistical Office) annual earnings surveys, and from Independent Schools Council censuses.
13. Interview, City of London School, 18 February 2013.
14. Telephone interview, 14 February 2013.
15. Telephone interview, 9 June 2014.
16. Calculation based on figures in Independent Schools Council 2014 census.
17. Telephone interview, 17 June 2014.
18. Telephone interview with head of Birkenhead School, 8 February 2013.
19. Telephone interview, London, 14 May 2013.
20. Martin D. W. Jones, *Brighton College 1845–1995*, Chichester, West Sussex: Phillimore, 1995, pp. 73, 94, 166.
21. Analysis of Independent Schools Council Censuses.

22. Cambridge University, Access Agreement with the Office for Fair Access (Offa) 2014–15.

23. Graeme Paton, 'Universities Handicap Private School Pupils, Says Head', *Daily Telegraph*, 3 October 2012.

24. Based on author's interviews with public school heads. David Levin of the City of London School, for example, mentioned quotas as a future possibility.

25. Independent Schools Council Census, 2014.

26. Interview, Dulwich College, 26 March 2013.

27. https://college.harvard.edu/financial-aid/how-aid-works/cost-attendance (accessed 14 October 2014).

28. http://news.bbc.co.uk/1/hi/uk_politics/2093448.stm (accessed 25 March 2014).

29. Telephone interview, 4 February 2013.

30. Independent Schools Council annual surveys. For the 1994 figure, I have included the eight schools in the Governing Body of Girls' Schools Associations, a now defunct body, whose heads were not also members of the Girls' Schools Association.

31. David Turner, 'Girls-only Private Schools Top Exam Grades at Co-eds', *Financial Times*, 13 September 2008.

32. John Charnley, 'The GCSE performance of independent school pupils: gender and school type differences', Curriculum Evaluation and Management Centre, 2008, http://www.cem.org/publications–4 (accessed 15 May 2013).

33. Interview, St James Senior Girls' School, 1 March 2013.

Chapter Ten: The Pauline and the Pasty

1. Will Hutton, 'Born poor? Bad luck, you have won last prize in the lottery of life', *Observer*, 15 July 2012; for the segregation argument, see also Hutton, 'Education: We All Lose When We Separate Our Children at the School Gate', *Observer*, 11 May 2013.

2. A. H. Halsey, A. F. Heath and J. M. Ridge, *Origins and Destinations*, Oxford: Clarendon Press, 1980, p. 4.

3. For example, interview with Fiona Millar, education campaigner, London, 15 May 2013.

4. For example, Geoffrey Walford, *Privatisation and Privilege in Education*, London: Routledge, 1990, Chapter Six.

5. 'Pathways to Banking Improving access for students from non-privileged backgrounds', research by the Boston Consulting Group for the Sutton Trust, January 2014.

6. The most detailed figures are in the Sutton Trust submission to the Milburn Commission on access, 'The Educational Backgrounds of Leading Lawyers, Journalists, Vice Chancellors, Politicians, Medics and Chief Executives to the Professions', March 2009.

7. http://www.bbc.co.uk/news/entertainment-arts–27924176 (accessed 23 June 2014).

8. 'Higher Education: the Fair Access Challenge', Social Mobility and Child Poverty Commission, June 2013, p. 5.

9. Lindsey Macmillan, Claire Tyler and Anna Vignoles, 'Who gets the top jobs? The role of family background and networks in recent graduates' access to high status professions', Institute of Education, University of London, December 2013.

10. Sutton Trust submission to the Milburn Commission on access, 'The Educational Backgrounds of Leading Lawyers, Journalists, Vice Chancellors, Politicians, Medics and Chief Executives to the Professions', March 2009.

11. 'Higher Education: the Fair Access Challenge', Social Mobility and Child Poverty Commission, June 2013, p. 16.

12. David Turner, 'Cambridge Attacks Poor-quality Teachers', *Financial Times*, 21 February 2009; http://www.timeshighereducation.co.uk/news/oxford-drops-below-cambridge-on-state-school-entrants/2012321.article (accessed 14 July 2014).

13. For example, 'Use of an aptitude test in university entrance: a validity study', National Foundation for Educational Research, on behalf of the Sutton Trust, September 2010.

14. Figures supplied by the Higher Education Funding Council for England, 4 March 2014. They relate to graduates who started full-time first-degree courses in 2007–8.

15. Figures supplied by Geoff Parks, director of admissions for the Cambridge colleges, 1 July 2012.

16. Macmillan, Tyler and Vignoles, 'Who gets the Top Jobs?'

17. Human capital theory was pioneered by Sir William Petty in the seventeenth century and Adam Smith in the eighteenth century, and developed further by economists including Gary Becker. See, for example, Gary Becker, *Human Capital: A Theoretical and Empirical Analysis, with Special Reference to Education*, Chicago: University of Chicago Press, 1980.

18. Rudolf Eliott Lockhart, 'Independent Schools and Exam Performance in 2011', Independent Schools Council, 2011.

19. E.g. Henry Deedes, 'Pasties Give Politicians Bellies, not Bottom', *Daily Mail*, 29 March 2012.

20. For example, Kevin Maguire, 'Posh David Cameron looks further out of touch than ever over pasty debacle', *Mirror*, 29 March 2012.

21. Press Association byline, 'Row Set to Hot up as Pasty Tax Comes into Force', *Independent*, 1 October 2012.

22. Independent Schools Council 2013 Census, p. 13; Department for Education, Schools, Pupils and Their Characteristics: January 2012, National Tables, Table 4A. Note that the author's own calculation, based on the Department data, is marginally different from that of the Independent Schools Council.

23. Telephone interview, 27 June 2014.

24. Interview with Tony Little, headmaster, Eton College, 4 February 2013.

25. Figures supplied by Charterhouse School bursar, 6 June 2013.

26. Figures supplied by Winchester College bursar, 15 May 2013.

27. For example, Andrew Adonis, Labour former education minister: see http://andrewadonis.com/2013/05/10/pupils-%E2%80%98segregated-from-society%E2%80%99-by-exclusive-private-schools/ (accessed 17 June 2013).

28. Author's own calculations, based on figures from Peter Davies, John Noble, Kim Slack and Katy Vigurs, 'Fee Remissions and Bursaries in Independent Schools', Institute for Education Policy Research, on behalf of the Sutton Trust, July 2010, p. 19.

29. Independent Schools Council Census, 2012, p. 12.

30. Telephone conversation with the bursar, 16 May 2013. Winchester calculates net income, after deducting tax and mortgage payments, for example. The government statisticians calculate gross income. Average net income would be considerably lower than £21,788.

31. Elizabeth Rigby and Andrew Bounds, 'Concerns over UK Conservatives' "Posh" Manifesto', *Financial Times*, 23 February 2014.
32. George Parker and Helen Warrell, 'Gove Takes Aim at Cameron's Etonians', *Financial Times*, 14 March 2014.
33. See, for example, Andrew Needham, *Core Tax Annual: VAT 2011/12*, London: A&C Black, 2011, p. 138.
34. Jose Harris, *William Beveridge: A Biography*, Oxford: Clarendon Press, 1977, p. 21.
35. Telephone interview, 16 June 2014.
36. Sutton Trust. 'The Educational Backgrounds of Members of Parliament in 2010', 2010.
37. http://blogs.telegraph.co.uk/news/matthewwholehouse/100218671/eton-boys-are-taught-they-were-born-to-rule-its-a-shame-so-many-are-not/ (accessed 16 July 2014).
38. Winchester College archives: 1957 annual report to warden and fellows.
39. Interview with Ralph Townsend, headmaster, Winchester College, 5 March 2013.
40. David Turner, 'Rival Exam Gains Favour with Private Schools', *Financial Times*, 22 August 2008.
41. David Turner, 'Watchdog Hits at GCSE Science', *Financial Times*, 26 March 2009.
42. Figures supplied by Independent Schools Council.
43. Email communication with Cambridge International Assessment, 20 March 2014.
44. Hannah Richardson, 'State Schools to Offer International GCSE Exams', 7 June 2010. http://www.bbc.co.uk/news/10258324 (accessed 11 March 2014).
45. Tim Ross and Graeme Paton, 'Michael Gove's A-level Reforms Condemned by Cambridge', *Daily Telegraph*, 23 January 2013.
46. Telephone interview, 20 June 2014.
47. https://www.kcs.org.uk/junior-school/clubs-and-activities/trips (accessed 16 July 2014). The Battle of Hastings trip is done by boys in the Junior School.
48. Telephone interview, 17 June 2014.
49. http://www.ofsted.gov.uk/news/changes-independent-school-inspection-ofsted-consultation (accessed 3 March 2014).
50. Alan Smithers and Pamela Robinson, 'Educating the Highly Able', Centre for Education and Employment Research, University of Buckingham, commissioned by Sutton Trust, July 2012, pp. 2, 6.
51. Katherine Sellgren, http://www.bbc.co.uk/news/education–22873257 (accessed 13 June 2013).
52. Graeme Paton, 'Gordon Brown: Failing Schools Face Closure', *Daily Telegraph*, 31 October 2007.
53. Smithers and Robinson, 'Educating the Highly Able', *passim*; for quotes from teachers, see pp. 16–17.
54. Graeme Paton, 'Gifted Pupil Scheme "Failing to Make the Grade" ', *Daily Telegraph*, 26 January 2008.
55. Telephone interview, 21 February 2013.
56. http://www.bbc.co.uk/news/education–28108153 (accessed 6 October 2014).
57. Davies, Noble, Slack and Vigurs, 'Fee Remissions and Bursaries'.
58. Social segregation in Swedish and Finnish schools observed on research visits to both countries while education correspondent at the *Financial Times*, 2007–10.
59. Interview, London, 15 May 2013.
60. http://blogs.lse.ac.uk/politicsandpolicy/archives/27103 (accessed 10 January 2014).

61. David Turner, 'Private Schools Urged on Academies', *Financial Times*, 3 October 2007.
62. Polly Curtis and Geraldine Hackett, 'Academies Sponsor ULT Ordered to Halt Expansion', *Guardian*, 5 November 2009; Richard Garner, 'One chief executive, two different schools of thought', *Independent*, 11 October 2012.
63. Richard Garner, 'A School Sponsored by an Independent Chain Fails its Inspection', *Independent*, 13 February 2012.
64. http://www.Independent Schools Council.co.uk/blog/the-contributions-of-independent-schools-to-team-gb-at-the-olympic-games-of–2000–2012 (accessed 23 June 2014).
65. http://www.bbc.co.uk/news/education–27928066 (accessed 23 June 2014).

Epilogue

1. Independent Schools Inspectorate on Winchester College, November 2009, paragraph 3.7.
2. Interview, Winchester College, 5 March 2013.
3. Email communication with Eton College archivist, 22 May 2013.
4. See school website, e.g., http://www.shrewsbury.org.uk/page/admissions (accessed 17 June 2013).
5. Interview, Eton College, 4 February 2013.
6. Sonia Purnell, *Just Boris*, London: Aurum, 2011, p. 46.

Select Bibliography

Interviews

John Clark, Birkenhead School
Jonathan Taylor, Bootham School
Richard Cairns, Brighton College
Roderick Mackinnon, Bristol Grammar School
Emma Taylor, Christ College, Brecon
David Levin, City of London School
James Whitehead, Downside School
E. M. George, Durham School
Tony Little, Eton College
Graham Hawley, Kelly College
Andrew Halls, King's College School
Angus McPhail, Radley College
Frances King, Roedean School
Laura Hyde, St James' Senior Girls School
Mark Turner, Shrewsbury School
William Phelan, Stamford School
Kenneth Durham, University College School
Anthony Seldon, Wellington College
Ralph Townsend, Winchester College
Christopher Barnett, Whitgift School
Fiona Millar, education campaigner

Archival material, school registers and conference proceedings cited in text

City of London

City of London School Chronicle

Dulwich College

Governors' Minutes
Dulwich College War Record 1914–1919, ed. McC. Christison

Eton College

Eton College Register 1441–1698, Eton: Spottiswoode, Ballantyne, 1943
Eton College Register 1753–90, Eton: Spottiswoode, Ballantyne, 1921
60/8/2/1/24 Provost and fellows Agenda Papers

Felsted school

http://www.felsted.org/OFMembersofParliament (accessed 14 May 2013)

Girls' Day School Trust

GDS/17/7/2
GDS/17/7/2
DC/GDS13/11/7
DC/GDS/5/1

Harrow School

Governors' minutes
HM/D/33, 34
Pouchée diaries
HM/W/FSD

Headmasters' Conference

1969 Report of the Headmasters' Conference

St Paul's

McDonnell, Michael J. F., *Registers of St Paul's School 1509–1748*, 1977, published by the
    school

Westminster School archives

Governors' minutes
A0002/24, Statutes of the Collegiate Church of St Peter
D63S1 Timetable Committee 1963–5

Winchester College

The Founder's Charter
1400 Statutes
Annual reports to warden and fellows
Winchester College, 1835–1906: A Register, Winchester: P.&G. Wells, 1907

School histories (arranged by school or education charity name)

Ackworth School, *So Numerous a Family: 200 Years of Quaker Education at Ackworth,
    1779–1979*, Pontefract, W. Yorkshire: Ackworth School, 1979.
Marett-Crosby, Anthony, *A School of the Lord's Service: A History of Ampleforth*,
    London: James & James, 2002.

David Gibb, *A School with a View: A History of Ardingly College 1858–2008*, London: James & James, 2008.

Holdgate, Martin W., *Arnold: The Story of a Blackpool School*, Kirkby Stephen: Hayloft Publishing, 2009.

Wake, Roy, and Denton, Pennie, *Bedales School: The First Hundred Years*, London: Haggerston Press, 1993.

Batten, Simon, *A Shining Light: 150 Years of Bloxham School*, London: James & James, 2010.

Bootham School, *Bootham School, 1823–1923*, London, Toronto: J.M. Dent & Co., 1926.

Jones, Martin D. W., *Brighton College 1845–1995*, Chichester, West Sussex: Phillimore, 1995.

Hill, Charles Peter, *The History of Bristol Grammar School*, London: Sir Isaac Pitman & Sons, 1951.

Quick, Anthony, *Charterhouse: A History of the School*, London: James & James, 1990.

Morgan, M. C., *Cheltenham College: The First Hundred Years*, Chalfont St Giles: published for the Cheltonian Society by Richard Sadler, 1968.

Avery, Gillian, *Cheltenham Ladies: A History of the Cheltenham Ladies' College*, London: James & James, 2003.

Bell, Moberly, *A History of the Church Schools Company*, London: SPCK, 1958.

Knight, Bernard, *The Story of Christ College, Brecon*, Brecon: The Society of Friends of Christ College, Brecon, 1978.

Hinde, Thomas, *Carpenter's Children: The Story of the City of London School*, London: James & James, 1995.

Christie, O. F., *A History of Clifton College, 1860–1934*, Bristol: J.W. Arrowsmith, 1935.

Magnusson, Magnus, *The Clacken and the Slate. The Story of the Edinburgh Academy 1824–1974*, London: Collins, 1974.

Allom, V. M., *Ex Oriente Salus: A Centenary History of Eastbourne College*, Eastbourne: Eastbourne College, 1967.

Card, Tim, *Eton Established: A History from 1440 to 1860*, London: John Murray, 2001.

Card, Tim, *Eton Renewed: A History from 1860 to the Present Day*, London: John Murray, 1994.

Maxwell-Lyte, Sir H. C., *A History of Eton College*, Fourth Edition, London: Macmillan, 1911.

Craze, Michael, *History of Felsted School*, Ipswich: W. S. Cowell, 1955.

Philp, Robert, *A Keen Wind Blows: The Story of Fettes College*, London: James & James, 1998.

Kamm, Josephine, *Indicative Past: A Hundred Years of The Girls' Public Day School Trust*, London: Allen & Unwin, 1971.

Howson, E. W., and Warner, G. T., *Harrow School*, London: Edward Arnold, 1898.

Tyerman, Christopher, *A History of Harrow School*, Oxford, New York: Oxford University Press, 2000.

Trott, Anthony, *No Place for Fop or Idler: The Story of King Edward's School, Birmingham*, London: James & James, 1992.

Miles, Frank, and Cranch, Graeme, *King's College School: The First 150 Years*, London: King's College School, 1979.

Wainwright, David Henry Edward, *Liverpool Gentlemen. A History of Liverpool College, and Independent Day School, from 1840*, London: Faber and Faber, 1960.

Wilmot, Darwin, *A Short History of the Grammar School Macclesfield*, Macclesfield: Claye, Brown and Claye, 1910.

Bentley, James, *Dare to be Wise: A History of the Manchester Grammar School*, London: James & James, 1990.

Hinde, Thomas, *Paths of Progress: A History of Marlborough College*, London: James & James, 1992.

Draper, F. W. M., *Four Centuries of Merchant Taylors' School, 1561–1961*, London: Oxford University Press, 1962.

Braithwaite, Roderick, *Strikingly Alive: The History of the Mill Hill School Foundation, 1807–2007*, Chichester: Published for the Mill Hill School Foundation by Phillimore & Co. Ltd, 2006.

Watson, Nigel, *And Their Works Do Follow Them: The Story of North London Collegiate School*, London: James & James, 2000.

Flower, Raymond, *Oundle and the English Public School*, London: Stacey, 1989.

De Zouche, Dorothy, *Roedean School, 1885–1955*, Brighton: Roedean School, 1955.

Rouse, W. H. D., *A History of Rugby School*, London: Duckworth & Co., 1898.

Anonymous, *St George's College Weybridge 1869–1969*, privately printed, 1969.

Bailes, Howard, *St Paul's Girls' School*, London: James & James, 2000.

McDonnell, Michael J. F., *A History of St Paul's School*, London: Chapman & Hall, 1909.

Mead, A. H., *A Miraculous Draught of Fishes: A History of St Paul's School*, London: James & James, 1990.

Drysdale, Richard (ed.), *Over Ancient Ways: A Portrait of St Peter's School, York*, London: Third Millennium Publishing, 2007.

Clarke, Henry Lowther, and Weech, W. N., *History of Sedbergh School 1525–1925*, Sedbergh: Jackson and Son, 1925.

Anonymous, *A History of Shrewsbury School*, 1889, Shrewsbury: Adnitt and Naunton, 1889.

Oldham, James Basil, *A History of Shrewsbury School, 1552–1952*, Oxford: Basil Blackwell, 1952.

Muir, T. E., *Stonyhurst College, 1593–1993*, London: James & James, 1992.

Page, G. G. H. (ed.), *An Angel Without Wings: The History of University College School 1830–1980*, London: University College School, 1981.

Watson, Nigel, *A Tradition for Freedom: The Story of University College School*, London: James & James, 2007.

Newsome, David, *A History of Wellington College, 1859–1959*, London: John Murray, 1959.

Carleton, John, *Westminster School*, London: Rupert Hart-Davis, 1965.

Field, John, *The King's Nurseries*, London: James & James, 1987.

Sargeaunt, John, *Annals of Westminster School*, London: Methuen, 1898.

Tanner, Lawrence, *Westminster School*, London: Country Life Publications, 1934.

Custance, Roger (ed.), *Winchester College Sixth-Centenary Essays*, Oxford: Oxford University Press, 1982.

Firth, John D'Ewes Evelyn, *A History of Winchester College*, London, Glasgow: Blackie & Son, 1936.

Leach, Arthur Francis, *A History of Winchester College*, London: Duckworth & Co., 1899.

Sabben-Clare, James, *Winchester College. After 600 Years, 1382–1988*, Winchester: P.&G. Wells, 1989.

Cowie, Leonard W., *That One Idea: Nathaniel Woodard and His Schools*, Woodard Corporation, 1991.

Flint, Lorna, *Wycombe Abbey School 1896–1986*, privately printed, 1989.

Other printed sources

Akers-Douglas, Lord (Chairman), *Report of the Committee Appointed to Consider the Education and Training of Officers of the Army*, 1902.

Anstruther, Ian, *Oscar Browning: A Biography*, London: John Murray, 1983.

Anstruther, Ian, *Dean Farrar and 'Eric'*, London: Haggerston Press, 2002.

Ashley-Smith, Joe William, *The Birth of Modern Education. The Contribution of the Dissenting Academies, 1660–1800*, London: Independent Press, 1954.

Aubrey, John, *Brief Lives*, ed. Richard Barber, London: Folio Society, 1975.

Bamford, T. W., *The Rise of the Public Schools*, London: Nelson, 1967.

Barker, George Fisher Russell, *Memoir of Richard Busby*, London: Lawrence and Bullen, 1895.

Beale, D., *Reports issued by the Schools' Inquiry Commission, on the Education of Girls. Reprinted . . . with extracts from the evidence and a preface*, London: David Nutt, 1869.

Bennett, Alan, *Plays 1*, London and Boston: Faber and Faber, 1996.

Benson, E. F., *David Blaize*, London: Hogarth Press, 1989.

Board of Education, *Private Schools, and Other Schools not in Receipt of Grants from Public Funds*, London, 1932.

Borer, Mary Cathcart, *Willingly to School*, Guildford and London: Lutterworth Press, 1976.

Boyd, David, *Elites and their Education*, Windsor: National Foundation for Educational Research, 1973.

Brauer, George Charles, *The Education of a Gentleman*, New York: Bookman Associates, 1959.

Brazil, Angela, *The Angela Brazil Omnibus Book*, London and Glasgow: Blackie & Son, 1937.

Butler, Samuel, *The Life and Letters of Dr Samuel Butler*, London: John Murray, 1896.

Cannon, John, *Aristocratic Century*, Cambridge: Cambridge University Press, 1984.

Charnley, John, 'The GCSE Performance of independent school pupils: gender and school type differences', Curriculum Evaluation and Management Centre, 2008.

Clarendon, Lord (Chairman), *Report of Her Majesty's commissioners appointed to inquire into the revenues and management of certain colleges and schools, and the studies pursued and instruction given therein*, 1864.

Clarke, Fred, 'The Recruitment of the Nation's Leaders', *Sociological Review*, 1936, p. 343.

Copley, Terence, *Black Tom: Arnold of Rugby: The Myth and the Man*, London: Continuum, 2002.

Creasy, Edward, *Memoirs of Eminent Etonians*, London: Richard Bentley, 1850.

Crouzet, François, *The First Industrialists: The Problem of Origins*, Cambridge: Cambridge University Press, 1985.

Cunningham, Hugh, *The Invention of Childhood*, London: BBC Books, 2006.

Dahl, Roald, *Boy: Tales of Childhood*, Harmondsworth: Penguin Books, 1986.

Davies, Peter, Noble, John, Slack, Kim, and Vigurs, Katy, 'Fee Remissions and Bursaries in Independent Schools', Institute for Education Policy Research, on behalf of the Sutton Trust, 2010.

Davis, Virginia, *William Wykeham: A Life*, London: Hambledon Continuum, 2007.

DeMolen, Richard L., *Richard Mulcaster and Education Reform in the Renaissance*, Nieuwkoop: De Graaf, 1991.

Department for Education, 'Schools, Pupils and Their Characteristics', various years.

Duckworth, Francis R. G., *From a Pedagogue's Sketch-Book*, London and Leipzig: T. Fisher Unwin, 1912.

Edwards, Anthony David, *The Role of International Exhibitions in Britain, 1850–1910: Perceptions of Economic Decline and the Technical Education Issue*, Amherst, NY: Cambria Press, 2008.

Ellis, Havelock, *Studies in the Psychology of Sex*, Vol. 2, Philadelphia: F. A. Davis, 1924.

Fleming, Lord (Chairman), *Report of the Committee on Public Schools appointed by the President of the Board of Education in July 1942*, 1944.

Fletcher, Frank, *After Many Days. A Schoolmaster's Memories*, London: R. Hale & Co., 1937.

Fox, Irene, *Private Schools and Public Issues: The Parents' View*, London: Macmillan, 1985.

Gathorne-Hardy, Jonathan, *The Public School Phenomenon, 597–1977*, London: Hodder & Stoughton, 1977.

Gilbert, Humphrey, *Queene Elizabethes Achademy*, London: Early English Text Society, 1869.

Gilpin, William, *The Regulations of a Private School at Cheam in Surrey*, 1752, BL L01000674783.

Girls' School Year Book, London: A&C Black, 1906 onwards.

Graves, Robert, *Goodbye to All That*, London: The Folio Society, 1981.

Greene, Graham (ed.), *The Old School*, London: Jonathan Cape, 1934.

Griggs, Clive, *Private Education in Britain*, London and Philadelphia: Falmer Press, 1985.

Gurner, R., *I Chose Teaching*, London: J. M. Dent and Sons, 1937.

Halsey, A. H., Heath, A. F., and Ridge, J. M., *Origins and Destinations: Family, Class and Education in Modern Britain*, Oxford: Clarendon Press, 1980.

Hare, Augustus J. C., *Memorials of a Quiet Life*, London: Strahan and Co., 1872.

Harris, Jose, *William Beveridge: A Biography*, Oxford: Clarendon Press, 1977.

Hoyland, Geoffrey, *The Man Who Made a School: Thring of Uppingham*, London: SCM Press, 1946.

Hughes, Thomas, *Tom Brown's School Days*, Cambridge: Macmillan, 1857.

Independent Schools Council Census, 1975 onwards.

Kendall, Guy, *A Headmaster Reflects*, London, Edinburgh and Glasgow: William Hodge & Co., 1937.

Kipling, Rudyard, *Stalky and Co.*, London: Macmillan, 1929.

Knox, Winifred, *A Little Learning, or A Victorian Childhood*, London: Faber and Faber, 1952.

Lambert, Royston, and Millham, Spencer, *The Hothouse Society*, Harmondsworth: Penguin, 1974.

Lawson, John, and Silver, Harold, *A Social History of Education in England*, London: Methuen, 1973.

Leathes, Stanley, *Report of the Committee Appointed by the Prime Minister to Enquire into the Position of Modern Languages in the Educational System of Great Britain*, Parliament Papers, IX, Cd9036, 1918.

Lee, C. H., *The British Economy Since 1700*, Cambridge: Cambridge University Press, 1986.

Leedham-Green, E. S., *A Concise History of the University of Cambridge*, Cambridge: Cambridge University Press, 1996.

Leinster-Mackay, Donald, *The Rise of the English Prep School*, London: Falmer Press, 1974.

Le Mesurier, John, *A Jobbing Actor*, London: Elm Tree Books.

Lockhart, Rudolf Eliott, 'A-level & GCSE Results 2010: Behind the Headlines', Independent Schools Council, 2011.

Mack, Edward, *Public Schools and British Opinion 1780–1860*, Westport, CT: Greenwood Press, 1973.

Mack, Edward, *Public Schools and British Opinion Since 1860*, New York: Columbia University Press, 1941.

Maclean, A. H. H., *Public Schools and the Great War, 1914–19*, London: Edward Stanford, 1923.

Macready, W. C., *Macready's Reminiscences*, ed. Sir Frederick Pollock, London: Macmillan, 1875.

Mais, S. P. B., *A Schoolmaster's Diary: Extracts from the Journal of Patrick Traherne, Sometime Assistant Master at Radchester and Marlton*, London: Grant Richards, 1918.

Mangan, J. A., *Athleticism in the Victorian and Edwardian Public School: The Emergence and Consolidation of the Educational Ideology*, Cambridge: Cambridge University Press, 1981.

Maybee, Bryan, *Pro Liberis, Independent Schools Association 1878–2010*, Woodbridge: John Catt Educational, 2010.

Milburn, Alan (Chair), 'Unleashing Aspiration: The Final Report of the Panel on Fair Access to the Professions', 21 July 2009.

Mokyr, Joel, *The Enlightened Economy, An Economic History of Britain 1700–1850*, New Haven, CT, and London: Yale University Press, 2009.

Mulcaster, Richard, *Elementarie*, ed. E. T. Campagnac, Oxford: Clarendon Press, 1925.

National Foundation for Educational Research, on behalf of Sutton Trust, 'Use of an Aptitude Test in University Entrance: A Validity Study', 2010.

Norwood, Sir Cyril, *The English Tradition of Education*, London: John Murray, 1931.

Norwood, Sir Cyril, and Hope, Arthur Herbert, *The Higher Education of Boys in England*, London: John Murray, 1909.

O'Donoghue, Jim, and Goulding, Louise, 'Consumer Price Inflation Since 1750', Office for National Statistics Economic Trends 604, March 2004.

Ogilvie, Vivian, *The English Public School*, London: B.T. Batsford, 1957.

Organisation for Economic Cooperation and Development, *Public and Private Schools: How Management and Funding Relate to their Socio-economic Profile*, Paris: OECD Publishing, 2012.

Orme, Nicholas, *Medieval Schools*, New Haven CT, and London: Yale University Press, 2006.

Parkin, George, *Edward Thring, Life, Diary and Letters*, London: Macmillan, 1898.

Phelps Brown, E. H., and Hopkins, Sheila V., 'Seven Centuries of the prices of Consumables', *Economica*, Vol. 23, No. 92, November 1956, pp. 311–14.

Public Schools Year Book, London, various years.

Purnell, Sonia, *Just Boris*, London: Aurum Press, 2011.

Rae, John, *The Public School Revolution: Britain's Independent Schools 1964–1979*, London: Faber and Faber, 1981.

Rae, John, *The Old Boys' Network: A Headmaster's Diaries 1972–1986*, London: Short, 2010.

Raikes, Elizabeth, *Dorothea Beale of Cheltenham*, London: Archibald Constable & Co., 1908.

Richards, Frank, *Billy Bunter of Greyfriars School*, London: Hawe Books, 1991.

Roach, John, *Public Examinations in England 1850–1900*, Cambridge: Cambridge University Press, 2008.

Rothblatt, Sheldon, *The Revolution of the Dons*, London: Faber and Faber, 1968.

Rubinstein, W. D., *Capitalism, Culture, and Decline in Britain, 1750–1990*, London: Routledge, 1993.

Sanderson, Michael, *Educational Opportunity and Social Change in England*, London: Faber and Faber, 1987.

Searle, Geoffrey, *The Quest for National Efficiency: A Study in British Politics and Political Thought, 1899–1914*, Oxford: Blackwell, 1971.

Sherington, Geoffrey, *English Education, Social Change and War, 1911–20*, Manchester: Manchester University Press, 1981.

Simon, Brian, *Education and the Social Order 1940–1990*, London: Lawrence & Wishart, 2010 edition.

Smithers, Alan, and Robinson, Pamela, 'Educating the Highly Able', Centre for Education and Employment Research, University of Buckingham, commissioned by Sutton Trust, 2012.

Social Mobility and Child Poverty Commission, 'Higher Education: the Fair Access Challenge', 2013.

Spinley, B. M., *The Deprived and the Privileged: Personality Development in English Society*, London: Routledge & Kegan Paul, 1953.

Stephens, W. B., *Education in Britain 1750–1914*, Basingstoke and New York: Palgrave, 1998.

Stevens, Charles, *The English Dialect of Winchester College*, London and New Brunswick, NJ: Athlone Press, 1998.

Stewart, W. A. C., and McCann, W. P., *The Educational Innovators. Progressive Schools, 1881–1967*, Vols 1 and 2, Basingstoke: Macmillan, 2000.

Taunton, Lord (Chairman), *Report to the commissioners appointed by Her Majesty to inquire into the education given in schools in England not comprised within Her Majesty's two recent commissions, and to the commissioners appointed by Her Majesty to inquire into the schools in Scotland, on the common school systems of the United States and of the provinces of Upper and Lower Canada*, 1868.

Teignmouth, John Shore, Baron, *Memoirs of the Life, Writings and Correspondence of Sir William Jones*, London: John Hatchard, 1804.

Thackeray, William Makepeace, *The Newcomes: Memoirs of a Respectable Family*, New York: Harper & Brothers, 1855.

Thomas, George, Earl of Albemarle, *Fifty Years of my Life*, London: Macmillan, 1876.

Thomas, Joseph John (Chairman), *Report of the Committee appointed by the Prime Minister to Enquire into the Position of Natural Science in the Educational System of Great Britain*, Parliament Papers, IX, Cd9011, 1918.

Timbs, John, *School-Days of Eminent Men*, London, 1862.

Tittler, Robert, *Nicholas Bacon: The Making of a Tudor Statesman*, London: Jonathan Cape, 1976.

Tupper, Martin, *My Life as an Author*, Edinburgh and London: Ballantyne, Hanson and Co., 1886.

Vachell, H. A., *The Hill*, London: George Newnes, 1905.

Vaizey, John, *The Costs of Education*, London: Allen & Unwin, 1958.

Various authors, *The Year Book of Education*, London: Evans Brothers, 1932.

Various authors, *The World of the Public School*, London: Weidenfeld and Nicolson, 1977.

Walford, Geoffrey, *Private Education*, New York: Continuum, 2005.

Walford, Geoffrey, *Private Education: Tradition and Diversity*, London: Continuum, 2006.

Walford, Geoffrey, *Privatisation and Privilege in Education*, London: Routledge, 1990.

Walford, Geoffrey (ed.), *British Private Schools Research on Policy and Practice*, London: Woburn Press, 2003.

Waugh, Alec, *The Loom of Youth*, London: Methuen, 1984.

Williams, Penry, *New Oxford History of England, The Later Tudors: England, 1547–1603*, Oxford: Clarendon Press, 1995.

Williamson, Jeffrey, 'Structure of Pay in Britain 1710–1911', *Research in Economic History*, Vol. 7, 1982.

Wodehouse, P. G., *Tales of St Austin's*, Harmondsworth: Puffin Books, 1972.

Worsley, T. C., *Flannelled Fool*, London: Hogarth Press, 1985.

Index

Perkin, William 132
Pestalozzi, Johann Heinrich 64
Peterborough, third Earl of 35
Pitt the Elder, William 31, 61
Pitt the Younger, William 61
Plato 100
Pope Pius II 11
Portsmouth High School 236
Powell, Baden 115–16
prefects 9, 55–8, 66, 94–9, 103–4, 109,
        134–5, 154, 179–80, 183, 201, 263–4
Prestwich, Mrs 52
Priest, Josias 52
Priestley, Joseph 77–8
Prince Arthur's Knights 18
Prior, Matthew 36, 45
public school accent 19, 117, 213
Public Schools, Commission of 1964
        213–14
Purcell, Henry 34, 52
Putney 52
Putney High 152, 167

Queen Elizabeth's Grammar School,
        Blackburn 252
Queen's College, Harley Street 125, 127

Radley College 139, 195, 205–6, 227, 250
    Angus McPhail (warden, 2000–14),
        225, 250
Ramsay, Agnata 152
religion, role of at schools 5, 93–6, 103,
        159–60, 204
Repton, Humphrey 74–5
Repton School 101, 232, 246–7
Ribbentrop, Joachim von 234–5
Roedean School 153–4, 188, 243
    Christopher Jonas (chairman of the
        board of governors) 251
    Frances King (headmistress, 2008–13)
        243, 251–3
Rogers, H. Lionel 139
Roman Catholic Relief Act of 1791 78
Rosebery, Lord, 99–100
Rossall School 106–7, 117, 140, 218
Rousseau, Jean-Jacques 64
Royal Military Academy, Sandhurst 56,
        110–11, 132, 158
Royal Military Academy, Woolwich 110
Rugby School vii, 172
    cruelty ix, 61–2, 84
    educational methods 71
    foundation 40
    headmasters

Thomas Arnold (1828–42) xi, 72,
        93–7
    Henry Hayman (1870–4) 72
    Henry Holyoake (1687–1730) 40
    Thomas James (1778–94) 71
    Archibald Tait (1842–8) 57
    rebellion 55–7, 109
Russell, Bertrand 84
Russell, 1st Earl 85–6
Rydal School 208
Rye, Marion de 2

St Alban's School 215
St Bee's School 185–6
St George's College, Weybridge 211
St James' Senior Girls' School 258
    Laura Hyde (headmistress) 258
St Leonard's School 152, 156–7
St Loe, Sir William 10
St Margaret's School, Bushey 176
St Mary's Convent School 207
St Paul's Girls' School 176–7, 222–3, 240,
        261
    high mistresses
        Heather Brigstocke 222–3
        Frances Gray 176–7
St Paul's School
    abuse allegations 212
    criticism 28, 43, 51, 268
    educational methods 43, 71, 74, 272
    foundation 13–14
    high masters
        George Charles (1737–48) 51
        Samuel Cromleholme (1657–72)
        43, 51
        Alexander Gill the Elder (1608–35) 28
        William Lily (1509–22) 14, 23
        John Sleath (1814–37) 71
        Martin Stephen (2004–10) 233
    old boys 23–5, 161
    pupils 114, 161
St Peter's School, York 186, 210, 229
Sanders, Nicholas 23
Sassoon, Siegfried 102
School Teachers Superannuation Act of
        1918 167–8
science, rise of (see also Modern sides) 80,
        111–12, 115, 126, 156–7, 200,
        206–7, 241–3
Scott, Walter 113
Sebright School 207–8
Second World War 187–91
Sedbergh School 159, 181
Sevenoaks School 244

Acknowledgements

My thanks to:

Heather McCallum, Tami Halliday, Candida Brazil, Rachael Lonsdale, Heather Nathan and the rest of the dedicated team at Yale University Press.

Andrew Turner, Philip Howard and Richard Heath, for reading my manuscript so carefully and making so many helpful suggestions.

Anne and John Turner, Colin Holloway, Mark Hitchens, Robin Reeve and Robert Tombs for educating me in matters historical, animal, vegetable and mineral.

Suzanne Foster, Angharad Meredith, Penny Hatfield, Elizabeth Wells, Terry Heard, Soraya Cerio and the archivists of the Institute of Education, for guiding me through their labyrinthine school archives.

The head teachers who kindly agreed to be interviewed by me. Their names are found in the Select Bibliography. Many thanks, too, to the pupils who took me on guided tours of their schools.

Fiona Millar, for kindly putting over the anti-public school view at her kitchen table.

The ex-public school pupils who kindly agreed to be interviewed by me. Your anonymity is preserved, but I am eternally grateful.